Icon, Brand, Myth:
THE CALGARY STAMPEDE

Icon, Brand, Myth:

THE CALGARY STAMPEDE

edited by Max Foran

AU PRESS

The West Unbound:
Social and Cultural Studies series

©2008 AU Press
Second printing 2010

Published by AU Press, Athabasca University
1200, 10011 – 109 Street
Edmonton, AB T5J 3S8

**Library and Archives Canada Cataloguing
in Publication**

Icon, brand, myth : the Calgary Exhibition and
Stampede / edited by Max Foran.

Includes bibliographical references and index.
Issued also in electronic format.
ISBN 978-1-897425-03-9 (bound)
ISBN 978-1-897425-05-3 (pbk.)

1. Calgary Stampede–History.
2. Calgary Stampede–Social aspects.
3. Calgary (Alta.)–History.
4. Calgary (Alta.)–Social conditions.
I. Foran, Max

GV1834.56.C22C3 2008   791.8'409712338   C2008-902106-1

This book is part of the The West Unbound:
Social and Cultural Studies series
ISSN 1915-8181 (print)
ISSN 1915-819X (electronic)

Printed and bound in Canada by AGMV Marquis
Cover and book design by Alex Chan, Studio Reface

All photographs and illustrations courtesy Calgary Stampede,
except for the following: Fiona Angus: p. 128; Max Foran:
p. 159, 160; Glenbow Archives: p. 8: NA-628-1; p. 21:
NA-81-1; p. 61: NA-446-111; p. 73: PA-1326-9; p. 89:
NA-5627-33; p. 101: NA-1722-2; p. 147: NA-2864-29706;
p. 274: NA-2376-1; p. 315: fig. 2; Stéphane Guevremont:
all photographs on pp. 266–267; Library of Congress: p. 175:
LC-USZ62-78721.

To my longtime friend, Doug Chapman

– Max Foran

Contents

Acknowledgements

I would like to thank the contributors to this volume, the genesis of which dates back to 2004 and the Faculty of Communication and Culture's inaugural course on the culture of the Stampede. Their time, effort, and co-operation are greatly appreciated. I would also like to acknowledge the support and co-operation of the Calgary Stampede and especially its generosity in supplying most of the visuals that appear in the book. Here a special thanks goes to Tracey Read, manager, Government Relations and Community Partnership, who helped me so much in so many ways.

Max Foran
University of Calgary
November 2007

Introduction

The idea for this book came as a result of the inaugural course on the Calgary Exhibition and Stampede (Calgary Stampede as of spring 2007) offered by the Faculty of Communication and Culture at the University of Calgary in the summer of 2004. This innovative course was based on guest lectures, many of which were delivered by members of the above faculty. At a get-together following the course there was general agreement among participants that the various lectures might serve a wider purpose if they were transformed into articles and made available to a larger audience. All of the contributors to this book either lectured or were the subjects of reference in the three Stampede courses offered in the summers of 2004, 2005, and 2006.

The course itself grew out of a growing awareness that the Stampede has evolved into a cultural phenomenon. Similar events are held annually throughout North America. Midways, rodeos, parades, performances, and agricultural and other exhibits are all part of an annual fairground tradition in countless cities and towns, yet none evokes reactions as does the Calgary Stampede. Growing up as a boy in Sydney, Australia, I visited the Royal Easter Show every year and was drawn in wonderment to scenes and events very similar to those I was to encounter later in another country and another city. Yet when I donned western garb to attend my first Stampede in 1964, feeling strange and out of place, I had already been imbued with the notion that I was now part of something special, a festive tradition unique to Calgary. In a way, my impression was valid. Unlike the Royal Easter Show, the Stampede was not simply attended; it was experienced. I learned my first and probably most important lesson about the Stampede that day: it had more to do with the act of participation than with offered opportunities. Paradoxically, it has been this capacity to embody a significance that transcends the sum of its various components that explains in part why the Stampede is held in such high and low regard.

The Calgary Stampede can claim many legitimacies. It hosts the premier event in a popular professional sport. In addition to being of significant economic worth to the city, the Stampede is based on a valid historic tradition that dates to the late nineteenth century and provides in many ways an interpretive window into the historical development of the prairie and foothills West. The Stampede has supported agriculture and the livestock industry for almost a century while promoting sports and western art and showcasing other events of cultural and social importance. Its capacity to solicit and organize phenomenal volunteer support is the envy of organizations worldwide.

And like it or not, the Calgary Stampede has become a world-class festival that spills out into the streets and carries its own messages within a spectrum of ritual, performance, celebration, and spectacle.

Yet as successful as the Stampede has been in attracting visitors and perpetuating its own popularity, it has also garnered considerable antipathy. Some criticize the Stampede for adhering to middle-class white Anglo-Saxon male values. Others view the Stampede as a money-making machine run by elites that exploits heritage in the interests of profit. A growing number protest the exploitation of animals. Some see the Stampede as little more than a giant hoax whereby illusions are cultivated, dressed up, packaged, and sold without shame. Still others wince at the folly of trying to embed a hokey, hackneyed event into the psyche and image of a dynamic city seeking global status.

Crucial in these allegiances and antipathies is the place of myth in the collective consciousness. Those who see the Stampede as a event during which fun and nostalgia mix freely do not recognize or care about myth. Similarly, those who appreciate myth, who see it as an agent for collective identification, a focus for the localization of universal values, or an entry point for personal interpretations, also have no difficulty accepting and participating in the Stampede cornucopia. Oppositely, it is the regenerating and exploitative capacity of this myth that draws the intense and largely recent criticism of the Stampede. Many cringe at its distortion of history, whereby fantasy is superimposed on fact with layers of glitz, bombast, and commercial hype. These critics see the Stampede as a giant hoax and an anachronism in an urban environment.

The following articles do not attempt to idealize or destroy this myth, nor is their intention to laud or denigrate the Stampede, although they do contain elements of all the above. With some overlapping, unavoidable in a collection of this type, the articles try to provide some perspectives of the enigma that is the Calgary Stampede. Collectively they attempt to answer several questions: What is the reality behind its origins and various components? What messages does the Stampede try to deliver? How did the Stampede go about cultivating its traditions? Where does the City of Calgary fit in? What can the Stampede tell us about First Nations and their treatment? Is the Stampede about more than rodeo, the midway, and artificiality? How can the rodeo and chuckwagon races be explained to urban and international audiences? Who is the cowboy? What are the Stampede organizers' visions for the future? The articles are wide-ranging in length, subject, tone, approach, and interpretation. Some focus on the Stampede and discuss it in a specific context. Others use the Stampede to explore pertinent themes. Together they furnish a heightened understanding and provide a useful forum for further discourse.

The opening article by Max Foran places the Stampede in its historical context and in effect sets the stage for the more focused articles to follow. He explains the Stampede's unusual composition and discusses its multiple origins. Foran emphasizes the Stampede's close relationship with agriculture and argues that it has been pivotal in ensuring Calgary's continuing importance as a livestock centre. He also feels that in order to appreciate the extent of the Stampede's contribution to Calgary, it is necessary to separate the ten-day July event from the larger year-round operations of its parent body.

Don Wetherell contends that the Stampede cultivated an invented tradition from the outset. He identifies the formative forces as the role of sport in ennobling manly characteristics, the legitimization of rodeo as a public spectator activity, and the ability of the inaugural Stampedes to inspire similar events elsewhere in the province. After 1923 the annual Exhibitions and Stampedes melded the values of the farmer and rancher with those of the rodeo performer to create both the iconic cowboy and the idealized sanitized virtues for which he stood. Wetherell locates this invented tradition within a risk-taking continuum. He also points out the exclusive place of risk-takers in the invented tradition paradigm. Minorities and the marginalized simply do not qualify.

The historic involvement of First Nations and the Stampede is documented by Hugh A. Dempsey, noted authority on the history of Plains Indians. Dempsey discusses the early involvement of First Nations people in Calgary fairs and traces their association with the Stampede to modern times. He deals extensively with the ongoing dispute with the Indian Affairs Department over the right of First Nations to participate in the Stampede, as well as conflicts between First Nations and Stampede administrators. However, while acknowledging the latter, Dempsey describes a mainly positive relationship and suggests that in many ways the Stampede acted to preserve First Nations traditions and artifacts.

Lorry Felske focuses on the parade that heralds the beginning of every Stampede. He discusses the importance of parades as statements of both diversity and homogeneity and examines the messages they embody. Most significantly, Felske argues that the first Stampede parade of 1912 did not begin a tradition, but rather was a continuing manifestation of a strong parading history in the city. In asserting that the inaugural Stampede parade simply built on existing practices, Felske locates an important dimension of the Calgary Stampede not in the tradition of the Wild West Shows and other vaudeville-type entertainment from which it grew, but in the daily life experiences and street culture of a small western Canadian urban community.

Noting the marginalized but important function of the midway, Fiona Angus sets the Stampede midway in historical and social context. She contends that despite its sanitization over the years, the midway's ambience has complemented the myth of the Stampede. Angus provides extensive details, both in the text and in endnotes, about the two major companies that have held the midway contracts for most of the Stampede's existence, describing the police investigation that led to the disappearance of Royal American Shows from Canada and the operations of its successor, Conklin Shows. Though she calls attention to the inherently exploitive nature of the relationship between the midway and its workforce, Angus also sees the midway as adaptable and flexible and credits Conklin with the ability to adjust to changing social mores, demands, and technologies.

In his article on the relationship between the City of Calgary and the Stampede, Max Foran dismisses the contention that the two were collusive. Instead, he argues that they were one and the same, which, he contends, explains their close co-operation. In a discussion of the two expansion issues, he also qualifies the popular perception that the city has consistently been a pawn of elitist Stampede interests. In an interesting speculation, Foran poses reasons why the two purposely keep their distance from each other: the Stampede because it does not want to be perceived as being an agent of the city, the city because it would prefer to see the Stampede take the brunt of public criticism over issues that involve them both.

Tamara Palmer Seiler examines the elusive identity of the Canadian cowboy. She locates him on a grid of influences characterized by values inherent in Canada's east-west nation-building processes, as opposed to those implicit in a continental north-south dynamic dominated by the United States. The Canadian cowboy necessarily emerges as a contradictory figure amenable to use and manipulation. In the Stampede he is at once an ideal marketing tool, a compatible ideological icon, and a personal embodiment of maverick Calgary and Alberta, while at the same time symbolizing that tantalizing "other" dimension that Canadians employ to distance themselves from Americans.

As its title suggests, Glen Mikkelsen's article takes the reader behind the chutes into the world of rodeo. He discusses the events and their rules and evokes the mystique of a sport that for all its excitement and danger is little understood by most spectators at the Calgary Stampede. Mikkelsen also probes rodeo at deeper levels. Elements of festival are captured in his discussion of rodeo clowns and the public tolerance of their socially unacceptable verbal exchanges. Mikkelsen's discussion of animal abuse issues underscores his major argument on the challenges facing rodeo. He speculates on how a sport viewed as anachronistic by many, whose rules are difficult to follow and whose human performers have little presence outside the arena, can continue to command its premier position at the Calgary Stampede.

Aritha van Herk explores the world of chuckwagon racing, an event pioneered by and most identifiable with the Calgary Stampede. She describes the event's origins, rules, development, and controversial image. She views chuckwagon racing as an activity firmly tied to a sense of place, with a close-knit community of participants and a unique iconic ethos. She also sees its development as local and accidental and "almost shyly naive." To van Herk, chuckwagon racing is a metaphor for hope, one that anticipates the peace that follows danger. It also touches the essence of a past era, possibly more than anything else the Stampede has to offer.

In his discussion of public art and monuments in Calgary, Frits Pannekoek argues that the best artistic statements about the Stampede are confined to the Stampede grounds, the rural hinterland, and the airport. Elsewhere, Stampede images are most visible in gaudy commercial signage. Pannekoek concludes that to Calgary's guardians of culture, the Stampede embodies a specific myth contrived for commercial purposes. While public art elsewhere in the city embodies historical and socio-cultural themes, emerging issues, and more refined myths, it has little to do with the Stampede and its rambunctious version of the city's "official" past.

Brian Rusted explores the controversial topic of western art and its marginalization by contemporary art institutions. He sees its robust survival as fitting evidence of a legitimacy that belongs outside more formal prescriptions. He discusses the Stampede's contribution to western art through several historic phases and manifestations, including the highly popular Stampede Western Art Show. Yet the results have not been entirely positive. Rusted points out that the Stampede's current efforts to promote itself through spectator-oriented visual representations have resulted in a popularized view of the West and a virtual abandonment of its relationship to art and visual culture.

In their "reading" of selected Stampede posters, Robert M. Seiler and Tamara Palmer Seiler show how visual texts can be sites of meaning. They see the Stampede posters as emphasizing both nostalgia for the past and a belief in progress and technology. The cowboy is incorporated into both these contradictory themes and thus emerges as an ambiguous figure. Within this context the authors suggest that the Stampede posters are much more open texts than might be imagined, and that the various images of the cowboy are central to the complex struggle over the meaning of western Canadian experience.

The closing article deals with Stampede as seen through its own eyes. Stampede Chief Executive Officer Vern Kimball offers some of his thoughts on where the Stampede has been and where it is going. Kimball acknowledges the past in a tribute to Guy Weadick. He also outlines the Stampede's plans for the future within parameters defined by Calgary's changing demographic and the challenges of the twenty-first century. Kimball links the Stampede's future to its success in developing a permanent physical presence, universally amenable and supportive of a vibrant urban-built form. More significantly, Kimball sees the Stampede as an ideal vehicle through which respect for a locally-grounded tradition can be integrated with the active promotion of the values it embodies. Specifically, these include western hospitality, commitment to community, pride of place, and integrity.

The Calgary Stampede is anything but bland. Some see it as a "ten-day party," a Disneyesque sham, and a commercial rip-off. Others hail it as "the greatest outdoor show on earth," a destination event, and a world-class festival rivalling Mardi Gras, Carnivale, or Oktoberfest. Could it be that all perspectives contain valid elements? It is its capacity to conjure up a wide spectrum of emotions; to symbolize the good, the bad, and the crass; to be anything one wants it to be that in part explains the Stampede's durability and, paradoxically, its popular appeal and denigration. The editor and authors hope this volume will contribute to further discourse about the nature of Calgary's controversial icon.

CHAPTER 1

The Stampede in Historical Context

Max Foran

A view of Stampede Park from Scotsman's Hill, ca. 1908.

"The Stampede is by and of the citizens of Calgary. It is for the world."

Calgary Herald, 5 July 1967

Like many events of its kind, the Calgary Stampede evokes widely divergent reactions. Some embrace the annual Stampede as "the greatest outdoor show on earth," a festive celebratory tribute to a bygone era. To others it is no more than Coney Island with a hokey cowboy flavour.[1] It seems fair to say that both viewpoints lack the understanding and appreciation necessary for a more realistic and reasoned assessment. It is the intent of this introductory discussion to touch on the composition of the Calgary Stampede as well as the formative forces and evolutionary trends that have helped define its essence over more than a century. This discussion also sets the stage for the more tightly focused articles to follow.

Composition and Structure

The Calgary Exhibition and Stampede, as it was known until 2007, occupies and operates several facilities on 55 hectares (137 acres) of land in Victoria Park a few blocks south of Calgary's downtown. Its operations, which generated revenues of over $85 million in 2004, fall loosely into three areas. Most notable is the Stampede itself, an annual ten-day festival built around a world-class rodeo, a modern midway, and a frontier western theme that spills beyond the grounds to the city itself. These ingredients absorb the bulk of media attention and inspire intermittent but persistent public debate over the merits or deficiencies of what has been popularly described as "ten mad days in July." Lost in these perceptions is the Exhibition. Thousands of visitors, after a day spent visiting the midway, watching rodeo, listening to rock bands, or playing blackjack, remain oblivious to the show ring where premier livestock compete for prestigious honours, the impressive art exhibition, or the hundreds of free educational opportunities afforded by diverse and sophisticated exhibits throughout the Exhibition grounds. Finally, the Calgary Stampede organization is a year-round operation. Indeed, in terms of annual attendance, the Stampede itself is not as pivotal as one might imagine. In 1975, for example, of the over three million people who visited the grounds, the Stampede itself accounted for fewer than nine hundred thousand. Over the years, the Exhibition and Stampede has hosted a variety of livestock shows and sales, sports events, trade shows, concerts, and public meetings, making it the undisputed entertainment and gathering centre for the City of Calgary.

The structure of the Stampede organization is a mystery to those who assume it is a private for-profit company. This misconception is understandable, since the Stampede in many ways does function like a private company. It is composed of shareholders who elect a governing board of directors that in turn decides on a president. In addition to the annual Stampede, the board of directors and permanent staff, plus over two thousand volunteers, manage and operate year-round activities and events in Victoria Park. What is not readily understood is the fact that the Stampede has always been a non-profit company. All senior positions are predicated on long tenure in lesser volunteer capacities. The board of directors receives no remuneration. No dividends are paid to shareholders, whose holdings are limited to twenty-five shares that originally sold for a dollar a share and now cost five dollars each. All surplus monies are redirected to operations and capital investment. The Stampede operates under a free lease and pays no taxes, an arrangement that means all buildings and property covered by the lease are under city title. The city protects its interests by including aldermen on the board of directors; two of them sit on the powerful executive committee. As will be indicated later in this volume, the relationship between the Stampede and the City of Calgary, though close, is very much a partnership of unequals.

Origins

The attention given to the Stampede component of the Exhibition and Stampede Inc., as it is legally known, has led to misconceptions about the organization's origins. Even some of the more knowledgeable people would cite the inaugural Stampede of 1912, although the real historical foundations lie in the Exhibition and a series of events that led to the amalgamation of the two components in 1923.

The Exhibition dates from 1886. A cornucopia of agricultural, sporting, and other festive activities, the Calgary Exhibition, like hundreds of others across the country, was designed to advertise district wealth, promote settlement, bring business to the host town, and provide an infrequent opportunity for social interaction and entertainment. Except for a brief period in the 1890s, the Exhibition was held every year, originally in the fall and after 1902 in July. By 1911, the year before the first Stampede, it had a home on city-owned land in Victoria Park, a capable permanent manager in the person of Ernie Richardson, and a free five-year renegotiable lease. More significantly, it had become a huge event in the rapidly growing city.

Calgary's Exhibition became big business in 1908 when the federal government as part of its national program to promote various areas of local government advanced $50,000 for a Dominion Exhibition in Calgary. When this was augmented by a provincial grant of $35,000 and a city donation of $25,000, organizers had an unprecedented budget with which to stage the biggest and best exhibition in western Canada. It lived up to its promise, drawing wide accolades and over one hundred thousand people. A year later, the Alberta Provincial Fair, dubbed as such to reflect government financial backing, drew praise as "the greatest spectacle in the history of the West," with special kudos reserved for the four-mile-long parade.[2] Again in 1911, the year before the first Stampede, the Exhibition was described as "the finest fair ever held in the city."[3] It appears, then, that the inaugural Stampede of 1912 should be looked upon not as a groundbreaking extravaganza, but as a variation in a sequence of highly successful fairs that reflected the city's rapid growth, rural prosperity, and disposable farm income.

During the Dominion Exhibition in 1908, people came to see the Strobel's airship. The hydrogen-filled, propeller-driven balloon made five successful flights over Victoria Park, but it exploded and burned on its sixth attempt.

The Stampede had its individual genesis at the Dominion Exhibition of 1908 in the unlikely person of an American-born former cowboy and showman, Guy Weadick. As part of the one-day event staged by Miller Brothers 101 Ranch Wild West Show, Weadick saw more potential in the vibrant young city than he did in his own future as a trick roper. He perceived that Calgary was ready for a different kind of Old West re-creation, a frontier celebration that replaced the fantasy and tricks of the Wild West show with authenticity and real cowboy skills presented via a rodeo. Record has it that he was dissuaded by H.C. McMullen, general livestock agent for the Canadian Pacific Railway, who felt that the time was not yet ripe for such an event.[4] Given the success of the Exhibitions at the time, one wonders at McMullen's caution. However, evidence suggests that public acceptance of rodeo may not have been as strong as one might expect. According to the *Morning Albertan* in 1910, rodeo was obsolete. In referring to a dismal rodeo in the city, the newspaper editorialized that "such entertainment is a thing of the past," and its elements of bull baiting and cruelty made it neither "elevating nor desirable."[5] The editorial was supported by a letter to the editor and a tongue-in-cheek article in the *Calgary Herald* that derided the contestants' amateurishness and lack of ability.[6]

So why was Weadick successful when he returned to the city in the winter of 1911–12 to follow his vision? The fact that rodeo had remained popular in smaller centres was only a partial reason, as was Weadick's considerable power of persuasion. Nostalgia was the key to the Stampede of 1912, nostalgia on the part of four cattlemen who had experienced the old days, who had lived through the horrendous winter of 1906–07, who had seen the open range give way to fences and wheat fields, and, most important, who had money. These four men, enshrined in the Canadian Agricultural Hall of Fame as the Big Four, had their own agenda when they backed Weadick's dream with a credit line of $100,000. While Weadick may have hoped that the Stampede of 1912 would blossom into an annual event anchored by a world-class rodeo, the Big Four saw it as a one-time party, a farewell gesture to a dying way of life. It is ironic that the Stampede with its vigour and unquestioned permanence should have been perceived as "a last hurrah" by the four men who enabled its birth.

In the inaugural Stampede held in September 1912, Weadick succeeded in moving the traditional Wild West performance in a new direction. His idea of re-creating the Canadian frontier experience, as opposed to the exaggerated U.S. model, and wedding it to a major professional rodeo competition was a highly successful innovation, one that he repeated seven years later in the Victory Stampede of 1919. As a postscript, it is unfortunate that in spite of Donna Livingstone's solid study, Guy Weadick remains underappreciated and understudied by scholars of history and popular culture.[7]

While the first bold move in creating the Stampede component is attributed to Guy Weadick, credit for blending it with the Exhibition is due to Ernie Richardson. As he continued to stage annual Exhibitions after 1913, Richardson found himself wrestling with two problems. By the end of 1922 both had become insurmountable. The first was economic and beyond his control. The collapse of the land settlement boom made staging the wartime Exhibitions expensive and risky. Effects of the collapse were compounded by enduring drought conditions after 1916 and a lingering post-war depression that sent hundreds of farmers and ranchers into bankruptcy. After incurring significant financial losses in 1921 and 1922, the Exhibition teetered on the brink of survival. The second problem Richardson faced concerned the Exhibition itself. Put simply, the traditional format of a fair built primarily around agriculture and augmented by Wild West travelling shows was losing its appeal to increasingly sophisticated urban audiences. In 1921 the *Albertan* summed up Richardson's problems succinctly when in reference to the failure of the recent Exhibition to attract crowds it noted, "There is real difficulty in discovering what the people want just now, and having decided on that the next difficulty is to get it."[8]

In desperation, Richardson opted for the tried and true by contacting Weadick and offering the travelling entrepreneur a proposal. Would he accept a contract to stage a Stampede in conjunction with the 1923 Exhibition? Weadick did so willingly and gave Richardson more than he expected. In the 1923 Exhibition and Stampede, Weadick added two ingredients that in time defined its uniqueness. First, the addition of the exciting and potentially dangerous chuckwagon races was inspired by the increasing popularity of high-speed auto racing. Second, Weadick's idea to have the whole city go western for the event put the Exhibition and Stampede in a wider urban festival context. The success and profitability of the inaugural Exhibition and Stampede led to public calls for its continuance. In September 1923 Richardson seemed to answer the *Albertan's* 1921 query when he told the board of directors, "Calgary has found something the people want, something peculiarly appropriate to our environment, and we only have to use our unique opportunities to the best advantage."[9]

In summary, the first Exhibition was in 1886, the first Stampedes in 1912 and 1919. The Calgary Exhibition and Stampede began in 1923. Weadick continued to return every year to stage the Stampede component until the organization dispensed with his services in 1932 and began operating both events as the Calgary Exhibition and Stampede Limited, a non-profit company incorporated in 1933.

Characteristics of the Calgary Stampede

The evolution of the Stampede is best explained by examining enduring features that have defined its purpose and operations. While other articles in this volume explore some of these, this discussion focuses on the Stampede's heritage dimension, its ongoing popularity, its agricultural component, and its role in bringing matters of wider concern and interest to the general public.

The Western Heritage Dimension

It would be foolish to deny that this dimension of modern Stampedes reflects hype and myth far more than any awareness of or conscious desire to replicate Canada's frontier heritage. The reason why has more to do with the absence of living embodiments of western Canadian history than with slick marketing or promotional campaigns. When the original characters passed from the scene, Stampede organizers looked for their replacements. Arguably, they chose unwisely. From another and more positive perspective, although here too there are critics who would affirm otherwise, the Stampede has managed to preserve many festival-type traditions commensurate with its origins and, indeed, the western Canadian experience.

Guy Weadick set the precedent for frontier authenticity in 1912 when he put together "the greatest gathering of men who participated in the laying of the foundation of the present great Western development."[10] They included Hudson's Bay Company factors, cowboys, whisky traders, buffalo hunters, and some frontiersmen who predated them. These individuals were given high priority both in the parade and on the grounds. During the 1923 Stampede, people who had lived in the settlement that became the town of Calgary in 1884 conducted tours of the city. The 1925 Stampede featured Mounted Policemen who had taken part in the great march west in 1873–74. When the Stampede decided to re-enact the history of the West in 1930, three of the Big Four were alive to share in it. In 1945 when the Exhibition and Stampede outlined its fourfold mandate, the first was "to perpetuate our frontier tradition,"[11] yet by the time the Stampede decided to celebrate

Guy Weadick, ca. 1912

its fortieth anniversary seven years later with an old timers' reunion, few remained who represented the founding days or the vigour and mystique associated with them.

The buoyant decade 1955–65 marked a significant change in the Stampede, one in which the authenticity of the Canadian frontier experience disappeared and was replaced by Hollywood's "Wild West." In this decade the American western myth took hold, especially among the younger generations due to the enormous popularity of westerns on television. Leading cowboy stars became high-profile drawing cards, presenting the Stampede with an opportunity that was just too good to pass up. Between 1958 and 1967, the Stampede hosted such western television heroes as the Cisco Kid (Duncan Renaldo), Bat Masterson (Gene Barry), Tonto (Jay Silverheels) of *The Lone Ranger*, Marshall Dan Troop (John Russell), *The Virginian* (James Drury), and Peter Brown of *Laredo*. They were feted and honoured for being what they represented: a mythologized embodiment of a West that never existed in Canada or, according to American scholars, in the United States.

As if to validate the new emphasis, a survey on the Stampede parade taken in 1968 relegated the old timers' section to last place.[12]

Since the 1960s, the Stampede has focused primarily on the generic western myth. Though signage on the grounds and the presence of attractions such as Weadickville pay lip service to a localized identity, little in the Stampede speaks of the western Canadian frontier experience. Allusions to lynchings or even the simulated gunfights have no Canadian precedents. The western lingo often used in the press (especially by Mayor Don Mackay in the 1950s) is hackneyed and inauthentic.[13] Western dress has become a creative statement rooted loosely in romantic perceptions more reminiscent of the American Southwest than the Alberta foothills. Most Canadians visiting the Stampede are more familiar with Dodge City than they are with High River, Longview, or Maple Creek, and they come away no wiser. In short, the Canadian West has largely disappeared from the Stampede.

More authentic statements have been made over time through formal and informal celebratory activities. Since 1925, when it honoured the fiftieth anniversary of the arrival of the North-West Mounted Police in Calgary, the Stampede has been mindful of the need to make historic statements. Later examples include a celebration of the British Empire in 1939, Western Canadian Old Timers in 1952, Alberta's fiftieth birthday in 1955, the fiftieth anniversary of the world's first military aircraft in 1959, and a March of Time Parade in 1962 to honour the Stampede's fiftieth birthday.

On a more informal level, the willingness to dress and adorn buildings in a particular fashion, to square dance in the street, or to partake in public breakfasts of hearty fare is ritualistic, to a degree transformational, and at the heart of true festival celebrations. The spin-off activities, most of which do not achieve permanence, are variations on the festival theme. Typical would be the buffalo sandwich breakfast (1923), the open-air cowboys' ball (1938), parking lot dances (1942), and, more recently, bar stool races on Second Street (2002) and Meadow Muffler Madness (1994), a raffle type of contest in which cows were encouraged to defecate on numbered squares arranged along Stephen Avenue Mall. The point is that Stampede fever is about a popularized theme that involves the citizenry, and attending the Stampede is perceived by many as "the thing to do." As columnist Peter Burgener noted in 2002, "The Stampede brings out a level of corporate and personal responses that are expressed physically, and that are participatory and responsible."[14] While critics of the Stampede might have no trouble documenting inauthenticity, they would find it much more difficult to prove contrivance rather than willing participation in its several off-grounds activities.

Ongoing Popularity

The enduring popularity of the Exhibition and Stampede is hard to explain. It offers nothing essentially different from features of other fairs and exhibitions across the country. For example, a visitor from another country might have difficulty discerning between the entertainment opportunities afforded by Klondike Days (Capital EX since 2006) in Edmonton and the Calgary Stampede, yet it has always been wildly popular. Except for a short dip in the early 1930s (and Stampede spokesmen were quick to point out that other fairs of comparative size did much worse), attendance at the Stampede has steadily risen. In the 1950s, for instance, record attendance figures were set every year. Three reasons for this continuing success can be identified. First, the Stampede enjoyed from the outset a media-created mystique. Second, it was promoted aggressively by a coalition of interests dedicated to enhancing business opportunities and tourism revenues. Finally, it was able to widen its overall appeal through non-Stampede activities.

The 1912 Stampede was the first event of its kind. Guy Weadick capitalized on its unique and heady mix of cowboys, Indians, frontiersmen, and thrilling rodeo competitions to attract two motion picture companies. The films they produced, described as the "most complete of any Wild West pictures ever exhibited in the city," were eventually shown to audiences across Canada, the United States, and Europe.[15] At least five more films were shot before 1950. *The Calgary Stampede* (1925), starring Hoot Gibson, became one of the most profitable movies in North America.[16] The CBC broadcast Stampede events a year after it was founded in 1936 and a year later used short-wave radio to send the same broadcasts to Great Britain. In 1958 CBC carried the first television images of the Stampede to the Canadian pubic. Over eighteen million Britons watched a fifty-five-minute BBC television special on the Stampede in 1965. Currently, a distinguished award-winning Polish director is interested in exploring the cowboy myth through a Stampede documentary.

One of the main reasons the Stampede has maintained a popular and high-profile image has been an incredible level of support from the local press. Newspaper articles on the Stampede were as effusive as they were persistent. Most of the time the local editors sold the myth, lapsing into hackneyed jargon and conjuring up fanciful images of wild and woolly days in the West. Sometimes thoughtful appraisals located the essence of the Stampede's appeal in local support and pride.[17] Extensive international press coverage also enhanced the Stampede's widespread appeal. Reporters from twelve countries and fifteen states covered the Stampede in 1954, and by 1973 the number of accredited photographers had jumped to over two hundred.[18] The Stampede was also featured in many books about western Canada, including several novels. In touting the Stampede's irresistible and universal appeal, the print media took every opportunity to quote luminaries who might not be expected to revel in the earthiness of the Stampede. "I have never seen anything like it," exulted the French ambassador to Canada in 1954.[19] Lord Louis Mountbatten was equally enthusiastic when he said in 1967, "The first time the Stampede comes to Royalty; the second time around Royalty comes to the Stampede."[20] This persistent and ebullient press support is one of the reasons why critics use the term "Sacred Cow" to denote the Stampede's inviolate status within the city.

Popularity was reflected in other ways. Almost from the beginning, the Stampede has been identified with personal statements. Slim Moorhouse chose the Stampede to display his thirty-six-horse team in 1924. Two years later a man walked from Toronto just to attend the Stampede. Another drove his tractor nine hundred miles for the same reason in 1954. As recently as 2004 a cowboy led a group of mounted riders all the way from Bandera, Texas, to the Stampede to make a statement about the faltering economies of small western towns. The Stampede is also a destination event. High school bands work diligently to make money so they can participate in the Stampede parade. California's Contra Costa County Sheriff's Posse dressed in uniform and arrived as a group in 1951. The Stampede has become a sought-after forum for both excellence and eccentricity, having hosted world championship events for blacksmiths and marching bands, an attempt to set a world record for the number of pancakes fed to guests in one hour, and even competitions for the most outlandish costumes.

The Stampede's commercial value was not lost on those who stood to profit by it. Ernie Richardson told civic officials in 1914 that the Exhibition existed to enhance the city.[21] Lindsey Galloway, senior manager of Corporate Communications and Stakeholder Relations, said the same thing in 2005. From the outset, the City of Calgary, the Chamber of Commerce, nearby businesses, livestock associations, and tourist agencies formed a powerful support group that complemented the Stampede by propagating its appeal whenever and wherever possible. One has only to note Mayor Don Mackay's correspondence in the 1950s, when he used his persuasive powers effectively to entice hundreds of Americans, mostly civic officials, to the Stampede.

The Stampede organization was proactive in furthering its appeal. It worked with the Calgary Tourist Bureau to find accommodation in private houses for visitors to the Stampede. It kept track of visitor movement within the mountain parks and lobbied the provincial government to improve road access to Calgary, particularly by roads that carried American visitors. In later years the Stampede tried to maintain its edge by commissioning studies and preparing long-range plans.

Another key to the Stampede's continuing success lay in its ability to attract prominent people. Usually they came in some official capacity, to open the Stampede, to act as honorary parade marshals, or simply to be guests of honour. From the first Stampede in 1912, when the viceregal guest was the duke of Connaught, Queen Victoria's son and the governor general of Canada, a steady procession of dignitaries has graced the Stampede. They included royalty, prime ministers, governors general, and premiers. In the 1950s, for example, the Stampede was attended in different years by Queen Elizabeth and Prince Philip, Prime Minister Louis St. Laurent, and Governors General Vincent Massey and Georges Vanier. The Stampede also successfully courted international celebrities whose presence in some official capacity contributed to crowd appeal. These included Prince Charles, the brother of the emperor of Japan, Lord Louis Mountbatten, Robert Kennedy, Douglas Bader, Walt Disney, Bob Hope, Bing Crosby, Rocky Marciano, Jack Palance, and Sam Elliott. As has been said on many occasions, "There's always someone to see at the Stampede."

Though the Stampede hosts many events on a year-round basis, the most popular are those related to sports. Nevertheless, the important role played by the Stampede in furthering sport in the City of Calgary has gone largely unrecognized.[22] For years the Stampede operated a hockey franchise; it was perhaps the pivotal agency promoting and staging the sport in Calgary. Between 1950 and 1981 the Corral and the Big Four Building were the largest facilities of their kind in the city. The Brier, the Canadian Men's Curling Championship, was held in the Big Four Building in 1961. Four years later the Corral hosted the Dominion Figure Skating Championship.

The Stampede's success in bringing increasing numbers of people to its grounds poses a significant dilemma for contemporary senior management. Larger audiences want more varied fare, but catering to all age and interest groups and trying to provide something for everyone may dilute features the rest of the world associates with the Stampede. As it seeks to become a major year-round venue, its western roots may well become just one element in a package of entertainment options. And largely mythical though they may be, these western connotations have been used to advertise and promote Calgary and the Stampede for almost a century. The Stampede will have to weigh popularity and the dollars that accompany it with the image it has historically conveyed. The two may prove to be more incompatible than present optimism suggests.

Agriculture

From its beginnings in 1886, agriculture and especially livestock have been of central importance to the Calgary Exhibition. Ernie Richardson was determined to maintain agriculture's priority after the Exhibition merged with the more entertainment-oriented Stampede in 1923. In 1942 the board of directors took special pride in the fact that the organization was making exceptional progress in "building up a plant for livestock and exhibition purposes second to none in Canada."[23] When the Exhibition and Stampede Limited published its four goals in 1945, the second was to foster the livestock industry. In 1977 a $30,000 commissioned study by Stanford Research Institute, a California-based entertainment consulting company, recommended that the future of the Exhibition and Stampede be vitally linked to its agricultural component. As late as 2002 the press noted that agriculture continues to be the backbone of the Exhibition and Stampede, yet changes have taken place. Though agriculture remains a component of Exhibition and Stampede activity, it has receded from its previous prominence.

An emphasis on agriculture is still a visible part of the Stampede. The barns, the show pavilions, and the concentration of educational agricultural activities still afford plenty of opportunities for visitors to acquaint themselves with purebred stock, to view agriculture-related performances, and to learn more about agribusiness. Today, the Calgary Stampede Agriculture Department presents over forty-five international stock show events during the Stampede. The Stampede is also important for sales. For example, in 1996 local company Alta Genetics sold $1.35 million worth of bull semen and embryo stock to buyers from fourteen countries.[24] In the same year, the chair of the Stampede Promotions Committee dealt with international buyers from twenty-nine countries who were interested in purchasing quality stock in order to rebuild their herds.[25]

The Stampede also enhanced Calgary's importance as a livestock centre. In 1927 it persuaded the Canadian Livestock Association to hold its annual convention in Calgary. After 1955 the breed associations were encouraged to hold their annual conventions around Stampede time through a policy that honoured a single breed annually. This succession of conventions was doubtless a factor in securing the World Charolais Federation meeting in 1967, which, according to the *Calgary Herald*, was attended by over one hundred international millionaires worth five billion dollars.[26] Two more world livestock congresses were held in conjunction with the Stampede in 1975 and 1978.

Most of the agricultural activity that occurs on a regular basis on the grounds throughout the year is organized and operated by the Stampede. Perhaps the most notable is the Calgary Bull Sale, which dates to 1901. Often described as the premier sale of its kind in North America, the Calgary Bull Sale grossed over two million dollars in 1994. The Stampede has also operated horse shows, sheep and swine sales, and seed fairs, and in the 1950s it promoted the sale of purebred stock to the United States.

The Stampede's association with agricultural education began when it hosted groups of farm boys in the 1930s. In the 1940s the Stampede's agricultural revue was designed to make children more aware of the attributes of prime livestock. Later emphasis was placed on promoting 4-H activity and, more recently, Aggie Days. Spokespersons for the Stampede now say their primary mandate is to find ways by which agriculture's message can be carried to an urban society. They are currently trying to develop innovative programs that will link consumers to the food they eat.

To maintain its status as an agricultural fair and its eligibility for government grants and concessions, the Stampede must include activities related to agriculture. In this sense it is no different from any small-town fair in Alberta. One could argue that the current annual provincial grant of ten million dollars in lottery monies had its historical roots in the allocation of horse racing and gambling privileges to agricultural fairs. Nevertheless, it is undeniable that agriculture figures less prominently in the Stampede's plans for the future. One could discern this in the late 1970s when its management opted for an all-purpose Round-Up Centre instead of the new Agricultural Building originally envisaged. To those directing the Stampede in the new millennium, promoting Calgary as a major entertainment and tourist centre seems to be a greater priority than showcasing or advertising agriculture.

A Wider Voice

Over the years the Stampede has incorporated issues of social interest and concern into its activities. First, it showcased modern technology in an age when people had few opportunities to attend trade shows or learn about inventions and innovations. Second, it drew public attention to larger national issues. Third, it has increasingly become associated with the wider concept of carnival itself.

The Stampede has been a vehicle for the display of technological advances. The 1935 parade, for example, was announced as the birth of the industrial era. In the same decade, the Stampede featured a robot that answered questions, a giant television twenty years before it was commercialized, car radios, wringerless washing machines, and the latest in automobile technology. Also in the 1930s, the Stampede's emphasis on automobile displays and the educational opportunities offered to viewers quite likely influenced buyer judgement and choice. Over the years, the Big Four Building and later the Round-Up Centre have continued to attract exhibits that feature state-of-the-art products.

The Stampede has also functioned as a catalyst for bringing public attention to contemporary events and issues. While the themed activities at Flare Square and the promotion of Canada's Centennial in 1967, the Commonwealth Games in 1978, and the Olympic Games in 1988 provide excellent examples, the most sustained demonstration of the Stampede's involvement in contemporary issues came during Second World War. In 1942 armed forces personnel opened the Grandstand Show, "On to Victory." Tanks were included in the parade that year, which concluded with a large float named The Float of Victory. The 1943 Stampede included demonstrations on commando tactics and parachute packing. The 1944 Grandstand Show was titled "Let Freedom Ring," and in the victory year, 1945, over five thousand troops led the parade. In the same year the chutes in the infield were adorned with flags of the allied countries, with the Hammer and Sickle right there in the centre beside the Stars and Stripes and the Union Jack. In conjunction with Canada's centennial in 1967, the Stampede hosted one of the first interdenominational church services in Calgary.

In more modern times, given the fractured interests of audiences and the sheer number of events competing for them, the Stampede has lost its capacity to be the catalyst it once was. This is unfortunate, especially given the Stampede's increasing focus on pure entertainment with all the shallowness and self-gratification it embodies.

The Calgary Exhibition and Stampede has always offered rodeo, exhibits, and entertainment. In this it is no different from a host of fairs across the North American continent. Its uniqueness, however, lies in several areas. One is the way it is organized and the relationship it enjoys with the City of Calgary. Also, while it is true that the Stampede has embraced a generic western mythology, it can also claim roots in the historic western Canadian ranching experience and a commitment to maintaining a strong focus on livestock.

A third important achievement concerns the way the modern Stampede has managed to capture the essence of carnival. In its rituals, messages, symbolic representations, and even in the language used to articulate the latter, the Stampede represents a merging of disparate values, of collective identities and individual statements. It has spilled beyond the grounds not just to events in shopping mall parking lots and Stampede breakfasts, but also to counter-cultural statements and parodies. For example, western clothing denotes participation and identification with a cultural tradition and therefore the status quo; the open disdain for Stetsons and boots evidenced by many young people is an implicit rejection of these same values. Other individuals and groups capitalize on the Stampede's popularity by promoting alternative activities and celebrations.

The Stampede adopts carnival traditions in other ways. Like Mardi Gras in New Orleans and ANZAC Day in Australia, the Stampede allows for a brief suspension of the constraints of everyday life. Role reversals in which dignitaries do ordinary things or suffer contrived humiliation are mockeries of accepted power relations. A suspension of the rules allows party-goers young and old ready access to situations in which marginal illegal activity is tacitly accepted. As Glen Mikkelsen points out, the rodeo clowns freely violate accepted social norms in their repartee with the spectators.

As a spectacle or celebration, as a ritual or performance, the Stampede is truly a carnival. The parade, fireworks display, midway, stage shows, and rodeo provide the best visual cornucopia of its kind in the country. United by contrived clothing and lingo and by the relaxation of norms, visitors to the Stampede, whether they be international or local, are suspended in a cultural vacuum, "pardners" in an unreal and temporary experience. Off the grounds beyond the Stampede statements, the pervading ethos of the myth reaches into other domains, carrying diverse messages and evoking different reactions. In this context, the Stampede is as much a time as it is an event.

Recently the Stampede has been trying to design an image that speaks of the past but which will resonate with larger and more diverse audiences. The two building blocks appear to be "community" and "western values." In 2006 the Calgary Stampede Board unveiled its plans for the redevelopment of Stampede Park to the north, where the inner-city suburb of East Victoria Park used to be. In a colourful brochure titled *Mapping Our Future*, the Stampede associated its plans for the future with "great development of surrounding inner-city neighbourhoods" that "will help build community at a time when community building is vitally important to Calgary."[27] In early 2007 Stampede President Steve Allan told a gathering at the Calgary Chamber of Commerce that community involvement is a universal responsibility. In announcing the Stampede's new brand in spring 2007, Stampede General Manager Vern Kimball noted that it is more than a logo: "It represents our commitment to preserve and promote the unique values of the Stampede and our community – western hospitality, integrity, commitment to community and pride of place."[28] It will be interesting to see how these grand plans unfold.

Notes

1. For contrasting views on the Exhibition and Stampede see James H. Gray, *A Brand of Its Own: The 100 Year History of the Stampede* (Saskatoon: Western Producer Prairie Books, 1985); Colin S. Campbell, "The Stampede: Cowtown's Sacred Cow," in *Stampede City: Power and Politics in the West*, ed. Chuck Reasons (Toronto: Between the Lines, 1984), 103–120.
2. *Calgary Herald*, 5 July 1909.
3. *Calgary Herald*, 30 June 1911.
4. Gray, *Brand of Its Own*, 35.
5. *Morning Albertan* (Calgary), 30 July 1910.
6. *Calgary Herald*, 30 July 1910.
7. Donna Livingstone, *The Cowboy Spirit: Guy Weadick and the Calgary Stampede* (Vancouver: Greystone Books, 1996).
8. *Albertan* (Calgary), 8 July 1921.
9. Minutes of the Calgary Industrial Exhibition Co. Ltd., Calgary Exhibition and Stampede Papers, box 1, 26 September 1923, Glenbow Museum Archives.
10. Guy Weadick to Mayor J. Mitchell, 13 June 1912, City Clerk Correspondence, Box 50, file folder 403, City of Calgary Archives (hereafter cited as CCA).
11. Calgary Exhibition and Stampede, Annual Report, 1945.
12. City Commissioners Papers, series V, box 104, file folder 4737, CCA.
13. The following extract from a letter written to the mayor of Vancouver is typical: "You can bet your dad-durned tootin' six shootin' guns and yore best little old spurs that you Vancouver cowboys and cowgals would have a wonderful time." He closes the letter with "yers trooly." See letter dated 11 May 1951, City Commissioners Papers, series IV, box 48, file folder E-1, CCA.
14. Peter Burgener, "Mixing Stampede into Perception," *Calgary Herald*, 3 July 2002.
15. News Telegram (Calgary), 17 September 1912.
16. Calgary Exhibition and Stampede, Annual Report, 1925.
17. See editorial, "The Spirit of the Stampede," *Calgary Herald*, 13 July 1954.
18. Calgary Exhibition and Stampede, Annual Reports, 1954, 1973.
19. *Calgary Herald*, 9 July 1946.
20. *Calgary Herald*, 7 July 1967.
21. E.L. Richardson to mayor, 28 February 1914, City Commissioners Papers, series I, box 50, file folder General Correspondence, January–June 1914, CCA.
22. For good discussion see "Hockey and Horses," *Calgary Herald Neighbors*, 13–19 July 1994.
23. Calgary Exhibition and Stampede, Annual Report, 1942.
24. *Calgary Herald*, 14 July 1996.
25. Ibid.

26. *Calgary Herald*, 7 July 1967.
27. Mapping Our Future: A Gathering Place for Calgary and the World (Calgary: Calgary Exhibition and Stampede, 2006).
28. "Brand Identity Built on Values," Saddle Bag 6, no. 1 (Spring 2007). The brand no longer contains the word "Exhibition." It consists of the words "Calgary Stampede" below a "C" and a "lazy S," the latter in recognition of the organization's agricultural roots.

CHAPTER 2

Making Tradition: The Calgary Stampede, 1912–1939

Donald G. Wetherell

The Big Four seen in this group of ranching elite: (far left) Archie McLean, A. E. Cross; (centre) the Prince of Wales (wearing jodhpurs) with George Lane and Pat Burns beside him.

Between 1912 and 1939 the Calgary Stampede increasingly influenced how Calgarians constructed their identity, and by the eve of Second World War the Stampede had become a permanent feature of Calgary life. Although the Stampede expanded and evolved after Second World War as part of the general reshaping of North American life in the wake of the war and Alberta's transformation by the oil boom, it had by the late 1930s already assumed many essential characteristics that have endured until the present.

The Stampedes of 1912 and 1919 were organized in Calgary as one-time events that served local commemorative and social needs. In contrast, the rodeo that was an entertainment feature of the Calgary Exhibition in 1923 and subsequent years created a different historical trajectory. While the 1912 and 1919 Stampedes provided historical legitimacy for those after 1923, the later Stampedes were also framed by their general cultural, economic, and historical context and by changing patterns in communications, transportation, mass entertainment, and sports. These Stampedes were also shaped by the economic benefits they offered Calgary, especially from an emerging tourism industry. Within this context, the annual Stampede gained popular acceptance as an expression of authentic local traditions and values. Whatever the merit of this view, the intersecting forces that gave the Stampede legitimacy in Calgary and Alberta meant that rodeo and a particular take on western history came to be accepted as a part of the city's self-definition.

The Calgary Stampede is, in historian Eric Hobsbawm's terms, an example of an invented tradition. The concept of invented tradition arose from Hobsbawm's inquiry into the ways that European counties in the eighteenth and nineteenth centuries had responded to the rapid changes demanded by the Industrial Revolution and the emergence of new states. When Hobsbawm looked at these societies experiencing extraordinary change, he realized that many of the events identified as ancient traditions, festivals, and rituals were, in fact, very recent.[1]

Invented traditions – activities that are actually recent but are accepted by the public as having a particularly long and resonant history and as representing something essential about a nation's character, values, and identity – arose from a widespread effort to justify the nation state, royal dynasties, and national boundaries by linking them, often tenuously and sometimes even falsely, with the past. These invented traditions often emerged fairly quickly and were accepted (or sometimes rejected) equally quickly by the population at large. Hobsbawm observed that invented traditions could be counted on to occur regularly because repetition implied continuity with the past.

Even so, invented traditions could not logically serve as the basis for the customs of everyday life because the social and economic links with the past that they supposedly represented had been irreparably severed by social, technological, and economic change. Nonetheless, these traditions were accepted as genuine expressions of how people viewed themselves and their place in the world. The invention of a tradition was not random. While the precise reasons why one tradition found public acceptance and another did not is not always clear, it is evident that traditions gained social sanction within certain parameters. Believability, for example, could only be secured by appealing to widely accepted interpretations – accurate or not – of history. Also, an event that challenged accepted social mores and attitudes or local political and social power was unlikely to be adopted.

To understand how invented traditions arise, it is important to attempt to isolate the stages through which an event evolves into a tradition. The Calgary Stampede moved through at least three stages towards being accepted as a legitimate and largely unquestioned part of Calgary's history and life. The process of entrenchment of this invented tradition can be further judged by the way it was imitated and reproduced elsewhere in the province.

The first stage in the invention of the tradition of the Calgary Stampede was a preparatory period from the late 1880s until 1912. During these two decades, crucial developments took place as rodeo emerged as a popular activity that was relevant, in part at least, to local conditions. Building on several decades of cowboy sports in southern Alberta, prototypes of the Calgary Stampede were enacted in 1912 and 1919, which marked a second stage in the evolution of an ideology that sustained the Stampede in Calgary and shaped its future development. The 1912 Stampede was very quickly replicated in other parts of the province, showing that its appeal was not merely a product of local idiosyncrasies. As well, while the 1912 and 1919 Stampedes promoted the social legitimacy of rodeo, they included elements that required amendment to achieve full social acceptability. The last stage in the Stampede's invention as a local tradition began in 1923, when it was first held in conjunction with the Calgary Exhibition as a formalized event that would be repeated without fail in subsequent years.

The Calgary Stampede was entrenched in Calgary's civic life by the late 1920s, and thus emerged relatively quickly as an invented tradition. Like the 1912 and 1919 Stampedes, those after 1923 offered a vision of ranching life and methods of production that had in fact existed for only a limited time in the province's history and now had little connection with contemporary social and economic systems, even in rural areas. Nevertheless, its believability and its public acceptance were sanctioned by a history of cowboy sports in southern Alberta, by the ongoing involvement of the Calgary elite in sponsoring the event, by its promise of economic benefit, by its appeal to a history that people wanted to have even if they personally did not, and by the entertainment that it offered the public, who faithfully crowded onto the Stampede grounds each year.

Making Rodeo Popular and Respectable

The development of ranching in southern Alberta began tentatively in the 1870s but grew significantly after the arrival of the railway in 1883. The Calgary Stampedes of 1923 and subsequent years were built on about forty years of cowboy sporting events in southern Alberta. As Canadian rodeo historian Claire Eamer notes, these events were the "simple contests among working men who had few other amusements." These were not rodeos – formal events with well-understood rules and competitive standards – but were informal and essentially disorganized.[2] Nevertheless, they spread quickly from the ranches and into the broader culture to create a public taste for cowboy sports that would ultimately take the form of rodeos. Local ranchers, for example, were heavily involved in the horse races held in conjunction with the Fort Macleod fair in 1886, and in addition to participating in the conventional races, they put on what was called a "cowboy race" between the first and second heats of the meet. This mile and a half race drew seven or eight contestants, and "the regulations required that this race be ridden in full cowboy costume." It was designed only as entertainment to break the tension of the real heats – the ones on which money was seriously wagered – and it was clearly secondary to the conventional races.[3]

This cowboy event was, however, significant in that it integrated local custom and history into the traditional Anglo-Canadian race meet and agricultural fair. The same pattern was seen at the week-long Calgary exhibition of 1894. As the *Edmonton Bulletin* reported, "the best drawing cards of the whole exhibition" were the bucking and roping contests. These events were still marginal to the more conventional aspects of the fair and each drew only six or seven contestants and lasted about one hour. The contestants divided naturally into two opposing groups, one from the north (Calgary and High River) and the other from the more southern areas around Fort Macleod. The lavish $100 prize for the roping contest indicates that a network of local fans was emerging. John Ware of High River was the star of the roping contests and drew "an enthusiastic crowd," many of whom had been present the year before when he broke "the best previous record" at the fair. Fans had by now begun to bet extensively on both the roping and bucking horse events; one of them wagered an extraordinary $300 on the northern group in the bucking contest. The betting, the large prizes, and the fact that some people remembered and kept track of local records of accomplishment were all signs that cowboy competitions were becoming locally entrenched as sporting events.[4]

The growing public appeal of cowboy events was further revealed by the fact that they were showing up at fairs, horse races, and sports days, and even as stand-alone events. Rodeos, which consisted only of cowboy contests, were not long in appearing. Raymond, Alberta, for example, claims that a "stampede" held on its main street in 1901 or 1902 was the first formal rodeo in Canada.[5] While such events drew upon regional ranching traditions, the popularity of cowboy sports was stimulated in a major way by other elements as well, especially commercial Wild West shows. The most famous of these were mounted by Buffalo Bill Cody beginning in 1882. When Cody gave up the business at the turn of the century, his imitators had made Wild West shows generic events, with troupes of actors travelling the continent putting on performances. Popular shows in Alberta included the Miller Brothers Wild West Show that brought riding and roping acts and dramatizations of the "Old West" to Calgary in 1908 and the Oklahoma Wild West Show that visited Red Deer in 1913. Travelling vaudeville shows also often included fancy roping, horse tricks, or other "cowboy" features.[6] Such shows doubtless stimulated popular interest in rodeo and helped legitimize local contests as fashionable and attractive mass entertainment.

Even so, the occasional lapse into vulgarity at these events confirmed a view that they were only marginally respectable. Respectability was a vague but powerful concept that shaped sporting life and reflected a complex mix of gendered and class attitudes about character, physical hardiness, social responsibility, and self-control.[7] When animals were involved in sport, the picture was further complicated by notions about the proper relationship between people and animals. An "alleged 'bucking contest' in the [town] square" in Fort Macleod in 1911, for example, prompted the local newspaper to argue that "when unwilling beasts have to be goaded and frightened into action, and are ridden about with blood from the spurs dripping from their flanks, the whole outfit responsible for the 'show' should be hauled up for cruelty to animals." The "days of the 'Wild West' are past," said the editor, "and the 'bucking contest' is a relic of barbarism."[8] Much the same reaction arose relative to the "cowboy sports," probably put on by travelling showmen, in Victoria Park (the site of the annual Calgary agricultural exhibition) in 1905. About a thousand spectators showed up, a significant number for a city with a population of around ten thousand, but the occasion was not without controversy and elicited a demand that cowboy sports conform to the etiquette and definitions of respectability acceptable to the community's leaders. An event in which "a huge cowboy grabs a steer by the nose with his teeth and throws the animal to the ground" drew particular outrage from the pulpit and the *Calgary Herald*. Indeed, the *Herald* reported that this spectacle had been seen previously and had aroused widespread feelings of "disgust." This negative reaction, noted the *Herald*, was "to the credit of the Calgary public," for "clean sports are liberally patronized in Calgary" and the city had no room for offensive displays. "Local colour can be introduced into these cowboy exhibitions without this sort of thing," warned the *Herald*, and "when a man is permitted to make an exhibition of this character in the presence of women and children, the finer sensibilities are outraged."[9] Such devotion to "clean sports" clearly trumped the value of "local colour," which seems to have been acceptable as a memento of place and historical moment, but not as a basis for civic life. Indeed, the episode demonstrated local determination to discard the uncouthness of the frontier, to prove that Calgary was a respectable town. It may have been new, but it had standards of social taste and civic life as high as those of more developed parts of Canada.

Interwoven into such concerns was a commonly expressed fear that recreational events and leisure time could be socially dangerous and must be managed in order to uphold and reinforce social conventions. In Canada, as in Britain and the United States, it was commonly argued that inappropriate use of leisure time would lead to social decay and would erode the central place of work in social life. This view held that recreation should be a re-creation of the individual for work. Since fun and play were necessary for a full life and for productive labour, "good" recreation could be defined as that which stimulated the mind and body and improved character, while "bad" recreation diverted people from work and led to dissipation or frivolousness.[10]

In hierarchies that ranked recreational activities by their social worth and utility, sport almost always met with approval. Sport built character, improved health through physical activity, and taught important lessons about the importance of good manners and how to be a graceful winner and a gracious loser. Team sports built character by teaching camaraderie, group loyalty, and obedience, while individual sports tested character and resourcefulness in combination with physical and mental skill. These virtues were also said to contribute to nation building and often evoked "Britishness," since Britain's success as an imperial power with a stable social order was attributed in part to its sporting traditions. A complementary notion held that amateur sports – sports played without monetary reward – were superior to those sullied by money. Although professional stars performed on the rodeo circuit, rodeo retained the aura of an amateur sport because many participants were local men and women who entered the contest for the glory of it. While participation was most important, spectatorship was also socially useful because those watching were given concrete evidence about how both winners and losers conducted themselves and how people could interact in a competitive environment.[11]

As a sport, however, rodeo was complicated because of its use of animals. Blood sports had been outlawed in Canada in 1870, but concerns about other forms of cruelty to animals had emerged by the late nineteenth century.[12] While these concerns influenced the way rodeo was practised, rodeo also tested horsemanship and livestock handling. In measuring and enhancing skills in these respects, it embodied many popular attitudes towards domestic animals – about controlling them, about being challenged by them, about dominating them, and about using them in the service of humans.

The Stampedes of 1912 and 1919

By 1912 Calgary was in the midst of a massive building boom, land prices were high, and economic forecasts were optimistic. It seemed that rodeo was well on the way to being purged of cruelty and vulgarity and becoming a socially legitimate and useful sport that could be popularized as part of the city's historical tradition. Over two decades of cowboy sports in southern Alberta and the development of a committed spectator audience further paved the way for the first Stampedes in Calgary in 1912 and 1919. The event also gained social and political legitimacy through its sponsors. Under the prompting of Guy Weadick, an American promoter and cowboy vaudeville performer, the 1912 Stampede was endorsed and bankrolled by leaders of the local elite, the so-called Big Four: George Lane, owner of the Bar U Ranch and Calgary businesses; Pat Burns, meat packer and owner of other businesses; A.E. Cross; rancher and owner of the Calgary Brewing and Malting Company; and Archie McLean, a rancher and provincial politician. Such sponsorship made the Stampede socially respectable. Ethnic background and class status were also relevant. The Big Four were apparently convinced that the Stampede would promote the history of British-Canadian ranching in southern Alberta and help the ranching elite confirm its legitimacy by appealing to a history that cast it as a local aristocracy and a founding group in the city.[13]

Preceded by a major marketing campaign, the 1912 Stampede ran for four days and offered an ambitious schedule of events that included a huge street parade of First Nations people, cowboys and cowgirls, floats, and various representatives of Calgary society. The rodeo events were relatively limited in comparison to those of later Stampedes: bronco riding, steer roping, and bulldogging, as well as various vaudeville-type acts such as fancy roping and trick riding.[14] A number of cowgirls participated in the competitions, reflecting that in Canada as in the United States, rodeo cowgirls were "pioneer professional athletes."[15] Weadick also managed to attract star visitors when he incorporated a scheduled visit to Calgary by the Governor General, the Duke of Connaught, into the Stampede. Purses that Weadick later claimed were "five times in excess of any that had been offered anywhere in the world up to that time" drew top contestants from across North America. The Canadian Pacific Railway (CPR) offered special half-fare excursion rates, and a reported forty thousand people from as far away as Winnipeg took advantage of them. Others drove from Fort Macleod and other centres in southern Alberta to take in the spectacle.

Local businesses found the arrival of thousands of out-of-town visitors a major boost to trade, but there were problems as well. As historian James Gray notes, the public grumbled that admission prices were too high and that the Stampede organizers had been lax about delivering value for money. Moreover, organizational problems, bad weather, and poor equipment and infrastructure (such as the lack of saddling chutes for the bucking horses) added to the confusion that dominated some events. Many observers objected to a gory display when "the bulldozed long-horn bulls spewed blood in all directions when the cowboys, wrestling them to the earth, tore their horns out by the roots."[16] While the Stampede's sponsorship and connection with the local elite, the quality of participants, and its advertising and marketing showed that the event had potential, its organizational and public relations problems indicated that it was not yet ready for incorporation into Calgary's life and mores. Thus, despite discussion about making it an annual event, a repeat Stampede was ruled out. The First World War soon followed, and war efforts precluded the possibility of another Stampede until 1919. Again bankrolled by the Big Four and managed by Guy Weadick, the second Stampede was designed as a "Great Victory Entertainment" to raise money for charities supporting veterans and children orphaned by the war.[17] While it was better organized and managed than the 1912 event, the 1919 Stampede sold only 57,456 admissions, not enough to cover expenses,[18] due to worrisome economic times, social uncertainty, and high gate prices.

Both the 1912 and 1919 Stampedes were considered successful, however, and they established a prototype that would be applied in the future. Both Stampedes offered the outline and content of an emerging invented tradition, a vision of the ranching and settlement years as a better time, the values of which continued to inspire society. In the hands of tourism promoters and others, this nostalgia soon led to a conflation of present and past that could be marketed as authentic and relevant. Yet, while ranching still dominated parts of the country around Calgary by the First World War and the city remained an important stock centre, most livestock operations no longer owed much to the open-range ranching tradition celebrated by the Stampede. After about 1906, the livestock industry began shifting towards feedlot and controlled production practices that in many ways owed more to industrial patterns of organization than to the history of open-range ranching.[19] By 1912 Calgary was a railway town that owed only a small part of its growth and wealth to ranching, although a family's ranching pedigree apparently conferred social status, especially when ranching money was combined with wealth earned from urban real estate, business, manufacturing, or transportation.[20] Calgary owed its growth as a major prairie city to its location on the CPR and its service to grain and irrigated farms in southern Alberta and mining and timbering areas in Alberta and the British Columbia interior.

While the 1912 and 1919 Stampedes were preludes to an invented Calgary tradition, they contributed materially to the emergence of such a tradition elsewhere as well. This seems to have been the case in Medicine Hat, where the first rodeo was held in 1917, but the history of the rodeo at Bruce, Alberta, which now advertises itself as "the biggest one-day rodeo in Canada," provides an even clearer illustration of this phenomenon.

Bruce is located slightly north of Camrose. The town was established in 1908, and every year beginning in 1909 it has held a sports day to celebrate its founding. In 1912 local men who had attended the Stampede in Calgary proposed that Bruce should add rodeo events to the annual sports day. This was in part simply the adoption of a successful event held elsewhere, but as with the Calgary Stampede in 1912, local conditions were in place to legitimize the event. Although mixed farming prevailed in the district, around 1912 drought in southern Alberta forced ranchers to drive their stock north to graze in the open land around Bruce. Cowboys who moved north with the cattle brought with them their recreational traditions.[21]

Thus, by 1913, factors that led to staging a rodeo in Bruce included local interest in the 1912 Calgary event and the cowboy culture of the men who accompanied the cattle from the south. There seems to have been some competition between the southern Alberta cowboys and local men, perhaps a story of outsider and insider that is always potent in small towns. As the local history of Bruce phrases it, "the ranch hands of the south were eager for some competition with the local cowboys." In this description it is interesting to note that the locals were the "cowboys" and presumably of higher standing than the outsiders who were mere "ranch hands."

The first Bruce rodeo was held on the fairgrounds. There were no bleachers, fences, or saddling chutes, and the loading pens at the railway station were used to hold the stock. The main feature of the day was a bucking horse competition. As at Calgary in 1912, there was no time limit and the rider just stayed on as long as possible. Prizes were paid to the top riders from a collection taken among the spectators. At first, these cowboy contests took place in conjunction with those customarily held at the sports day, such as baseball, but soon the cowboy contests took over and the event became a rodeo. In 1919 it was still called the Bruce Sports Day, but by 1920 it had become known as the Bruce Stampede, and although ball games continued for a few years to be a feature of the day, they disappeared in the late 1920s, leaving the event dominated by rodeo.

As Bruce's rodeo demonstrates, the Calgary Stampede of 1912 had sparked imitators, indicating that rodeo was becoming part of a more diffused tradition in Alberta. The 1912 Stampede was not yet an invented tradition, however; it was only the prelude to one because it lacked the continuity that could frame its ideology and give it consistent expression in local life.

Beyond Spectacle: The Calgary Stampede, 1923–1939

While the Stampedes of 1912 and 1919 inspired rodeos in other parts of Alberta and confirmed the social and sporting legitimacy of rodeo, the 1923 Stampede gained further legitimacy by tapping into the historical traditions of agricultural fairs in Canada. This elevated it beyond mere spectacle enacted for the enjoyment of a crowd and the promotion of immediate local needs into an activity intimately connected with a venerable and deeply symbolic tradition in Canadian rural life.

Agricultural fairs were organized in most parts of Alberta as part of the culture transplanted by Anglo-Canadian settlers. Beginning in 1885, and with few interruptions, annual fairs were a feature of summer life in Calgary and surrounding areas. Fairs symbolized ideals of rural collective purpose, sociability, and community. Mounted by local agricultural societies, they were officially seen as opportunities for farmers to meet, show their livestock and grain, compare experiences, and learn about efficient farming techniques and the improvement and reform of rural society.[22] As such, agricultural fairs merited the support of the state, and the federal government, as well as the territorial and later the provincial governments, provided grants to support them.

Beyond such objectives, the fairs clearly offered fun and diversion at the midway, sports events, and grandstand show. Keeping educational and entertainment functions in appropriate balance was sometimes a matter of public concern. Some critics contended that while fairs should be enjoyable, they should above all be useful. Cowboy contests were a distraction – no different from a midway or a horse race – luring people away from sober recreations that would leave them better prepared to work. As H.A. Craig, the superintendent of fairs and institutes for Alberta, remarked in 1908, government grants were justified because "the agricultural fair is an edu-cational institution." And, he warned, it was important that this character be preserved and that the fair not be an occasion when "things relevant to agriculture are side-tracked, and horse races, fakirs' shows, ball matches etc. take their place."[23]

At the same time, pragmatism forced everyone to recognize that enter-tainment at fairs had to be tolerated because it attracted visitors who might benefit from the more serious objectives of the fair. While government grants were important, fair boards knew that a fair could not survive without sub-stantial gate receipts. Such pragmatism became even more important in the early 1920s, when the provincial government reduced the amounts it paid in grants to agricultural fairs. In the case of the Calgary Exhibition Associa-tion, the grant for 1923 fell from $10,000 to $8,000. Given the losses the Exhibition had chalked up between 1920 and 1922, its board of directors realized that the fair had to bring in more people or be abandoned due to falling attendance and rising debts. The Exhibition Association had featured trick riding and roping in its 1921 spring horse show to increase its audience, and public enthusiasm led to the expansion of these features in the follow-ing year. This, along with the precedents of the 1912 and 1919 Stampedes, persuaded the directors that if they added "a really outstanding stampede as an exhibition attraction, we could recoup our losses and build up an institu-tion which would be as important in building up Alberta as the Canadian National Exhibition is in Eastern Canada."[24]

The Stampede held in 1923 in conjunction with the agricultural fair was so successful that attendance increased dramatically. Indeed, the fair associa-tion soon began to remake its identity by calling itself the Calgary Exhibition and Stampede. In 1922 the Calgary Exhibition had attracted about 97,000 people. In 1923, the first year it included the Stampede, it drew nearly 138,000. The course was set; in subsequent years attendance continued to increase, reaching 223,425 by 1938. Further cuts in government funding in the late 1920s and suspension of all grants for a few years in the early 1930s made rodeo entertainment essential to the survival of the fair as a profitable event.[25]

As a means of enhancing the popularity and profits of the Calgary Exhibition, the 1923 Calgary Stampede emerged from a different context and rationale than had the 1912 and 1919 Stampedes. The Stampedes of 1923 and subsequent years could be smoothly integrated with the traditions of an agricultural fair. The inclusion of cowboy performances did not challenge the ideal of the fair as an educational event that promoted social good and the health of the farming community. Indeed, while clearly entertainment, rodeo had recognizable connections to rural life, and while these connections may have been overdrawn, they legitimized rodeo within the traditions and functions of prairie agricultural fairs.

. Rodeo had become a familiar and welcomed public sport by the early 1920s. And it was truly a sport. It involved physical exertion, it measured skill against standards of performance, it was competitive, and it applied uniform rules (at first only locally), all within a recreational framework. To be sure, the Stampede blurred the lines between amateur and professional sport, but rodeo contests had long presented an amiable mix of working cowboys and cowgirls and professional rodeo stars who travelled the North American rodeo circuit. In any case, the lines defining professional and amateur in sport were beginning to blur in the 1920s as North American sports became more professionalized and commercialized, with a star system, monetary and/or professional rewards, and accurate historical standards of competitive excellence. Indeed, as cultural historian Karen Wall has noted, an important theme in the history of Canadian sport after the First World War is that traditional sports such as cowboy contests that were local, often spontaneous, and unorganized were regularized into scheduled and predictable events.[26]

In the case of the annual Calgary Stampedes after 1923, such regularization also contributed to a framework within which the Stampede could become part of an invented tradition. With its elevation to a regular, rather than occasional, sporting event, the Stampede after 1923 transcended the more limited traditions of cowboy sports, local rodeos, and the Stampedes of 1912 and 1919. Moreover, the regularization of the event allowed the Stampede to become an accepted part of civic life. As sociologist Eric Dunning comments, sports spectators construct not only personal identities but also communal ones by forming bonds with other spectators that articulate their interdependence. Indeed, Dunning notes, sport "has come to be important in the identification of individuals with the collectivities to which they belong."[27] When annualized and formalized, such conditions are intensified, and although they are most apparent in team sports, an annual sporting event itself – especially when always held in the same place, such as the Calgary Stampede – creates a similar set of relationships. In other words, an event and the competitions it contains can contribute equally to civic identity.

The Calgary Stampede management's policies, whether by accident or design, reinforced these characteristics of organized sporting events. The Stampede's management carefully guarded the high quality of the rodeo programs. Cash prizes were reduced from those that had been offered in 1912 and 1919 to save money, but perhaps also to reflect respect for the Anglo-Canadian traditions of amateur sport. While cash was still offered, championship titles and prizes such as saddles, buckles, and other items donated by famous people such as the Prince of Wales and Mary Pickford and by local businesses were also given to reward success.[28] E.L. Richardson, the general manager, recalled that although many people had been "sceptical" that public interest in rodeo events would last, "the secret of its success is that it is not a show put on by paid performers, but is a real competition" located in Calgary, "the ranching centre of Alberta," and drawing contestants from Canada and the United States. The cowboys, he noted, "know that it is conducted on the level" and see the Stampede's trophies as honours in their own right. In keeping with this sporting ideal, the management of the Stampede ensured that the best judges were hired and provided excellent quality stock and horses.[29]

Even so, the characterization of the rodeo events at the Calgary Stampede as national and international was, in some respects, self-referential. Until 1929 each rodeo was independent and had its own rules; no centralized records were kept. While terms such as "World Championship" were commonly used, they were largely meaningless. The major rodeos in North America, such as at Calgary and Cheyenne, were important enough that their claims to represent important championships were recognized by rodeo contestants and the public alike, but this did not equate to comparative measurement of skill or recording of accomplishment. In 1929, however, the creation of the Rodeo Association of America made it possible to regulate events and establish greater uniformity across different venues.[30] This trend was rapidly confirmed in the next few years through the creation of similar organizations that dealt with regulations, qualifications, and rules, such as the Cowboy's Insurance Association in 1944 (later called the Cowboy's Protective Association and now the Canadian Professional Rodeo Association) and, shortly afterwards, the Canadian Stampede Managers' Association.[31] As a result, by the late 1940s the Calgary Stampede could rightfully be ranked as one of the great sporting events in North America.[32]

The regularization of the Stampede and its linkages to past rodeos, the traditions of the prairie agricultural fair, and the evolving world of sport helped create conditions favourable to its emergence as an invented tradition. Success was also assured by hiring Guy Weadick as manager of the Stampede. Compliance of the local elite was guaranteed, and impartiality and fairness ensured, by recruiting the Big Four who had backed the 1912 and 1919 Stampedes as rodeo judges along with the president of the Western Stock Growers' Association, the head of the Alberta Stockyards, and four members of the Calgary Exhibition Association board of directors.[33] Mindful of complaints in 1912 and 1919 that the Stampede had been something of an expensive and deceitful shill, Stampede organizers were determined to keep the event affordable and honest. Advertisements for the 1923 event promised "Positively No Advance In Hotel Or Restaurant Rates. No Sting Attached To This Celebration."[34] The Calgary Auto Club offered free camping for visitors, while a free accommodation bureau helped others find rooms. Free events were always featured on the Stampede grounds, and admission fees were kept at reasonable levels. In 1927 admission to the grounds and a reserved seat at the grandstand enclosure could be had for $1, which gave rise to the claim that "nowhere in the world can such a wonderful programme be seen for five times this price."[35]

The traditional fair programs – livestock shows and displays of grain, farm produce, and industrial materials – were maintained and in some cases enhanced in order to keep the event dynamic and community oriented. For example, a livestock review before a grandstand audience was instituted and children's programs, such as school spelling bees, were incorporated into the fair. A lavish street parade launched the Stampede, while the rodeo program included the same range of events that had been staged in 1912, such as bucking horses, roping, and steer riding, but in greater number and variety. Many additions reiterated traditional rodeo events; others were simply invented but came to be accepted as representing a genuine "tradition" of the Old West. The chuckwagon race, the most famous of these invented events, has come to define the Stampede's public image as representing the vigour, manliness, and danger of western life.[36] So too, the re-gendering of rodeo into a male preserve was another transformation, albeit not unique to the Calgary

Stampede. By the Second World War, cowgirls' participation in rodeo had almost entirely disappeared due to forces that included the Hollywood image of the range as a male preserve and the disdain of most professional rodeo associations towards women's participation.[37]

Blanche McCoughey, Bertha Blanchett, and Dolly Mullens competed in the 1912 Stampede.

The Stampede of 1923, like that of 1912, was dominated by a self-conscious nostalgia for past times. Stampedes of the interwar years refined this nostalgia into a pursuit of identity through a critique of modernity, perhaps expressing a search for authenticity and certainty in a time of rapid social and technological change. Such reactions were not unique; they had been expressed with varying intensity throughout Western Europe and North America since the nineteenth century and had given rise to the invention of many traditions. As Ian McKay demonstrates in his study of the construction of new identities in Nova Scotia in the interwar years, appeals to local folk customs and practices served various social objectives and economic interests, including the tourism industry.[38] Although there were many variants — concerns for early architecture, folk songs and practices, and handicrafts — nostalgia found its expression in the Calgary Stampede through an appeal to simpler times with better values and higher social purposes than those found in industrialized society. Subtitling the event as an "Old Timers' Re-Union and Pioneer Jollification," the advertising for the 1923 Stampede set a pattern that would be followed for many years.[39] As an article in the *Farm and Ranch Review* (a farm journal published in Calgary) claimed,

> First of all, there is no place in the West that has the
> natural location, with such scenic embellishments, right
> at its door, the historical data to work upon, such as the
> Hudson's Bay Company frontier activities, the honoured
> traditions of the Royal North West Mounted Police,
> the native reservations practically at the city limits, the
> cowmen in their picturesque work, and last, but not least,
> the great number of old-timers, both men and women,
> who still live in the vicinity; men and women who are
> the actual pioneers of this Last Best West whose untiring
> efforts and strenuous undertakings in a primitive country
> are the real cause of the wonderful development that
> has been attained in the country in comparatively few
> short years.[40]

What this meant in practical terms was illustrated in various ways, all linked by a particular view of the role of history in contemporary civic life. Weadick persuaded Calgarians to dress in western clothing and to decorate the streets and storefronts of downtown Calgary with planks and other "pioneer" materials. The fairgrounds featured an Indian Village set up and staffed by local First Nations people dressed in colourful and elaborate costumes, but while First Nations provided colour, the history that the Stampede referenced was always the Euro-Canadian conquest of the land. The effective erasure of the Aboriginal past by its relegation to spectacle was central in the historical interpretations and traditions that the Stampede promoted. Such presentations helped to link the Calgary Stampede to an often imagined regional past that was seen as romantic and colourful. Euro-Canadian history was focused in part on the Old Timers' Cabin located near the Indian Village and maintained by the Southern Alberta Old Timers' Association, where pioneers could gather and reminisce. More directly, the parades often featured historical floats and references, and that of 1925 was one of the most elaborate in this respect. The parade of riders, floats, bands, and dignitaries took an hour and forty minutes to pass one point. At its core

A cowboy cooks breakfast on a downtown street in 1923.

were thirty floats that "pictured the romantic story of the West" and "made many a heart throb and long for some magic wand to turn back the clock of time." But the parade was more about the present than the past. It asserted the triumph of the Euro-Canadian settler and the celebration of the present through a sentimentality in which "color, romance, glamour was there aplenty, with pathos, humor and a hundred memories tender and stern for the men and women who have made this city grow since the days of old Fort Calgary." The floats were organized in an equally presentist fashion – the first portrayed the West before the arrival of whites, while the remaining twenty-nine celebrated in rough chronological order the achievements of Euro-Canadians. All the predictable themes were there: "the explorers," the North-West Mounted Police, the Hudson's Bay Company (which in fact had only a minor presence in southern Alberta), missionaries, whiskey traders, Fort Calgary, and the signing of the treaties. Other floats dealt with the CPR, land surveyors, early retail operations, transportation, newspapers, town councils, and, among others, the Turner Valley oil field. The parade ended triumphantly with a float on the theme of "Calgary today." As further evidence of the demands and standards of the present, the parade was led by Guy Weadick and Hoot Gibson, the Hollywood cowboy movie star, and was filmed so that it could be included in one of Gibson's films.[41]

Hoot Gibson was no less a part of an invented tradition than was the Stampede's vision of the past, but he represented an enduring pattern in which the Stampede celebrated famous personalities or powerful individuals and the structures that buttressed Anglo-Canadian order. Parade themes or special events were identified to create a unique identity for each Stampede and maintain a particular view of Calgary's history. Themes included the sixtieth anniversary of confederation in 1927, the Royal Canadian Mounted Police, and the founding of Fort Calgary. Pat Burns was honoured in 1931 on the occasion of his seventy-fifth birthday, and in 1939 the theme was set as the "British Empire" in honour of the visit of King George and Queen Elizabeth to Canada.

Such evolving themes not only served to reinforce a particular view of past and present, but also helped to keep the Stampede dynamic in order to encourage repeat visits year after year by locals and outsiders alike. Despite their sentimentality about earlier times, the Stampede of 1923 and those that followed were made possible by the technology that they implicitly decried. The presentations of Calgary's history as one of authentic colour and romance had wide appeal and could be marketed effectively because, as was noted in 1924, "Calgary is a Western town and proud of it." The city welcomed thousands each year to the Stampede and entertained them "in a true Western manner, and her very location and history prove that Calgary is about the one place in the Canadian Northwest that can properly indulge in such a Western holiday."[42] An important part of twentieth-century tourism has been a quest for authenticity, for "genuine" experiences that reveal "true" local conditions. The achievement of such experiences involves complex undertakings on the part of hosts and visitors alike, and many critics have argued that the pursuit is inherently futile.[43]

Whatever the case, many tourists, like local residents, apparently accepted the Stampede as representing an authentic, or at least attractive, experience. While statistics about the origins of visitors to the Stampede are unavailable, the Stampede rapidly became a regular part of many Albertans' vacation plans. By 1931 the Stampede attracted about 198,000 admissions, and after declining in the next two years because of the Depression, the number reached almost 215,000 in 1936. In 1939 more than 240,000 people were admitted to the Stampede grounds. Since the population of Calgary in the 1930s was approximately 85,000, these attendance figures greatly exceeded the city's population. While some of the admissions represent repeat visits, they nonetheless indicate that a large number of outsiders came to the city for the event.[44] By 1927 the Crowsnest Pass area, for example, contributed as usual "a heavy quota of visitors" who travelled to the Stampede by train or by car, and people from other nearby points, such as Claresholm, were making a visit to the Stampede an annual event.[45]

The Stampede also attracted visitors from further away. The CPR offered special passenger fares between Calgary and all points in Saskatchewan, Alberta, and eastern British Columbia. Visitors from other points were able to take advantage of the CPR's special summer tourist fares to Banff and Lake Louise, which included stopover privileges in Calgary during the Stampede. By 1939 a hard-surfaced road from the U.S. border via Waterton connected American tourists to Calgary and Banff and Lake Louise, Canada's "famous mountain playground."[46] In their tourist promotions, Stampede organizers eagerly seized on the fortuitous proximity of Banff. As E.L. Richardson, the Stampede's general manger, told Premier Brownlee in 1927,

> Each year the number of tourists [visiting the Stampede] increases considerably and they come from greater distances. The business at the Kananaskis gate of the Banff National Park during and immediately following our annual Exhibition dates is phenomenal and is increasing very rapidly every year. We have had on our grounds at one time automobiles with licenses from as many as fifteen states and five provinces. The tourist business is now recognized as of such great value that Alberta cannot afford to miss an opportunity to try for her full share of that traffic ... The marvellous mountains at Calgary's door give us an opportunity unexcelled by other cities on the continent.[47]

As with the Stampede of 1912, one measure of the success of the 1923 and subsequent Stampedes was the imitators they inspired. By 1946 thirty-eight district Stampedes were held in western Canada, of which well over half took place in Alberta, many of them no doubt inspired by the increased popularization of rodeo at the Calgary Stampede.[48] As illustrated by one rodeo in the Peace River Country, these events also represented the intersections of local culture and place with contemporary attitudes and needs. A rodeo begun in Teepee Creek (northeast of Grande Prairie) in the early 1930s developed into one of the most attractive summer events in the southern part of the region.

Bucking horses, horse racing, and pulling contests were the central events, but baseball, boxing, tug-of-war, bathing beauty contests (sometimes featuring men's and women's events), drinking, and a dance helped draw crowds and competitors from near and far. One resident humorously recalled the story of one of these outside competitors:

> "All of us poor old farmers around here had on work
> boots and patched coveralls, but we were having a real
> good time. Then this great big, slim, would-be cowboy
> stepped up. He was from Calgary and he was going to
> show the locals how to ride. He was all dressed up fit to
> kill, and bragged around to everybody how he could ride.
> Now Burns had an old work horse at the time, and that
> horse could buck! He'd just bawl and paw when he hit the
> ground. Anyway, they got that horse all saddled up and
> that cowboy aboard and let him buck. Well, that horse
> went up once and the horse came down, but the cowboy
> kept on going up and up. When he finally came down,
> he landed just the way he had been on the horse – and he
> landed hard. He picked himself up and he left and after a
> hearty laugh, the local riders kept on with the show."[49]

In this recollection it is notable that while the local rodeo owed its popularity to the precedent of Calgary's stampede, it transcended these origins to express local sensibilities and attitudes. The Calgary cowboy – Alberta's new version of a city slicker – was no match for rural wiles or traditions; farmers were the salt of the earth and thus would survive, while the city boy's fancy gear and smart talk only hid incompetence. This old story confirmed the superiority of rural honesty, and perhaps rural guile, but it was also another demonstration that the forms events took had different meanings in different locations and contexts and that invented traditions could be reworked by others to serve their own particular needs.

Such adaptability reveals the strength of the myth of the cowboy that rodeo promoted. Even so, no rodeo in Alberta was as successful as Calgary's was in defining place and history and the meaning of time. The Stampede of 1923 was the first in a series that has continued to the present day. While it built on a long history of cowboy sports in southern Alberta and the precedents of the 1912 and 1919 Stampedes, the 1923 event was the true beginning of the institutionalization of the Stampede as a part of Calgary's myth about itself. This myth was a flexible one, but its core was and remains the myth of the frontier and of the figures who supposedly made it. In this sense, the Stampede conflated farming and ranching pioneers into a common story of struggle and success. That each group was bitterly opposed to the other in the nineteenth century, and that each group saw itself as part of a cultural vanguard and its opponents as regressive forces, has not restricted the myth making that smoothed over these divisions and joined historically opposing groups within a common story of struggle and triumph.

The tradition of preparing pancake breakfasts continues on.

Contemporary virtues of hard work, individual success or failure, and risk taking can be lauded by appealing to a sanitized past, a world of unquestioned and peaceful social relations, meaningful and inspiring community cohesiveness, sociability, straightforwardness, and pragmatism. Such myths have become central tenets for a society trying to adapt to almost continuous technological and social change while also attempting to establish its own presence and identity. In times of flux, myths of constancy, of a presence on the land and continuity with what came before, and of successful engagement with an often hostile climate, retain their potency. Such myths can also nicely accommodate the power relations in society. The myth of the pioneer, especially of the pioneer as risk taker, remains a central part of Calgary's and Alberta's view of itself. It is remarkable how slight a shift has been required to extend an appreciation of the homesteaders' perceived rural character and perseverance into a justification of the activities of Calgary capitalists. The notion of risk has now become central in the idealization of the Stampede. The contestants are described as fearless risk takers and the Stampede's history itself as proof of the virtues of high-powered marketing, good management, and the well calculated risk taken by the Exhibition managers in 1923.[50]

The invented traditions that the Stampede promoted and described as full of pathos and tears missed the true pathos and the truly important questions about Alberta's history. In contemporary Alberta, pioneering – in whatever form – connotes the victory of Euro-Canadians. The invented past of the Stampede portrayed Indians as a source of colour, but not humanity or inspiration. It posited that rodeo represented the essence of the Anglo-Canadian Protestant conquest of the West and saw open-range ranching (not railways, wholesaling and distribution, mining, irrigation, wheat farming, and land development, among other elements) as the formative cultural and economic event in the history of southern Alberta. Only hard work, not hard work along with luck, ethnicity, social and political power, and an economic system that offered most of its rewards within a highly specific social and economic framework, shaped the past and the present. True, the dominant culture of the region was Anglo and Protestant; true, ranchers had worked hard and faced difficulties, but so too had First Nations people and Czech and Ukrainian miners and Chinese navvies and Mormon farmers and failed homesteaders and countless others who were forgotten in this celebration of success and whose lives raised often uncomfortable questions about who had won and why, and who had lost and why, and what those wins and losses have meant.

Notes

1. Eric Hobsbawm, "Mass Producing Traditions: Europe 1870–1914," in *Representing the Nation: A Reader: Histories, Heritage and Museums,* ed. David Boswell and Jessica Evans (London and New York: Routledge and The Open University, 1999), 61–86.

2. Claire Eamer and Thirza Jones, *The Canadian Rodeo Book* (Saskatoon: Western Producer Prairie Books, 1982), 6.

3. *Macleod Gazette*, 19 October 1886.

4. *Edmonton Bulletin*, 2 August 1894.

5. Eamer and Jones, *Canadian Rodeo Book*, 7.

6. Donald G. Wetherell and Irene R.A. Kmet, *Useful Pleasures: The Shaping of Leisure in Alberta, 1896–1945* (Regina: Canadian Plains Research Center, 1990), 332; Donna Livingstone, *The Cowboy Spirit: Guy Weadick and the Calgary Stampede* (Vancouver: Greystone Books, 1996), 6–10.

7. On respectability in sport, see Colin D. Howell, *Blood, Sweat and Cheers: Sport and the Making of Modern Canada* (Toronto: University of Toronto Press, 2001), 28–50.

8. *Macleod Advertiser*, 8 June 1911.

9. *Calgary Herald*, 6 July 1905.

10. Wetherell and Kmet, *Useful Pleasures*, 3–10.

11. Ibid., 163–86.

12. Howell, *Blood, Sweat and Cheers*, 11–13.

13. Guy Weadick, "Origin of the Calgary Stampede," *Alberta Historical Review* 14, no. 4 (966): 21; Vincent Varga, "Gentleman Ranchers – High Class Cowboys," *Journal of the West* 23, no. 4 (1984): 55. On Weadick's life, see Livingstone, *Cowboy Spirit*.

14. Hugh Dempsey, *The Golden Age of the Canadian Cowboy: An Illustrated History* (Saskatoon: Fifth House, 1995), 129.

15. Mary Lou LeCompte, "Home on the Range: Women in Professional Rodeo, 1929–1947," *Journal of Sport History* 17, no. 3 (1990): 318.

16. James Gray, *A Brand of Its Own: The 100 Year History of the Calgary Exhibition and Stampede* (Saskatoon: Western Producer Prairie Books, 1985), 39–41. See also Weadick, "Origin of the Calgary Stampede," 21; *Macleod Spectator*, 5 September 1912.

17. "Stampede in Calgary in September" (1919) and "Calgary Exhibition and Stampede," Clipping File, Glenbow Museum Archives.

18. Gray, *Brand of Its Own*, 52–53.

19. Maxwell Foran, *Trails and Trials: Markets and Land Use in the Alberta Beef Cattle Industry, 1881–1948* (Calgary: University of Calgary Press, 2003), 1–27.

20. See, for example, Henry C. Klassen, *Eye on the Future: Business and People in Calgary and the Bow Valley, 1870–1900* (Calgary: University of Calgary Press, 2000), 149–84.

21. This and following material on the Bruce Rodeo is taken from *Hurry to Bruce: A History of Bruce and Area* (Bruce: Bruce History Book Committee, 1988).

22. David C. Jones, *Midways, Judges, and Smooth-Tongued Fakirs: The Illustrated Story of Country Fairs in the Prairie West* (Saskatoon: Western Producer Prairie Books, 1983), 6.

23. *Farm and Ranch Review*, February 1908.

24. Richardson to Brownlee, 26 October 1927, Premier's Papers (PP), file 417, Provincial Archives of Alberta (cited hereafter as PAA); Gray, *Brand of Its Own*, 58, 60.

25. Minister of Agriculture to Buckle, 10 December 1930, 73.307, file 244 (box 20), PAA; Superintendent of Fairs to Patterson, 26 January 1937, 73.307, file 248, PAA.

26. Karen Wall, "The History of Sport in Alberta," Unit 1, Part B (typescript, unpublished research report, Royal Alberta Museum, n.d.), n.p.

27. Eric Dunning, *Sport Matters: Sociological Studies of Sport, Violence, and Civilisation* (London: Routledge, 1999), 3–6.

28. Gray, *Brand of Its Own*, 61.

29. *Farm and Ranch Review*, June 1945.

30. LeCompte, "Home on the Range," 318.

31. Wall, "History of Sport," Unit 1, Part B, n.p.

32. Gray, *Brand of Its Own*, 147.

33. *Farm and Ranch Review*, 20 June 1923.

34. *Farm and Ranch Review*, 5 June 1913 (advertisement).

35. *Farm and Ranch Review*, 25 June 1927.

36. Dempsey, Golden Age, 129; Gray, *Brand of Its Own, 100; Twenty-Third Annual Meeting of the Canadian Association of Exhibitions*, Toronto, November 24 and 25, 1949 (pamphlet), copy in PP, file 1768, PAA.

37. LeCompte, "Home on the Range," 324–25.

38. Ian McKay, *The Quest of the Folk: Antimodernism and Cultural Selection in Twentieth Century Nova Scotia* (Montreal: McGill-Queen's University Press, 1994). On such expression in twentieth century Canadian architecture, see Nicola Justine Spasoff, "Building on Social Power: Percy Erskine Nobbs, Ramsay Traquair, and the Project of Constructing a Canadian National Culture in the Early Decades of the Twentieth Century" (Ph.D. diss., Queen's University, 2002).

39. *Farm and Ranch Review*, 5 June 1923 (advertisement).

40. *Farm and Ranch Review*, 20 June 1923.

41. *Farm and Ranch Review*, 25 July 1925.

42. *Farm and Ranch Review*, 25 June 1924.

43. Formative studies in the large literature on authenticity and tourism include O.J. Boorstin, *The Image: A Guide to Pseudo-Events in America* (New York: Harper and Row, 1964); D. MacCannell, *The Tourist: A New Theory of the Leisure Class* (New York: Schocken, 1976); and Edward Bruner, "Abraham Lincoln as Authentic Reproduction: A Critique of Postmodernism," *American Anthropologist* 96 (1994), 397–415.

44. "Alberta Fairs 1931–1939," 73.307, file 245, PAA.

45. *Coleman Journal*, 7 July 1927; *Claresholm Local Press*, 20 June 1930.

46. *The UFA*, 3 July 1923 (advertisement); *Claresholm Local Press*, 22 June 1939.

47. Richardson to Brownlee, 26 October 1927, PP, file 417, PAA.

48. *Farm and Ranch Review*, May 1946.

49. Quoted in Donald G. Wetherell and Irene R.A. Kmet, *Alberta's North: A History, 1890–1950* (Edmonton: University of Alberta Press, 2000), 293–94.

50. See, for example, Ralph Klein, "The Stampede Adds Colour to Our Towering Offices," *Calgary Herald*, 12 June 2005, A16.

CHAPTER 3

The Indians and the Stampede

Hugh A. Dempsey

Indian races were a highlight of early Stampedes.

Indians[1] have been a part of Calgary's entertainment life ever since the town began in 1883. As soon as the first shops were opened on Stephen and Atlantic avenues, some of the merchants began to sponsor dances in front of their stores to attract customers. Indians gathered in a circle and performed various types of dances, commonly called "grub dances" or "tea dances." Afterwards they were given food by the store owner. In 1885, when eastern troops were stationed in the town during the Riel Rebellion, at least one dance was held. According to a reporter, "There was a grand pow-wow of thirty Sarcees to-day in front of the fort. The 9th battalion and Col. Smith's men of the Winnipeg Light Infantry were drawn up in front to enable the men to see the war dance."[2]

The relationship between the Indians and townspeople during the 1880s was one that was kept at arms' length. The Indians – particularly the Sarcees – were welcome at treaty time when they came to spend their money or at any time when they had legitimate business to conduct. Those who simply camped near town were periodically warned away by the police and sent back to their reserves. The result was that communication was limited.

The only exceptions were in the fields of sports and showmanship. Not only did the Sarcees and Blackfoot swarm into town if there was some holiday, but a few also competed actively in such events as foot and horse racing. For example, a Blackfoot named Little Plume began winning foot races in Calgary in 1883 and was sent as far as Winnipeg by local gamblers. In 1886 another Blackfoot runner named Deerfoot started his impressive career in Calgary, which gave him everlasting fame.[3]

In 1884 the idea of holding an annual fall fair resulted in the formation of the Calgary and District Agricultural Society. In 1886 the first fair was held and included "a few Indian and cowboy horse races thrown in for good measure."[4] Over the next several years, Indian races were part of the program, although these were considered simply as a form of amusement for the crowd rather than a sport. For example, in 1894 the *Calgary Herald* commented, "An Indian pony race was the next and as usual set the occupants of the grand stand into a fit of laughter. The race was to the half mile post then turn and come back, and it furnished lots of fun for the sports loving people."[5] And a few years later, "This race was well contested and brightened up the crowd. The best horse won. The owner's name was not furnished in the papers. If translated perhaps it would not have sounded parliamentary."[6]

By the end of the 1890s the role of the Indians began to change due to an increasing town population and a desire to broaden the fair's program beyond horse racing and agricultural exhibits. In 1899 the Calgary Agricultural Society became the Inter-Western Pacific Exhibition and the date of the fair was moved from autumn to mid-summer. In 1900 a large parade of mounted Indians took place in front of the grandstand in honour of a visit by Territorial Lieutenant-Governor A.E. Forget. A year later a public parade was held at the opening of the exhibition. The *Albertan* reported the presence of Stoney, Blackfoot, and Sarcee Indians.

> They were there in tens and hundreds in every conceivable description of raiment and combination of colors, except those who were color blind, and they developed their eccentricity by appearing with as little clothing as was conducive to their liberty in a civilized community. Truly the exhibition company is to be congratulated for their round up of these natives of the plains. Why not offer prizes for the best dressed Indian, the handsomest squaw, the fattest papoose, and the largest family of papooses? This would further increase the interest the Indians take in affairs of this kind.[7]

While the exhibitions were organized for the entertainment of the towns-people, the Indians thoroughly enjoyed the chance to participate. They performed social dances and war dances; had tug-of-war contests, races, and other athletic events; showed off their finery; and visited friends from other reserves. The trip to the fair gave them an opportunity to relieve the monotony of reservation life, to get away from the boredom of farming and gardening, and to relive some of the exciting days of the past.

A few years later, a reporter recalled these visits:

> The [Indians] used to camp on what was then the outskirts of the town. The favorite camping place of the Sarcee Indians was the plateau above Twentieth or Royal avenue, where some of the finest residences of the city now stand. The Stoney tribe used to occupy a vast empty space between Shaganappi and Fourteenth street west. Others were to be found camped on the outskirts of the town in other directions. They came in thousands and ranged their tented towns in more or less systematic order.

Small, very dirty children and thousands of dogs seemed
to be the chief inhabitants of these Indian encampments....Calgary's white population used to visit these
encampments in the evenings by the hundreds. Many
were the hard bargains driven by the untutored redskin
with a white brother newly arrived from the east for
some trifling souvenir. It is the echo of this past that the
Stampede brings to Calgary.[8]

One of the first to publicly complain about Indian participation in the
Calgary fair was Sarcee missionary Henry Gibbon Stocken. In 1903 the
Anglican clergyman railed against the "baneful...influence of such exhibitions upon their morals"[9] and wanted the fair boycotted. His letter to the
editor was responded to by Crispin E. Smith, one of the parade marshals.
"Why should the poor red man have all the amusement taken out of his
life?" he asked. "Is a tug of war demoralizing? Is a foot race wicked? Is a horse
race as ridden by Indians not as moral as other races?"[10]

After that exchange of letters, matters settled down for the next five years,
even though Indians appeared to be visiting or participating in the fair in
increasing numbers. This was apparent in 1908 when Calgary became the
one city in Canada chosen as the site for the Dominion Exhibition. As a
result, the Exhibition Board went all out in planning the biggest celebration
yet. The parade and Indian participation were organized by the Rev. John
McDougall and Crispen Smith. As stated by the *Herald*, the Indians were the
hit of the parade:

Indians from every tribe in Alberta were out in the old
trappings of their bygone life on the open prairies and
hills. Clad in skins, tanned with the fur on and off, with
their old rifles thrown over their shoulders and powder
horn and bullet pouch slung by their sides, leading their
huskies packed for the trail. Following the Indians on foot
came a war party under two chiefs arrayed in their great
war bonnets, hung with feathers and beads and buckskin
fringe, painted into hideous nightmare and riding after
the most approved Indian fashion, on a pad or bareback,
guiding their horses by the thong through the mouth.

Following the chiefs came the braves stripped to the waist, their bodies covered with red and yellow ochre and their hands holding spears, bows and rifles.

In the rear of the war party came the camp following of squaws and papooses on horseback and with travois and following these came four old trail-worn braves, clad in a smothering heap of furs, carrying the full paraphernalia of the Indian chase and bent with years.

Rev. John and Mrs. McDougall rode on horseback behind their dusky charges.[11]

In the 1890s pressure had been applied to suppress the Sun Dance and other religious activities and attempts were made to replace them with local sports events. After the turn of the century, no distinction was made between religious and secular events. If they harkened to the past, they were to be discouraged. In 1900 Blackfoot Indian Agent G.H. Wheatley had complained that fairs exposed his wards to temptation and degradation.

Until 1908, the involvement of Indians in fairs and parades had been only a minor irritation to officers of the Indian Department, but the Dominion Exhibition spectacular emphasized all those features that the Indian agents were trying to discourage. There was nothing in the Indian Act that specifically prevented Indians from going to fairs, but the "feathers and war paint" presentation contrasted sharply with the government's attempt to promote farming and to encourage Indians to give up their relics and practices of the past.

One of the men who launched a long and aggressive campaign against Indian participation in fairs was J.A. Markle, inspector of Indian Agencies for Alberta. As far as he was concerned, the fairs occurred when the government wanted the Indians to be busy haying or working in their fields. He also saw the events as an encouragement for Indians to retain old customs which, in his opinion, had no place in the new world which the government had laid out for them. His negative remarks brought support from some churches and moral reform leagues that sided with the Indian Department, while local boards of trade, newspapers, and local promoters resented the interference. Public opinion was divided; some saw Indian participation in parades and fairs as an embarrassing reminder that these people still existed, while others were impressed by their costumes, horsemanship, and unique culture.

One of the strongest supporters of Indian participation in fairs was the Rev. John McDougall, Methodist missionary on the Stoney Reserve. In 1908 he not only endorsed the idea of Indians going to Calgary, but also visited the various reserves to encourage them to go. However, he had no support from Methodist headquarters in Toronto, where the Committee on Temperance and Moral Reform went on record as being "unalterably opposed to taking Indians from reservations and giving exhibitions at Western fairs and introducing the practices formerly associated with pagan customs."[12]

The Calgary Exhibition ignored complaints and in 1909 another six hundred Indians joined in "The Greatest Spectacle in the History of the West."[13] Inspector Markle was angry about their participation and the fact that some newspapers were now describing Indians as "degenerate remnants of a noble race" and painting them as beggars and people without dignity.[14]

Even the 1908 "spectacle" was overshadowed by events of 1910, when the fair included a re-enactment of the signing of Treaty Seven, organized as a five-act play and including some two thousand Indians. Inspector Markle lodged an official complaint with Ottawa, charging that the Calgary Exhibition was doing irreparable harm to the Indians. He said that the Peigans had abandoned their fields, predicted a crop failure, and said that women were being demeaned by being referred to as "squaws."[15]

As the dispute between Markle and McDougall hit the southern Alberta press, public attitudes gradually shifted to the government's viewpoint. Even the *Calgary Albertan*, which had taken a strong stand on Indian participation, changed its tune. "The attraction is a good one," it stated, "but if it is harmful, or if the people mostly in active charge of the Indians believe that it is harmful it would not do to take such a risk."[16] McDougall responded sadly, "I do not want to see with the eyes of Mr. Markle or the Indian Commissioner on this question. I would not use the lenses of their thought on this matter, not by any means. They view the Indian not as a fellow man, a being just as capable as themselves in distinguishing between right and wrong, but as an inferior to be treated as a child."[17]

After getting reports from Indian agents and hearing Markle's complaints, Indian Department Secretary J.D. McLean sent a letter to the Calgary Exhibition early in 1911, asking it to stop using Indians as its featured attraction. E.L. Richardson of the Exhibition company disagreed with the implications of the letter, saying that Indians "are not slaves and have the same right to attend an exhibition as anyone else."[18] However, the adverse publicity must have taken effect, for in the summer of 1912, the only native event featured was Indian pony races.[19]

This would seem to be an inopportune time for Guy Weadick and his local promoter, H.C. McMullen, to plan a huge one-time-only Stampede that would be quite separate from the annual Calgary fair. They already had received word that the Duke and Duchess of Connaught would attend the show, and they wanted the Indians there as well. Accordingly, in May 1912 Calgary Mayor J.W. Mitchell wrote to the Indian Department asking for permission to invite Indians to participate. "I am...aware of the fact," he said, "that the Department of Indian Affairs does not look with any degree of favour upon cities encouraging them to leave their reserves and come to the cities for celebrations [but] I can safely assure you that no unseemly entertainment will be indulged in which would have a tendency to excite or degrade the Indians."[20]

Calgary officials believed they had a good argument in that a Royal Visit would coincide with the Stampede. Mayor Mitchell pointed out that Indians had been a main feature during the visit of the Duke and Duchess of Cornwall and York in 1901.

The immediate response from the bureaucrats was negative. Western Chief Inspector Glen Campbell repeated the stand that it was hard to keep the Indian farmers at work with haying and harvest, and that the fairs themselves were demoralizing. He suggested to Ottawa that the Duke of Connaught, who was Canada's governor general, be encouraged to tell the Indians to stay on their reserves. However, the viceregal monarch would not be drawn into the fray. In fact, his aide was quite sarcastic when he observed that,

> ...the chief objection to the Indian display is that it stulti-
> fies the work of the Emigration Department who spend
> much time in [telling] settlers that there is no such thing
> as an Indian in Canada. The crops and hay-fields will not
> take much hurt from a few days neglect in mid-October,
> and if the missionaries have not got better hold on the
> Indians by now, then...I do not suppose they ever will.[21]

Thwarted by the governor-general, the Indian Department nevertheless sent a notice to all its agents in southern Alberta, informing them that "it has been decided that it will not be advisable to allow Indians of your Agency to take part in the Frontier Days celebration...."[22] However, when the Black-foot Indian agent passed the information along to the Mounted Police, any hope of any co-operation from them was quashed. "Some Indians will inev-itably leave the Reserve," commented R. Burton Deane, Mounted Police superintendent in Calgary. "They cannot lawfully be prevented by force from doing so, nor when they have left the Reserve, can they be lawfully coerced to return."[23]

When Weadick learned that the Indians would be discouraged from attending the Stampede, he turned to political influences. First, Sir James Lougheed, a Calgarian and member of the federal cabinet, appealed directly to the Hon. Robert Rogers, who was the superintendent-general of Indian Affairs, asking him to overrule his civil servants. This was followed by a note from R.B. Bennett, member of Parliament and later the prime minister of Canada, and a telegram from the Hon. Francis Cochrane, minister of Railways and Canals. The pressure was too great for Rogers to ignore. On August 8, less than a month before the Stampede, he announced that not only would the government withdraw any objections, but it also would actively assist in bringing Indians to the Calgary Stampede. Chief Inspector Glen Campbell was placed in charge of the task and toured each reserve to gain the co-operation of reluctant Indian agents.

Four members of the Treaty 7 First Nations at the 1912 Stampede.

Indian scouts were engaged to be in Calgary to patrol the camps; chiefs and councils were invited to meet the governor general; and Indians were told they could take part in the parade, sign up for the rodeo events, or simply go as spectators. It was a complete about-face for the federal authorities.

The Methodist Church was appalled at the decision. Writing from Toronto, its general secretary complained:

> I am informed that...permitting these Indians to take part in the Stampede at Calgary will result in hundreds of acres of grain being neglected. Besides, there is all the degrading, disgusting immorality which is so openly practised upon these Indians, who are wards of the Government, by immoral and vicious white men. Many of the Indians...are ruined by these parades that they are never restored to the position and character they formerly held.[24]

But the decision was made, and there was no turning back. The delighted Indians flocked to Calgary by the hundreds on September 2. Dozens of men and women brought their finest costumes and horse gear for the parade and put on a delightful show. The Toronto *Globe* commented that the "gorgeous display of paint, beads and colored blankets was made by the six tribes of Indians who formed the bulk of the parade, and lent a historic picturesqueness to the modern city street with its thousands of thronging spectators."[25]

During the six-day event, the Indians were everywhere. Their tepees were located next to replicas of a Hudson's Bay Company post and a whiskey fort, and they offered daily dances and joined in parades. At the first grandstand performance, they put on a spectacular show.

> Yelling and brandishing rifles, lances and shields, the red men galloped into the arena. Time and time again they circled the fence at the gallop, crossing and recrossing, twisting, turning and shooting in all directions, finally pulling up their war ponies with a flourish directly in front of the three tom tom players in the centre of the area. Then they dismounted and to the steady beat of the tom tom and the weird chant of the squaws, a regular war dance was indulged in.[26]

In rodeo, the most outstanding competitor was Tom Three Persons, from the Blood Reserve, who won the bucking horse championship and became the only Canadian to reach the finals. Others took part in the Indian races, relay races, and special events. For example, winning the one-mile bareback wild horse race was a Stoney named David, while in the half-mile, Philip Big Swan, Joe Three Suns, and Tom Spotted Bull were the top three.

Officials estimated that an impressive eighteen hundred Indians had attended the six-day Stampede, yet there had only been seven arrests under the Indian Act – all for liquor offenses – during the entire period. This caused an Indian Department official to comment that "if the white men who were in Calgary during that week had been under the same [liquor] regulation... there would not have been jails enough in Canada to hold them."[27]

When it was over, the Indians went home happy and encouraged by the government's apparent willingness to co-operate, but the 1912 decision had been politically influenced and in no way affected the intransigence of the bureaucrats. In fact, right after the Stampede, Inspector Markle unleashed a diatribe against the fair. "Somebody made about $50,000 out of the Calgary Stampede," he said. "Yes, somebody made a pretty big thing out of that, and it was we who supplied material for the show. It is futile to attempt to raise Indians and to lower them at the same time."[28] His attitude was obvious a year later when the Indian Department refused to assist Guy Weadick when he wanted to take some southern Alberta Indians to the Winnipeg Stampede. Not only did it refuse, but in 1914 Ottawa officials revised the Indian Act to make such participation in fairs and parades illegal unless permission was given by the local Indian agent. The Act stated,

> Any Indian in the province of Manitoba, Saskatchewan, Alberta, or British Columbia, or in the Territories who participates in any Indian dance outside the bounds of his own reserve, or who participates in any show, exhibition, performance, stampede or pageant without the consent of the Superintendent General [Minister] or his authorized agent, and any person who induces or employs any Indian to take part in such dance, show, exhibition, performance, stampede or pageant, or induces any Indian to leave his reserve or employs any Indian for such a purpose, whether the dance, show, exhibition, stampede or pageant has taken place or not, shall on summary conviction to be liable to a penalty not exceeding twenty-five dollars, or to imprisonment for one month, or to both penalty and imprisonment.[29]

The impact on the Calgary Exhibition was immediate and absolute. Indians no longer figured in the parades, and if they attended as spectators, the fact went unnoticed in the Calgary press. The only significant reference to

Indians between 1914 and 1919 was an account of Indian horse races at the fair in 1916.[30]

In 1919 promoter Guy Weadick was back in Calgary, this time to put on a Victory Stampede marking the end of the First World War. Like the 1912 extravaganza, it was not a part of the Calgary Exhibition but was a one-time celebration. Weadick's plans included inviting the continent's best cowboys as well as the Indians from southern Alberta. When confronted with federal regulations banning Indian participation, he did not simply acquiesce, as the Calgary Exhibition authorities had done, but looked for ways to get around the law or, if necessary, to merely ignore it. Presumably he assumed that if a thousand Indians showed up, the government would be hard pressed to fine them all, and if Weadick himself was charged, the penalty was only twenty-five dollars.

In the end, Weadick's plan was a simple one. Indians would not be officially invited, but if they showed up they would be free to participate. At the same time, the Stampede would make a concession to the Indian Department by praising the advancement of native people. As Weadick explained to the press, "The Indians will not be allowed as a tribe or tribes to take part in the Stampede, but individually they wish to be present, as it will be a spectacle that which there is none dearer to them."[31] In another press release, the Stampede stated, "Although they will not officially take part in the Stampede, yet their appearance in the coming celebration is necessary to make the event a complete success, as no showing where the wild life of the west is depicted would be complete unless they were present."[32]

To mollify the Indian Department, the Stampede added a few comments about the Sarcees who, "under Big Belly's leadership and the competent direction of federal government's officials, including the agent for the Sarcees, William Gordon, have taken to agriculture of late years and are doing very well. They have been fitted out with implements, work horses and all the other requisites to modern farming and their progress has been very satisfactory." Yet Weadick could not resist adding a dig, saying that "they will one day be in position to solve their own problems fairly well without extraneous assistance."[33]

However, all pretence of the Stampede's passive involvement was discarded once the Indians were on the scene. "The encampment of Indians which has been organized by the Stampede management at Victoria park," said the *Herald*, "lends to the atmosphere of the western festivities. Here we have some of the best known chiefs in western Canada, living under their own canvas, with their wives, children, horses, dogs and other odd members of the retinue in attendance."[34] Among those identified from the Blackfoot were head chief Yellow Horse, interpreter Joe Calf Child, Boy Chief, Three Suns, Duck Chief, and White Headed Chief. From the Sarcees came head chief Big Belly, Jim Starlight, Big Crow, Big Knife, and Fox Tail. From the Bloods came One Spot and Black Plume. No reference was made to either Stoneys or Peigans being in attendance, but virtually all leaders of the Blackfoot and Sarcee were on hand.

In the opening parade, Guy Weadick was at the front, with Yellow Horse at his side. Following them was the large contingent of Indians, some on horseback and some afoot. After them rode the Mounted Police, old timers, cowboys, and floats. "The Indians were the feature which attracted the greatest attention during the march through the city," said a reporter. "The chiefs were attired in their best regalia, and all carried their various badges of office." The reporter added that "without them it would have been pretty tame."[35]

The Victory Stampede drew tremendous crowds, but this had no apparent effect upon the Calgary Exhibition's decision to abide by the government regulations and not to press for Indian participation. Instead, the fairs of 1920, 1921, and 1922 continued to feature horse racing and agricultural displays. The attendance was dismal.

Seeking a solution to the lagging interest in the fair, the Exhibition Board decided to add the highly successful Stampede to the program. Organized under the direction of Guy Weadick, it immediately added cowboys, rodeo events, a buffalo barbeque, and Indians to the 1923 show. E.L. Richardson contacted Minister of the Interior Charles Stewart, who "provided 5 buffalo [for the barbeque] and 3 buffalo hides, and granted permission for the Indians to take part in the celebration."[36]

The Calgary Exhibition and Stampede went all out to promote the show. For days prior to the event, tipis were pitched on the lawn beside the CPR station and Indians in full regalia posed for photographs on the station platform. Inside the fairgrounds, some sixty tipis were pitched beside the replica of a Hudson's Bay Company store, and more than seven hundred Indians were part of the show. On parade day, "Stoney, Sarcees, Peigans and Blackfeet...made the air resound with their weird and wonderful war songs."[37]

With apparent approval from the Indian Department, the Stampede continued its Indian and cowboy theme into 1924 in a presentation that was even larger than that of the previous year. Exhibits of beadwork were on display under the grandstand, prizes were given for best-dressed Indians, and the evenings featured "Indian pony, teepee Travois, and squaw races."[38]

But the problems with the Indian Department were not over. While its former nemesis, James Markle, was now arranging land surrenders, the

A view of the Indian Village during the 1912 Stampede.

Stampede now had to cope with W.M. Graham, who had recently been appointed Indian commissioner for the prairie provinces. He was even more autocratic than Markle and wielded a greater amount of power. Throughout his career he was unalterably opposed to native religious ceremonies, dances, and other activities that he believed were a hindrance to progress. Stated his biographer, "In 1909 he emphasized to Department Secretary J.D. McLean that religious dances should not be allowed under any circumstances. Not only did he feel that such activities would 'demoralize' the Indians but on a practical level they would waste time better spent on agricultural pursuits."[39]

In 1925, according to historian James Gray, Graham denied permission for Indians to participate in the Stampede. As Gray notes,

> the edict sent panic shock waves through Victoria Park.
> This was the 50th anniversary of the arrival of the NWMP
> and the future site of Calgary. That was to be the theme
> of the 1925 exhibition. The historical pageant which was
> organized in cooperation with the parade was the most
> ambitious ever attempted. In addition the Mounties

brought in their musical ride and the countryside was
combed for surviving members of the Great Trek of
1874–75. To try to stage such a celebration without
Indian involvement was unthinkable.[40]

A compromise was eventually reached, as indicated by the Stampede's 1925 Annual Report: "Through the cooperation of Mr. W.M. Graham, Indian Commissioner, an arrangement was made to have a number of Indians camped on the grounds and take part in the pageant; so as to interfere as little as possible with work on the Indian reservations, Mr. Graham arranged to have only the older Indians, who as a matter of fact are most interesting from a tourist standpoint, participate in the festivities."[41] Reports of the fair, however, indicate that in the parade, the Indians "were there in hundreds – a motley, whooping, crew, proudly sporting every clashing color of the spectrum."[42]

The near-boycott continued for as long as Graham remained commissioner. For example, the 1926 Annual Report of the Stampede noted that "Mr. Graham insists that only a certain number come from each reserve to camp on the grounds and only such Indians as are unfit to work on the land are included among this number."[43] The press made reference to a diminished representation and a list of prize winners includes mostly elders. Awards for best dressed and best travois went to the Stoneys Hector and Mrs. George Crawler, Jonas Rider, and Mrs. Eliza Hunter; the Sarcees Big Knife, Joe Big Plume, Mrs. Eagle Plume, Mrs. Old Sarcee, and Mrs. Dick Starlight; and the Blackfoot White Headed Chief, Duck Chief, Mrs. Bear Chief, and Mrs. Spring Chief.[44]

Subsequent reports from 1927 to 1932 continued to thank the Indian commissioner and agents for their cooperation. Finally, after a bitter bureaucratic fight with Deputy Superintendent-General Duncan Campbell Scott, Graham abruptly retired as commissioner late in 1932. He was replaced by Howard W. McGill, who chose to delegate responsibilities for such matters as fairs to M. Christianson, regional director for Alberta, whose office was in Calgary.

Suddenly the sun began to shine on the Calgary Stampede. Unlike Graham and Markle, Christianson had no objection to Indian participation in fairs and other events. Although the prohibitive regulations were still on the books, Christianson had full authority to grant permission, and he did so. A short time later, he joined the Exhibition and Stampede Board as a director, becoming even more intimately involved with the activities of the natives in the Stampede. By the time he left office several years later, Indian participation in the Calgary Stampede was an established tradition.

Meanwhile, Indian participation in rodeo had been an entirely different matter. There seems to have been no objection to native involvement in Indian races, or even in professional rodeo events. Apparently the lack of cultural or religious significance of rodeo superseded any government objection to young athletic men leaving their reserves during farming season. Similarly, the young men themselves usually remained outside the sphere of the Indian Village. They competed with white cowboys and usually lived with them in or around the barns. Their dress was that of cowboys, not Indians, and their identity as native was secondary to that as cowboys. Marilyn Burgess sees this separation of Indian and rodeo events at the Calgary Stampede as a division between the prehistoric past and the historical past. "These rodeo performances produce the historical past of white colonization," she writes, "while relegating Native meanings of the land to an inaccessible pre-history, of little relevance to the modern nation."[45]

From the 1920s through to the 1950s, many Indians took top titles at the Stampede. Among them was two-time calf roping champion Pete Bruised Head, steer decorating champion Jimmy Wells, King Bearspaw, Johnny Left Hand, Bill McLean, Fred Gladstone, Jim Spotted Eagle, and others.[46]

Pete Bruised Head with trophy, 1927

During the 1930s the Stampede established routines that became part of the Indian Village program. The three tribes – Stoney, Blackfoot, and Sarcee – took the lead in opening day parades, travelling separately and sometimes interspersed with brass bands. Each day thereafter, Indians from a different tribe paraded to the downtown area, where they performed dances and sometimes took up collections from the spectators. At the village, a volunteer group of non-Indian judges inspected each tipi and gave awards for the best. Once a day, two or three tipis were open for inspection by the public, a bowl placed at the entrance of each to receive donations. Over the years, various activities came and went – dancing; meat cutting competitions; tipi raising; children's races; hand games; demonstrations of cooking, tanning, and beading; flag raising with honouring songs; Sunday church services; and others. Those involved in midfield events participated in buffalo riding, tug-of-war, pony racing, travois racing, rawhide racing, and various re-enactments.

The number of tipis in the village was limited to ten each from the three tribes. In 1962, during the fiftieth anniversary of the Stampede, the Bloods and Peigans were added to the encampment.[47] But this "official" camp was just a faction of the entire Indian attendance at the fair. Others came for pure entertainment, just as other Albertans enjoyed the show.

Methods of reaching the Stampede changed over the years. Although some Indians owned automobiles and trucks in the 1930s and 1940s, the preferred method of travelling for many years was by horse and wagon. For example, the *Calgary Herald* noted in 1944:

> Along the Banff highway this morning, scores of wagons,
> saddle horses and ponies could be seen as the Stony Indian
> contingent headed for the Indian village at the stampede
> grounds. Some will arrive now, others Sunday morning....
> The Sarcees were also packing up while east of Calgary
> hundreds of Blackfoot Indian wagons could be seen head-
> ing for Calgary.[48]

A gradual change in transportation methods became evident in the postwar period, as noted by this comment in 1948: "East and west of Calgary, long lines of Indian wagons could be seen on the trails this morning as Blackfoot Indians from the Gleichen reserve and Stony from the Morley reserve made an early start for their overland haul to Calgary....Some of the wealthier braves were travelling in automobiles."[49]

By the 1950s the tide had shifted in favour of motor vehicles as the main form of transportation. In 1953 reports were that some Blackfoot "will make the 79 miles driving with horses, while some will come in cars and trucks."[50] Ben Calf Robe preferred horses, travelling as far as Langdon the first night and reaching the Stampede grounds the following day. His distinctive tipi, showing a wolf attacking a buffalo, was usually the first one erected in the village. By the 1980s the use of trucks was so commonplace that a number of Blackfoot led by Leo Pretty Young Man "re-enacted" the horse and wagon trip with a Stampede Trail Ride from the reserve to the village. "This ride is very important to our people," Pretty Young Man told the press. "For me it brings back the past days, of the way things used to be. In those days our traditions and our culture were very sacred things; this ride can give other people an understanding of that."[51]

When they arrived in Calgary, those who were part of the official village went to the village site at the northwest entrance to the grounds. The camp was in a low-lying area with a high fence to the north, show buildings to the west, barns to the east, and the midway to the south. The camp was split by a row of trees, with the Sarcees on one side and the Blackfoot and Stoney camps to the east. In this latter area was a stage built beneath a huge tree which was called the Sun Tree. At one time on the eastern edge of the village were a Mounted Police detachment and a replica of a trading post.

The pitching of tipis on the day before the Stampede was popular entertainment for onlookers. "Hundreds of curious Calgarians will watch the Indians raise their tipis," said a reporter in 1949, "with old women of the tribe in charge of the proceedings. This is one of the few occasions when male members of the tribe take orders from the womenfolk."[52] As an example, Mrs. Maggie Gunny Crow, an 87-year-old Blackfoot, was seen "giving her grandson some pointers on setting up their tepee."[53]

For those who were not part of the camp, there were various places where tents could be pitched. These, of course, changed as the city grew. In the earlier period, the Stoneys were at Shaganappi, the Sarcees in the Mission district, and the Blackfoot across the Bow near the present Memorial Drive and Deerfoot Trail. One man recalled camping across the river and taking a streetcar to go to the grounds during the 1930s.[54]

By the 1940s the Blackfoot tribes had moved to the valley south of the Stampede grounds to an area that extended all the way to the present Manchester district. At the north of the settlement was the Sunshine Auto Court. In 1942 artist Mildred Valley Thornton went in search of Crowfoot's daughter, who was in one of the camps. She wrote, "A half-hour ride took me to the auto camp, but where were the Indians? I could see a tepee or two on the hill overlooking the camp so, laden with my painting kit, I started in that direction. When I reached the heights a bewildering panorama met my eyes. Far and near were tents, not tepees."[55] Undismayed, she began walking south. Over the first hill she came to one camp, then to another, but did not find her subject. She walked through herds of horses in a coulee and at the next hill she was given directions. After passing another camp with an overabundance of noisy dogs, she finally found her subject on a high hill at the southern extremity of the camps. As a reporter stated, "Hundreds of Indians...pitched tents on the hills flanking the Macleod Trail south of the AMA auto camp."[56] However, by 1951 the Manchester area was becoming so built up that the Indians were obliged to move back to their old location across the Bow. It was not a desirable site but remained in use until motor vehicles turned Stampede visits into day trips.

For those living on the grounds, life was a flurry of activity from the time they arrived. They were paid for bringing their camp gear, given a corral for their horses, issued rations, and expected to adhere to the rules of the village. Although these varied over the years, the list for 1961 is a good example. Owners were required to have a painted tipi and all the furnishings. If they left before the end of the show, they would not be invited back. They had to be prepared to take part in parades, downtown shows, and camp activities. Abuse of alcohol or drugs could result in dismissal from the camp. The right to be a tipi owner could be inherited.[57]

The village at the entrance to the grounds had its drawbacks. It was located beside the midway, making it hard for parents to keep track of their children and even harder to sleep at night. Also, the area was wide open, so tipi owners were often pestered by drunks and troublemakers. The undesirable location was discussed on a number of occasions, but nothing was done.

Then in 1950 a heavy downpour caused flooding in the camp. James Gray noted,

> The area where the Indian village was located was a notorious low spot that had once been a sunken garden. By the middle of the week some of the teepees were standing in a foot of water and their occupants had to be moved into the Arena to dry out.[58]

A year later there was another flood, particularly in the low-lying area occupied by the Blackfoot. The damage again was extensive. In 1963 I noted in my diary, "there was a terrible thunderstorm which raged for most of the night. It was clear by morning but the Indians were late [for parade judging] because the rain had soaked the camps."[59] Two years later, on July 11, 1965, I wrote, "A heavy downpour in the late afternoon flooded out the Peigans and caused damage to the other lodges."[60] This downpour resulted in the loss of more priceless costumes and artifacts. When my wife and I visited the camp that evening, soggy buffalo robes, damaged buckskin dresses, and other objects had been dragged outside the tipis in an attempt to save them. When immediate settlement was not forthcoming, some angry tipi dwellers formed the United Indian Committee to seek compensation. Leonard Crane, Daisy Crowchild's son, said damage ranged from $150 to $700 but implied the Stampede was offering as little as $50. The Stampede Board claimed Crane's group had no standing and it would deal only with individuals.[61] In the end, some sort of settlement was reached and the United Indian Committee dissolved.

Not until 1974 was the problem completely resolved when the village was moved to a new site at the south end of the grounds, across the Elbow River. It offered excellent drainage, and the fenced area provided security and nighttime protection for members of the camp.[62]

Flooding was not the only problem facing the Stampede Board over the years. There were frequent complaints about the amount of money received, many tipi owners indicating that it actually cost them money to come to the Stampede. Others complained about the rations and the way they were distributed. In 1947 tipi owners submitted a petition outlining the contributions they were making to the success of the Stampede and seeking more money, but nothing came of it.[63]

In 1950 the Board reacted to Indian complaints about drunks bothering tipi owners and tourists by cancelling free admission to all Indians other than tipi owners and their families. Until this time, Indians could enter the grounds simply by showing their treaty cards. The Stoney Indians were so angry about the ruling that they boycotted the 1950 Stampede. Coincidentally, the Stampede that year was subjected to a terrific rain and hail storm, giving rise to the story that the tribe had put on a "rain dance."[64] Late in the year, a meeting was held with the Stoneys, who denied the stories. Tom Kaquitts said the rains were not caused by the Indians, "but came from someone above, far over the blue mountains."[65] Regardless of their guilt or innocence, no change was made in the admittance ruling. The only concession was to provide the tipi owners with large blocks of day passes that they could give to their friends.

James Gray claims the boycott resulted in the Stampede Board finally waking up to the need for changes. He wrote,

> The prize list for all Indian events was gone over and the budget doubled. Moreover the practice was abandoned of dumping the Indians' food into flour sacks, a practice that

went back to the way in which starving Indians were given famine relief in the first days of the North West Mounted Police. In its place a system was installed for providing the Indians with specially prepared and packaged hampers containing food that made for a varied and balanced diet.[66]

In 1961 rations consisted of beef, tea, sugar, bread, jam, and potatoes.[67]

Other problems plagued the Stampede Committee in the 1960s and 1970s as dissatisfaction over money and Indians' use of the press to publicize their concerns made these matters a public issue. Complaints over insufficient payments for coming to the Stampede had been expressed for years, but they seldom got beyond the grounds. In 1961, however, the head chief of the Blackfoot, Clarence McHugh, publicly demanded more money and threatened to form a group of tipi owners to boycott the show. He commented, "The small amount given us hardly covered the costs of moving and keeping us in supplies for the week. [The amount] worked out at 60 cents a day per person."[68] McHugh, a Second World War veteran and successful farmer, was an active leader in native provincial politics. However, he made the mistake of announcing his demands and threat of withdrawal before consulting with the tipi owners. The Stampede Board immediately lobbied to keep the other owners on side, and the demonstration failed. Only McHugh left the camp in the following year.

A more serious confrontation took place in 1972, when Dave and Daisy Crowchild, two of the most popular people in the village, were suspended for a year and their tipi site given to someone else. The problem arose when they moved out of the village before the Stampede was over. According to one report, Dave's wife was ill, so he took her home and later to hospital.[69] Another explanation is that they went to an Indian gathering at Daisy's home reserve in Manitoba.[70] Even though they left their tipi in place, they were told they had broken the rules and had lost their rights as tipi owners. There was a great outcry from the general public, for these two people were well known as leading goodwill ambassadors between the native communities and Calgary. The Crowchild Trail had been named in their honour. Finally, under intense pressure from the press, an invitation was extended for them to return, but they never did.

There also were growing complaints that the members of the Indian Events Committee and the judges, all of whom were non-Indians, were engaged in a master-servant relationship with tipi owners that was not unlike that of Indian agents. Finally, in 1970, four Indians were added to the committee as advisory members, and in short order some prize monies were doubled and horses were provided with barns for the first time.[71] A year later, these four tipi owners and another two became members of the committee itself, and by 1985 all tipi owners automatically were members of the Indian Events Committee.

In 1989 tipi owner Bruce Starlight complained publicly that events had become "dull and routine" because the Indians did not have enough input. Although they were now members of the committee, "All they're doing is picking our brains and making decisions for us even though the activities are ours."[72] In 1972 City Councilman Eric Musgreave complained that Indians at the Stampede were used as a "tourist gimmick" and that they were being exploited.[73] His claims were immediately challenged by members of his own council. In 1991 *Calgary Herald* columnist Catherine Ford unsuccessfully suggested that Indians should reject the Stampede.[74] In 1999 Roy Little Chief, former head chief of the Blackfoot, reportedly claimed that conditions at the village were "appalling," that elders were being forced to dance, and that tipi owners had no influence. His comments were immediately rejected by tipi owners such as Ed Calf Robe, who said, "The only thing bad about this Stampede was the weather."[75]

In spite of discomfort, adverse weather conditions, and other problems, the Indians have always loved the Stampede. When asked in 1946 why she came, Inez Hunter said, "I come to the Stampede for two reasons – my husband Judas is a chief, and I must come to put up the tent and keep it tidy for him. It is most important that he be here. Then I like the Stampede because once again I meet all my friends and we can talk over old times."[76] "This is my summer holiday," is the way Mrs. One Spot described her trip to the Stampede.[77]

I first became involved with the Indian Village in 1962 as a judge, and over the years I have had ample opportunity to see the relationship between the Indians and the Stampede. It is, in many ways, a love affair. The tipi holders are proud of their role in the Stampede and point out they often are the third and fourth generations of families involved with the village. The prize ribbons given at the parades and the village are taken quite seriously. I can recall the elation throughout the Stoney camp when one of their tipis was chosen for the first time as the best in the whole camp. Most do not mind having their pictures taken; at one time they expected they would be paid for it, now it is optional.

I found no examples where people felt they were being "used" by the Stampede or were mere pawns for the benefit of attracting tourists. Rather, they believed it was an opportunity to show off their culture and their individual expertise in bead working or costume making. While outsiders have claimed that native culture was being commercialized, the Stampede actually proved to be an important factor in preserving it. During the 1950s and 1960s, when native culture was at a low ebb and people were disposing off their relics, tipi owners refused to sell because they needed them for the Stampede.

A hoop dancer performs during a ceremony at the Indian Village.

There can be no doubt that attitudes towards Indian participation have changed drastically since the 1890s. Initially Indians were considered amusing sidelights to the real show, with even their pony races being held up to ridicule. The press was no better than the general population in making snide and sarcastic remarks about native participation. During government attempts to suppress Indian involvement, references were made to the demeaning way they were treated and how women were insulted.

Much of the change in attitude can be attributed to Guy Weadick. He saw the Indians as colourful and positive assets to the Wild West show. He had personal friendships with many Indians and saw their virtues extolled and publicized at the 1912 and 1919 Stampedes. When the Calgary Exhibition and Stampede was formed in 1923, Weadick continued with this positive and laudatory approach to the Indian participants. He may have had showmanship in mind when he insisted on Indian participation, but the results fostered a positive image for the Indian. Another development in favour of the Indians occurred when Ed Hall was placed in charge of Indian events.

This began a half-century dynasty with his son Tom, his son-in-law Roland Bradley, and his grandson Ron Hall successively providing continuity and intimate knowledge of the camp and its functions.

Many changes have been noted in the past forty-five years. Some people bring their campers and spend the night in them, rather than their tipis. Events such as the North American Chicken Dancing Competition have become a major part of the week. Booths have been added to sell bannock and handicrafts, and vouchers are issued instead of rations. In short, most of the changes have been made for the benefit of the tipi owners. But it is still the Stampede, and to paraphrase from a popular movie, "If you build it, they will come."

Notes

1. To be politically correct today, one uses such terms as "First Nations," "Native Americans," etc. Tribal names gaining popularity include Siksika (Blackfoot), Nakoda (Stoney), Tsuu T'ina (Sarcee), Kainai (Blood), and Pikuni (Peigan). However, as this article provides a historical overview, the author has used those names and titles commonly in use at the time. This avoids the confusion of calling a tribe one name in direct quotations and another in the main text.
2. Hugh A. Dempsey, ed., "Calgary and the Riel Rebellion," *Alberta History* 33, no. 2 (Spring 1985): 14.
3. Hugh A. Dempsey, "Deerfoot and Friends," in *The Amazing Death of Calf Shirt and Other Blackfoot Stories* (Calgary: Fifth House, 1994), 161–85.
4. *Calgary Herald*, 5 July 1939.
5. *Calgary Tribune*, 25 July 1894.
6. *Calgary Herald*, 5 September 1902.
7. *Calgary Albertan*, 13 July 1901.
8. *Calgary Herald*, 20 August 1919.
9. *Calgary Herald*, 24 July 1903, cited in W. Keith Regular, "'Red Backs and White Burdens': A Study of Indian and White Relations in Southern Alberta, 1896–1911" (master's thesis, University of Calgary, 1985), 155.
10. Regular, "'Red Backs,'" 155.
11. *Calgary Herald*, 1 July 1908.
12. *Lethbridge Herald*, 9 June 1909. Cited in W. Keith Regular, "On Public Display," *Alberta History* 34, no. 1 (Winter 1986): 3.
13. *Calgary Herald*, 5 July 1909.
14. *Calgary Albertan*, 5 July 1909.
15. Regular, "Public Display," 4.
16. *Calgary Albertan*, 12 August 1910.
17. *Calgary Albertan*, 28 October 1901, cited in Regular, "'Red Backs,'" 6–7.
18. Cited in Regular, "'Red Backs,'" 8.
19. *Calgary Herald*, 4 July 1912.
20. J.W. Mitchell to J.A. Markle, 6 May 1912, Indian Affairs, RG-10, vol. 3826, file 60,511-3, Library and Archives Canada (hereafter cited as LAC).
21. Lieutenant Colonel H.C. Lowther to Superintendent-General of Indian Affairs, 2 August 1912, Indian Affairs, RG-10, vol. 3826, file 60,511-3, LAC.
22. J.W. McLean to Blood, Blackfoot, Peigan, Sarcee, and Stoney Indian agents (circular letter), 9 July 1912, Indian Affairs, RG-10, vol. 3826, file 60,511-3, LAC.
23. R.B. Deane to Indian Agent J.H. Gooderham, 18 July 1912, Indian Affairs, RG-10, vol. 3826, file 60,511-3, LAC.
24. T. Albert Moore to J.W. McLean, 30 August 1912, Indian Affairs, RG-10, vol. 3826, file 60,511-3, LAC.

25. *Globe* (Toronto), 4 September 1912.

26. *Calgary News-Telegram*, 5 September 1912.

27. Glen Campbell to Hon. Thomas Crothers, 12 May 1913, Indian Affairs, RG-10, vol. 3826, file 60,511-3, LAC.

28. *Bow Valley Call*, Gleichen, 24 October 1912.

29. Canada, *The Indian Act Consolidated for Office Purposes* (Ottawa: King's Printer, 1949), Sec.140A/2, p. 49. This regulation remained on the statute books until the passage of a new Indian Act in 1951.

30. *Calgary Herald*, 3 July 1916.

31. Ibid., 21 August 1919.

32. Ibid., 20 August 1919.

33. Ibid., 21 August 1919.

34. Ibid., 25 August 1919.

35. Ibid., 27 August 1919.

36. Report of the Manager of Calgary Exhibition to the Directors, 26 September 1923, Calgary Exhibition and Stampede Papers, M 2160, Glenbow Museum Archives.

37. *Calgary Herald*, 10 July 1923.

38. Ibid., 5 July 1924.

39. "Introduction," by James Dempsey, in William M. Graham, *Treaty Days: Reflections of an Indian Commissioner* (Calgary: Glenbow Museum, 1991), x.

40. Gray, *Brand of Its Own*, 80–81.

41. Gray, *Brand of Its Own*, 80.

42. *Calgary Herald*, 6 July 1925.

43. Calgary Exhibition and Stampede, Annual Report, 1926, CES Papers, Glenbow Museum Archives.

44. *Calgary Herald*, 5 July 1926.

45. Marilyn Burgess, "Canadian 'Range Wars': Struggles Over Indian Cowboys," *Canadian Journal of Communication* 18, no. 3 (1993): 351–64.

46. Glen Mikkelsen, "Indians and Rodeo," *Alberta History* 35, no. 3 (Summer 1987): 15.

47. *Calgary Albertan*, 29 January 1962.

48. *Calgary Herald*, 8 July 1944.

49. Ibid., 3 July 1948.

50. Ibid., 4 July 1953.

51. Ibid., 7 July 1989.

52. Ibid., 9 July 1949.

53. Ibid., 7 July 1964.

54. Jasper Many Heads, interview in *Calgary Sun*, 15 July 2004.

55. Mildred Valley Thornton, *Buffalo People: Portraits of a Vanishing Nation* (Delta,

BC: Hancock House, 2000), 147.

56. *Calgary Albertan*, 8 July 1945.

57. "Indian Events on the Exhibition Grounds 1961," copy in Dempsey files. See also "Tipi Holders Policy," April 26, 1989, in author's possession.

58. Gray, *Brand of Its Own*, 128.

59. Diary of Hugh A. Dempsey, 8 July 1963, in author's possession.

60. Diary of Hugh A. Dempsey, 10 July 1965, in author's possession. The author was one of the judges at the Indian Village at the time.

61. *Calgary Herald*, 18 August 1965.

62. Ibid., 5 July 1974.

63. Ibid., 5 July 1947.

64. Gray, *Brand of Its Own*, 128.

65. *Calgary Albertan*, 8 December 1950.

66. Gray, *Brand of Its Own*, 128.

67. "Indian Events on the Exhibition Grounds 1961," copy in Dempsey files.

68. *Calgary Herald*, 14 July 1965.

69. *Calgary Albertan*, 8 February 1973.

70. Interview with Mrs. Pauline Dempsey, June 19, 2005. Mrs. Dempsey was a member of the Indian Events Committee at the time.

71. *Calgary Albertan*, 20 July 1970.

72. *Calgary Herald*, 12 July 1989. In 1991, Starlight was involved in further controversy when he ran for a seat on the Calgary Stampede Board of Directors. The custom was for people to put their names forward for two or three years before being accepted, but when Starlight was rejected on his first try, a campaign was launched through the press to have him installed. As a result of intense pressure, he was elected in the following year.

73. *Calgary Herald*, 18 February 1972.

74. Ibid., 24 November 1991.

75. Ibid., 18 July 1999.

76. Ibid., 11 July 1946.

77. Ibid., 13 July 1956.

CHAPTER 4

Calgary's Parading Culture Before 1912

Lorry W. Felske

A float in the Dominion Exhibition parade, 1908.

The Stampede parade is a unique public event in the Canadian urban landscape. On the first Friday morning of July, the parade draws over three hundred thousand spectators to Calgary's centre in anticipation of the rolling pageant of western Canadian icons. At dawn keen spectators loaded with lawn chairs claim prime front-row seats, then latecomers crowd sidewalks or stake out aerial perches from office windows, apartment balconies, rooftops, ladders, newspaper boxes, or the beds of trucks parked conveniently at each cross street. At earlier parades agile enthusiasts climbed telephone poles for a more commanding view. As the parade ambles past, the core components of First Nations, red-coated Mounties, and cowboys and cowgirls are mixed with a variety of other ingredients: clowns, business and community floats, chuckwagons, bands, horses and other animals, vehicles, and a roster of dignitaries (governmental, military, and royal) and celebrities (local, national, and international). Taking nearly three hours to pass, the parade's finale comes with the flashing lights and whooping sirens of fire engines, police cars, and street sweepers scooping up the mounds of horse manure and other parade debris. Spectators flood the parade route and disperse. Most herd tired families towards cars or public transit for the ride home; others trot to the Stampede grounds to view exhibits, stroll the midway, grab scarce casino seats, climb the grandstand to watch rodeo events, or buy tickets for the chuckwagon races later in the evening. When the parade concludes, the Stampede begins.

In the writing about the Stampede that annually mesmerizes Calgarians, the parade receives frequent but indirect treatment; it is usually lodged in a variety of different contexts: the exploitation of First Nations, the confluence of American and Canadian cowboy culture, the historical evolution of the exhibition organization, or the biographies of important Stampede organizers such as Guy Weadick, Ernie Richardson, and C.W. Petersen.[1] One dominant theme is the interpretation of Stampede events as a performance discourse narrating the arrival and success of European settler culture in the Canadian West and the suppression of First Nations cultures. In this framework the parade becomes a one-sided story about the European colonization of western Canada, "a mindset that demanded continual repetition."[2] Certainly a good portion of Calgary parade history lauded European colonization, but the Stampede parade had a local urban context as well. Unlike the competitive rodeo events created especially for the first Stampede, parades were an integral part of Calgary culture before 1912. Apart from the participation of more cowboys, cowgirls, and First Nations people, the 1912

Stampede parade did not stray far from Calgary parading traditions, and in the years that followed, the Stampede parade borrowed heavily from the first Calgary parades.

To appreciate the wider context of the Stampede parades it is useful to consider studies of performance activities in other cultures. One individual who explored this area was Eric Hobsbawm, who was interested in the invention of traditions in modern society. According to Hobsbawm, invented traditions include a wide variety of rituals (parades included) whose purpose is three-fold: to accomplish social cohesion, to legitimize institutions, and to teach values and conventions of behaviour.[3] These invented rituals spring from the need to reconcile constant change in the modern world with the desire for stability and traditional understandings about society. Usually controlled by a society's elite groups, invented traditions resolve conflict by presenting new values or by showing how old values apply to new situations. The cathartic qualities of the 1935 Stampede parade are described by a spectator:

> We enjoyed everything, but I could not help but notice
> the extra expression of heartfelt pleasure when the
> cow-boys and old-timers' section of the parade came
> into view. One could…feel the vibration of good feeling
> running all through the crowd … It vibrated along the
> side-walks, echoed and re-echoed from the tops of trucks
> and businesses and on up to the windows and roofs of the
> buildings that lined the avenue.[4]

Other works exploring ritual performances make similar assessments of their stabilizing effects. In *How Societies Remember*, Paul Connerton emphasizes that rituals such as parades use interpretations of the past to legitimize a particular social order. Connerton argues that "control of a society's memory largely conditions [or supports] the hierarchy of power" in a society.[5] In this regard, "making sense of the past is a kind of collective autobiography...a master narrative that is more than a story told and reflected on, it is a cult enacted."[6] In an extensive study of ritual activities, Catherine Bell describes events such as parades as a means of achieving community consensus. In Bell's typology of rituals, parades fall within a group that deals with "feasting, fasting and festival." In this category, Bell sees events such as parades as "cultural performances" or "social dramas" in which people "express publicly – to themselves, to each other, and sometimes to outsiders – their commitment and adherence to basic...values."[7]

In the case of the parade, Bell is careful to note that understanding the content of the parade is important, but the experience of viewing the parade, of being part of the crowd that witnesses the parade, is also a crucial part of the ritual. Events such as parades "draw together many social groups that are normally kept separate and create specific times and places where social differences are either laid aside or reversed for a more embracing experience of community."[8]

Implicit in these interpretations of parades as ritual is the assumption of an underlying need to demonstrate community solidarity. Hobsbawm argues that the invention of traditions occurred "when a rapid transformation of society weakened or destroyed the social patterns for which 'old' traditions had been designed."[9] Other observers of ritual, such as A.P. Cohen, make a similar observation that ritual becomes important when "community boundaries are blurred or undermined."[10] Still others see ritual as a way to deal with growing differences in a culturally diverse society. Dominic Bryan, who has studied Orange Parades and other ritual festivals in Europe, notes that "the more internally diverse the community, the more elaborate and regular the attempts to define it."[11] In the case of new societies such as Calgary that were experiencing rapid growth and sudden reversals, conditions of upheaval and social confusion spawned ritual as a means of achieving social communication and stability.

Historical Background of Calgary Parades

Over the period of Calgary's development from an outpost of the North-West Mounted Police in 1874 to an urban centre by the early 1920s, rapid economic, social, and political transformations occurred. Economically, the Calgary region evolved from a minor centre in the western fur-trading economy, to an intensive cattle-ranching area, and then to a prosperous market-driven agricultural district with an industrial and service support system that included railways, coal mines, and banks. By the 1920s the growing oil and gas industry promised even more change. These economic shifts contributed to major political developments, particularly after provincial structures replaced territorial governance when Alberta became a province in 1905. From a small community dealing with practical issues such as livestock roaming its streets, Calgary was becoming a major urban centre with fundamental urban problems. Drastic social transformation continued as well, as Calgary's economic development boosted its population from 4,400 in 1901 to 50,000 by 1912. Ranching attracted newcomers from central Canada, Great Britain, and the United States. The development of an agricultural economy and its supporting services and industries accelerated immigration from European countries to Calgary and the surrounding area. With the neighbouring First Nations population already on the scene, Calgary's cultural mosaic was complex. Over the period before the First World War, many different groups found parading a convenient way of staking claim to Calgary's identity.[12]

Layered on these local situations were national issues and events that made the life of Calgarians even more challenging. Severe economic downturns in 1907–08, 1913–15, and 1920–23 complicated Calgary's growth. The First World War (1914–18) brought further disruption to the city and to all of Canada, as the city and country attempted to adjust to the departures of soldiers, their injuries and deaths, and the reintegration of returning soldiers. With the rise of an urban economy, class tensions became more significant; people talked of working-class revolution and the "Bolshevik menace." Additional social concerns such as prohibition, prostitution, and crime also claimed the attention of Calgary residents. Certainly other Canadian cities experienced these problems, but in western Canadian cities, relatively new creations with shorter histories of governance and leadership, they were significant challenges.

In the context of these developments, the emergence of Calgary parades as a device for community communication occurred early in the city's history. The Stampede parades of 1912 and 1919 and those that followed continually from 1923 emerged from a local civic culture and history of parading. The eventual success of the Stampede parade was due partly to the skills of key individuals such as Ernie Richardson and Guy Weadick, but it depended fundamentally on an established Calgary parade habit that grew with the city. Calgary certainly was not alone in this regard; most western Canadian communities organized, participated in, and witnessed parades of various types and sizes before the first Stampede parade in 1912. Photographs of parades by specific groups such as Masons, Orangemen, trade unionists, military units, and the Mounted Police; ethic communities such as the Chinese; and small local bands, usually from fire or police departments, are found frequently in western archives and described often in the region's newspapers.[13] Indeed, as Susan Davis observes, "parades were an important, varied and popular mode of communication in nineteenth century cities" in North America.[14] In the absence of other institutions, parades in newly created western Canadian urban centres, small and large, were an easy way to express, and to some extent challenge, the meaning of community and to articulate urban accomplishments, plans, and anxieties about the past, present, and future. Local and regional parading culture developed prior to 1912, and the additional elements that emerged during the First World War greatly influenced the Stampede parades that became a regular part of events from 1923 onward. Although the 1923 parade marked the beginning of Stampede parades held continually in association with the annual Exhibition, a massive 1925 parade celebrating the arrival of the North-West Mounted Police (NWMP) in Calgary finally corralled a parade within the realm of Stampede festivities.

British and American Influences

One important source of inspiration for the Calgary parading culture was the British Empire. In this early period the annual celebration of Victoria Day, two coronations (Edward VII and George V), the occasional royal or aristocratic visitor, and to some extent Dominion Day all generated Calgary parade activity. From the earliest days of settlement in the Calgary area, connections with the British Empire had deep roots. In the 1880s and 1890s the British presence in southern Alberta sprang from general interest in investing in all parts of the Empire, from the South African gold fields to the Australian outback. Interest in the possibilities of the prairies was boosted by a visit by the Marquess of Lorne, Canada's youngest governor general (1878 to 1883) and the husband of Queen Victoria's fourth daughter, Princess Louise (who gave Regina its name and after whom Lake Louise is named). Lord Lorne toured the West in the summer of 1881 with "a bevy of British journalists."[15] Overwhelmed by their experiences, the writers and Lord Lorne encouraged British investment in the West just as the Canadian government was offering cheap land leases to promote large cattle ranches. Arriving in significant numbers, British investors in southern Alberta soon rode beside Canadians and Americans and their cowboy work force.[16] Polo and cricket became popular sports in the foothills of the Rockies. When Albert, the fourth Earl Grey, visited Calgary in 1889, his public ride through the city passed beneath a specially constructed triumphal arch.[17] Grey's visit was one of the first instances of Calgarians taking to the streets to acknowledge a significant event. (Grey became governor general of Canada from 1904 to 1911.)

With these local British connections and Canada's key membership in the Empire, it is easy to understand why the Victoria Day celebrations emerged as significant Calgary activities. Already by 1901 the Victoria Day parade had reached substantial size and its format foreshadowed many aspects of other Calgary and Stampede parades. Despite rain the previous day, the 1901 parade "splashed manfully along," moving east and west on the city's major avenues. The parade began at the fire hall and went west on Northcote (Fifth) Avenue to First Street West, south to Stephen (Eighth) Avenue, east five blocks to Fourth Street East, south to Atlantic (Ninth) Avenue, west five blocks to First Street, north to Northcote Avenue, east another five blocks back to Second Street East, and south to City Hall, where it disbanded. Although held to mark Victoria Day and to preface the various sporting events and competitions held later in the day, the parade had a special western theme. As Territorial Premier F.W.G. Haultain and a "large majority of members" of the Territorial Legislature were visiting the city, the organizers seized on the opportunity to herd them into the first section of the parade under the direction of Major Saunders of the NWMP. Led by the twenty-five-piece Calgary Fire Brigade Band, the lieutenant governor of the North-West Territories, Amédée Forget, followed with the legislative members and Calgary Mayor J.S. Mackie, all in horse-drawn carriages.[18]

Each section of the 1901 parade that trooped behind government officials had a separate marshal and a marching band. The second subdivision of the 1901 Victoria Day parade was led by J.W. Mitchell (who became Calgary's mayor in 1911) and the Medicine Hat Band. Decidedly military in nature and demonstrating the Empire connections, this section featured a contingent of thirty South African veterans led by Captain Inglis, along with a contingent of Mounted Police and a group of high school cadets. The third section, with P. Campbell as marshal and the Edmonton Fire Department Band providing music, was for sportsmen such lacrosse and football players and bicyclists, contestants for the competitions to be held later in the day. The fourth section, under the control of Parade Marshal W. McKenzie, moved to the accompaniment of the coal miners' band from the neighbouring town of Canmore and contained all the float entries (mercantile and comical), followed by a selection of livestock. The final parade section, marshalled by J. Laycock, was more diverse; accompanied by a band from Olds, a town north of Calgary, the last section featured "citizens in their carriages," Indians on horseback, and students from the local Calgary Indian Industrial School.[19]

For many of those participating in the 1901 Victoria Day parade, as in nearly all Calgary parades, prizes were offered. The best decorated bicycle, ridden by Ida Allan, won $3; the best decorated horse, pulling the fire department's chemical pump, also won $3; the best decorated horse team, another fire department entry pulling the hose wagon, won $6. Although the brewery float handing out liquid refreshment was a crowd favourite, it lost the best comical float prize ($10) to the Darktown Fire Brigade. Reflecting the racial prejudices of the era, fire department members, with faces painted black, sprayed water on themselves and onlookers as they moved along the route. Prizes for the best representation of a trade float and the most handsome float, each worth $10, went to the Great West Saddlery Company. Its float featured two wagons lashed together, on the decks of which craftsmen demonstrated the construction of a saddle and a buggy bridle as they moved along the crowded route. The prize for the best mercantile entry went to the Hudson's Bay Company float featuring the interior of an early trading post complete with stacked canned goods, rifles, blankets, and a rum jar, as well as a live white-haired fur trader and Indians engaged in smoking tobacco.

The final prize offered by the 1901 parade committee rewarded participation in these festivities by the Calgary community: $20 went to the best decorated building, the Calgary Hardware Company.[20] The interest in civic decoration continued in the Victoria Day parade, with "many stores and residences decorated in honour of the occasion."[21] By the 1908 Exhibition parade, everyone expected street decorations, and the *Daily Herald* chastised businesses that did not participate.[22] The peak of civic decoration came with the Coronation parade for George V in June 1911, a year before the first Stampede parade. City Hall was swathed in bunting, and decorations adorned the post office, library, educational institutions, stores, and "private residences in the suburbs." Eighth Avenue from Second Street West to Second Street East was "one streak of colour." Although a light rain the day before the parade wilted some outdoor drapery, the city streets were walls of red and white bunting, especially the parade route from Mewata to Victoria Park, down Sixth Avenue, and under the Second Street East subway beneath the Canadian Pacific Railway (CPR) tracks.[23]

An estimated six to ten thousand people marched in the 1911 Coronation parade for George V. Calgary's entire school population of two thousand pupils participated, including students from Crescent Heights Collegiate, the boys wearing "merry widow hats" and the girls carrying Japanese parasols. Organized by Fire Chief John "Cappy" Smart, the parade comprised five sections, each led by a prominent citizen and a band. The school children led the procession, followed by civic officials. Next came two sections of military units that had gathered that week for training exercises on the outskirts of the city. The last division, led by the Salvation Army, contained Calgary's fraternal and friendly societies. At least two floats graced the 1911 Coronation parade: the electrical workers built an illuminated Britannia pulled by six horses, and the Parks Department constructed a forest scene populated with grazing deer.[24] These contributions were not as extensive as those in the 1902 Coronation parade for Edward VII that featured ten company floats, with the Calgary Brewing Company taking the prize for best trade float.[25]

Claiming that the 1911 Coronation parade "was the largest of its kind to be organized in the west," *Albertan* reporters estimated that thirty thousand people lined streets and the Second Street subway was "beetled black with spectators." The expectation that so many Calgarians would attend the parade had prompted Police Chief J.S. Mackie to warn everyone to leave houses and businesses "securely fastened" to eliminate opportunities for theft by nefarious types. Mackie also cautioned Calgarians about setting off firecrackers during the parade, as "several thousand horses" clomping along the route could be spooked. Despite these anxieties, George V's Calgary Coronation parade, "a moving panorama of gay colour," proceeded without incident and Fire Chief Cappy Smart reeled in the accolades for his efforts.

In the Victoria Day and Coronation parades, many elements of later Stampede parades were already evident: the parade's role as the opening event for activities that followed,[26] the thematic divisions within the parade, the important place of government officials at the beginning of the parade, the presence of the military and Mounted Police, and the floats and bands oriented to the area's history, local businesses, and nearby towns. A sense of frivolity and caricature had also emerged in Calgary parades, and citizens were encouraged to wear costumes and put up decorations to provide the dramatic backdrop for each parade. Overall, the parade stressed civic achievements in the context of connections with the British Empire.

Receiving significant but less intense parade treatment in these years before 1912 was another, newer empire with strong links to the Calgary area. The important role of American settlers was acknowledged by including them in various parades throughout these years. On some occasions separate parades were held to celebrate the Fourth of July and special days were set aside during the annual Exhibition to honour American settlers. In February 1908 a Calgary American Association emerged, "not to stimulate an admiration for American institutions and laws," but to encourage a "love for Canada" among all its residents. In 1908 the association produced an American float for the Exhibition parade on July 1 and a parade on July 4 celebrating American themes.

Led by I.G. Ruttle, an American cartage company owner who participated widely in other Calgary parades and activities, the parade on July 4, 1908, was extensive, featuring the Iowa Regiment Band as well as bands from Lethbridge and Camrose. One parade stunner was an elephant symbolizing the Republican Party, with "President Taft" riding on its back, while "William Jennings Bryant" rode less regally alongside on a mule, the symbol of the Democratic Party. The official American float for the July 4 parade, which also appeared in the July 1 Exhibition parade, was in two parts: the first section was a boat filled with immigrants of all nationalities; the second part showed the results of "training in Uncle Sam's school, the moulding of the rough material into lawyers, doctors, engineers, carpenters, blacksmiths, policemen and even politicians."[27] Another float featured Miss Liberty against the background of a large version of the Stars and Stripes. Two gentlemen dressed as Uncle Sam and John Bull, who had made a previous appearance in the 1906 Exhibition parade,[28] passed by in a carriage waving energetically to the crowd.

In addition to nearly fifty cowboys and a number of First Nations participants, walking and on horseback, the July 4, 1908, parade also had commercial floats previously seen in the parade that opened the Exhibition week on July 1. Along with a number of local citizens in carriages, the parade ended with the Canadian and American fat ball teams, men weighing over 200 pounds who competed during the Exhibition. The American team sported a large sign proclaiming that "We are Yanks...about to wallop the stuffing out of the Canadian Fats" and challenging the crowd to attend the game and watch its victory that evening.[29] Missing among the spectators for the July 4, 1908, parade was a group of Spokane businessmen and their families whose attendance had been arranged by Calgary's American Association. Delayed by a disabled train engine and too many glasses of liquid hospitality at a Fort Macleod breakfast,[30] they arrived just after the parade, but were an important part of the 1908 Exhibition activities that followed. Among this group were Andrew Laidlaw and C.F. Clough, who had investments in the Crow's Nest Pass coal district in southwestern Alberta.[31]

While both American and British connections were an accepted part of Calgary's culture, signs of local tension spawned by competing loyalties did occasionally surface. In 1911, shortly after the Coronation Parade, a car flying American flags roared up and down Eighth Avenue, the city's main street, angering bystanders on a day so clearly devoted to warm Empire feelings. Constable Finlayson of the Calgary Police stopped the car and grabbed some of the flags, snapping their poles over his knee and ripping the banners to pieces, all to the delight of onlookers. With a warning from the constable and the approach of more officers, the car quickly vanished.[32] This scene was repeated in 1912 at the Victoria Day celebrations when a Mr. Pyles appeared on Ninth Avenue in a car with American flags in an elevated position of prominence over the Union Jack. Police arrested the apparently drunk Mr. Pyles after pushing their way through a crowd of nearly a thousand people, most of whom had gathered to threaten Pyles with bodily harm. In an effort to mount an expedition to the city jail to force his release, his defenders unsuccessfully sought help from the American consul, who, probably with good reason, had made himself scarce.[33] Generally, though, the Americans were welcome visitors, and the Duke of Connaught recognized their contributions to southern Alberta when he visited Calgary during the 1912 Stampede. In his brief speech, the Duke observed,

> There are around me – I well know – a great number of
> our American cousins from across the border, who have
> been drawn here by the numerous attractions presented
> by the Province of Alberta; and I wish to tell them that
> they are very welcome, and that we readily extend to them
> the hand of hospitality which they have extended to our
> young men in the Western States during the past.[34]

Labour Day Parades

Another expression of the realities, and to some degree the growing tensions, in the Calgary community were the Labour Day parades that had also become regular Calgary events. The impetus to include all aspects of the community was strong. David Bright's study of the Calgary labour movement, for example, found the city's Labour Day parade had porous boundaries. Begun in 1902, Calgary Labour Day parades were dominated by unionized workers, but other groups, politicians, children, animals, and even employers were regularly included. At the platform events that followed the 1902 Labour parade, for example, Conservative R.B. Bennett and Liberal Arthur Sifton joined with Calgary clergy in proclaiming their working class sympathies. A similar mixture of other community groups and attractions occurred in the 1906 Labour Day parade, which had one thousand participants. In addition to the floats such as that of the Boilermakers Union, with its complete forge-equipped boiler-making workshop, there were also eighteen city officials, school children, mounted military cadets, Boy Scouts, and a zoo float "complete with goat and bear cub."

In the 1907 Calgary Labour Day parade, the dual purpose of representing both labour and the wider community in which it worked was again apparent. A large parade with two to three thousand marchers and an audience of ten to fifteen thousand people, the 1907 parade started off with city police representing the "power of the law" and also included a group of city officials.[35] The latter group, however, did not impress a possibly labour-sympathetic *Daily Herald* reporter, who felt that "the pomp and chivalry of power was effetely expressed...by the city legislators. They rode in chariots, [with] the dull somberness of the landaus unlighted [sic] by a tinge of color. They looked sad and depressed."[36] Also near the front of the parade were W.H. Cushing, minister of public works in Alberta's provincial government, and M.S. McCarthy, a Calgary Conservative politician.[37] In this parade school children again took part; "decked out in their best, [they] tramped stolidly along in the ranks of labor" along with mounted khaki-clad military cadets. There was also a section of local clergy, undoubtedly included because of their growing sympathy for the social gospel movement, an increasingly popular theological position that promoted church involvement in practical social issues.

Once the opening sections of the 1907 Labour Day Parade had passed, the main body of Calgary's workers made their way down the city's avenues. The list of workers' unions eager to express their skills and contribution to the Calgary community was extensive. One of the parade's highlights, at it had been in 1906, was Boilermakers Union's huge wagon pulled by six white horses, with men busily hammering metal at glowing forges. Equally impressive were the Stonecutters, with two monster stones "weighing many tons" that had been locally quarried and wrestled atop wagons for the parade. The Lathers Union float featured a miniature house constructed by its members. The Typographical Union float carried a foot press used to pump out handbills that union men tossed enthusiastically to spectators along the route. Bakers' and butchers' wagons were joined by a large contingent of building labourers that reflected the hectic growth in the city's housing and business infrastructure. Finally, there were company floats, entries by a number of Calgary lumber firms that indicated, along with the police, legislators, and clergy, the inclusive nature of the Labour Day parade. Adding humour to the parade were the water wagons used to douse the city's dusty streets. Riders on these wagons sprayed the parade audience on a hot September morning without regard for social rank.[38]

Labour's participation in Calgary's parading culture was not limited to this one annual parade. The 1901 Victoria Day parade included a "best of trade" prize category; the 1902 Coronation parade, in addition to business floats, also had "labor men: 31 strong."[39] Organizers of the 1902 Exhibition created a special day for labour at Victoria Park, as the event was held during the Labour Day weekend. The crossover between parades of different types occurred again in the 1908 Exhibition parade when the Trades and Labour Council entered a float.[40] The most amazing example was the 1912 Stampede parade, which was scheduled for the same weekend as the Labour Day holiday. The Trades and Labour Council and Guy Weadick's Stampede management group agreed to hold a joint parade, the enticement for unionists to join the cowboys and First Nations allegedly facilitated by a $1,500 payment to the council.[41] Hundreds of unionists marched in the parade that really should be referred to as the Stampede and Labour Day Parade of 1912.

A feature of the Labour Day parades by 1907 was the participants' costumes. Members of a number of unions were donning identical clothing to distinguish themselves from other tradesmen. The leatherworkers wore white suits, red hats, and blue sashes; the tinsmiths donned tin hats; the railway workers wore new overalls; and the blacksmiths wore dark clothing suited to their trade. Special clothing also appeared in other parades. In the 1908 Dominion Exhibition parade, cowboys from the Miller Brothers 101 Ranch Wild West Show, who were hired to perform during the week, dressed in a way that "lent an air of supreme western[n]ess to the [parade] spectacle."[42] Costume prizes were awarded as early as the 1902 Labour Day parade, and they became standard for the larger Calgary parading events. For example, the 1908 Exhibition parade offered prizes for the "best decorated cowboy" and the "best decorated Indian." The adoption of special clothing also extended to school children, who were dressed in white for the Exhibition parades of 1908 and 1909 and the 1911 Coronation parade, and members of various military groups, who appeared in uniform. The clothing worn by the First Nations was described in detail in local newspapers from the very first years of their participation in Calgary parades. In the 1912 parade special attention was accorded to Chief Yellow Horse, with his top hat, cavalry trousers, and yellow shirt. Decoration of the parade route, which had started early in Calgary's parade history, and greater numbers of costumed participants made the parades increasingly spectacular. By 1912 the alteration of reality by decoration and costume had become a normal part of Calgary parade protocol. The eventual dominance of cowboy garb developed from these early patterns.

Impromptu and Charitable Parades

Parades marking Labour Day and the Empire were major celebrations in Calgary. Other occasions, however, were commemorated by parades of a less spectacular nature. These included parades by local fraternal organizations and more quickly organized processions to greet dignitaries arriving at the train station for a short visit and tour of the city. One such visit to Calgary was by Robert Borden in June 1911, a few months before the federal election that would make him prime minister. After greeting him at the CPR station, the Calgary Citizens' Band led Borden's carriage on a brief tour through city streets before he opened Calgary's new sandstone city hall. Borden was then taken back to the train for a quick run to High River. When he returned, three bands led him to the Sherman Auditorium rink, where he gave a speech.[43]

Another example of such an event occurred in the spring of 1912, when the city was suddenly overrun with American Shriners making their way back from their annual convention in Los Angeles to the eastern United States by way of Canada. Within a three-day period, several hundred Shriners disgorged from the railway station. Their Calgary counterparts greeted them with great enthusiasm and paraded them through the city streets, stopping at City Hall, where the Illustrious potentate of each temple received a three-foot golden ceremonial key to the city. Thousands of Calgarians lined the streets to watch the processions. Some Shriners, including those from Philadelphia's Lulu Temple, also had marching bands. The "most demonstrative of all the visitors" were the New Yorkers, who were "armed with cowbells, dinner gongs, tin horns and almost every conceivable kind of noise producing instrument."[44] The New Yorkers ignited firecrackers on the platform before boarding the train and set off firecrackers attached to its caboose as they pulled out of town.

A procession that annually wound its way along Calgary streets was the Hospital Parade. Started by Mayor John Emerson, the parade on Hospital Sunday advertised the campaign to solicit funds for the city's hospitals, and eventually to raise money to build the General Hospital. The event held on Sunday afternoon, September 1, 1907, was typical. Organized by Fire Chief Cappy Smart, the parade was led by the Salvation Army Band, followed by Mayor Arthur Cameron and his aldermen in carriages, the fire brigade, guest speakers in carriages, and prominent citizens in their automobiles and carriages. Accompanying the procession were people wearing hospital fund badges and carrying donation boxes for collecting money from the crowd. Twenty-five hundred spectators followed the parade to Victoria Park to listen to speeches by the guests and politicians. Mayor Cameron reminded everyone that "three things in every community go to show what advancement the citizens had made...and these were the quality of the religious institutions, the quality of the educational institutions, and the quality of the medical intuitions." The parade through the city centre served its community purpose well, as over $1,000 flowed into the Hospital Fund.[45] What is also interesting about this parade is that it was held the day before the 1907 Labour Day parade that brought more than half the city's population onto its streets. Calgary parade organizers apparently had no concerns about staging two parades in two days. Parades were the accepted way to reach the general public.

First Nations and the Parades

The First Nations had a longstanding interest in Calgary's celebrations and fairs. According to the memoirs of Fire Chief Smart, interaction with the First Nations in the summer months dated from the 1880s. Smart remembered that as soon as the snow melted each spring, Sarcee and "halfbreed" families camped on Moccasin Flats (the area now known as the Mission District), where they held bucking horse riding contests and horse and foot races.[46] When Calgary's first horse track was constructed on Jim Owen's farm (where the Elbow Park district stands), it became a "mecca of Calgarians of all ages." First Nations people were active participants known for being "square shooters" who did not fix races, as did some other horse owners.[47]

Once the annual Calgary Exhibitions reached significant size, the First Nations were quick to participate. In 1906 "Indians by the hundreds" attended the displays in the pavilion, and both Indians and ranchers were of great interest to Calgarians and visitors to the city.[48] According to the *Morning Albertan*, the "extremes meet in the ranchers with their peculiar get-ups and the Indians with theirs."[49] As Calgary's sense of civic and/or urban identity emerged, those who resided beyond its borders were increasingly seen as different, perhaps even exotic. In 1906 many Calgarians gathered to watch the First Nations as they "left in a body at six o'clock [p.m.] making quite a fine show as they drove out in every variety of cart and wagon ... "[50] The departure of the First Nations from the 1906 celebrations may have inspired the decision to include them more directly in later Exhibitions.

The integration of the First Nations into the city's parading events emerged from a long context of local interaction. The parades organized by the Calgary Exhibition Society for the 1908 Dominion and 1909 Provincial exhibitions were large, intricately organized, and detailed, similar in many aspects to the later Stampede parades. Following the segmentation patterns previously seen in Calgary processions, the 1908 parade began with a star-studded opening section dominated by politicians and other representatives of powerful western institutions.[51] Waving and smiling from their carriages at the head of the 1908 parade were Alberta's Lieutenant Governor George Hedley Bulyea, Premier A.C. Rutherford, Chief Justice Arthur Sifton, Senator James Lougheed, Exhibition President I.S.G. van Wart, Hon. W.H. Cushing, Mayor A.L. Cameron and his city council, Colonel Sam Steele, Superintendent R. Burton Deane of the NWMP, and rancher A.E. Cross.[52] The "great feature of the parade," "the star performers," however, came next, an estimated one thousand Indians from all the tribes of Alberta.[53] Led by the

Ninety-first Highlanders Band "in full uniform," the First Nations presented a varied collection of images. Organized by the "indefatigable" Reverend John McDougall and his wife, who rode on horseback at the end of this section and received "round after round of applause,"[54] the First Nations displayed

> the old trappings of their bygone life on the open prairies and hills. Clad in skins, tanned with the fur on and off, with their old rifles thrown over their shoulders...leading their huskies packed for the trail...came a war party under two chiefs...following the chiefs came the braves stripped to the waist, their bodies covered with red and yellow ochre and their hands holding spears, bows and rifles ... in the rear...came squaws and papooses on horseback and with travois.[55]

Blackfoot people in Calgary Stampede parade, ca. 1923.

The First Nations' place in the parade stimulated a wide range of responses in local newspapers. Although the First Nations were given some credit for surviving in a difficult plains environment, they were depicted as a fading culture that had been replaced by a greater European civilization. Juxtaposed in the parade against the "new" phase of western Canadian reality (ranching, farming, and the increasingly dominant urban landscape), the First Nations fared poorly. Local newspapers depicted the First Nations and European cultures as passing each other: one culture in decline, the other in advance; an uncertain future for the first inhabitants of the prairies, a clear sense of the boundless destiny for settlers. It should be noted, however, that the First Nations were not the only group seen as marginalized. According to the *Calgary Herald*, the First Nations section of the 1908 parade also included pioneers in "traveling equipment," early missionaries in "pioneering outfit," the Hudson's Bay Company, a "halfbreed" hunting party in Red River carts and on horseback, members of the Mounted Police from 1874, and an earlier form of western transportation, pack horses, an entry organized by H.C. McMullen, who would be a key organizer of the 1912 parade. At the end of this historical section was a "posse of Cowboys and their outfit."[56] Colonial judgments about what was inferior, out of date, or a precursor of true progress were applied to these "pioneer" European groups by including them with the First Nations. Not walking in the parade, but meant to complement its historical elements, was a buffalo herd corralled on the Exhibition grounds for everyone to see.

Calgary's other major newspaper, the *Morning Albertan*, expressed similar colonial disparagement of the First Nations. The *Albertan*, however, also acknowledged the importance of the First Nations, "who figured in the story, who were at one time factors in this great country" in the era of the fur trade. The *Albertan* saw the First Nations as people to be admired; their story was not solely the narrative of the vanquished. Columnists respected the uniqueness of First Nations culture and recognized the qualities that had been necessary for survival in the West.

> The Indians showed to the greatest advantage. It is believed that the pageant of yesterday saw the last great parade of the great Indian race. If so, the Indians went at it as though it was the swan song of the race and they made the effort supreme to leave on the records that are to come that the [First Nations] race had many grand and noble qualities, that the pages of history and romance describing these people, which told of deeds and heroism and renown, were in no ways exaggerated.[57]

Although the *Albertan*, like the *Herald*, relegated the First Nations to the category of the noble savage,[58] the *Albertan* was more astute in its observations of First Nations people in the parade: Chief Crowfoot was at the head of one group of Blackfoot, Chief War Eagle led another group. Most First Nations people were from the Blackfoot community, along with the Stoneys and Sarcees. In lesser numbers in the parade were members of the Cree, Peigan, and Blood communities. Leading the Sarcees was Chief Bull Head, whose political acumen was singled out for recognition. The *Albertan* noted that he had "checked on every occasion the efforts of the Calgary Board of Trade to open a portion of the reserve for settlement."[59] As well as knowing who was in the parade, the *Albertan* was also aware that the First Nations had a sense of their own interests and were capable of protecting those interests. Their political skill was evident in the payment arranged for participating in the parade. To the First Nations, most of which came by train to Calgary, went a variety of foodstuffs: 1,800 pounds of flour, 200 pounds of sugar, 30 pounds of tea, 1,500 tobacco plugs, one and a half sides of beef, 200 pounds of bacon, two barrels of fish, one tub of mince meat, 200 pounds of "evaporated" apples, and "an amount of cordials and essences."[60] Overall, the conclusion of the *Albertan* was that the Indians were in the very best form: "There was nothing in their part of the performance that deserves any kind of criticism, except praise. They passed along [the parade route] with the greatest dignity ... "[61]

Although Marilyn Burgess has argued that the participation of the First Nations in these events was exploitive, a way of broadcasting the narrative of superior European settler culture that justified the usurpation of First Nations lands, other perspectives must be considered. It was certainly true that Calgary promoters sought participation of the First Nations as a means of providing a spectacle. Evidence of this objective is provided by their letters to Indian agents, especially those in the Calgary area. But it is also clear that these events sustained traditional practices. While the Department of Indian Affairs was determined to obliterate the cultures of First Nations peoples and set them on the trail to modernization, the Calgary parades helped preserve aspects of their traditions, although undoubtedly with some distortion. Those wishing to exploit the First Nations in parades or other events were, ironically, their allies against officials in Indian Affairs who were firmly committed to assimilation.

An example of these cross purposes can be seen in 1903, when Indian Agent A.J. McNeill refused to co-operate with Calgarian Crispen Smith, who was trying to organize Indian horse races. McNeill suspected "indian fights – War dances, sham fights" were also planned. McNeill explained that such things went against government policy, which was to teach the First Nations "to forget their Savage habits and customs and make them peaceful members of society." McNeill opposed turning the "Sarcees into a Circus troop...[or]

'wild west show' just to entertain some of the residents of the town."[62] McNeill informed Smith that these things were all contrary to the Indian Act and that they also disrupted haying and other summer work on the reserve. McNeill reminded Smith, "had you to live on a Reserve like myself, I think you would expect a little sympathy and backing from your White neighbors, instead of having them make it harder by encouraging the Indians to keep up their old customs which are so prejudicial to their advancement."[63]

McNeill eventually came to view the participation of the First Nations in such events in a more positive light. A request in 1906 from Cappy Smart to have the Sarcees take part in the Fourteenth Annual Convention of the Pacific Coast Fire Chiefs Association in Calgary was approved. McNeill informed Smart,

> I shall read your letter to Head Chief 'Bull's Head' and
> principal men of the Sarcee Band. I have no hesitation
> in saying that they will do what is required of them. The
> Sarcees generally come home pleased with their holiday,
> and recently the Pennsylvania Editor's Committee used
> them so well I am sure all will be happy to do their very
> best and will turn out with their 'best clothes' as you so
> ably put it.[64]

In 1909 an incident illustrating the conflict between the goals of Indian Affairs and the plans of local promoters caused one local Mounted Police inspector, Arthur M. Jarvis, considerable grief. Members of the Exhibition parade committee and important local chiefs approached Jarvis to request that three members of the Blackfoot reserve be released a few days before the end of their thirty-day sentence for public drunkenness to participate in the parade. Knowing this was a somewhat unusual procedure, Jarvis intercepted Alberta Chief Justice Arthur Sifton at the courthouse to ask if it was possible. Jarvis took this action because his own superior, Captain R. Burton Deane, was away on special duty. Sifton told Jarvis early release would probably be acceptable, but he should contact the Alberta attorney general about the matter. Jarvis then telephoned S.B. Woods, the deputy attorney general, who gave his approval.

The decision Jarvis made to accommodate local citizens organizing the parade and chiefs who had done several favours for the Mounted Police ignited a serious controversy that eventually put his career in jeopardy. Upon learning of the men's release, Gleichen Indian Agent J.H. Gooderham filed a complaint with his superiors, who immediately contacted the commissioner of the Mounted Police, Major A.B. Perry, a stickler for correct protocol. Perry ordered a Special Inquiry into the incident, and after reading its report concluded that Jarvis should have asked him, the commissioner, for permission to release the prisoners. Jarvis had mistakenly assumed that the province had jurisdiction because Alberta courts sentenced the men and paid the NWMP to house provincial prisoners. However, as the jails were run by the NWMP, Perry concluded that Jarvis should have requested permission from within the police hierarchy. In Perry's opinion, Jarvis

> by his ill-considered actions, had brought discredit on the Force; has shewn [sic] decided lack of sound judgement; and exhibited qualities which render him unfitted [sic] for the responsibilities of a commanding Officer...I propose to remove him from Calgary to some point of less importance and where he will not be called upon to exercise the functions of command.[65]

After further consideration, moreover, Perry decided Jarvis deserved even harsher punishment for facilitating the participation of these individuals in the Exhibition parade. Perry ordered Captain Deane, the Calgary commander, to arrest Jarvis for possible charges of violating internal rules of discipline. Deane, however, "one to whom controversy...[was] the spice of life," refused to obey. Deane argued that Jarvis had acted responsibly by consulting provincial officials, and if any mistake was made, Alberta's deputy attorney general was at fault. Perry promptly responded by attempting to charge Deane with insubordination, but arguments about procedural conventions seem ultimately to have thwarted charges against both Deane and Jarvis. Perry settled for a clear instruction to everyone in the force that "the Attorney General's Department in Alberta does not control the guard rooms of this force; that the Department has no authority to issue instructions to Officers of the force with regard thereto."[66] Deane, who did, indeed, have a nose for confrontation, soon used this regulation to cause Perry new grief. When the superintendent of immigration asked Deane to deliver up a prisoner for deportation, he refused, citing Perry's previous instruction that orders for release must come from Perry. Although nothing in the file indicates the outcome, Perry's commitment to proper procedure was about to increase his administrative workload, thanks to Deane.[67]

The Department of Indian Affairs opposed the participation of First Nations in other arenas as well during this period. Another dispute arose when Reverend John McDougall, the well known Morley missionary among the Sarcees, encouraged and organized First Nations communities to participate in summer festivals in Calgary, Banff, and other western towns. McDougall's activities were opposed not only by Indian Affairs; within his church and the wider community, many criticized him for perpetuating pagan cultures and beliefs. Appearing in their traditional outfits, playing drums, singing, and carrying weapons were all seen as detrimental to the spiritual welfare of the First Nations. John Maclean, McDougall's biographer, noted McDougall's response. McDougall wrote that he "felt that there were sufficient safeguards at the Stampede and [other] Pageants to protect the natives; the amusement would relieve the monotony of life on the Reserve, while the knowledge obtained would prove beneficial to them all."[68] Keith Regular documents McDougall's keen defense of the right of First Nations to demonstrate and practise their culture. In a series of letters to various papers, McDougall forcefully stated his conclusion that the Department of Indians Affairs and others

> view the Indian not as a fellow man, a being just as capable
> as themselves in distinguishing between right and wrong,
> but as an inferior to be treated as a child ... I will not
> treat them as inferiors not yet will I approach them with
> feelings of bigotry or religious intolerance ... [69]

McDougall argued further, and in a startling manner for someone supposedly supporting colonization by arranging their participation in these events, that

> while some Indians are Catholics and some Protestant,
> there are many who still cling to the old faith, and
> these...have as much right to join in the sun dance or the
> thirst dance as a Methodist has to join a camp meeting.
> We fought hard for the privilege of civil and religious
> liberty and the Indian is just as much entitled to religious
> freedom as a white man.[70]

Despite McDougall's ferocious and admirable defense of the First Nations' religious and civil rights, and in the context of these many conflicts, the Department of Indian Affairs amended Section 149 of the Indian Act in 1914 to prohibit participation in exhibitions, stampedes, and pageants. As Regular points out, however, this was a hollow victory; the penalties for soliciting participation were lessened, established practices were not included, and the local Indian agents could grant exemptions. Regular concludes that the colonization campaign had been defeated by advocates for the Indians such as McDougall, by parade organizers who requested their presence at urban celebrations, and by less than unanimous support by Indian agents themselves. "[A]ll indications suggest that the Indians did not feel particularly exploited by their association with the exhibitions. There were no impassioned pleas to stop the fairs … "[71]

Participation of First Nations in the Calgary parades, and in those of other western communities, is not a simple tale of exploitation by European colonizers. Those intimately involved with these arrangements, such Reverend McDougall, took a pragmatic and culturally tolerant approach to their inclusion. It was certainly true, however, that the First Nations and the Europeans who shared an early prairie history with them were not generally viewed by the wider Calgary public as contributing to the future development of the West. That future was reserved for those who controlled ranching, agriculture, and urban activities.

Celebrations of Progress

Devotion to progress was expressed in many Calgary parades, most clearly in sections of the 1908 parade dedicated to "Modern Conditions," which to parade organizers were epitomized by machines. As the 1908 parade began, an airship sixty feet long holding eight thousand cubic feet of hydrogen gas flew above the crowd, piloted by an American, Jack Dallas. Although it later caught fire and burned while on the ground, it was an impressive sight. Other modern elements were represented by "an automobile procession, as beauteous as a tropical garden" (one car smothered in pink rosebuds and another driven by Norman Lougheed adorned with chrysanthemums)[72] and an assortment of decorated bicycles.

Joining these machines depicting modern times was a large section of floats representing Calgary's ethnic communities – a visual buffet of cultural diversity. The recent inclusion of ethnic floats in contemporary Stampede parades is nothing new in this regard. The Calgary Citizens' Band led this section, followed by the Imperial float featuring Miss Hattie Massander as Britannia, seated in the centre dressed in white, with a beaver and a live bulldog at her feet, surrounded by British military veterans representing "British possessions ruled by Britannia [South Africa, Australia, and India]; the power of Britain on land and sea; the industry and tenacity of the British people."[73] The Canadian float carried several young women, one for each province, and portrayed the Dominion as an "unfinished" task, "a fairy-like creation with gossamer wings, carrying a basket of luscious fruits."[74] The theme of the English float was nautical, Lord Nelson's flagship H.M.S. *Victory*, with the motto that "England this day expects every man to do his duty." The "Scotch" float decorated with the plaid of the Gordon Highlanders depicted Prince Charlie's departure from Flora McDonald, with William Wallace and other warriors following on foot.[75] The prize-winning Scandinavian float recreated a Viking ship complete with raised prows, billowing sail, shield-adorned sides, and costumed rowers captained by a stand-in for Leif Ericsson. Unfortunately, low-strung wires on Calgary streets claimed the ship's mast and sail, along with the more highly placed flags on the Imperial float.[76] Nevertheless, enthusiasm for Calgary's new multicultural mosaic poured forth from the *Morning Albertan*:

> Calgary streets last night were a living exemplification
> of the fact that the West is a cosmopolitan community.
> All sorts and conditions of men and women, too, good
> naturedly jostled each other, side stepped, sashayed and
> ducked, laughed, jollied, apologized, and forgot. Wharf
> rats from Lunon [London], coal-heavers from Lancashire,
> farmer boys from the Midlands met, jostled, exchanged
> repartees and passed on. Scotties frae ... [77]

Well before the 1912 Stampede, parading in Calgary had become a significant part of annual spring, summer, and fall celebrations, and parading was clearly considered a fundamental means of expressing various messages. The basic form of a parade – the juxtaposition of past, present, and future – was clearly in place before the 1912 parade. Historical pageantry had become a prominent part of many of these parades, which included fur traders; the ranching community with its cowboys, cowgirls, horses, and cattle; the NWMP; the military; the first European settlers; the government officials who had guided and still represented ongoing development at all levels; contemporary business and ethnic communities; individuals or floats representing the area's external connections; and the First Nations and, it should be noted, the Métis community.

Key Individuals in Parading Culture

Before the 1912 Stampede, parades had already become a venue in which talented and influential persons emerged, took control, and represented a variety of interests. Ernie Richardson[78] became the managing director of the Calgary Exhibition in 1907, just as the Exhibition Committee won the right to hold the Dominion Exhibition in 1908. Richardson was the consummate organizer, a clear communicator and skilled planner capable of overseeing the increasingly large parade and the events associated with the Exhibition. He was, for example, keenly aware of the importance of advertising in making the Exhibition and events such as parades successful. For the 1909 Exhibition, Richardson convinced R.R. Jamieson, chairman of the Calgary Board of Commerce, to distribute seventy thousand copies of a ten-page pamphlet throughout the province.[79] In 1911 Richardson decided to distribute flags, "so popular last year," to every school district in Alberta.[80] In addition to his general awareness of factors such as advertising, Richardson was a master of detail. After the accounts for the 1909 Exhibition reached his desk, he pursued apparent over-billing by the police department. For their services on the grounds, Calgary police invoiced fifty cents per meal and claimed three meals each day, while the fire department asked for only twenty-five cents and not always the maximum number of meals. Richardson wrote the new police chief, J.M. Mackie, "I wish to be absolutely fair in paying accounts, but do not wish to be imposed upon."[81] He expressed similar sentiments to the mayor about this matter, explaining that "we certainly do not wish to appear small in a matter of this kind, but on the other hand do not wish to be considered easy, and allow people to receive payment for accounts which we have reason to believe are not correct."[82]

Richardson was certainly an important figure in the Exhibitions and later Stampedes, and his skills complemented those of Guy Weadick, about whom a considerable amount also is known. Weadick, who originated the idea of a "Stampede," was an entertainer and promoter who had travelled widely in North America. Weadick had planned a western show for Calgary as early as 1908, but shelved the plans for a variety of reasons. With the financial backing of the Calgary ranching community's "Big Four," Weadick finally pulled off the first Stampede in conjunction with the Exhibition organization in 1912. Weadick's showmanship skills and Richardson's management abilities welded the Stampede permanently to the Exhibition from 1923 onwards.

Harry C. McMullen has received less attention, although he was very involved in parades and Exhibition activities before 1912 and shared

Weadick's interest in developing a western show for Calgary, or anywhere else that might be enticed into such a project. McMullen was an American who had "found his way to Alberta with the first cattle drives from Montana in the late 1870s"[83] and eventually became the general livestock agent for the CPR.[84] In this powerful position, McMullen traveled widely in the West and made numerous contacts in the ranching and wider western community. In 1908 McMullen produced an infield show for the grandstand audience based on the idea of a mounted military corps. McMullen's men rode into the infield, where they set up a camp, lit a fire, and posted a sentry. Moments later the sentry spotted the enemy and sounded the alarm and the men broke camp, saddled and packed the horses, and made their getaway over a number of hurdles.[85] In its basic form this event was similar to the camp break-up that started the chuckwagon races added to the Stampede in 1923. McMullen was a confidant of Guy Weadick's as early as 1908,[86] and his letter about Calgary's booming economy in 1912 convinced Weadick that the time was ripe for a "Stampede" event. Because of his contacts in the ranching industry, McMullen was able to introduce Weadick to the Big Four in order to arrange financing for the event.[87] For this assistance and for his role as director general of the Stampede in 1912, McMullen received a share of the profits.[88] Alberta McMullen, his daughter, won the award in 1912 for the Champion All Round Canadian Cowgirl.[89]

Previously introduced in this narrative was another significant individual in parading activity before and after 1912, James "Cappy" Smart. Born in Scotland, Smart emigrated to Calgary in 1883 to live with his uncle, Thomas Swan, working at different jobs until he finally landed at the fire brigade in 1885. By 1898 Smart was fire chief, a position he held until 1933. Enthusiastic about community activities, Smart participated in many early athletic competitions and organized games for the 1901 Victoria Day event. In his efforts to promote fire safety and the role of the fire brigade, Smart pushed the Calgary fire brigade and its band into participation at parades and other public festivities.[90] By 1902 the fire brigade seems to have been expected to take the organizational lead in such matters. The fire brigade postponed the 1902 Victoria Day Parade because of bad weather and plans to celebrate the Coronation Day of Edward VII in August of that year. At the Coronation Day celebrations, Smart's Fire Brigade Band headed the parade, followed by Chief Smart riding in a carriage with Alderman Hatfield.[91] At the 1905 celebrations Smart's fame was enhanced when the city awarded him a gold medal "for heroic service" in stopping a runaway team of fire brigade horses that had bolted while being hitched.[92] As the organizer of the Exhibition parade in 1908, Smart "showed himself to be a man of great executive ability and his staff of assistants were most efficient."[93] He remained closely involved with the yearly parades and led the procession for a number of years, walking alone at the front. In an undoubtedly wise moment of reflection, he declined fulfilling this leadership function on the back of a donkey.[94]

The 1912 Stampede Parade

By the fall of 1912 the culture of celebration and the practice of parading were well established in Calgary and in other western communities. The Stampede theme rode comfortably on a format already well established within the Calgary community. For example, the participation of the First Nations in Calgary events was clearly normal, and not something newly created in 1912, although Weadick did move them nearer to the beginning of the parade. However, they were still behind an introductory section led by the Calgary's Citizens' Band and a collection of Stampede officials that included the director general of the Stampede, H.C. McMullen, and Stampede manager Guy Weadick, his wife, and several cowgirls.[95] Fifteen hundred First Nations people came next, following Reverend John MacDougall[96] and Superintendent of Indian Affairs Glen Campbell. The 1912 parade was scheduled to begin at nine o'clock in the morning, but McMullen and Weadick, preoccupied with details, made it to the starting point just after ten o'clock. Waiting for them were eighty thousand spectators, most lining the streets seven to eight rows deep, some climbing up the girders of the new Hudson's Bay store, where they looked like "a telegraph wire...with swallows in the migratory season."[97] With the delay, "kodakers were given a fine chance to snap the different groups"[98] of First Nations assembled at their Sixth Avenue and Ninth Street starting point. Popular in this photographic frenzy was Chief Yellow Horse of the Blackfoot nation, who proudly wore two medals, one given to him by Queen Victoria and one by the King, formerly the Duke of York (probably during his visit to Calgary in 1901). As the First Nations participants moved along the avenue, some walked, some rode horses, and some travelled in carts, singing and beating their drums. Guy Weadick had also "imported a hundred Indians from the United States who gloried in parading around in their war paint."[99]

As the procession headed east along Sixth Avenue, a series of other groups marshalled on intersecting cross streets joined in the parade. At Eighth Street, falling in behind the First Nations, a group representing the first Europeans in the West comprised Hudson's Bay Company men, miners, fur traders, and other "old-timers"; a wagon pulled by oxen; a stagecoach with six horses driven by Colonel Murphy that had been used in the 1860s and 1870s on the run from Fort Macleod east, "when the country was often extremely dangerous with hostile Indians"; a whiskey trade outfit; and a team of buffalo hitched to a Roman chariot driven by Major Yokum.[100] The buffalo chariot illustrated the *Calgary News-Telegram*'s claim that the "Stampede is a marvelous exposition of the human subjugation of animal nature in its wildest moods, and is a wonderful exhibition of what man can do in rendering the most fractious of the animal kingdom subservient to his will."[101]

At Seventh Street the parade acquired a section that included veterans of the NWMP who made the march across the prairies to southern Alberta in 1874. Led by Major Page and Colonel James Walker, these men looked to be "in the prime of life," with "none of the harrowing exhibitions of senile decay usually witnessed at a review of military veterans." Along with this group came bull trains and surveyors, then Senator Lougheed, with his wife by his side, driving a democrat (light wagon pulled by horses) and seeming "to enjoy the experience." Next in the parade was a detachment of Mounted Police drawn from Calgary and the surrounding area as a special guard for the visit by the governor general of Canada, the Duke of Connaught, Queen Victoria's third son, formerly Prince Arthur. Another parade through Calgary streets, complete with triumphal arch, was held especially for the duke and duchess later in the week. The Cowboy Band from Pendleton, Oregon, which captured a great deal of attention during the week that followed, and a large "roundup outfit of cowboys and cowgirls" were added to the parade at Sixth Street.[102]

Where the 1912 parade differed significantly from other Exhibition and Victoria Day parades was in its final section, which joined the procession at Fifth Street. As the Stampede was held during the first week of September in 1912, the Labour Day parade was accommodated in this procession. The annual Labour Day parade and athletic contests had reached significant levels in 1911, when they "surpassed any previous demonstrations of the local labor men,"[103] so the negotiations for this joint parade must have been intense. According to Gord Tolton, the Trades and Labour Council was paid $1,500 to relinquish its own parade plans and join the McMullen march.[104] At the head of the labour section was the Painters and Paperhangers Union float, decorated in several colours and "very much admired," with members of the union marching behind the float two abreast, each "nattily attired in smart…suits with caps to match." Next came the Brotherhood of Painters and Decorators, then the Carpenters and Joiners, all sporting white caps. The

Militia in Calgary Stampede parade, 1912.

Brewery Workers Union float came next, with a tiered display of bottles and casks. The Electrical Workers float included displays of motors, dynamos, arc lights, "vari-colored incandescent lights," and a telephone exchange. Also included in the labour section of the parade was the International Union of Moulders, its members wearing black vests, dark shirts, and overalls. Following them were a boys' brigade and a float with 20 young women, graduates of western educational institutions, with their teachers. Some real estate and furniture companies also had floats in this section, along with the delivery wagons of the Ontario Laundry Company and a float of Martin-Orme Company pianos. Most impressive in this section, however, was the Sheet Metal Workers Union, with each member wearing new overalls and holding a soldering hammer in his right hand. The cross-pollination of Stampede and labour themes was succinctly expressed in their headgear: they wore "Stetson hats made of tin with copper bands delicately riveted in the sides."[105]

Moving at a fast pace, the two miles of parade participants took over an hour to complete their march. Although the parade column moved smoothly along, it was interrupted twice by streetcars that were still providing service despite the parade. The streetcar motormen "became the embarrassed object of impatient hoots and cries" before stopping their cars and moving them on to side streets. Although Director General McMullen's "indefatigable efforts...[were] largely responsible for the magnitude of the Stampede" and he was a thoroughly happy man at the end of the parade, he probably wished that streetcar service had been suspended.[106] As the parade neared its conclusion at Victoria Park, the labour section of the parade broke off and continued west along Seventeenth Avenue. The rest of the parade marched forward for a review by Pat Burns, Archie McLean, George Lane, H.C. McMullen, and "other old-timers," who received a "great ovation and waving of hands from the cowmen and cowgirls."[107] In a very basic way the division of the parade represented the future split in the city's interests, one clearly tied to the urban economy and the other linked to the rural hinterland.

Messages of the Parades

During the turbulent years from Calgary's emergence as a settlement site in the 1870s until the early 1920s, flexible institutions such as parades were a means of reflecting issues and realities that preoccupied the community. Parades of various kinds were the dominant social activity in this period; a great deal of time and effort was expended in organizing, staging, and attending them. In a very basic sense Calgary parades were an allegory of the local community, an iconic repertoire of the near and distant past mixed with a glimpse of the future. Central to this story of Calgary beginnings were the First Nations, who were portrayed not as a civilization defeated by force, but as a civilization in decline. However, the First Nations were not alone in this categorization. The Métis and the first Europeans were often linked with the First Nations in parades and other civic endeavours, all seen as remnants of a way of life that was coming to an end on the plains. The narrative of past times fading also included the homesteaders, the early mine prospectors, the first Mounted Police, and the first ranchers.

As well as origins, Calgary parades addressed the contemporary scene, often revealing the tensions that emerged in this period of western Canadian development. During the years before 1912, the gap between rich and poor widened considerably, as Calgary evolved from a town in which everyone was looking for opportunities to a city in which some had succeeded and others had not. The city's parades addressed this disparity with the floats of businesses celebrating entrepreneurial success and those of workers' organizations that displayed pride in their skills, the contribution of the working class to western development, and the implicit message that everyone should share equally in the fruits of those accomplishments. David Bright points out in *Limits of Labour*, however, that class polarization in Calgary was never as extreme as in other prairie cities such as Winnipeg.[108] Other entries in Calgary parades by organizations such as the Salvation Army and advocates of Prohibition promoted their values as social goals around which the community could unite. As the city's population diversified, the parade also functioned as an interpretative guide for newcomers and a means for them to proclaim their participation in Calgary's community. The most common parade message was faith in progress, with the implication that future growth would erase present differences; everyone would succeed in the end. The egalitarian cowboy, the first pioneers, and even the area's First Nations, were unifying booster images in western Canada.

A rambunctiously growing society also needed boundaries. Calgary parades always included the symbols of order and constraint in the form of the Mounted Police, military representatives both domestic and international, local fire and police departments, and officials from various levels of government. After the beginning of the First World War in 1914, the parades became even more military in nature. The Exhibition's close association with the armed forces continued after 1918 and intensified during the Second World War. To this day, the Mounties and the military are still a presence as participants in the parade and exhibitors on the grounds.

Calgary parades, Stampede and otherwise, also provided residents with symbolic representations of connections with others: local, regional, and international. The Stampede parade consistently included entries from outlying towns and cities, their participation facilitated by expanding railway lines and roads. Very early in their development, the Calgary Exhibition and Stampede Board realized that their events could be associated with other tourist and recreational attractions such as the national parks to the west of the city. Internationally, ties with Great Britain's empire remained fundamentally important despite the devastating loss of life in the First World War. Associations with another empire, the American one, were also apparent in the early parades, and the American presence continued in the following decades, eventually overshadowing, but not completely erasing, British participation.

In a new society such as Calgary's in the first two decades of the twentieth century, parades were a flexible institution that could address a variety of important community issues and accomplishments. Calgary's vibrant street culture set the stage for the successful development of the Calgary Exhibition and Stampede; the Stampede parade has become one of its major components. That street culture resurfaced with intense vitality in 2004 when thousands of Calgary Flames fans crowded the Red Mile – the Seventeenth Avenue district. These celebrations and the early ones that occurred in Calgary before 1912 emerged in very similar circumstances, those of a city experiencing rapid growth and the issues it produces. In the absence of other institutions, or the slowness or incapacity of other institutions to respond, citizens in both periods took to the streets to define, refine, and express their vision of Calgary and western Canada: its past, its present, and its future. Calgary parades were, and still are, bulletin boards where messages about identity are exchanged among segments of Calgary's community.

Notes

1. Robert Seiler and Tamara Seiler, "Managing Contradictory Visions of the West: The Great Richardson/Weadick Experiment," in *Challenging Frontiers: The Canadian West*, ed. Lorry W. Felske and Beverly Rasporich (Calgary: University of Calgary Press, 2004), 155–81; David R. Jones, "C.W. Petersen," in *Citymakers: Calgarians After the Frontier*, ed. Max Foran and Sheilagh Jameson (Calgary: Historical Society of Alberta, Chinook County Chapter, 1987), 183–96; Grant MacEwan, "Calgary's 'Cappy' Smart," in *Citymakers: Calgarians After the Frontier*, ed. Max Foran and Sheilagh Jameson (Calgary: Historical Society of Alberta, Chinook County Chapter, 1987), 70–78.; Lorain Lounsberry, "Wild West Shows and the Canadian West," in *Cowboys, Ranches, and the Cattle Business*, ed. Simon Evans, Sarah Carter, and Bill Yeo (Calgary: University of Calgary Press, 2000), 139–32; James H. Gray, *A Brand of its Own: The 100 Year History of the Calgary Exhibition and Stampede* (Saskatoon: Western Producer Prairie Books, 1985); Fred Kennedy, *The Calgary Stampede Story* (Calgary: T. Edwards Thonger, 1952); Donna Livingstone, *The Cowboy Spirit: Guy Weadick and the Calgary Stampede* (Vancouver: Greystone Books, 1996).

2. Marilyn Burgess, "Canadian 'Range Wars': Struggles over Indian Cowboys," *Canadian Journal of Communication* 18, no. 3 (1993): 2.

3. Eric Hobsbawm and Terence Ranger, eds., *The Invention of Tradition* (Cambridge: Cambridge University Press, 1983), 9.

4. Calgary Exhibition and Stampede Fonds (hereafter cited as CESF), M2160/41, Newsclippings file, 1910–1941, Glenbow Museum Archives (hereafter cited as GMA).

5. Paul Connerton, *How Societies Remember* (Cambridge: Cambridge University Press, 1989), 1.

6. Ibid., 40.

7. Catherine Bell, *Ritual: Perspectives and Dimensions* (New York: Oxford University Press, 1997), 120.

8. Ibid., 127.

9. Hobsbawn and Ranger, *Invention of Tradition*, 5.

10. A.P. Cohen, *The Symbolic Construction of Community* (London: Tavistock, 1985), 50.

11. Dominic Bryan, *Orange Parades: The Politics of Ritual, Tradition, and Control* (London: Pluto Press, 2000), 11–12.

12. Max Foran, *Canada's Frontier Metropolis: An Illustrated History* (Calgary: Windsor, 1982); Henry Klassen, *Eye on the Future: Business People in Calgary and the Bow Valley, 1870–1900* (Calgary: University of Calgary Press, 2002).

13. *Morning Albertan*, 2 July 1906. The 1906 Red Deer parade, led by the mayor and the Red Deer Band, featured 40 business floats. The Calgary Salvation Army

Band led the city's Orange Parade in 1906, which was reported as the largest ever held in Alberta: Ibid., 12 July 1906. Another Orange parade occurred in 1908: Ibid., 13 July 1908. On 24 May 1903, the annual Church parade of the Sons of England took place just prior to the Victoria Day parade. *Calgary Daily Herald*, 25 May 1903.

14.   Susan G. Davis, *Parades and Power: Street Theater in Nineteenth-Century Philadelphia* (Philadelphia: Temple University Press, 1986), 3.

15.   Gray, *Brand of Its Own*, 4–5.

16.   Gray, *Brand of Its Own*, 4–5; Sheilagh Jameson, "The Social Elite of the Ranch Community in Calgary," in *Frontier Calgary: Town, City, and Region, 1875–1914*, ed. Anthony W. Rasporich and Henry C. Klassen (Calgary: University of Calgary Press, 1975), 56–70. For views of the British and American influence in the western ranching communities see David Breen, *The Canadian Prairie West and the Ranching Frontier, 1874–1924.* (Toronto: University of Toronto Press, 1983), and W.M. Elofson, *Cowboys, Gentlemen, and Cattle Thieves: Ranching on the Western Frontier* (Montreal: McGill-Queen's University Press, 2000).

17.   Donald B. Smith, *Calgary's Grand Story: The Making of a Prairie Metropolis from the Viewpoint of Two Heritage Buildings* (Calgary: University of Calgary Press, 2005), 41.

18.   *Albertan,* 25 May 1901; Photograph NA-1113-1, GMA. This photograph shows the Calgary Fire Brigade Band at the head of the parade.

19.   *Morning Albertan*, 25 May 1901.

20.   Ibid., 29 May 1901.

21.   *Daily Herald,* 25 May 1905.

22.   Ibid., 1 July 1908. The dominant department store in town, the Hudson's Bay Company, received praise for its efforts.

23.   *Albertan,* 22 June 1911.

24.   There was controversy over credit for building the float; the *Albertan* got it wrong and the correction appeared in the *Herald*.

25.   *Albertan,* 13 August 1902.

26.   Lounsberry discusses the role of a parade in the opening of Wild West shows and touring circuses in "Wild West Shows."

27.   *Morning Albertan*, 4 July 1908.

28.   Ibid., 4 July 1906.

29.   Ibid., 4 July 1908.

30.   *Daily Herald,* 4 July 1908.

31.   *Morning Albertan,* 4 July 1908. See Lorry W. Felske, "Studies in the Crow's Nest Pass Coal Industry from its Origins to the End of World War I" (Ph.D. thesis, University of Toronto, 1991), Chapter 2, for details of American entrepreneurial development in the Crow's Nest region.

32. *Morning Albertan,* 6 June 1911.

33. Ibid., 25 May 1912.

34. City Clerk's Correspondence, City Clerks Department Fonds, box 50, file 403. City of Calgary Archives (hereafter cited as CCA).

35. David Bright, *The Limits of Labour: Class Formation and the Labour Movement in Calgary, 1883–1929* (Vancouver: UBC Press, 1998), 63–66. Winnipeg's Labour Day Parade had five thousand participants in 1907.

36. *Calgary Daily Herald,* 3 September 1907.

37. *Albertan,* 3 September 1907. See Smith, *Calgary's Grand Story,* 116, for background on M.S. McCarthy.

38. *Albertan,* 3 September 1907; *Calgary Herald,* 3 September 1907. The unions represented in the parade included those of the Tailors, Typographical and Pressmen, Bakers, Leather Workers, Soap Workers, Warehouse Workers, Blacksmiths, Teamsters, Boilermakers, Maintenance of Way Men, Machinists and Railway Carmen, Electrical Workers, Laborers, Lathers, Plumbers, Stone Cutters, Carpenters, Quarry Workers, Bricklayers, Tinsmiths, Plasterers, Painters, Engineers, Civic Employees, and General Machinists.

39. *Albertan,* 13 August 1902.

40. *Morning Albertan,* 1 July 1908.

41. Gord Tolton, "Dreams of a Showman," *Canadian West Magazine* 9, no. 1 (1993): 43.

42. *Morning Albertan,* 1 July 1908.

43. *Calgary Daily Herald,* 23 June 1911.

44. *Morning Albertan,* 23 May 1912.

45. *Morning Albertan,* 2 September 1907. Before the 1911 Coronation Parade, the YWCA collected money from Calgarians.

46. "Cappy Smart: I Remember Calgary When," magazine section, *Calgary Herald,* 3 December 1932. According to Smart, the area known as Moccasin Flats included all the land west of First Street West to Sixth Street West and from Seventeenth Avenue south to Rideau and Roxboro.

47. Ibid., 31 December 1932.

48. Members of the First Nations in the Calgary area participated in the 1901 Victoria Day Parade and First Nations students at the Calgary Indian Industrial School were in the 1902 Coronation Parade.

49. *Morning Albertan,* 7, 9 July 1906.

50. Ibid., 11 July 1906.

51. There were seven divisions in the parade under Fire Chief James Smart: First Division, H.B. Wilson; Second Division, Crispin E. Smith and J. Morrison; Third Division, H. Hewer; Fourth Division, H. McClelland and R. Morrison; Fifth Division, W. Gillespie; Sixth Division, H.P. Swain; Seventh Division,

Mr. Rees. Labour Day parades followed the same arrangement. *Calgary Herald*, 1 July 1908. In 1911 the first part of the parade included the Citizens' Band, the press, members of Parliament, candidates for the House of Commons, sport judges, the mayor, commissioners and aldermen, city employees, city officials, friendly societies, and the trade unions. The parade was led by two mounted policemen and the parade marshall, J.G. Lubbil. *Morning Albertan*, 4 September 1911.

52. *Calgary Herald*, 1 July 1908. Also in the first section were Attorney General Cross, Hon. W.T. Finlay, Judge Mitchell, the judges of the Exhibition, the directors of the Exhibition, two carriages of ex-mayors, and two carriages conveying the pageant committee. Eight former mayors in these carriages included George Murdock, Calgary's first mayor. *Morning Albertan*, 1 July 1908.
53. *Morning Albertan*, 1 July 1908.
54. Ibid.
55. *Calgary Herald*, 1 July 1908.
56. Ibid.
57. *Morning Albertan*, 2 July 1908.
58. Emma LaRoque, "When the 'Wild West' is Me: Re-viewing Cowboys and Indians," in *Challenging Frontiers*, ed. Lorry W. Felske and Beverly Rasporich, 136–55.
59. *Morning Albertan*, 1 July 1908.
60. Ibid.
61. Ibid., 2 July 1908.
62. A.J. McNeill to the editor, newspaper clipping, no name or date given, RG10, vol. 1627, Library and Archives Canada (hereafter cited as LAC).
63. A.J. McNeill to Crispin Smith, 10 July 1903, RG10, vol. 1627, LAC.
64. A.J. McNeill to Chief Cappy Smart, August 2006, RG10, vol. 1627, LAC. McNeill also seemed happy to cooperate with John de Sousa of the Inter-Western Pacific Exhibition Company, Calgary. To de Sousa he wrote, "I shall arrange to get as many Indians in as possible to attend your exhibition, but had you given me longer notice I could have done better. Owing to the Indians being scattered over their Reserve at haymaking, some being 15 miles west...the bad condition of the trails and crossings, it is no easy matter to collect them in a hurry. I shall do the best I can however." A.J. McNeill to John de Sousa, 30 August 1903, RG10, vol. 1627, LAC.
65. A.B. Perry to Comptroller of RNWMP, 5 January 1910, R.G. 18, series A1, vol. 390, file 237-10, LAC.
66. A.B. Perry to Comptroller of RNWMP, 9 September 1909 , R.G. 18, series A1, vol. 390, file 238-10, LAC.
67. A. Burton Deane to A.B. Perry, 25 November 1909, R.G. 18, series A1, vol. 390, file 238-10, LAC.

68. John Maclean, *McDougall of Alberta: A Life of Rev. John McDougall, D.D., Pathfinder of Empire and Prophet of the Plains* (Toronto: Ryerson Press, 1927), 260.

69. Keith Regular, "On Public Display," *Alberta History* 34, no. 1 (1986): 7.

70. Ibid., 6.

71. Ibid., 9.

72. *Morning Albertan*, 1 July 1908.

73. Ibid.

74. Ibid., 2 July 1908.

75. Ibid.

76. *Calgary Herald*, 1 July 1908.

77. *Morning Albertan*, 1 July 1908.

78. Seiler and Seiler, "Managing Contradictory Visions."

79. Board of Commissioners Papers, series I, box 2, file R.R. Jamieson, 1909, n-z, CCA.

80. Clipping, n.d., n.a., M2160/41, GMA.

81. Ernie Richardson to J.M. Mackie, 3 August 1909, Board of Commissioners Papers, series I, box 2, file R.R. Jamieson, CCA.

82. Ernie Richardson to Mayor R.R. Jamieson, 3 August 1909, Board of Commissioners Papers, series I, box 2, file R.R. Jamieson, CCA.

83. Gray, *Brand of Its Own*, 35.

84. *Morning Albertan*, 6 July 1908.

85. Ibid., 2 July 1908.

86. Lounsberry, "Wild West Shows," 146.

87. Tolton, "Dreams of a Showman," 39; Guy Weadick, "Origin of the Calgary Stampede," *Alberta Historical Review* 14, no. 4 (Autumn 1966): 21.

88. CESF, M2160a, series I, 17 April 1912, GMA; Guy Weadick, letter to editor, *High River Times*, 8 February 1940; CESF, M2160/41, Newsclippings file, 1940–1941, GMA. McMullen and Ad Day (Addison P. Day), the arena director, were each due 25% of the net profits. As this number shrunk to $15,000 and the Big Four had promised $5,000 to the Hospital Fund, they demanded that McMullen forfeit $2,500 of his share: Tolton, "Dreams of a Showman," 43–44. Guy Weadick was adamant about the role of H.C. McMullen in organizing the 1912 parade, as Cappy Smart, who had been in on so many Calgary parades, was starting to get the credit by 1940: Guy Weadick, letter to the editor, *High River Times*, 8 February 1940, CESF, M2160/41, Newsclippings file, 1940–1941, GMA.

89. Gray, *Brand of Its Own*, 38.

90. *Calgary Daily Herald*, 25 May 1901.

91. *Albertan*, 13 August 1902.

92. *Calgary Daily Herald*, 25 May 1905.

93. *Daily Herald*, 1 July 1908.

94. James Gray notes that Smart was chairman of the parade committee and grand marshal from 1903 until two weeks before his death in 1939. Gray, *Brand of Its Own,* 109.
95. *Calgary Daily Herald,* 9 September 1912.
96. Gray, *Brand of Its Own,* 37. McDougall received $390 for his services, but it is unclear if this was to cover expenses or a personal payment.
97. *Calgary Daily Herald,* 3 September 1912.
98. Ibid.
99. Gray, *Brand of Its Own,* 37; Guy Weadick, "Origin of the Calgary Stampede," *Alberta Historical Review* 14, no. 4 (Autumn 1966): 23. Weadick, *Calgary Daily Herald,* 3 September 1912.
100. *Calgary Daily Herald,* 3 September 1912.
101. *Calgary News-Telegram,* 3 September 1912.
102. *Calgary Daily Herald,* 3 September 1912.
103. *Morning Albertan,* 2 September 1911.
104. Tolton, "Dreams of a Showman," 43.
105. *Daily Herald,* 3 September 1912; *Morning Albertan,* 2 September 1912. The unions for the 1911 Labour Day Parade included the Leatherworkers, Machinists, Allied Printing Trades, Bricklayers and Masons, Stonecutters, Brotherhood of Carpenters, Lathers, Amalgamated Carpenters, Plumbers and Steamfitters, Electricians 348, Metal Workers, Barbers, Plasterers, Railway Carmen, Painters, Bakers, Horseshoers, Electricians 416, and Brewery Workers.
106. Guy Weadick, letter to editor, *High River Times,* 8 February 1940, CESF, M2160/41, Newsclippings file, 1940–1941, GMA.
107. *Calgary Daily Herald,* 3 September 1912.
108. Bright, *Limits of Labour.*

CHAPTER 5

Midway to Respectability: Carnivals at the Calgary Stampede

Fiona Angus

Beckoning the crowds to enter the grounds of the Calgary Stampede, the carnival midway rides act as highly visible markers of the presence and the promise of excitement for Stampede participants. Curiously, however, despite this visibility, carnivals at the Stampede have been largely neglected in historical records and sociological analysis. For example, in James H. Gray's comprehensive history of the Calgary Stampede, *A Brand of Its Own: The 100 Year History of the Calgary Exhibition and Stampede,*[1] various wider cultural and economic influences are expertly interwoven with historical facts to demonstrate the remarkable evolution of the Stampede from a relatively small agricultural exposition to the multi-faceted and internationally renowned event that is seen today. However, interspersed among Gray's historical facts are only a few tantalizing but rather brief references to the carnivals that have played at the Stampede over the past century. One might be left with the erroneous impression that this component of the Stampede is, indeed, marginal and only incidental in the grander scope of the annual Calgary spectacle.

A strong case could be made that the midway at the Stampede is, in many ways, peripheral to the central themes of the Stampede. The midway has rarely reflected the same contradictory, albeit highly successful, guiding principles as those of the Stampede: the vision of a retrospective (and historically inaccurate) glorification of the myth of the Wild West, combined with contemporary notions of what constitutes social and technological progress. Despite its ideologically segregated status at the Stampede, however, the history of the midway and its many carnival occupants is an equally evolving phenomenon, one that reflects broader cultural beliefs and practices that largely focus on issues of morality and respectability. Like the Calgary Stampede, which has evolved over the decades in response to economic and political dynamics and the perceived need to maintain a vibrant balance between nostalgia for the past and celebration of the economic and ideological promise of the future, carnivals have also responded to changing beliefs and public demands that centre mostly around issues of decency and general social acceptability.

As a component of the Stampede that has always been considered a necessary yet fundamentally separate entity, the midway at the Stampede has never felt the same need to share in the overall Stampede vision and its outward manifestations of emphasized themes of celebratory Prairie West traditions (with the exception of some of the earlier Wild West shows). As a strictly profit-oriented entity, the carnival at the Stampede has always had only one goal – to generate money by offering affordable and irresistible entertainment to fairgoers. This vision, a reflection of the tenets behind all carnival companies in North America, was the impetus behind the earliest travelling carnival companies, and continues to this day. What has changed, however, are two central features: the types of entertainment offered by carnivals and, even more profoundly, the social influences relative to morality, deviance, and overall respectability. This examination of carnivals at the Calgary Stampede demonstrates the gradual evolution of an entertainment activity that began as tantalizingly deviant and, over time, has moved from the cultural margins to a place of relative public respectability, while continuing to retain an aura of mystery, excitement, and diversion.[2]

Definitions and Brief History of Carnivals and Midways

Before exploring the various carnivals that have played at the Stampede, it is important to clarify what is meant by the term "carnival"[3]: "a traveling collection of amusements which include games of chance, sideshows, and thrilling rides"[4] or (less formally) "a lusty busty bawdy bitch...who has kicked up her frolicsome heels and masqueraded under many guises and names."[5] The constituent parts of carnivals have changed significantly over the past century – changes that have, for the most part, been in response to a variety of technological advances and, more significantly, fluctuating beliefs about morality and decency. Fundamentally, however, the term "carnival" refers to the actual physical entities that have occupied midways since the late nineteenth century.[6]

It is also salient to contextualize the carnivals at the Stampede in a brief historical discussion of carnivals in North America, the genesis of which is located in the 1893 World Exposition in Chicago. Although small travelling circuses were common from the mid-nineteenth century onward, carnivals per se were non-existent until after the Chicago World's Fair. The central purpose of the 1893 World's Fair was to educate and impress the masses with contemporary technological innovations. However, a segment of the World's Fair named the "Midway Plaisance" was devoted to many free entertainment attractions and side shows.[7] This first midway, one and a half miles long and "a block wide,"[8] comprised a Ferris wheel, merry-go-round, and other attractions such as "fat ladies," fortune tellers, and games of chance.[9] Thus, although the terms "carnival" and "midway" are often used interchangeably, there is a distinction: "midway" is the actual geographical location, while "carnival" refers to the entities that occupy the midway. Although the midway proved to be highly attractive to fairgoers and generated significant revenue for the World's Fair, it was also seen as vulgar and somewhat immoral. It was, therefore, geographically segregated from "the serene and aristocratic Court of Honor,"[10] despite being wrapped in a cloak of respectability through the use of an idyllic name for the assemblage itself and attempts to display many of the rides, sideshows, and attractions "in the romantic style of the fancy waistcoat era."[11]

The financial success of the midway at the Chicago World's Fair led to a proliferation of smaller travelling carnival companies in the ensuing years that continued to use the name "midway" to refer to their entertainment offerings. Most of these early carnivals did not survive for long, as their dependence on guaranteed crowds and money was significantly challenged by the sparse population outside urban centres in North America. Many of the smaller carnival groups joined together, thereby creating a single carnival company, which made them far more attractive to the general public and guaranteed them more bookings over the carnival season.

The Midway on the Margins: The First Half of the Twentieth Century

By 1902 twenty-four carnival companies were operating in the United States. Many of these companies also travelled to western Canada as part of their route. The growth of railway lines, threading their way across both Canada and the United States, facilitated the movement of the carnivals. The companies offered a motley collection of rides and "freak" and "girlie" shows, games, and other concessions. The ride component tended to be quite small, mainly due to the expense of travel. The largest segment of most travelling carnivals was the tented sideshows. Vaudeville stage shows comprising comedians, musicians, and variety acts were common features of early twentieth-century carnivals, as were gambling booths and other games of chance.[12]

The partnership between agricultural fairs and carnivals was formed during the early part of the twentieth century and continues to this day. During the first two decades of the twentieth century, carnival companies realized that by negotiating contracts with larger agricultural fairs, they would be guaranteed a more secure income. The carnival season was May through to October, but most agricultural fairs took place from August to October, a practice that continues today. Carnival companies often struggled financially from May to August as they attempted to find "still dates," smaller venues of short duration. Lucrative still dates were difficult to find. This sometimes led to debt acquisition or even bankruptcy for many smaller carnival companies before the official agricultural fair season had even begun.[13]

The alliance of agricultural fairs and carnival companies throughout most of the first half of the twentieth century was rarely harmonious. Each entity needed the other to survive financially. Carnivals were usually considered by agricultural fair boards to be "a necessary evil,"[14] essential for the financial success of a fair, but ideologically contrary to the fundamental principles of the agricultural fairs, which were to educate the mainly rural fairgoers and provide a venue in which farmers could show their stock. The midway presence was seen as a distraction from these lofty ideals, and from the early 1900s onwards there were ongoing conflicts between moral entrepreneurs (in the form of agricultural purists, churches, and fair reformers) and agricultural fair boards and the general public, which supported the carnival presence, the former for financial reasons and the latter for entertainment purposes. A manifestation of these contradictory dynamics was the location of carnivals at the agricultural fairs. They were often positioned just inside the main entrance to agricultural fairgrounds in order to be the first to take advantage of the money brought onto the grounds. In the case of the Calgary Stampede, for example, most of the carnival games and sideshows were located at the northern end of the Stampede grounds, so that people entering at the main gates (northwest on the grounds) would have to pass by the carnival tents and games en route to the more "wholesome" agricultural activities and displays.[15]

Most opposition to carnivals centred on fears that the midways were dominated by con men (known as "grifters" or "fakirs").[16] There were concerns that female fair-goers would be lured into white slavery and men would be morally debased by the sight of the semi-clad women in the girlie shows.[17] In contrast, little moral indignation was demonstrated towards the freak shows, no doubt a reflection of cultural beliefs dominant in the early twentieth century, which sanctioned the display of so-called human oddities with no concerns about exploitation.

The freak shows that comprised a significant portion of carnivals for the first half of the twentieth century consisted of both animals and people with abnormal physical features, such as "fat people, dwarfs, half men-half women, two-headed creatures, Siamese twins, and just about anything the mind could imagine."[18] Animals and people from "exotic" locales were very popular because most fair attendees (largely from the farming communities) did not travel much beyond their immediate regions and were duly entranced by live attractions ostensibly from foreign lands.[19] Many of the people and animals were, indeed, imported by carnival promoters from around the world. However, a significant number of these live exhibits were quite bogus;

for example, it was not uncommon for Aboriginal peoples to be presented as people from Africa or India, costumed in suitable clothing and makeup; as Scott claims, "historical [and geographic] accuracy [were] not always a strong point in the sideshow business."[20] Gambling was another source of contradiction and consternation.[21] All the prairie provinces had legislation that discouraged gambling, but most exhibitions ignored the statutes, as they needed the revenue from gambling (in the form of midway games, as well as horse racing) to survive economically.[22]

Carnivals at the Calgary Stampede

Although it would be fair to speculate that many of the travelling carnivals described above frequented the smaller agricultural fairs in the western provinces during the late nineteenth century, the earliest account of a carnival-like presence on the midway at the Stampede is found in Gray, who states that, in an attempt to attract larger crowds to the Exhibition in 1901,

> The freelancing merry-go-round and ferris wheel opera-
> tors, snake-oil pitchmen, and other itinerant merchants
> were gradually brought into the operation. But not always
> with favorable results. Public grumbling developed over
> the crookedness of some of the gambling games and it was
> universally resolved that greater emphasis had to be placed
> on elevating the moral standard of all the attractions at
> the fair.[23]

Typical of most carnivals, then, the midway occupants at the Stampede tended to be viewed with varying degrees of suspicion[24] as lurid repositories of sin, sexuality, and moral degradation. An illustration of the outrage expressed by the agricultural purists is the following from the *Farm and Ranch Review*, published in Calgary in 1915:

> One of the most repugnant experiences which can befall
> the average man or woman is afforded by a tour of the
> midway at any of our Western agricultural fairs. Raucous-
> voiced vendors megaphone the merits of their show. From
> weather-beaten tents emerge girls in misery, who, at a word
> from the official orator, force their faces into smiles and
> dance on a crazy platform ... All this is done, and linked up

with the name of progressive agriculture. Is it that our exhibition boards consider this banal form of entertainment in keeping with the standards of rural people? Or is it that the financial success of the exhibition is made precarious without the presence of the midway?...The matter of abolishing the unquestionably immoral effect of the midway should commend itself to our social reform leagues.[25]

Although moral entrepreneurs made ongoing attempts to "clean up" the midway, they rarely had much success, as fair organizers became increasingly dependent on the revenue from the carnivals.

From its earliest days, the Stampede locale was visited by various forms of small travelling entertainment entrepreneurs, specific details of whom were rarely recorded. Most were independent, transient sideshow operators who disappeared as quickly as they appeared on the midway, making their way to the next potentially lucrative location. The practice of bringing diverse entertainment groups to the Calgary Exhibition existed for many years prior to 1920. Examples include the Miller Brothers 101 Ranch Wild West Show in 1908, a "three-girl motorcycle act in which the girls raced each other around the inside of gigantic wire cage,...acrobats, and Howard's Dogs and Ponies" in 1909.[26] In the same year (1909), the Exhibition also included what appears to be the first formal carnival operation, the C.W. Parker Carnival Shows,[27] as well as Al G. Barnes's wild animal circus.[28]

According to historical records, the main carnival companies that played at the Calgary Stampede in the twentieth century are as follows:

1920	Johnny J. Jones Exposition
1921	C.A. Wortham's No. 1 Show
1922–1924	Johnny J. Jones Exposition
1925	Rubin & Cherry Shows
1926–1929	Johnny J. Jones Exposition
1930	Morris & Castle Shows
1931	Johnny J. Jones Exposition
1932–1933	Castle-Ehrlick-Hirsch Shows (reorganization of Morris & Castle Shows)
1934[29]–1940	Royal American Shows
1941–1945	Conklin Shows
1946–1975	Royal American Shows

1976–present   Conklin Shows (which became part of North American Midway Entertainment in 2005)[30]

The carnival companies listed above were augmented by many independent carnival acts, a practice that continues today. Most travelling carnivals subcontracted a variety of rides and concessions. However, there is very little extant evidence of precisely who the early "independents" were. The informality of historical record-keeping reflects the quite loose arrangements made between a carnival owner and the independents that he employed.[31] The independents themselves also tended to move from one carnival company to another in their ever-present search for the most viable spots at which to set up their tents.

A significant turning point for the carnival companies that subsequently played at the Calgary Stampede was the formation of the western summer fair circuit.[32] According to Gray, the Calgary Exhibition suggested a need for a set route for carnivals, which became established in 1911. The "A Circuit" (or route) comprised Calgary, Edmonton, Prince Albert, Saskatoon, and Regina.[33] The establishment of the route system that endures, albeit in modified form, today was beneficial to both carnival companies and the exhibitions. Benefits to carnival companies included the right to bid on the circuit and to acquire contracts that guaranteed them at least five weeks of work for a set number of years.[34] For exhibitions, the advantage of the circuit system was that they were able to attract larger carnival companies rather than often having to accept smaller companies with fewer attractions and a higher likelihood of illicit business practices. The circuit system, therefore, set the stage for moving the travelling amusement companies from the cultural margins (out of which grew the image of carnivals as inherently evil and criminal) towards the centre of legitimacy, crucial to the financial success of both the carnivals and the exhibitions that hired them.[35]

As the largest of the western exhibitions, Calgary was considered the ideal starting point for the western Canadian route, as it could include both Dominion Day (July 1) and the Fourth of July (the latter date attesting to the large American presence at the Calgary Exhibition). The Edmonton Exhibition, however, challenged this on the grounds that it was equally entitled to be the Dominion Day location for the carnival. The parties reached a compromise, which was "to alternate the first weeks of July between Calgary and Edmonton."[36]

Most of the carnival companies that worked the Canadian circuits from 1914 onwards were American. A typical carnival route for the American shows was to cross the border at Emerson, Manitoba, in June, travel west through the southern prairies to the Rocky Mountains, and then travel east as far as Ontario before returning to Minnesota.[37] Some small Canadian carnival companies operated in the prairies, an example of which is the Moyer Amusement Company from Assiniboia, Saskatchewan, which provided four rides in the 1928 season and was no doubt attached as an independent to the larger American companies.[38]

Between 1918 and 1932 there appears to have been intense competition for the entire A Circuit. The competition is reflected in the fact that, occasionally, the successful A Circuit bidder also achieved the highly-sought-after Canadian National Exhibition (CNE). In other years, the carnival company that successfully outbid its predecessor for the A Circuit had played at the CNE in the previous year. Performance at the CNE provided a potent source of revenue that enabled companies to build ride inventories and thus assured a stronger presence in subsequent contract bids. Some unsuccessful A Circuit bidders were awarded the B Circuit (smaller agricultural fairs) instead, before acquiring the A Circuit. Gregg Korek, vice-president of The Canadian Midway Company,[39] adds a further explanation for the number of carnival companies that played the A Circuit, a pattern that eventually gave way to the dominance of Royal American Shows:

> Jones [Johnny J. Jones Exposition] had the circuit for
> the most number of years, seemingly being given a break
> every few years while the circuit tried out a new show.
> They must not have been satisfied because they kept going
> back to Jones until Johnny Jones died in 1930. The Jones
> show quickly went downhill after that. Morris and Castle
> Shows I think bought out Wortham early in the 1920's
> and eventually changed the name. Castle-Ehrlich-Hirsch
> Shows is the successor to Morris and Castle. The carnival
> companies that then serviced the Calgary Stampede were
> certainly no match for the powerhouse Royal American
> and lost their contracts for Western Canada. To my
> knowledge, there was not a bidding process. Royal at that
> time had a far superior product and won the opportunity
> to play the lucrative Western fair route. Royal had a
> fantastic Stampede in 1934. The new show proved to
> be very popular with Calgarians and, for that matter,
> Western Canadians.[40]

Carnivals changed rapidly in the 1930s in a profoundly Darwinian fashion, as the economic effects of the Great Depression resonated throughout the entertainment industry. The smaller shows simply could not survive without sufficient revenue from the public. Technology was also salient to the changing form of carnivals: a component of carnivals that began to decline in the 1930s was the collection of variety acts that showcased singing, dancing, and humour, victims of the invention of the radio and the growing film industry.

During the 1950s the freak shows began to disappear from carnivals, in reaction to mounting public opinion that the display of "abnormal" human beings was fundamentally immoral. Another key component of carnivals that diminished significantly from the 1950s onwards was the girlie shows. Carnival operators were being pressured to present more wholesome entertainment. As well, televisions and movie theatres presented images of women that largely rendered the burlesque-type revues obsolete and no longer titillating to the heterosexual male population. A further factor that influenced changes on the midways was the growing competition from amusement and theme parks, particularly in the United States and eastern Canada, the consequence of which was that carnival companies focused strongly on expanding the number and variety of rides, which were far less expensive to transport and operate than the live bands, vaudeville acts, and water shows, all of which required large numbers of people and which were becoming increasingly less profitable to carnival companies. Only the larger carnival companies could afford this necessary expansion in carnival rides and games, which spelt the demise of many of the smaller travelling shows and ushered in a new era of carnivals.[41]

Moving from the Margins of the Calgary Stampede: The Second Phase (1950–1975)

The presence of Royal American Shows at the Calgary Stampede was another critical turning point in the evolution of carnivals not only at the Stampede, but throughout Canada. Gregg Korek provides the background of Royal American Shows' acquisition of the Calgary Stampede contract:

> In late 1931, Carl Sedlmayr [owner of Royal American
> Shows] and a contingent of his people came to Western
> Canada to visit the fairs in Brandon, Calgary, Edmonton and
> Regina, although not Winnipeg, as the date in Winnipeg

was not a fair yet but a Kinsmen fundraiser. Carl
presented a midway to these fairs that was unmatched
anywhere in North America. The fairs in Western Canada,
including the Stampede, of course, were impressed with
Royal's lineup of rides, sideshows and games. Also, Carl
was a very good salesman and a very likeable guy. In
the late summer of 1932, representatives from Calgary,
Edmonton and Regina exhibitions attended the State Fair
of Minnesota, while the fair was in operation, to see the
show and again visit with Carl. During the Minnesota
visit, Carl cemented a deal that would bring his show
to Canada for the 1934 season to Brandon, Winnipeg,
Calgary, Edmonton, Regina and I think Saskatoon.[42]

Founded by Carl J. Sedlmayr, who was born in Nebraska in 1886, Royal
American Shows was one of the largest American carnivals throughout most
of the twentieth century.[43] Although Royal American's first contract with the
Calgary Stampede was in 1934, the company was unable to travel to Canada
from 1942 to 1945, during the Second World War, as it relied on a large
train (up to 90 rail cars) for transportation.[44] During the war, use of the rail
system was restricted by the United States government to the movement of
military personnel and equipment.[45]

In 1967 Royal American Shows was at its pinnacle in terms of size, "over
800 people along with livestock and equipment and over 80 railroad cars,"
and by 1971, "Royal American Shows carried the greatest number of flatcars
ever carried by any traveling amusement organization in the world."[46] The
show travelled with a full complement of "carpenters, canvas men, electricians, painters, full working machine shops with mills, lathes, drills, weld-
ers, mechanics, cookhouse, portable showers, [and] mail department."[47] A
somewhat sentimental history of Royal American Shows takes a sad turn as
the author describes how the changing economy in the latter 1970s led to a
loss of revenue for Royal American Shows, "due to longer distances involved
in the carnival's season, culminating in the loss of its Canadian route in
1977 [sic] during a tax evasion scandal that led to Carl Sedlmayr's arrest.
Although Carl Jr. was fully exonerated, Royal American was now locked out
of Canada."[48]

In fact, the "tax evasion scandal" proved to be far more than an anomalous
incident in the history of Royal American Shows. The alleged tax evasion

not only resulted in numerous charges being laid, but also launched a Royal Commission[49] (known informally as the Laycraft Inquiry, named after the Commissioner, Justice James H. Laycraft) inquiring into the affairs and practices of Royal American Shows in Alberta.[50] The results of the inquiry led to the formation of the Alberta Gaming Commission (the first of its kind in Canada) and permanently changed many of the historical practices of carnivals in Canada.

The following quotation from the introduction in the report of the public inquiry demonstrates the magnitude of the investigation and its findings:

> On July 24, 1975, at 2:00 A.M., a force of more than 130 police officers of the Edmonton City Police and Royal Canadian Mounted Police converged on the carnival midway of Royal American Shows Inc. then situated at the grounds of the Edmonton Exhibition Association Ltd. Acting under a Search Warrant issued in Alberta Provincial Court late on the previous day, the officers seized from R.A.S. and from a number of independent midway concessionaires operating on the midway under arrangement with R.A.S. several thousand documents and large sums of money. For the most part, the documents consisted of accounting records. Using evidence derived from this seizure, some 87 charges under the Criminal Code of Canada and under The Income Tax Act were subsequently laid against individuals and R.A.S.[51]

The seizure and arrests were the culmination of many years of suspicion and surveillance spanning British Columbia east to Manitoba and conducted by various policing bodies (RCMP and several city police departments) as well as the federal Department of National Revenue. Suspicions of illegal accounting practices heightened in 1974 when, on several occasions, RCMP officers at the Vancouver airport recorded the transportation in suitcases of large sums of cash by persons associated with Royal American Shows.[52] Carrying significant amounts of money was not illegal. However, the source of the cash was sufficient to raise strong suspicions in various government bodies. The primarily cash-only basis[53] of carnivals had long confounded law enforcement agencies as well as the Department of National Revenue.[54] As Laycraft states,

The traveling carnivals from the United States had always presented the D.N.R. [Department of National Revenue] with a difficult audit problem. Not only were carnivals a business about which little was known, but the duration of their stay in Canada afforded little opportunity for examination. R.A.S. was a typical example. It visited four cities in three provinces over a period of six weeks, dealing almost entirely in cash. A tax audit involved not only R.A.S. itself but also each of the independent concessionaires. When the fair closed in Regina, the whole carnival operation moved overnight into the United States.[55]

After a lengthy and highly complex set of meetings that involved RCMP in Ottawa, British Columbia, Saskatchewan, Manitoba, and Alberta, as well as various Department of National Revenue agencies, the decision was made to single out Royal American Shows for intense investigation, as it was the largest in western Canada (although all carnival companies were considered equally suspect). A Task Force was formed to investigate three main areas: income tax fraud, fraud against exhibition boards (in the form of not paying them the amount designated in contracts), and the presence of illegal games.[56] One of the main intentions of the Task Force was "to set up surveillance to detect the 'skimming' of money from carnival operations or from the casinos" in each of the main exhibitions.[57]

Winnipeg was the first operation to be watched, followed by Calgary. The Task Force arrived in Calgary on June 26, 1975, to set up its surveillance for the beginning of the Calgary Exhibition and Stampede on July 3, 1975.[58] Its main objective at the Stampede was to watch the movement of tickets from the rides and shows. Calgary Exhibition and Stampede officials were aware of this and gave their full co-operation. Nothing illegal was observed, reflected in Laycraft's finding that "careful monitoring of the rides and shows over several days disclosed that the accounting made by R.A.S. [Royal American Shows] to C.X.S. [Calgary Exhibition and Stampede] for rides and shows was accurate and that C.X.S. was obtaining its proper share of the gross revenue derived from them."[59]

As well as the lack of sufficient evidence of illegal activities, another reason why the eventual "take-down" of Royal American Shows did not take place in Calgary was due to inferior telecommunications technology. During their surveillance in Winnipeg, the Task Force had strong suspicions that it was being monitored by Royal American Shows, which appeared to have better equipment than the Task Force members.[60] In Calgary, the Task Force attempted to monitor communications among the various carnival employees, using "better equipment obtained from Ottawa together with two civilian radio technicians to operate it."[61] Despite the improved telecommunications technology, the monitoring project was further hampered by local citizens' band (CB) radio transmissions, which resulted in Royal American Shows changing frequencies several times, thereby creating even more difficulties for the Task Force, which decided to abandon radio surveillance in Calgary and resume it in Edmonton. However, some arrests were made at the Stampede that year due to the presence of the Task Force. Calgary City Police shut down two of the midway games that were considered illegal under the Criminal Code, and four people running the games were prosecuted.[62]

The Task Force's investigation in Edmonton resulted in Royal American Shows being charged with six counts of defrauding the Edmonton Exhibition of a total of $52,164.63, along with many other Criminal Code charges.[63] Royal American Shows never returned to its Canadian route after 1975.[64] Following their release on bail, the people who were charged returned to the United States. Had the carnival come back to Canada, the individuals would most certainly have been arrested and detained at the border. The carnival equipment seized from the 1975 raids at Edmonton and Regina was held in storage until the mid-1990s, at which time the assets were sold at auction and the proceeds were used to pay the outstanding fines.[65] Royal American Shows continued to operate in the United States for the next twenty years, diminishing in size over time; its last show was in Lubbock, Texas, in October 1997.[66]

Royal American Shows played at the Calgary Stampede from 1934 to 1975, except during most of the Second World War, when Conklin Shows replaced it at the western Canadian exhibitions. The disappearance of Royal American Shows after a total of thirty-five years of playing at the Stampede opened the way for Conklin Shows to take on the A Circuit, which it continues to hold to the present day.

The Modernized Midway at the Calgary Stampede: 1976 to the Present

Conklin Shows' acquisition of the A Circuit was the result of complex negotiations, as the spectre of Royal American Shows' illegal activities had garnered much negative publicity for carnivals and created the need for a more cautionary approach by exhibition boards. In order to understand fully how Conklin Shows was able to acquire and retain the profitable A Circuit, however, it is necessary to place its success in a historical and economic context. Conklin Shows' ability to stay well ahead of its competition is unique in many ways, but perhaps the most singular characteristic is its consistently astute business acumen combined with a keen awareness of the need to present an image of respectability to the public as well as its business partners.

The originator of Conklin Shows was James Wesley "Patty" Conklin, born in Brooklyn, New York, in 1892.[67] He was born Joe Renker and, like Carl Sedlmayr Sr. of Royal American Shows, began working in the carnival industry as a sideshow talker in New York and, later, a gambling game operator in carnivals in Texas and Oklahoma. He formed a partnership with carnival show-owner J.W. Conklin in 1916, but the carnival company did not survive economically, ending in 1920. Patty, however, was treated like a family member, which is why he changed his name to Conklin, and when Conklin Sr. died in the fall of 1920, Patty continued working with the Conklin family.

With Conklin's widow and her son Frank (eleven years younger than Patty), Patty ran the small carnival operation for the next year. After a plan to join Wortham Shows (which had the western Canada A Circuit) at the Winnipeg Exhibition did not materialize, the trio unexpectedly encountered and joined a small carnival show named the International Amusement Company,[68] which was playing at St. Boniface, near Winnipeg, and remained with it through the rest of its Canadian route that year.

Shortly thereafter, Patty Conklin partnered with Speed Garrett from Seattle to form Conklin & Garrett Shows; from 1924 to 1930 the carnival grew from two railway cars to fifteen. During the Depression, the show travelled to the Maritimes. Although it did not fare well economically,[69] it was able to take advantage of plentiful cheap labour. In 1932 Patty moved the carnival to Ontario, eventually making the show's headquarters in Brantford.

Despite occasional setbacks, the company continued to grow over the next forty years, expanding throughout both Canada and the United States. By the 1980s, Frank Conklin (Patty's grandson) had reconfigured the American route to the point that the Canadian and American Conklin operations had become autonomous business entities. The Canadian operation continues to be headquartered in Brantford, Ontario, while the American company, under the leadership of Frank Conklin,[70] is based in West Palm Beach, Florida.

Another factor contributing to Conklin Shows' procurement of the A Circuit (which included the Calgary Stampede) was that two years prior to the 1975 takedown of Royal American Shows a group of Canadian carnival operators headed by Heinz Oldeck lobbied the western Canadian fairs and exhibitions to contract Canadian, rather than American, carnival companies. Their argument was that the significant financial revenue should remain in Canada, rather than go south to the United States. During the 1975 Stampede, newspapers in Calgary reported that the 1976 Calgary Stampede would be the first fair in the West to include a Canadian midway company, in conjunction with the larger Royal American Shows.[71] Korek states that "this decision rocked the ranks of management of Royal American for they had a lock on midways in the west for over forty years."[72]

After the raid on Royal American Shows in Edmonton in July 1975, the pro-Canadian carnival contingent realized that the western Canadian fairs were going to have to find a replacement for Royal American Shows.[73] The Canadian midway lobbyists' attempts escalated, leading to a meeting in Calgary in mid-September 1975 headed by George Hughes, general manager of the Edmonton Exhibition, and Bill Pratt, general manager of the Calgary Stampede. Decisions were made to attempt to book a Canadian carnival company by inviting submissions from Canadians and to book an American company only if a Canadian carnival could not supply the same level of equipment. Although the original intent was to keep the A Circuit intact, by November 1975 it was "every man for himself,"[74] as the Western Fairs Association realized it would be highly unlikely that it could provide midways for all the A Circuit fairs. Pratt and Hughes, as a result, sought carnival companies for the midways at Calgary and Edmonton, hoping that the other cities involved (Brandon, Winnipeg, Regina, and Saskatoon) would follow suit.[75]

In late November and December 1975, the International Association of Fairs and Exhibitions held its annual meeting in Las Vegas, during which Pratt and Hughes engaged in discussions with various Canadian carnival companies, including Conklin Shows, that eventually resulted in compact between Conklin Shows and the Calgary and Edmonton boards. In mid-December 1975 the Calgary Stampede invited Conklin Shows to a final meeting in Calgary, at which Jim Conklin, Sheila McKinnon, Alfie Phillips, and Colin Forbes came to a final agreement. Almost immediately, Jim Conklin held a meeting in Ontario with senior Conklin Shows management to develop a show for the West in 1976; within a week, Conklin Shows had acquired agreements with fairs in Brandon, Winnipeg, Calgary, Edmonton, and Regina.[76]

From January to March 1976, Colin Forbes, Joe Piggott (Conklin Shows' legal counsel), and Alfie Phillips organized the contract. This was particularly significant because public exposure of the illegal practices of Royal American Shows had cast a wide shadow over all carnivals in Canada and "authorities

Alfie Phillips

of every description wanted to make sure that Conklin Shows was not going to be a repeat performance of 1975."[77] Evidence of the reluctance of the fair boards (both Calgary and Edmonton) to commit to a long-term contract is that by early April 1976, Piggott and Forbes emerged from negotiations with only one-year contracts for each of the fairs, to ensure that there was at least a carnival company in place for the fast-approaching 1976 Calgary Stampede and Edmonton Klondike Days.[78]

Further evidence of the intensified suspicion of carnivals following the Royal American Shows investigation was the fact that, even two years later, in 1978, the RCMP and auditors from Revenue Canada followed Conklin Shows for the entire summer. Phillips states,

> There was forty of them [police and auditors]. They came
> in 1978 to investigate our show. There wasn't any serious
> offences [noted]. What they did was try to follow the
> money, from the game, to the office, to the bank, and they
> also tried to monitor all our cash operations so they could
> estimate how much revenue was coming in. So they'd send
> out two auditors and they'd spend the whole time at one
> game. And they'd also audit our ticket operations, too, and
> our game operations. We had an interesting summer. They
> followed us right to Winnipeg, and then they followed
> us right through to Toronto. It must have cost them a
> fortune: forty people, staying in hotels.[79]

A central reason that Conklin Shows emerged unscathed from the close scrutiny of authorities in 1978 was that an important aspect of the contract negotiations in 1976 had been the inclusion of much more transparency with regard to the financial arrangements between Conklin Shows and the fair boards.[80] Conklin Shows offered the fair boards a percentage of the revenue taken from the games and the rides.[81] Further incentives offered by Conklin Shows were considered extremely progressive: the midway Guest Relations Booth and colour-coded canvas on all the rides and the games were features that remain today.[82]

As the aforementioned negotiations attest, the success of Conklin Shows was, and is, a direct consequence of its ability to recognize cultural and economic changes in wider society and respond to them well by continually modifying and adapting the carnival company to meet societal needs and demands. In fact, the smaller carnivals' inability to react and adapt to wider cultural conditions is the primary reason why only the largest carnivals continue to exist today.

The evolution of Conklin Shows into a more corporatized entity reflects its adaptation to the difficulties all contemporary carnivals face.[83] Alfie Phillips outlines the many factors involved in the increasingly expensive costs of running a carnival: the long distances that the carnival equipment has to be moved,[84] the rising costs of gasoline, premiums for liability insurance, and the costs involved in meeting required standards of operation.[85] The larger carnival companies, such as Conklin Shows, are scrutinized more closely by authorities because of their high visibility, as well as pressure by the various agricultural boards that standards meet the overall criteria for the large exhibitions. One advantage for Canadian companies of the higher costs of running carnivals is that the large American shows are reluctant to come to Canada, as the costs are even more prohibitive due to the devalued American dollar plus the Canadian goods and services tax (GST). This is in addition to the problems often encountered at the border relative to carnival workers who may not meet the requirements of Immigration Canada.[86]

Another difficulty that Conklin Shows has encountered concerns the labour force needed to run such a large operation. Historically, carnivals have relied heavily on a small but relatively stable core group of workers who tend to stay with the carnival for its entire season and a more transient group of workers who are often hired locally at each carnival spot. Hiring local workers as a reserve army of labour has been a common practice at most seasonal exhibitions, fairs, and carnivals for many years. Gray refers to "a small army of unemployed single men [being] rounded up and put to work"[87] in

1931 at the Calgary Stampede, which was "the start of a continuing role for the Calgary Industrial Exhibition Company: acting as an unemployment relief agency."[88] Contemporary carnival companies also rely heavily on local workers, especially for the labour-intensive teardown of the carnival before it moves on to its next location.

A critical factor in the availability of casual workers is economic conditions, which presents a somewhat ironic situation for carnivals: a buoyant economy usually means a large turnout of people and, consequently, larger revenues. However, it also often means a shortage of available local workers. This has been the case for many years for Conklin Shows with regard to the Calgary Stampede, especially as the agricultural basis of the Alberta economy gradually gave way to the emerging oil industries. As Phillips states, "we have always had problems with the workforce here [in Calgary]; nobody wants to work here because the economy is too good."[89] Conklin Shows holds job fairs in Calgary and Edmonton to hire local workers for positions such as ticket sellers, office staff, food concessions staff, and game and ride operators. Approximately 600 or 700 local workers are hired for Conklin Shows at the Calgary Stampede, including 100 ticket sellers and approximately 100 people working in Kiddy Land (children's rides).[90]

The shortage of local workers for temporary employment is not the only impediment encountered by Conklin Shows. It has also had difficulty finding sufficient full-time workers because "young people today don't want to do this kind of work."[91] Conklin Shows now looks beyond North American borders for its workforce, and for the past several years has brought in workers (mainly young white males) from South Africa.[92] Despite some difficulties in finding both temporary and full-time workers, Conklin Shows remains nonetheless a dominant carnival company in western Canada and the United States.[93]

Conclusion

In 1939 H.W. Waters, an American carnival historian, argued that carnivals would eventually become bland and boring when neutralized of their more deviant components to meet legal and societal standards. Waters predicted that moral entrepreneurs would eventually succeed in their quest to rid midways of their sinful temptations. Positing also that "younger people lose interest [in carnivals] at a certain age," Waters states,

> Attempts have been made to refine and dignify the midway. It has here and there been dressed up in a more sedate coat and it has been given a new name, and such an air of respectability that it has lost its carnival or festival spirit which in the past has been the secret of its success. Long experience has shown that the more successful the carnival owner is in creating the carnival atmosphere at the fair the more successful he will be financially.[94]

Waters did not entertain the possibility that carnivals would prove to be one of the most durable and flexible of human social creations. It can be strongly argued that carnivals in North America have never become sufficiently sanitized in either image or substantive content that the public has lost interest. Certainly, many of the early smaller carnivals did not survive, but it was not due to public disinterest. Inefficient or overtly illegal business practices were the main reasons for their disappearance, rather than any significant successes by agricultural purists in ridding the midway of its "slippery vermin."[95]

This examination of the carnival companies that have played at the Calgary Stampede has demonstrated that the successful carnivals have adapted to changes in technology, public morality, and the ebb and flow of the economy. Indeed, as the largest agricultural fair and exhibition in the western provinces, the Calgary Stampede has attracted the largest carnival companies in North America, thereby opening up what quickly became an extremely lucrative carnival route with mutual advantages for the carnivals and the various fair boards.

Once the mainstay of early twentieth-century carnivals, the tented sideshows displaying "freaks" and girlie shows have disappeared, with carnival rides and games of chance now dominating the midway at the Stampede. For most Stampede attendees, however, the midway continues to emanate an aura of decadence, particularly at night, with the overwhelming noise, bright lights, and nostalgic smells of popcorn and candy floss. One might conclude, therefore, that the ambience is rooted in the same confluence of myth and nostalgia that envelops the Stampede in its entirety, and that the midway has indeed reached the centre of respectability and legality. Most of the illegal activities have been purged from carnivals due to closer scrutiny by authorities and the general public's refusal to either tolerate or sustain interest in some of the more dubious attractions and practices. However, an issue that has remained problematic, although largely invisible to the general public, is what could be characterized as exploitation of a largely powerless carnival workforce. As stated earlier, carnivals have relied on a small core of permanent workers, augmented by temporary employees at the larger exhibitions and fairs. With no protection from unions, carnival employees tend to work between twelve and sixteen hours a day, for a fixed weekly wage, seven days a week, and with little time off.[96] Historically, the workers have tended to accept these conditions as normal and natural, as many of them are used to working in marginal unskilled labour. However, in 2005 some of these conditions came to the attention of the general public when a large number of the South African workers at Conklin Shows spoke to the press and, eventually, left the carnival in Edmonton.[97] The consequence was an investigation by Alberta Human Resources and Employment, which showed that "the company failed to maintain proper payroll records, record employees' breaks or limit individuals' work to twelve hours."[98] Conklin Shows was issued a warning. In 2006 Alberta Human Resources and Employment continued to monitor working conditions at the Calgary Stampede and Edmonton's Capital EX (formerly Klondike Days).[99]

The fact that the wages and working conditions of carnival workers are largely ignored by the general public (and the media, until the issues are brought to their attention) is a consequence of the enduring belief that carnival workers occupy a very low social class location and continue to be seen, and portrayed, as a quasi-criminal element of carnivals. North American Midway claims that "the workers are hired from abroad [South Africa] because they are energetic and dedicated, and an important aspect to changing the image of the dirtier, grumpier 'carnie' that people associate with midways."[100] The people hired by the carnival, therefore, are yet another projection of the image that carnivals attempt to attain, along with the bright lights, music, and family-oriented ambience. Carnivals, including all the shows that have played at the Calgary Stampede over the past century, have always been an illusory social phenomenon. From their earliest manifestations as sinful and decadent through their gradual evolution towards more mainstream entertainment, the carnivals at the Calgary Stampede will, no doubt, continue to simultaneously repel and entice fairgoers with their paradoxical nature, appealing to our desire to be entertained within the margins of respectability.

Notes

1. James H. Gray, *A Brand of Its Own: The 100 Year History of the Calgary Stampede and Exhibition* (Saskatoon: Western Producer Prairie Books, 1985).

2. It is salient to point out that the evolution of a phenomenon that defies societal definitions of respectability towards legitimacy may, in fact, be the consequence of more sophisticated *illusions* of proper conduct: what the general public is meant to perceive. It is also important to point out that, although the focus of this chapter is the Calgary Stampede, the history of carnivals at the Stampede is representative of and, indeed, embedded in a broader Albertan and western Canadian sociocultural context. Therefore, the Stampede's carnival history cannot be singled out as unique or extraordinary. Rather, the dynamics that have shaped the evolution of the midway or carnival component of the Stampede are those that informed the entire carnival and agricultural fair industry in the West over the past century.

3. It is difficult to define a carnival precisely because carnivals vary tremendously in size and components and have altered in meaning over time. The word "carnival" originates in fifteenth-century celebrations of pre-Lenten meat-eating, but developed a broader meaning in "the commonplace American sense of gaudy and somewhat disreputable pleasure." See Samuel Kinser, *Carnival, American Style: Mardi Gras at New Orleans and Mobile* (Chicago: University of Chicago Press, 1990), 3–4.

4. Kinser, *Carnival*, 3.

5. Joe McKennon, *A Pictorial History of the American Carnival* (Sarasota: Carnival Publishers of Sarasota, vol. 1, 1972), 11.

6. It is important to point out that carnivals have existed in many forms for hundreds of years in other countries and societies. While most European carnivals have roots in religious ceremonies, most North American carnivals have had one purpose: the procurement of revenue through the provision of entertainment.

7. David C. Jones, *Midways, Judges, and Smooth-Tongued Fakirs: The Illustrated Story of Country Fairs in the Prairie West* (Saskatoon: Western Producer Prairie Books, 1983), 52. See also Judith Adams, *The American Amusement Park Industry: A History of Technology and Thrills* (Boston: Twayne, 1991), 28; and H.W. Waters, *History of Fairs and Expositions: Their Classifications, Functions and Values* (London, ON: Reid Bros., 1939), 128. Waters spells the term "The Midway Pleasaunce."

8. Jones, *Midways, Judges,* 52.

9. Waters, *History of Fairs,* 128.

10. Adams, *American Amusement Park Industry,* 28.

11. Waters, *History of Fairs,* 128.

12. Guy Scott, *Country Fairs in Canada* (Markham, ON: Fitzhenry and White-side, 2006), 65. Scott states that the musicians frequently wandered around the fairgrounds, playing between the performances on stage, as well as during inclement weather in order to sooth the nerves of agitated livestock.

13. Ibid., 62.

14. Ibid., 127.

15. Gregg Korek, vice-president, Canadian Midway Company, personal communication with author, July 2006. In the earlier years, the carnival shows and sideshows set up rather arbitrarily on the Stampede and Exhibition grounds. There is little historical record of where the earlier carnivals were located. However, Gray refers to the midway in a photograph taken in 1912, describing it as "a ramshackle affair in which the carnival games and 'grease joints' [food concessions] were located in the middle of Indian Village by the main entrance," which supports Korek's statement (Gray, *Brand of Its Own*, 39). As carnival companies grew, much more planning was needed to find the right location and adequate space for the rides and games. Currently, the arrangement is that the Stampede asks Conklin Shows to submit a preliminary lot layout for the rides before April 1. The Stampede may suggest changes or sanction the initial submission, so, in essence, the Stampede and Conklin Shows negotiate to come to a mutual agreement on the placement of the carnival rides and games. Alfie Phillips, interview with author, 13 July 2005.

16. Scott, *Country Fairs,* 77. The term "fakir" comes from the Arabic meaning "beggar" and refers to a religious mendicant; "how this term was transferred to a carnival con man defies explanation." See also Jones, who refers to "bean-in-the-nutshell operators, known collectively as fakirs or fakers" in *Midways, Judges*, 4.

17. Ibid., 81–82.

18. Ibid., 72.

19. Ibid., 74.

20. bid., 74.

21. For example, in 1905, there was enormous opposition to gambling on the midway at the Calgary Exhibition, although the same carnival company had provided gambling games in Edmonton. The carnival company paid the Calgary Exhibition Association $500 for the "privilege" of setting up the games for three days. After some young boys were observed near the gambling games, a citizens' group headed by Reverend G.W. Kerby complained. Rev. Kerby enlisted the help of the mayor and other citizens. They told the chief of police that they would charge the mayor with impeachment unless the game operators were arrested and punished. However, the usual outcome of such moral outrage was that judges

told the offenders to leave town, and the situation would then repeat itself the following year. See Faye Reinberg Holt, *Awed, Amused, and Alarmed* (Calgary: Detselig Enterprises, 2003), 179–80.

22. Jones, *Midways, Judges,* 54.

23. Gray, *Brand of Its Own,* 19.

24. Gray states that, in 1920, "one of the continuing problems of the Calgary Exhibition" was with the midways. "The rides were a super attraction, and along with the rides were the so-called games of chance. All were capable of being rigged to ensure that the 'marks' left their money with the operators.... Floating along the midways from town to town were a motley gang of sneak thieves, pickpockets, and hustlers." Gray, *Brand of Its Own,* 100.

25. "In the Name of Agriculture," *Review* (6 September 1915): 499, in Jones, *Midways, Judges,* 51–52.

26. Gray, *Brand of Its Own,* 31.

27. The C.W. Parker Carnival was typical of the travelling carnivals of the early twentieth century that played in both the U.S. and Canada. Charles W. Parker, the carnival owner, entered the carnival business initially by manufacturing amusement devices, including making improvements on existing models such as merry-go-rounds. He is also the originator of the "High Striker," still found in most carnivals. He formed a carnival company in Kansas in 1902 under the name of C.W. Parker Amusement Company, which grew into the Great (and later, "Greater") Parker Shows. A website covering the history of Charles W. Parker reproduces the following item from William E. Connelley, *A Standard History of Kansas and Kansans* (Chicago: Lewis Publishing Company, 1918): "At the present time Mr. Parker is the largest private owner of amusement cars in the United States, His factory at Leavenworth is the largest in the world devoted exclusively to the manufacture of amusement devices." *http://skyways.lib. ks.us/genweb/archives/1918ks/biop/parkercw.html* (accessed 28 January, 2006).

28. Gray, *Brand of Its Own,* 31.

29. Gray, *Brand of Its Own,* 100. The date of 1934 for Royal American Shows conflicts with that given by Gray, who states that "over the years, Calgary and the other western fairs tried several midways before settling in 1936 for the Royal American Shows which seemed, at that time, to be a cut above most of its competition."

30. Jim Conklin via e-mail message from Ron Getty to author, 4 February 2005.

31. The writer uses the male pronoun deliberately. Almost all carnival owners over the past one hundred years have been male.

32. The original circuit system consisted of three circuits: A, B, and C. The A Circuit was considered to be the largest and most profitable carnival route, consisting mostly of large annual exhibitions. The B Circuit comprised

smaller exhibitions and agricultural fairs, often in relatively remote small towns. Little is known about the C Circuit, but one can assume that this route included even smaller towns and fairs with less profitable opportunities. The A Circuit still exists today in western Canada (the Calgary Stampede being considered the largest spot). The B Circuit also still exists, albeit on a much smaller level than in the twentieth century. The C Circuit no longer exists. The evolution of the various circuits can be explained by the evolving demographic changes in western Canada, as the populations in cities grew, often at the expense of the near-depletion of many of the once-thriving smaller rural towns that formed the basis of the B Circuit. Interestingly, the Canadian National Exhibition (CNE) held in Toronto was often part of a package acquired by the successful A Circuit bidder. Ontario has always had far more carnival companies, as it has had the population base to support companies that often did not have to travel out of the province in order to survive economically. However, it is probably the case that none of these carnivals were large enough to play at the CNE, which is probably why the CNE contracts were seen as an entity separate from the other Ontario locations for carnivals.

33. Gray, *Brand of Its Own,* 33. Changes over the years with regard to cities in the A Circuit reflect changes in these cities' exhibitions. For example, by 1918 Winnipeg and Brandon were added to the A Circuit, and Prince Albert was excluded (Jim Conklin via e-mail message from Ron Getty to author, 4 February 2005). The same cities remained in the circuit for the next few years. However, of note is the absence of Calgary in the 1922 A Circuit (Jim Conklin via e-mail message from Ron Getty to author, 4 February 2005), for which there is no extant explanation. In 1923 the Western Canada Association of Exhibitions was formed, with the A Circuit consisting of the same cities, including Calgary.

34. The process of bidding by carnival companies for contracts has varied over time. In western Canada, there does not seem to have been a bidding process per se until about the middle of the twentieth century. Agricultural fairs did not have much from which to select and tended to choose the largest, most spectacular carnival company available, which was usually American until Conklin Shows grew in size and scope. Although bidding itself was virtually non-existent until relatively recently, contracts were drawn up with the selected carnival. There appears to be no historical record of the contracts between some of the earlier carnivals, such as the Johnny J. Jones Exposition, with the Calgary Stampede (Ron Getty, Stampede Archives, e-mail correspondence 3 February 2006). However, Gregg Korek recalls that in 1946, Royal American Shows returned to the Calgary Stampede and the other

western fairs with agreements based on five-year terms with a two-year extension (Gregg Korek, e-mail message to author, 2 February 2006). According to Jim Hobart, midway and exhibits manager at the Calgary Stampede, the standard term length for Stampede contracts currently is three to five years. Hobart, e-mail message to author, 26 January 2006.

35. It is important to point out that much of the alleged legitimacy was merely a camouflage for continued illegal activities.

36. Gray, *Brand of Its Own,* 33.

37. Jones, *Midways, Judges,* 52. See also Donald G. Wetherell and Irene Kmet, *Useful Pleasures: The Shaping of Leisure in Alberta, 1896–1945* (Edmonton: Alberta Culture and Multiculturalism, 1990), 321.

38. Wetherell and Kmet, *Useful Pleasures,* 321.

39. This is the corporate name of Conklin Shows' Canadian operations.

40. Gregg "Scooter" Korek, e-mail message to author, 2 February 2006.

41. McCain Library and Archives, University of Southern Mississippi, *www.lib.usm.edu/~archives/m329.htm* (accessed 14 January 2006).

42. Korek, e-mail message to author, 2 February 2006.

43. There is very little recorded history of the show, and most of the information on it is found on a website created by a former employee of the show, Carl LeMay, who cites as his source Joe McKennon's *A Pictorial History of the American Carnival* (Sarasota: Carnival Publishers of Sarasota, vol. 1, 1972; vol. 2, 1972; vol. 3, 1981). See LeMay, *Royal American Shows: The Worlds [sic] Largest and Most Brilliantly Illuminated Midway,* accessible at http://home. tampabay.rr.com/lemay/royal.htm (accessed 7 September 2005).

    As a young man, Sedlmayr obtained a job as a sideshow talker at an amusement park in Chicago. To repay a debt owed to him, the owner of Siegrist-Silbon Shows (a circus) granted Sedlmayr ownership of the circus in 1921. Sedlmayr chose a new name for his show, Royal American Shows, in order to appeal to both Canadians and Americans. In 1923 he sold brothers Elmer and Curtis Velare an interest in a partnership that continued until the early 1940s. By the 1930s Sedlmayr and the Velare brothers had created an impressive carnival "dedicated to the principle of carrying clean, high-class entertainment to the public." Sedlmayr then took on a new partner named Sam Soloman, and Sedlmayr and Soloman bought and ran the Rubin & Cherry Show for two years. (This conflicts somewhat with LeMay's historical account implying that Royal American Shows remained in its original format as a travelling carnival throughout its tenure.) However, it was very common for carnivals throughout most of the twentieth century to change names or to change ownership while retaining the same name. It could very well be the case, consequently, that the Rubin & Cherry show carried the Royal

American banner during that time period. It was not until after the Second World War that Sedlmayr ran Royal American Shows as the sole owner. Circus, Minstrel and Travelling Show Collection, M329, McCain Library and Archives, University of Southern Mississippi, *www.lib.usm.edu/~archives/ m329.htm* (accessed 14 January 2006).

44. This was typical of larger carnivals in North America, which travelled long distances with massive amounts of equipment and a large number of workers.

45. Korek, e-mail message to author, 2 February 2006.

46. LeMay (accessed 7 September 2005).

47. Ibid.

48. Ibid.

49. Alberta, Royal Commission of Inquiry into Royal American Shows, *Royal American Shows Inc. and Its Activities in Alberta: Report of A Public Inquiry / James H. Laycraft, Commissioner* (Edmonton, 1978) (hereafter cited as Laycraft, *Royal American Shows*).

50. Evidence of the length of the inquiry can be seen in the following comments from Laycraft: "I spent one year of my life on this Royal Commission. On days that were otherwise somewhat dull it made the front pages of all Alberta newspapers" (Laycraft, e-mail message to author, 24 January 2006).

51. Laycraft, *Royal American Shows*, A-1.

52. For example, in 1974 James Breen flew out of Saskatoon "carrying a satchel containing $25,000.00, Benjamin Mayers of Vancouver traveled from Winnipeg to Vancouver carrying approximately $100,000.00, [and] on another occasion, Mayers and Breen left Edmonton carrying approximately $200,000.00." Laycraft, *Royal American Shows*, B-2.

53. It is also important to point out it was not unusual for senior carnival employees to be carrying large amounts of cash. Carnival companies rarely used banks through much of the twentieth century. Based on a cash economy, carnivals traditionally paid their employees directly with cash, and made purchases in a similar fashion. Travelling from location to location in a semi-autonomous fashion also created a practical need to have ready cash on hand, rather than conducting transactions or making deposits at banking institutions. Carnival owners were also very well aware that banks did not particularly trust them and, given the often tumultuous and unpredictable economics of the carnival business, banks were usually loathe to extend loans to carnivals. This practice of avoiding banks continued until well into the 1980s for many of the smaller carnivals in Canada (and, one can speculate, in the United States). Fiona Angus, "Key to the Midway: Masculinity at Work in a Western Canadian Carnival" (Ph.D. thesis, University of British Columbia, 2000), 111.

54. Police had always been highly suspicious of all carnivals since the turn of the century. However, they often turned a blind eye to the illegal activities, safe in the knowledge that the "grifters" would soon be leaving town. It was only when carnival companies grew larger and their presence far more visible that provincial and federal authorities became more vigilant.
55. Laycraft, *Royal American Shows,* B-5.
56. Ibid., B-7.
57. Ibid., B-11.
58. Ibid., B-11.
59. Ibid., B-11–12. In a telephone conversation with the author in February 2006, Gregg Korek said that he had been told anecdotally that the Edmonton Exhibition had been selected for the raid because the Calgary Stampede area was considered too close to the U.S. border for any potential escapees, and that Edmonton's relative isolation was seen as being less likely to provide an easy exit for alleged carnival criminals. The overall impression given in Laycraft's report is that the surveillance in Winnipeg and Calgary was motivated by the need for concrete evidence of illegal practices by Royal American Shows. For example, the report states that after the Task Force left Winnipeg for Calgary on June 26, 1975, a "confidential source [supplied]... the location of the R.A.S. records." One can surmise, therefore, that had sufficient evidence been collected prior to their arrival in Calgary, the Task Force might have decided to conduct its raid of Royal American Shows at the Calgary Stampede, rather than at the Edmonton Exhibition.
60. Laycraft, *Royal American Shows,* B-11.
61. Ibid., B-12.
62. Ibid., B-13–14. Another event that occurred in Calgary during the Stampede also resulted in charges being laid later: "On July 11 [1975], two persons, William Goggin and James Breen, who had been described in criminal intelligence reports of the previous year as 'bagmen', arrived from Saskatoon. On July 12, they went to the Calgary Airport with $70,000.00. They presented this money to the R.C.M.P. Airport Detachment for a private inspection for flight clearance. The Airport Detachment noted the license number of a rented car being used by the two men and passed the information on to the Task Force." This incident became very significant in the subsequent raid at Klondike Days in Edmonton, as the rented vehicle was tracked and found in the parking lot of the Edmonton Plaza Hotel, leading the Task Force towards the eventual uncovering of a highly complex set of transactions involving several individuals connected with moving the money from the various exhibitions to points south of the border, and out of the jurisdiction of Canada's Department of National Revenue.

63. The entire endeavour, however, was not without numerous and complex problems. Even before the Task Force began its work of monitoring Royal American Shows, it was beset by internal conflicts and disagreements among the various Task Force members with regard to jurisdictional issues and other legal aspects. After the Task Force exposed the alleged illegalities in Royal American Shows in Edmonton, ongoing difficulties arose with regard to loss of continuity of documentation, largely because of the aforementioned tension among the Task Force parties. Further evidence of the distrust that appears to have existed among the various Task Force members (particularly between the RCMP and local police departments) is "The Northstar Incident," in which the RCMP was accused by Edmonton City police officers of spying on their activities at the Northstar Inn in Edmonton in December 1975, during the ongoing legal proceedings following the July 1975 investigation of Royal American Shows' activities at Klondike Days. This was not an insignificant issue, as it led directly to the alleged tainting of documentation and information that effectively ruled out court admissibility. In fact, the issue of court admissibility in the form of both "loss of continuity" and "non-disclosure of documentation" is cited in Laycraft's report as the reason why charges stemming from evidence of criminal activities against Albert Anderson, the general manager of the Edmonton Exhibition, were stayed. Charges against Anderson arose after the Task Force's seizure of the "black book" containing information written by Peter D. Andrews, Royal American Shows concessions manager, between 1973 and 1975. In essence, the book contained records of bribes in the form of money and gifts given to various people of significance, some of whom were named, while others were indicated by an office only. Laycraft states the following in his report: "In the case of some cities in the United States substantial sums of money were shown as having been given to various named or designated individuals. In Canada, the book showed sums of money ranging from $50.00 to $300.00 as having been given to a number of named Calgary policemen. Three other Canadians are shown as having received money. Two are not identified by name. The other person named was Albert J. Anderson, then General Manager of the E.X.A. [Edmonton Exhibition Association]." Ibid., B-22–67. Anderson was charged with "unlawfully and corruptly accepting awards, advantages, or benefits of goods and money from Sedlmayr, Andrews, and Demay as a consideration for showing favour to Royal American Shows Inc.," charges which, as mentioned above, were stayed due to allegations of improprieties with regard to the continuity of documentation. Ibid., B-24.

64. The raids by the Task Force on Royal American Shows continued in Regina after Royal American left Edmonton.

65. Korek, e-mail message to author, 2 February 2006.
66. Minstrel and Travelling Show Collection, M329, McCain Library and Archives, University of Southern Mississippi.
67. Unless otherwise noted, most of the historical data on Conklin Shows is derived from the extensive history of the show compiled by Gregg Korek, Jim Conklin, and John Thurston (www.conklinshows.com/history.htm). Korek states that Thurston, from Ottawa, is currently writing a book on the history of the Conklin Shows. Korek, e-mail message to author, 23 February 2006.
68. The writer was unable to locate any information on this particular show, but its name reflects the tendency of carnival owners in the late nineteenth and early twentieth centuries to select grandiose names for quite small carnival operations.
69. Economic downturns are particularly difficult periods for carnivals, and many carnival companies disappeared during the Great Depression. Carnival companies, then as now, depend on an often unpredictable number of customers to survive. Poor economic conditions as well as inclement weather have a significant impact on any carnival's seasonal revenue and, often, its chances of survival.
70. Jim Conklin retired in 1996, which is when Frank took over the American operations. However, Jim remains actively involved in the Ontario operations of Conklin Shows, which are known as The World's Finest Shows (Phillips, interview with author, 13 July 2005).
71. Korek, e-mail message to author, 2 February 2006.
72. Ibid.
73. After the raids in Edmonton and Regina, the western fairs assumed that Royal American Shows would return (albeit in a sanitized form) for the upcoming season.
74. Korek, e-mail message to author, 2 February 2006.
75. Ibid.
76. Ibid.
77. Ibid.
78. Korek stated that there were proposals from other midway companies in the fall of 1975. One proposal was from Jerry Murphy's United States Shows, which appear to have attempted to meet the Canadian carnival criterion by creating a Canadian midway called "Canadian Carnivals." There were also proposals from Heinz Oldeck's company and Bingo Hauser's West Coast Amusements. Korek states, "I believe in total that there were twelve submissions that were presented by carnival operators." Korek, e-mail message to author, 2 February 2006.
79. Alfie Phillips, interview with author, 13 July 2005.

80. A stark example of the alleged "skimming" by Royal American Shows is found in Gray's statement that in 1975 the midway revenue was $208,933 (the amount declared by Royal American Shows) yet, one year later, in 1976 (when Conklin Shows had the midway contract), the midway revenue was $502,000, "an indication surely that something more than mere tax juggling had been taking place in the Royal American Shows' counting house." Gray, *Brand of Its Own,* 169.

81. Phillips, interview with author, 13 July 2005. Historically, carnival companies have used a variety of ways to pay fair boards their portion of the revenue. Often the agreements were very informal, with somewhat arbitrary percentage commissions being placed on the carnival ride components and the games (the general "rule of thumb" was that the more lucrative the carnival component, the larger the commission demanded by the fair board). Alfie Phillips states that one arrangement is for carnival companies to deposit the ride money (money from ride tickets) into the fair board's bank account, and then the carnival company keeps the concession (games) money. Under this arrangement, payment is not made on a percentage (commission) basis, but on a flat basis where "you rent 100 feet and you pay so much money to the office for 100 feet."

   "Sullivan Amusements" (pseudonym), the carnival I researched in 1996, used a percentage system between the carnival company and the fair boards, and also between the independent carnival operators and the show itself. During the research, I asked how a financial figure was arrived at in order to compute the agreed-upon percentage at the end of each spot, given that Sullivan Amusements was a strictly cash-run operation. The office employee at Sullivan Amusements told me that, in both sets of circumstances, a check with the previous year's figures provided the carnival with a kind of benchmark figure to go by, while also considering any mitigating factors such as weather that might affect the revenue. The employee advised me that there was an unspoken acknowledgment between the carnival and its contractees that the figure was never completely accurate, but close enough to the previous year so that disputes could not develop. The arrangements for the more itinerant independents were even more loose and informal: handshake agreements with the owner of Sullivan Amusements to give a percentage (known as "points") of their day's take, called "the nut." (The word "nut" has an interesting derivation. The Sullivan Amusements worker told me that "years age, when circuses came into town, the mayor of the town would get upset when circuses would head out without paying, so he would take one nut off of every wheel of every trailer and when the circus trainer brought his money in, his rent, the mayor would give him his nuts back.") Percentages/

points varied tremendously from 20 percent to 45 percent depending on how well-known and well-liked the independent contractors were by the carnival owner. Angus, "Key to the Midway," 95.

82.   In the past ten years, Conklin Shows has added other features, such as machines that dispense hand lotion and the sale of bottled water. Alfie Phillips commented, "Patty Conklin would roll over in his grave if he knew we were selling bottled water! Roll over in his grave! Three dollars for a bottle of water!" Phillips, interview with author, 13 July 2005.

83.   The carnival business, in general, has struggled over the past fifty years to survive, with so many other entities competing for entertainment dollars (e.g., television and other electronic technological advancements and, increasingly, casinos and gaming in general). Jeff Blomsness, chair of the Outdoor Amusement Business Association, stated in 2000 that the Cypress Group carnival company merger was a very positive step towards the survival of the carnivals involved. Blomsness said, "We're hurting. Two-thirds of the ride manufacturers are out of business, and some that did 60% or 90% of their business with carnivals are now doing 10%, or even less. The whole industry is hurting, and it will trickle down to fairs." Tom Powell, "Farrow, Conklin, Thebault-Blomsness to consolidate," *Amusement Business*, 15 October 2004, *www.amusementbusiness.com/amusementbusiness/industrynews/article_display.jsp* (accessed 22 January 2006).

84.   The Conklin Shows website states that "the cost of moving rides, from fair to fair, even before the increase in gas has become almost prohibitive. Last year [2003], to move the show the 20,000 miles from Florida to the Calgary Stampede and back cost in excess of $5,000,000." Conklin Shows, *www.conklinshows.com/rides_secrets.htm* (accessed January 12, 2005).

85.   Alfie Phillips characterized this as "government interference," stating that "in some provinces, it's excessive. For example, in Manitoba, they come and visit our office, about seventeen regulatory bodies, and in Toronto, it's twenty-two, such a wide span...that we touch on all these different areas of government regulations [such as] the fire marshall, health department, police department, health and safety people, people auditing us. It's just a myriad of regulatory bodies that descend upon us." Phillips, interview with author, 13 July 2005.

86.   Ibid.

87.   Gray makes frequent references to the reliance of the Stampede over the years on both casual and volunteer workers.

88.   Gray, *Brand of Its Own,* 90.

89.   Phillips, interview with author, 13 July 2005.

90.   Ibid.

91.   Ibid.

92.	The company used by Conklin Shows is "Away 2 Xplore," which offers "international staffing solutions" and recruits "a large portion of [its] candidates from South Africa's middle class working families" (*www.away2xplore.org*, accessed 5 August 2005). The South African workers fly into the southern U.S. initially, usually in January, work on ride maintenance and restoration for Conklin Shows at West Palm Beach, and then begin the carnival company's season by working in spots in Miami, eventually making their way north to the Calgary Stampede in July and continuing on the show's route for the remainder of the season. The South African workers then fly back to South Africa in November. The workers are brought in under employer-sponsored seasonal worker visas (known as H-2Bs), which are given to workers employed by companies that claim they are unable to find suitable or available workers domestically.

93.	Another sign of the evolution of Conklin Shows into a more corporatized entity is its merger with North American Midway Entertainment in January 2005. North American Midway Entertainment comprises Conklin Holdings, Farrow Amusement Company (of Jackson, Mississippi), and Thebault-Blomsness Inc. (of Crystal Lake, Illinois), and is a wholly owned subsidiary of Stone Canyon Entertainment Corp., a company formed by former Ticketmaster Group chairperson and CEO Fred Rosen and The Cypress Group, a New York-based equity firm. North American Midway held contracts, as of October 15, 2004, for 142 annual fairs and exhibitions in seventeen U.S. states and four Canadian provinces. Powell, "Farrow, Conklin."

Jim Hobart, midway and exhibits manager for the Calgary Stampede, states that "Conklin Shows' last contract with the Stampede was for five years (2000–2004). With Conklin Shows being an integral part of the merger brought together by North American Midway Entertainment, the Calgary Stampede entered into a one-year contract for the 2005 Stampede with The Canadian Midway Company (Conklin Shows) and North American Midway Company to bridge the gap. The Calgary Stampede and [The Canadian Midway Company] are currently in negotiations to go forward with a new contract. The length of the contract is one of the terms to be determined." Jim Hobart, e-mail message to author, 24 February 2006.

In a press release dated October 15, 2004, The Cypress Group states, "Conklin is the largest midway operator in North America with a large presence on the East Coast and throughout Canada, operating rides and concessions at 17 shows with attendance of approximately 8.4 million." The Cypress Group/Private Equity Investing, *www.cypressgp.com/pr_2004_10_15.htm* (accessed 22 January 2006).

Conklin Shows played for the first time as The Canadian Midway Company, the northern unit of North American Midway Entertainment, in the summer of 2005, although its public banner continues to be Conklin Shows.

94. Waters, *History of Fairs*, 129.
95. Jones, *Midways, Judges,* 54.
96. Angus, "Key to the Midway."
97. William Lin, "Carnival Staff Walk Out Over Poor Conditions," *Edmonton Journal*, 31 July 2005.
98. Trish Audette, "Midway Operator's Violations 'Minor,'" *Edmonton Journal*, 3 August 2005.
99. Elise Stolte, "Long Hours Leave Midway Workers Barking," *Edmonton Journal*, 15 August 2006. Stolte states, "Employment Standards officers started working with the company earlier this month when they set up at the Calgary Stampede. When provincial officials looked at records ending July 14 [2006], they found midway employees had not been paid Alberta's $7-per-hour minimum wage or overtime pay, a minimum one and a half times the regular pay. On July 21, that was corrected and employees got back pay for their time in Alberta ... Officials will prosecute if the travelling company does not limit a worker's day top twelve hours." Interestingly, the *Calgary Herald* had no coverage of this issue from 2005 to 2007.
100. Brad Linn, "Overseas Workers Perk Up the Midway," *Calgary Herald*, 16 July 2006.

Special thanks from the author to Gregg "Scooter" Korek, Alfie Phillips, and the Honourable James H. Laycraft, Q.C., LL.D, for their valuable information and contributions to this chapter.

CHAPTER 6

More Than Partners:
The Calgary Stampede and the City of Calgary*

Max Foran

Victoria Park neighbourhood, 1977

* This article appeared in Urban History Review 34, no. 2 (2006): 30–42, and is reprinted with permission.

No one would dispute the powerful influence of the Stampede on Calgary.[1] Every July, a ten-day celebration of heritage, cowboy culture, and western mythology transforms an energetic corporate metropolis into a relaxed, fun-loving "Cowtown." A phenomenon unrivalled in the country in terms of global publicity, the Stampede also contributes significantly to Calgary's identifiable, if controversial, urban image. Given this important connection, it is surprising that so little is understood about the relationship between Calgary's civic government and the Stampede. Solid studies such as James H. Gray's *A Brand of Its Own: The 100 Year History of the Calgary Exhibition and Stampede* or more popular treatments such as Fred Kennedy's *Calgary Stampede: The Authentic History of the Calgary Exhibition and Stampede, "The Greatest Outdoor Show on Earth," 1912–1964* do not analyze this relationship. Others, such as Colin Campbell's "The Stampede: Cowtown's Sacred Cow," in *Stampede City: Politics and Power in the West*, reiterate a common, largely unsubstantiated view that the city is a pawn of elitist Stampede interests.[2] Even informed observers are unsure how the two corporate bodies actually interact.[3] In 1966 a spokesman for a group of concerned citizens said the Stampede Board was "some sort of quasi public body though no one is entirely sure."[4] In reality, discussion of the complex relationship between the City of Calgary and the Stampede falls historically into three broad categories: the powerful ties that have always bound them; their disagreements, which are less obvious; and their cultivation of a separateness that is more apparent than real. This popular perception has prejudiced the Stampede more than the City.

Background of the Stampede

Annual fairs and exhibitions were part of the European and North American historical experience. Their continuing importance today can be seen in the serious competition for world fairs and expositions. The German corporation Frankfurt Messe, for example, organizes over one hundred trade fairs a year throughout the world. In Canada, exhibitions historically filled a variety of needs. They enabled social interaction and provided important entertainment opportunities.[5] Through press coverage they advertised regional wealth and potential to the outside world. They also brought global products to specific audiences. Most significantly in terms of the host town or city, they were mediums for civic promotion or boosting, particularly during the early twentieth-century settlement boom.[6] Historian Paul Voisey notes how fairs "served the boosters' purpose" in Alberta small towns of that period.[7] While they varied in size and scope from blue-ribbon events such as the Royal Agricultural Winter Fair in Toronto and the Pacific National Exhibition in Vancouver to smaller regional and local fairs such as those in Brandon, High River, or Kelowna, the various exhibitions were uniform in their desire to cultivate a close identification with the cites and towns that hosted them. The Calgary Stampede, as one of Canada's major exhibitions, has been no exception to this rule.

Calgary's economy was based first on livestock and later on its ability to serve as the major distributing centre for rural south and south-central Alberta. In the modern era the city has added oil and natural gas extraction, tourism, and high-technology activity to its economic portfolio. The Stampede has been the primary vehicle by which these economic priorities were promoted and consolidated, a fact duly recognized and abetted by civic government.

The Calgary Stampede is also a festival in that it exports a cultural product with roots in the past and celebrates a specific localized perception of this heritage. The conscious deployment of cultural capital and the success of some cities in utilizing it has led to emulation and the rise of a festival industry. In short, cities worldwide, large and small, now seek to "sell" themselves by the deliberate manipulation of culture via festivals to enhance their appeal to tourists, potential investment capital, business interests, and affluent residents.[8] Successful cities have managed to brand themselves through identification with their annual festivals. To many, the names of cities such as Rio de Janeiro, New Orleans, and Munich are associated with Carnivale, Mardi Gras, and Oktoberfest, respectively. The same could be said for Calgary and the Stampede.

According to Harvey Molotch and John Logan, who studied the political economy of place, exhibitions and festivals are "growth engines." Their promotion and advancement are facilitated by a combination of specific interest groups that see mutual advantage in the attendant economic spinoffs.[9] In this context, civic governments continue to be particularly supportive of exhibitions and festivals, since they generate local spending, increase civic revenues, and offer employment opportunities. Mardi Gras, for example, is worth a billion dollars a year to the city of New Orleans. Japanese governments are anticipating that their focus on cultural extravaganzas such as the 1100-year-old Gion Festival in Kyoto will help boost tourist numbers to eight million by 2007. Each of the several events in Edinburgh's International Festival brings Scottish culture to an audience twice the size of the population of the city. In Canada, the Festival of Murals in Chemainus, British Columbia, has shown how a small town has managed to sell itself to tourists by giving the flagging lumber industry a high heritage profile. In 2003 the Calgary Stampede informed the public that for every dollar of revenue generated from Stampede activities, another $2.60 is spent elsewhere in the city.[10]

The Calgary Stampede owes its survival to the City of Calgary. In 1889 the federal government sold ninety-four acres in Victoria Park for $235 to the Calgary Agricultural Society for its Exhibition, with the stipulation that the land could not be subdivided into town lots.[11] The agricultural society subsequently mortgaged the land to build a race track, but in 1896, amid generally depressed conditions, it had to relinquish the mortgage to Canada Permanent Savings Company. Following a four-year hiatus in which no fall fair was held, several local businessmen formed the Inter-Western Pacific Exposition Company Limited to revive the Exhibition, Its first order of business was to petition the city to redeem the mortgage. In 1901, following negotiations with Richard Bedford Bennett acting for Canada Permanent Savings Company, the city took ownership of the exhibition grounds for the sum of $6,500.[12] For the next nine years the City of Calgary maintained the grounds and collected entrance and rental fees. Through lease arrangements in 1911, the Exhibition, now the Calgary Industrial Exhibition Company Limited, took over the management of the grounds.[13] In 1933 the name was changed to the Calgary Exhibition and Stampede Limited. Under this new title, the company assumed expanded powers under the Companies Act of Alberta (1929), except those limited by the lease. This situation has continued to the present day.

Given the fact that the city owns the land on which the Stampede operates and the fact the latter pays no property tax on land within its lease, it is not surprising that the two enjoy a unique relationship. On the one hand, the Stampede enjoys little political interference because it operates at arm's length from the city; on the other hand, the two are indistinguishable. One Stampede president went so far as to equate the Stampede with a city utility.[14] In 1965, when the Stampede was applying for city-owned land in Lincoln Park, prominent real estate man Kent Lyle wondered how the city could treat the Stampede like a private party. To Lyle, the application was misleading and even moot, since the Stampede and the city were one and the same.[15]

One has only to note the active presence of senior city officials within the Stampede organization. Not only the mayor and aldermen, but also the city commissioners and other high-level officials were often associate directors and/ or shareholders and sometimes occupied positions on the Stampede Board of Directors during their tenure of office. The current city manager, Owen Tobert, is both a Stampede shareholder and a senior associate. Moreover, city officials usually retained their Stampede positions after relinquishing their civic duties. Conflict of interest was not a problem for the city or Stampede; the public questioned the relationship between them only during the two expansion issues, and in both instances this was confined to the communities most affected by the expansion plans. In practical situations, neither thought it was necessary to keep at arm's length, as shown by a traffic access issue in 1960. In order for the city to "keep closely in touch with the Exhibition's plans," the Stampede agreed to make a city planner an associate director and then place him on its traffic committee. The same applied to Chief Commissioner John Steel, who was made an associate director so he could serve on the Stampede's grounds and development committee.[16] To both bodies, this represented neither collusion nor conflict of interest, but simply one agent of the city co-operating with another to effect better communication.

Another factor binding city officials to the Stampede was its high public profile. This was due in large part to its astonishing level of success in attracting wealthy and influential citizens to volunteer leadership positions. When Mayor J.W. Mitchell referred to arrangements for the 1912 Stampede as being "in the hands of our most wealthy citizens," he was articulating a pattern that was to be repeated over and over again.[17] Drawn from exclusive business, ranching, social, and civic circles, the list of committee chairmen and associate directors was a who's who of Calgary and area. For example in 1966–67 its directorship and committees boasted luminaries including Alberta Premier Peter Lougheed, Senator Harry Hays, prominent businessmen Max Bell and Carl Nickle, cattlemen Angus McKinnon and Don Matthews, and Justice M.M. Porter, to name just a few. The value of associating with such high-powered figures was not lost on city spokesmen. The aldermanic appointments to the Stampede Board provide a good case in point. Considered the "plums" of all appointed committees, they were hotly contested.[18] In one year the members of the committee charged with placing aldermen on committees came under attack in Council for assigning themselves to the Stampede Board.

The presence of well-known figures on the Stampede's board and committees attracted others like them. Four outcomes are discernible. In addition to elite recruitment, the Stampede moulded its leaders through its associate directorships and volunteer service, often making the point that the presidency could not be secured via influence or money. Second, these disparate but high-profile individuals were bound together through association and time by a firm belief in the Stampede's worthiness. Third, they in turn influenced the public to volunteer. Reinforced by a friendly press, this combination of elite recruitment, focused leadership, and broad citizen participation gave civic officials a host of reasons to support the Stampede. Finally, the prestige of its management bestowed an air of independence. To the public, the Stampede appeared more as a dynamic private organization than a subsidiary of the city, as witness the fact that many today believe the Exhibition and Stampede is a private corporation.[19]

The Stampede's success in cultivating an image of independence aroused periodic hostility within City Council. At times, aldermen challenged the Stampede's apparent indifference and high-handedness. In August 1943 Stampede President T.A. Hornibrook referred to relations between the two as warranting "a better understanding."[20] Civic departments sometimes voiced their displeasure when their budgets were affected by Council decisions relative to the Stampede. On rare occasions, a civic department made adverse recommendations.

Co-operation

Co-operation between the City of Calgary and the Stampede was rooted in the belief that the latter benefited the former commercially. In 1896 the Board of Trade wanted the city to buy the Exhibition grounds because a fair would encourage and promote business interests.[21] The impact of the Stampede on streetcar revenues in depressed times is a case in point: the Stampede pointedly informed the city that they were worth $25,008 between 1919 and 1921 and $1,136 during Stampede week alone in 1935. Persistent rhetoric had the same goal. According to Guy Weadick, the man behind the 1912 Stampede, the event was "a great scheme for the publicity and general welfare of Calgary."[22] In 1919 Stampede Manager Ernie Richardson proudly stated that Calgary benefitted from the Exhibition "to a considerable extent without any expense.[23] Stampede President C.M Baker noted in 1935 that the Stampede was "taking a long stride forward in the development of the city,"[24] and in 1972 a Stampede document argued that it was "difficult to understate the importance of the Stampede to the citizens of Calgary."[25]

City officials reciprocated with equal enthusiasm. In 1944 Mayor Andrew Davison said the Stampede had done more to advertise Calgary than any single agency. His successor three years later noted that the Stampede "has been part and parcel of the life of our city," and in 1948 referred to its value in advertising Calgary to all four corners of the continent.[26] The press was equally supportive. According to Robert Konrad's article "Barren Bulls and Charging Cows: Cowboy Celebrations in Copal and Calgary," the Stampede "has a recognized status as 'sacred cow' for the media."[27] This ongoing adulation has contributed to a widespread opinion that the Stampede was different from other entertainment and civic events and deserving of special consideration. It mattered not that that some thought the Stampede was not as good for business as popularly believed or that the tourist impact may not have been as great as the rhetoric indicated.[28] The city and the Stampede remained close partners in endorsing Ernie Richardson's prophetic words when in reference to the success of the 1923 Exhibition and Stampede, he said, "Calgary has found something the people want, something peculiarly appropriate to our environment,…and we only have to use our unique opportunities to the best advantage."[29]

The city has been generous with its leases to the Stampede. First, it extended their tenure. The 1911, 1916, and 1921 leases were for five years; they went to ten years in 1924, to thirty-two years in 1947, and to fifty years in 1960. Second, leases were renegotiated before their expiry date. The 1921 lease was renegotiated and extended in 1924 in response to a request by the Stampede for city support regarding insurance premiums. Financial issues also motivated later negotiations. When Crown Trust expressed nervousness about lending $500,000 to the Stampede for the construction of the Corral, the city amended its charter to allow the thirty-two year lease.[30] The fifty-year lease in 1960 was arranged through another amendment mainly for the same reasons. Third, lease provisions widened the powers of the Stampede. The 1960 lease is a good example, as it allowed the Stampede Board to acquire land not directly adjacent to the grounds. The purchase of the Stampede Ranch near Hanna was one result. The initial land acquisition for expansion purposes south and west was another. The 1960 lease also removed stipulations on the disbursement of surplus monies. Finally, it widened the Stampede's options with respect to sports franchises and subleasing the grounds.[31] In the mid-1970s when the lack of expropriation power prevented Stampede officials from completing house purchases in Victoria Park, the city amended the enabling agreement and did it for them.[32]

Money bylaws for capital and other projects were of inestimable value. Had the city not acquired the fairgrounds in 1901, the Inter-Western Pacific Exposition Company Limited might well have folded. Between 1902 and 1910 four money bylaws appropriated over $75,000 for grounds improvements.[33] In 1911 another bylaw for $55,000 was approved for a stock pavilion and horse barns. In 1914 ratepayers endorsed a substantial bylaw for $360,000 to construct a grandstand, barns, and sale pavilion and recon-figure the race track.[34] However, the largest single expenditure occurred in 1968 through a bylaw granting the Stampede Board four million dollars over twenty years for expansion purposes.

The city also furnished direct grants. Between 1908 and 1919 the Exhibition Board received over $73,000.[35] Considering the fact that the Exhibition lost money in more years than not during this period, the city grants were crucial to its survival. There would have been no Exhibition in 1915 if the city had not provided money.[36] Manager Ernie Richardson told the Exhibition Board in 1919 that he hoped "the Calgary Exhibition has now developed to such a stage that it will not be necessary to ask the city for an annual grant,"[37] yet as late as 1951, when the recent construction of the Corral caused a shortfall, the Stampede Board again approached the city for financial help.[38]

The city helped the Stampede financially in other ways. It used its favour-able credit rating to secure low-interest loans and pass on substantial interest savings to the Stampede. The Dominion Works Programme on the Exhibition Grounds in 1939 was enabled by a $46,950 loan at 2 percent interest secured by the city for the Stampede.[39] In 1977 the Stampede saved over $100,000 in interest payments when the city borrowed money from the province at 8 percent and used it to defray a Stampede bank loan held at 11.25 percent. The city also set up lower interest financing for capital projects through the Alberta Municipal Financing Corporation[40] and lent $700,000 in 1976 at lower than bank interest rates so the Stampede could construct the necessary green space buffer between its expansion boundaries and the rest of Victoria Park.[41] In 1978 the city secured a grant for which the Stampede was ineligible and passed it on to the board to allow the construction of the Jaycees infield park.[42] Even when the city made the Exhibition Company pay insurance after 1921, it still provided a credit line of $6,000 in case of default, and for a time in the 1930s re-assumed the cost of the premiums. In 1975 it contributed $25,000 towards a study by Stanford Research Institute that ultimately led to a Stampede Master Plan.[43] With Stampede expansion infringing on the Victoria Park Community Centre in 1975, the city paid $65,000 for its relocation.[44] In 1950 the city took over responsibility for erecting the street decorations. Eleven years later it was persuaded to increase its financial contribution from $4,000 to $5,500, and in 1979 agreed to assume half the cost of the decorations or $100,000 over a five-year period.[45]

Co-operation occurred in less significant areas. In 1956 the city acquired the Sunshine Auto Court east of the Elbow River for the reasonable sum of $45,000 and then passed it on to the Stampede at the same price.[46] A potential buyer and member of the Stampede Board backed off so as not to prejudice the transaction.[47] Whether it be oiling thoroughfares and installing fire alarm boxes inside the grounds, erecting bandstands or supplying building materials, buying advertising space in a promotional brochure, allowing paid public parking on recreation areas during Stampede, lending fowl from the zoo for poultry exhibitions, or even tolerating construction "non-conformities," the City of Calgary was a ubiquitous presence in Stampede activities.[48]

The Stampede reciprocated, generally making its buildings, equipment, and manager available upon request by the city. In the First World War the grounds housed Canadian troops. Stampede buildings served as an isolation hospital in 1921, and a shelter and kitchen for the unemployed in 1932 and the On-to-Ottawa trekkers in 1935. During the Second World War, the Provincial Institute of Technology and Art relocated some of its classrooms there. In the early years, the Exhibition acted as the city's agent in preparing civic exhibits for other fairs in western Canada. Over the years, the Stampede became a focal point for organized sports, and it was a pioneer in encouraging competitive hockey in the city. Currently, the Stampede Foundation supports several local community youth and education groups.

Tensions

Despite their generally positive relationship, the city and the Stampede have had their issues. First, the elitist nature of the Stampede Board rankled aldermen whose frequent requests for financial statistics indicated critical interest. Sometimes these questions amounted to direct challenges. Furthermore, the presence of city-operated facilities on the Exhibition grounds was contentious and ultimately of financial cost to the Stampede. The most serious issue, however, was related to Lincoln Park.

The assumption that what was good for the Stampede was also good for the city aroused periodic hostility. Some aldermen and certainly segments of the public in proposed Stampede expansion areas saw the Stampede Board as an elitist, inconsiderate group indifferent to alternative opinion and not averse to browbeating the city. For example, in spite of a public vote endorsing another name for the Corral in 1951, the Stampede Board stood firm.[49] In 1932 a labour newspaper called for a campaign to "get the parasites [Stampede] off taxpayers' property."[50] Accusations of connivance were not uncommon.[51] The notion of an "Old Boys Club" wielding enormous and indiscriminate leverage was exacerbated in City Council by the Stampede Board's admitted secrecy and lack of community consultation. For example, during the Lincoln Park issue one alderman felt that "the Board was controlled by a group of influential rich men who moved in exclusive circles." Another thought the board was not close enough to the people.[52] Mayor Rodney Sykes' executive secretary wrote in 1974 that the Stampede Board "was inclined to do as it wants."[53] This perceived elitism polarized Council on sensitive issues. The Lincoln Park and Victoria Park expansion controversies are excellent cases in point.

An early confrontation set the stage for future dialogue. In 1911 the city audited the Exhibition Company's books as a condition of its annual $5,000 grant. The subsequent report documented laxity and improper accounting procedures. Some aldermen on City Council were incensed and called the Exhibition's management practices into question. In angrily refuting these allegations, General Manager Ernie Richardson attacked his accusers for their lack of experience or knowledge about running an Exhibition.[54] The critics fell silent and a precedent was set. Henceforth, the Exhibition and Stampede was to broach little interference by the city.

Another civic attack on the Stampede in 1943 was linked to projected spending on an artificial ice rink operation that had been sublet in the arena on the grounds. On August 12 Stampede General Manager Charles Yule approached Council requesting a ten-year extension on the current lease, which was due to expire in November. Yule argued that additional security of tenure was warranted before $6,000 was expended on improving the heating facilities in the arena where the ice rink was located.[55] A day later the city commissioners endorsed Yule's request. On August 16, when the issue was brought to Council, Alderman W.G. Southern, a former Council representative on the Stampede Board, requested an audit of the Stampede books. Furthermore, by querying the city's right to negotiate a lease at all, let alone at a nominal cost, Southern essentially called the Stampede's right to exist into question.[56] Southern likely was incensed that the Stampede intended to profit by subleasing what was essentially city property, yet according to a fellow alderman, Southern had little knowledge of Stampede activities and had attended only two meetings in four years.[57] A stunned Council complied by ordering a complete external audit and asked the city solicitor to advise it on the legal questions.

On August 20 the city solicitor upheld the existing leasing arrangements but cautioned that under its present terms the lease could not be terminated before expiry except by mutual consent.[58] A week later an extensive audit revealed no irregularities in the Stampede's books.[59] Southern then countered with a suggestion that the Stampede pay $20,000 a year rent, an amount roughly commensurate with the annual interest the city was paying on the capital debt on the Stampede buildings.[60] Matters came to a head on September 8 during a meeting between the Stampede Board and City Council's Legislative Committee. The board had complied willingly with the audit request but balked at paying a $20,000 annual levy on a new lease. Threatening to abandon the Stampede altogether, President T.A. Hornibrook informed the committee, "Our board has reached a stage where it is prepared to quit right now and you can have it like that if you wish."[61]

Faced with this ultimatum, Council opted to save face. Though it agreed in principle to renewing the lease under existing arrangements, it also insisted on some modifications. In a new ten-year lease approved by a narrow 6 to 4 vote on December 20, 1943, the Stampede Board agreed to an increase in Council representation on its executive board from one to two, and to a clause that specified conditions by which a lease could be terminated before its expiry date. In the Stampede Finance Committee's annual report released in November, E.D. Adams adopted a familiar refrain in censuring the city:

> It is to be hoped that City Council while conducting the
> affairs of the city will allow the directors of the Stampede
> to continue their efforts without undue hindrance bearing
> in mind that the Stampede is only a voluntary company
> and that all its shareholders have but one thought in mind
> – to work for the good of the community, and spend what
> money they are fortunate to earn to be of benefit to the
> City of Calgary and the community at large.[62]

Self-righteousness and the emphasis on its voluntary and therefore unimpeachable intentions were the Stampede Board's main weapons whenever its motives were called into question.

An ongoing area of contention between the Stampede Board and the City of Calgary concerned the location of non-exhibition facilities on the fairgrounds. Over time, the city had appropriated about seven acres in the designated exhibition grounds for storage, a power house, and streetcar barns. The Exhibition had sought a legal opinion on this non-exhibition use in 1912 but was informed by Richard Bedford Bennett that the city's actions were within its power even though they might be "contrary to the spirit of the patent."[63] By the 1940s the Stampede had a facility-space problem. Following extensive and not always progressive dialogue, the city agreed to give up the space, but not without a price. It cost the Stampede $50,000 to move the streetcar barns to Eau Claire in 1948.[64] Ten years later the Stampede had to agree to pay the city a further $100,000 to free up the remaining space.[65] The idea of making the Stampede pay for land that was originally part of the lease runs counter to the usual co-operation extended by the city. In all likelihood, the civic departments affected wanted to offset the costs of replacing the facilities.

The Lincoln Park Issue

The failure of the Stampede's Lincoln Park expansion proposal in 1964–65 was its greatest setback at the hands of the city. The extension of the Stampede from seven to nine days in 1966 and to ten days a year later was a direct response to this failure and to the need to accommodate more people on the grounds. For the city, it was a matter of weighing economic, financial, and political odds. In this balancing act, the Stampede emerged as a minor player. Also, by this time, the city also had other relocation ideas for its favourite child.

In December 1963 federal Minister of Defence Paul Hellyer announced in the House of Commons that the government was downsizing its Royal Canadian Air Force facilities across the country. Calgary's Lincoln Park was one of the casualties. By July 1964 Council had decided to accept the federal government's offer of first choice on the 426 acres located in the Lakeview district in the city's southwest. Originally, the city wanted to maintain the facility as a municipal airport. In September, after the Department of Transport declined to operate the proposed airport, the city entertained vague notions of converting the land into a residential area and light industrial complex.[66] When Mayor Grant MacEwan and Chief Commissioner John Steel negotiated a price of $750,000 for the purchase of the land, the Stampede seized what it thought was a golden opportunity.[67] On October 23 it gave notice that it was prepared to buy Lincoln Park for the city and relocate its operations there. It even enclosed a $75,000 cheque as a down payment.[68]

Though this move was sudden and unexpected, the Stampede had already been influenced by prior civic action. By the 1950s the most serious problem facing the Stampede was a lack of space on the grounds.[69] Correspondence between the board and commissioners indicated clearly that the former expected the city to furnish a solution either by providing a new site elsewhere or by allowing expansion in its present location. It was also equally obvious by 1960 that the city preferred the second solution. Commissioner Steel made this quite clear during a meeting in March with Stampede officials.[70]

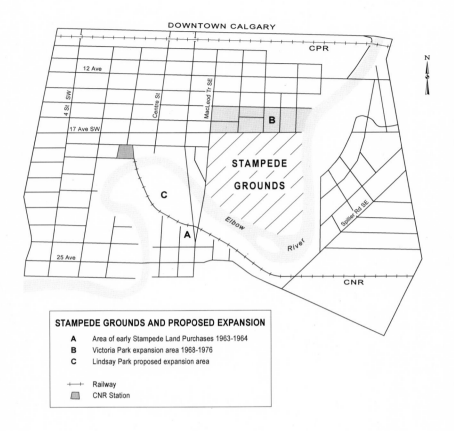

STAMPEDE GROUNDS AND PROPOSED EXPANSION

A   Area of early Stampede Land Purchases 1963-1964
B   Victoria Park expansion area 1968-1976
C   Lindsay Park proposed expansion area

┼─┼─┼   Railway
▨   CNR Station

Using its expanded powers under the 1960 lease agreement and a half-million dollar bank loan, the Stampede began acquiring properties in nearby Lindsay Park to the south and west of the grounds in the spring of 1963.[71] This program stalled for three reasons. One was the high price asked by the largest landowner, Canadian National Railway. Difficulties also arose over the feasibility of diverting the Elbow River that snaked through the area. However, the most formidable obstacle was raised when John Steel told the Stampede Board the city was not prepared to consolidate the land parcel by effecting the necessary street closures.[72] Only hours after hearing this news the Stampede opted for Lincoln Park.

The Stampede's offer was received favourably by the city commissioners, who recommended the purchase of Lincoln Park to Council.[73] The aldermen, however, were not so sanguine. Instead, Council took the prudent route and ordered its Planning Department to undertake a study on the future of Lincoln Park. The $75,000 cheque was returned.[74] The Stampede took its own precautions by hiring a consultant to prepare its brief to Council and to assess the feasibility of other sites.[75]

Public reaction was quick and vehement. The October 26 meeting of City Council faced an audience of 150 unhappy Lakeview residents whose noisy interjections almost caused Mayor Grant MacEwan to clear the chamber.[76] In addition to threatening legal action if the Stampede were allowed to relocate

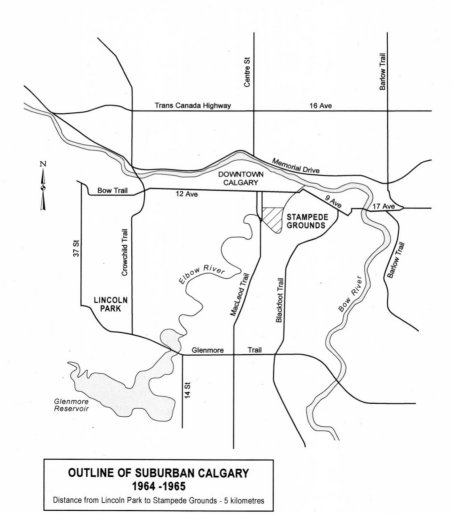

OUTLINE OF SUBURBAN CALGARY
1964 -1965

Distance from Lincoln Park to Stampede Grounds - 5 kilometres in Lincoln Park, the Lakeview Community Association protested everything from odours and traffic congestion to water problems and falling land prices. Also, other parties soon expressed their interest. ATCO Industries was prepared to pay $750,000 for only one hundred acres. Robin-Nodwell wanted thirty-seven acres for a tracked-vehicle plant. Developers interested in a shopping complex offered over two million dollars. Mount Royal Community College saw Lincoln Park as a possible site for its relocation. In all, twenty-three applications were received for property parcels including two museums and a Bible college.

The Stampede's cause was not helped by a bitter controversy within Council. Since all four aldermen on the Stampede Board had voted in favour of the proposal, they were excluded from voting or even discussing the issue in Council. George Ho Lem and Ernie Starr sought a judicial declaration that they were not disqualified under the City Act from voting on "questions affecting a company of which they are directors." Under an injunction granted on May 17, 1965, Council debate on the subject was suspended pending a decision. The issue went to trial after the city tried unsuccessfully to challenge the injunction. The judge's ruling on June 10 upholding the city's decision to exclude the aldermen from voting came just a few days before the release of the Lincoln Park study.[77] The Stampede Board could not have been happy with the publicity; the trial proceedings revealed that both aldermen had been shareholders as well as directors.

Nevertheless, the Stampede pressed its case in a spirited campaign. In a brief to City Council in late March it unveiled detailed and grandiose plans for the new facilities at Lincoln Park. It also lobbied heavily for public support. The $45,000 spent on advertising was accompanied by radio broadcasts and the first phone-in television show in Calgary.[78] President Don Matthews and several directors toured the affected communities in an effort to make their case personally.[79] These measures, however, were countered by mounting public opposition and demonstrations. With the tide turning, the Stampede tried to convince Mount Royal College of the advantages of relocating in Victoria Park rather than in Lincoln Park. During a series of secret meetings, Stampede officials focused on the college's interest in remaining in the downtown area and intimated that the province might be willing to provide 90 percent of the cost or $5.4 million to relocate the college there.[80]

The Lincoln Park Report was released on June 16. Of the four proposals considered, the Stampede's was ranked last.[81] The report recommended that the land be given over to housing, high-rise apartments, ATCO Industries, Mount Royal College, and other public facilities. As for the Stampede, the report noted, "It is the least compatible. It yields much less direct benefit to the city than all the other alternatives and carries with it the smallest economic benefit to the city at large." Also revealed was the city's preference for future Stampede expansion. According to the report, Stampede needs would be best served through expansion "in contiguous areas – perhaps in conjunction with pending urban renewal plans."[82]

Why did the Stampede lose Lincoln Park? To many civic administrators, moving the Stampede there seemed like a logical solution to a vexatious problem. City engineers thought the site was suitable in terms of access and discounted claims that water contamination was a possibility. Despite all its promotion, the Stampede must take a share of the blame. Perhaps its greatest mistake was in expecting recompense from the city. Estimating that a successful bid would mean abandoning land and facilities in Victoria Park worth six million dollars, the Stampede Board unwisely suggested that the city provide the money. Some aldermen, not understanding the Lindsay Park situation, thought the Stampede's bid was too sudden. Others saw it as self-serving and arrogant. Lakeview residents resented "rich men flexing their muscles." Knowing the importance of the issue, the Stampede Board should have avoided all taint by excusing the aldermen from discussions. It also did little to counter suggestions for alternative sites. No clear case was laid before the public giving the reasons why other possibilities had already been considered and rejected.

But even considering the above, politics and the lure of potential revenue worked against the Stampede. It made little political sense to anger a well-organized, articulate, middle-class neighbourhood. More likely, however, financial considerations doomed the Stampede's proposal. Set against the Stampede's bid of $750,000 for tax-free land, the prospect of receiving three million dollars in land sales and substantial annual taxes was simply too much to resist.

For the first time, the Stampede had failed to advance its interests with the city on a major issue. It was a bitter blow, as evidenced by its president, Don Matthews, who equated the Planning Department's report with the end of the Stampede. The board of directors met on June 20 to consider a response. Amid practical comments such as "We should bow out gracefully" and "It would be futile to continue," the Stampede Board decided to abandon its interest in Lincoln Park.[83] This was seen by the press as a generous gesture since, in effect, it reinstated the voting powers of the four aldermen and enabled a truly representative Council to adopt the Planning Department's recommendation.[84]

The failure to secure Lincoln Park necessitated a change in the Stampede's strategy. Given its consultant's report that Lincoln Park was the only suitable outside site, the Stampede redirected its focus to its existing premises.[85] In the fall of 1965 the Stampede reopened negotiations on a Lindsay Park site but was thwarted by city traffic plans that effectively isolated it from the existing grounds. In December 1965 the Stampede Sites Committee reported to the Executive Committee that the only viable solution lay in rapid transit from outlying parking reserves.[86] But when it also mentioned that expansion north was "a partial solution," the focus began to shift to an entirely new debate.

Victoria Park

Between 1968 and 1976 the Stampede acquired eight blocks in residential Victoria Park directly north of the grounds. This marked the beginning of the end for this older working-class neighbourhood. The intrusion into a deteriorating yet well-established community aroused spirited opposition from residents who did not want to leave. The Victoria Park expansion issue provides the best single example of the complex relationship between the Stampede and the city. Co-operation, antagonism, and distance were all observable in this emotional and protracted public issue.

Following the Lincoln Park setback, the Stampede began pressuring the city for a solution to its space problems. By 1967 expansion on the existing site was an accepted fact. In an astounding move in March 1968, the city commissioners asked the four aldermen on the Stampede Board to settle the future of the area "for once and for all."[87] Their subsequent recommendation to allow the Stampede to expand into residential Victoria Park was accepted by the commissioners and endorsed by Council. Under an agreement reached in July 1968, the city provided four million dollars at $400,000 a year to the Stampede to enable the purchase of eight blocks east of Macleod Trail between Seventeenth Avenue and Fourteenth Avenue in Victoria Park.[88] The agreement also contained alternative accommodation provisions for displaced tenants who were allowed to remain in the purchased houses until they were ready for demolition, which was to occur by block and not until most of the land was in the hands of the Stampede. The city was to approve all purchases and retain the title to all acquired lands. Later, when a few stalwart residents refused to sell, the 1968 agreement was amended to allow the city to use expropriation where necessary.[89]

Land acquisition was a protracted and painful process. It took over seven years for the 229 properties to be acquired. In 1976 the former home to twelve hundred people was a jumble of ruined empty spaces interspersed with dilapidated houses awaiting demolition. Across Fourteenth Avenue to the north the deterioration extended to the rest of Victoria Park.[90] Most residents were convinced that it was only a matter of time before the same fate awaited them. [91] Caught in the limbo of uncertainty, many sold out to speculators who offered low rent and little maintenance. All in all, it was grim evidence of a partnership process dedicated solely to property acquisition.

The election in 1969 of an antagonistic mayor inflamed the conflicts between the Stampede and the city, causing delays and internecine strife. Rodney Sykes blamed the Stampede Board for its cavalier attitude towards powerless residents and City Council for its endorsement. Noting that he got little support from Council, Sykes aligned himself with the Victoria Park citizens' group in an attempt to halt the land purchases. His failure to influence any change was due in large part to a confrontational style and abrasive personality that alienated many aldermen and civic administrators.[92] The Planning Department also opposed the expansion. A study released in 1971 recommended abandoning the entire expansion project in favour of other options,[93] but Council ignored that study and a subsequent report in 1974 that recommended extensive rehabilitation outside the expansion zone as a way of preserving Victoria Park from further encroachment by the Stampede.[94]

Unarguably, the Stampede was partly responsible for the destruction of Victoria Park. It could have gone elsewhere. Lincoln Park was not the only outside solution. In 1967, for example, the board of directors gave scant consideration to a proposal to relocate in the recreational area of Happy Valley on the western fringe of the city.[95] The lack of a master plan meant that the Stampede had moved to destroy a community without forethought. The fact that expansion was linked primarily to parking was a major irritant.[96] As it was, the present grounds were largely empty except during the Stampede and the board had to defend the validity of turning a residential neighbourhood into a parking lot while already possessing abundant underutilized parking space. According to the citizens' committee formed to fight the expansion, the Stampede had acted pre-emptively and was unconcerned about offering market prices for the houses instead of replacement value. The committee described the Stampede Board as confrontational and accused it of using "block busting" and intimidation tactics to force residents from their homes.[97] It also alleged that acquired houses were poorly maintained and allowed to deteriorate so people would be encouraged to move.[98]

However, the city was more responsible than the Stampede for the fate of Victoria Park. It had favoured a northerly expansion as early as 1960. In a meeting with the Stampede, Commissioner John Steel referred to Victoria Park as "a depressed residential area" and suggested a northerly expansion from Seventeenth Avenue all the way to Twelfth Avenue.[99] By 1965 the city was clearly bent on amalgamating the Stampede expansion plans with large-scale redevelopment of Victoria Park under urban renewal. A 1965 land-use map of the city slated all of Victoria Park for redevelopment. The Stampede did not mention Victoria Park as a possible expansion area until late 1965, and even then referred specifically to this as a city decision. It was only when the federal and provincial governments proved less than enthusiastic about urban renewal for Victoria Park that the city forced its hurried solution.[100] Furthermore, the city's lack of a consistent long-range vision for Victoria Park made it virtually impossible to protect the rest of the community in the post-expansion phase. The city's first general plan in 1963 made no provision for the central area. The 1970 plan implicitly recognized the Stampede Board's encroachment.[101] An updated plan released in 1973 specifically stated that expansion would not be allowed north of Fourteenth Avenue,[102] yet in a map accompanying a further update in 1977, the whole of Victoria Park had been given over to the Stampede.[103] The area's integrity was threatened by other civic policies that included a commitment to redevelopment rather than rehabilitation in spite of contrary recommendations.[104] The proposed light-rail transit system through the community was another potential dividing influence.

The Victoria Park issue concerned the reversion of private land to the city and a civic decision to deploy it in the Stampede's interests. In short, it was an initiative conceived and sanctioned by the city but executed by the Stampede, and the bulk of the public criticism fell on the latter. The Stampede, rather than the city, was generally perceived as the architect of residential ruin. That the city had had plans for a northerly expansion since 1960 did not figure in the public debate. Neither did the city's original proposal to absorb the entire community. The public was not aware of the haphazard decision-making process nor of the dereliction of duty by the city commissioners. As with Lincoln Park, the city was quite prepared to treat the Stampede as a private body instead of a junior partner. Interestingly, the Stampede made no effort to shift the burden of blame to the city. Given its elitist nature, it probably preferred "to take the heat" rather than admit chattel status.

Though not acknowledged at the time, the Stampede's expansion into Victoria Park also sealed the future of the rest of the neighbourhood. By 1998 the rest of Victoria Park up to Twelfth Avenue had fallen into the Stampede's hands. Despite an effort to rehabilitate the area in the late 1970s, the city's reversal of policy in allowing the Olympic Saddledome to be constructed there in 1982 marked the beginning of the end for this small low-rent community. The city's subsequent indecisiveness, combined with the Stampede's aggressive (and secret) $12 million land purchase program in 1987–88 allowed the area to lapse to the Stampede almost by default. In August 2004 the Stampede announced a $500 million plan to "transform Stampede Park into a 193 acre multi use community park zoned with entertainment, educational, discovery, exhibition and agricultural facilities."[105] There was no mention of housing. Though a few people still occupy crumbling dwellings and small apartments, East Victoria Park now awaits demolition.[106] The presence of a few neat, well-kept, attractive houses is a poignant reminder of what might have been.

Conclusions

Several broad conclusions follow from this discussion. First, it is undeniable that the Stampede's huge success in "selling" the city was due in large part to the co-operation it received from city hall. However, the fact that the Stampede was able to operate at arm's length from the city when it came to policy making allowed it freedom and flexibility not enjoyed by similar institutions. For example, the structure of the Edmonton Exhibition made it far more susceptible to political interference.

Though it could easily have done so through lease provisions, the city has never used its position to change Stampede priorities or practices, especially with respect to minority groups. Does the Stampede consciously freeze First Nations in time in the interests of tourists?[107] First Nations participants were asked not to wear glasses during the 1968 parade.[108] Do ethnic groups and women have restricted access to the portals of power within the Stampede? The first time a woman was elected to the board of directors or invited to the annual Stampede president's luncheon was in 1979.[109] As late as 1995, only one woman sat on the board of directors. Did the interests of property and the Stampede count more than those of the poor and disadvantaged in Victoria Park? Though it could be argued that the Stampede is now responding to criticism, the city's silence speaks volumes.

Calgary's "Cowtown" image, for good or bad, is closely linked to the Stampede. Through its support, the city has consciously endorsed this image. During the years of rapid growth between 1950 and 1970, Mayor Don Mackay was the Stampede's best publicity agent. His folksy correspondence with mayors and politicians in Canada and the United States was full of Stampede and western allusions. Other mayors in this period, such as Harry Hays, cattleman and founder of the popular Hays Stampede breakfast; Grant MacEwan, agriculturalist and widely-read western author; and home-grown Jack Leslie, grew up with horses and publicly advertised their strong identification with the western spirit. The civic support behind business participation in Stampede activities, the half-day civic holiday, and the willingness to adopt western civic symbols were all linked to a desire to support not only the Stampede, but also the image it was trying to promote.

The Stampede's board of directors and its associate directors are an impressive aggregation of local business and social elites. Their ongoing interaction has produced a powerful coalition of interests, influence, and ideology that has advertised and even branded the city. The ideological dimension has particular relevance to the ranching and oil and gas industries. Each has always been interested in the other. Ranchers have been inveterate investors in the oil and gas industry, while the oilmen have always nurtured an ongoing fascination with ranching and the outdoor western ethos it embodies. The Stampede provides an urban forum in which these two ideologically compatible groups can work together and with the city to serve the "common interest." In this sense, the civic emblem of the white Stetson hat may have more validity than popularly imagined, although it is not the cowboy who is wearing it – it is the rancher, and by extension his ideological counterpart, the oilman.

Notes

1. In the interests of brevity, the word "Stampede" is used throughout this discussion to refer to the Calgary Exhibition and Stampede. It also the most common term used to identify the Exhibition and Stampede. Indeed, the word "Exhibition" was recently dropped from the Stampede's logo.

2. See Colin S. Campbell, "The Stampede: Cowtown's Sacred Cow," in *Stampede City: Power and Politics in the West,* ed. Chuck Reasons (Toronto: Between the Lines, 1984),103–20.

3. Rebecca Aizenman, a vociferous opponent of Stampede expansion in Victoria Park, wrote a long letter to the city asking for clarification on the relationship between the two.

4. Notes of Citizens' Meeting, Victoria Park, 4 December 1966, Board of Commissioners Papers, series V, box 262, file folder 7200, City of Calgary Archives (CCA).

5. See Faye Reineberg Holt, *Awed, Amused and Alarmed: Fairs, Rodeos and Regattas in Western Canada* (Calgary: Detselig Enterprises, 2003).

6. Alan F.J. Artibise, "Boosterism and the Development of Prairie Cities, 1871–1913," in *Town and City: Aspects of Western Canadian Urban Development*, ed. Alan F.J. Artibise (Regina: Canadian Plains Research Center, 1981), 209–35.

7. Paul Voisey, "Boosting the Small Prairie Town, 1904–1933: An Example from Southern Alberta," in *Town and City: Aspects of Western Canadian Urban Development*, ed. Alan F.J. Artibise (Regina: Canadian Plains Research Center, 1981), 154–55.

8. Gerry Kearns and Chris Philo, eds., *Selling Places: The City as Cultural Capital, Past and Present* (Oxford: Pergamon Press, 1993); Philip Kotler, Donald H. Haider, and Irving Rein, *Marketing Places: Attracting Investment, Industry and Tourism to Cities, States, and Nations* (Toronto: Maxwell Macmillan Canada,1993).

9. John R. Logan and Harvey Molotch, *Urban Fortunes: The Political Economy of Place* (Berkeley: University of California Press, 1987).

10. See Calgary Stampede's *2003 Report to the Community.* Tourist spending in Calgary in 2003 was estimated at around $900 million. In 2003 the Stampede's 1,500 permanent and part-time employees and 2,000 volunteers managed 450 events in Stampede Park and participated in numerous other community programs.

11. For good treatment of the early years, see Linda Christine English, "The Calgary Exhibition and Stampedes: Culture, Context and Controversy, 1884–1920," (M.A. thesis, Department of History, University of Calgary, 1999).

12. City Clerk's Correspondence, box 3, file folder 27; box 4, file folder 36, CCA.
13. Ernie Richardson to City Commissioners, 12 November 1910, City Clerk's Correspondence, box 35, file folder 272.
14. Stampede President to City Commissioners, 8 October 1946, Board of Commissioners Papers, series IV, box 48, file folder E-1.
15. Lincoln Park Expansion, Board Submissions, correspondence dated 30 April 1965, Board of Commissioners Papers, series V, box 84, file folder 4100.1.
16. Minutes of a Meeting Held at City Hall, 14 March 1960, Board of Commissioners Papers, series V, box 22, file folder 175.
17. Mayor J.W. Mitchell to E.A. Cruickshank, Commander Military District #13, 26 June 1912, City Clerk's Correspondence, box 50, file folder 403.
18. "Stampede Board Postings Spark First Bitterness on New Council," *Calgary Herald*, 20 October 1964.
19. Private poll taken by author in the summer of 2004. Well over one-third of those polled believed that the Stampede was a private operation.
20. T.A. Hornibrook to Mayor Andrew Davison, 20 August 1943, City of Calgary Papers, box 8, file folder 44, CCA.
21. City of Calgary Papers, box 15, file folder 19.
22. Guy Weadick to Mayor J. Mitchell, 13 June 1912, City Clerk's Correspondence, box 50, file folder 403.
23. Ernie Richardson to Mayor R.C. Marshall, 18 August 1919, Board of Commissioners Papers, series I, box 89, file folder M-S, April–December 1919.
24. C.M. Baker, President, to E.A. Hookway, City Comptroller, 26 February 1935, City of Calgary Papers, box 29, file folder 277.
25. "Stampede: A Proposal for Long Range Development," Board of Commissioners Papers, series VI, box 71, file folder Calgary Exhibition Board 1972, file 1 of 2.
26. Board of Commissioners Papers, series III, box 13, file folder E-1, Stampede 1945–49.
27. Robert Konrad, "Barren Bulls and Charging Cows: Cowboy Celebrations in Copal and Calgary," in *The Celebration of Society: Perspectives on Contemporary Performance*, ed. Frank Manning (Bowling Green: Bowling Green State University Press, 1983), 161.
28. Letter to Mayor, 17 July 1928, Calgary Exhibition and Stampede Fonds, box 2, file folder 5, Glenbow Museum Archives (hereafter cited as GMA).
29. Minutes of the Calgary Industrial Exhibition Co. Ltd., 26 September 1923, Calgary Exhibition and Stampede Fonds, box 1, GMA. To be fair to Richardson, it should be added that he always equated the value of the Stampede with its success in advertising and coalescing the agriculture and livestock industries.

30. Board of Commissioners Papers, series IV, box 21, file folder 1 of 2, Calgary Exhibition and Stampede 1953–59.

31. City Solicitor's Office to Commissioner Dudley E. Batchelor, 23 May 1958, Board of Commissioners Papers, series IV, box 21, file folder 1 of 2, Calgary Exhibition Board 1953–59.

32. Board of Commissioners Papers, series VI, box 72, file folder Calgary Exhibition Board 1975. The 1968 expansion agreement with the city was amended to allow the city to assume the direct responsibility for securing the remaining land in the area effective 5 October 1975.

33. Board of Commissioners Papers, series I, box 18, file folder General Correspondence, Jan.–June, A-D, 1911.

34. Minutes of the Calgary Industrial Exhibition Co. Ltd., Discussion on the Exhibition Bylaw 1632, 28 August 1913, Calgary Exhibition and Stampede Fonds, box 1, GMA. Due to wartime conditions the first bonds on the bylaw could not be sold until after the war.

35. "Stampede Limited, Examination of Accounts to Mayor and Council of the Corporation of the City of Calgary," Henderson, Teare and Waines, Chartered Accountants, 26 August 1943, City Clerk Files, box 339, file folder 2207, CCA.

36. Minutes of the Calgary Industrial Exhibition Co. Ltd., 22 January 1915, Calgary Exhibition and Stampede Fonds, box 1, GMA.

37. Ibid., 20 October 1919.

38. Charles Yule, Managing Director, to Mayor Don Mackay, 2 June 1951, Board of Commissioners Papers, series IV, box 48, file folder E-1.

39. Annual Report, 1939, Calgary Exhibition and Stampede Fonds, box 2.

40. Board of Commissioners Papers, series VI, box 73, file folder Stampede Board 1980.

41. Board of Commissioners Papers, series VI, box 72, file folder Stampede Board 1976.

42. Ibid., file folder Stampede Board 1978.

43. Board of Commissioners Papers, series VI, box 73, file folder Calgary Exhibition Board 1978.

44. City Council Motion, 17 December 1975, City Planning and Building Department, series VIII, box 17413, file folder Victoria Park 1976, CCA.

45. Correspondence dated 26 May 1961, Board of Commissioners Papers, series V, box 22, file folder 175; City Council Minutes, 5 April 1979, Board of Commissioners Papers, series VI, box 73, file folder Stampede Board 1979.

46. Correspondence dated 2 May 1955, Board of Commissioners Papers, series IV, box 48, file folder E-1 1954–55.

47. Correspondence dated 9 March 1955, Board of Commissioners Papers, series IV, box 48, file folder E-1 1954–55.

48. The "non-conformities" concerned extensions to the grandstand in 1967. See correspondence of L.S. Walker, Chief Building Inspector, to Commissioner Ivor Strong, 9 November 1967, Board of Commissioners Papers, series V, box 22, file folder 125.

49. Maurice Brown to J.B. Cross, President, Calgary Exhibition and Stampede, 11 January 1951; Mayor Don Mackay to Maurice L. Brown, 18 January 1951, Board of Commissioners Papers, series IV, box 48, file folder E-1.

50. "Exhibition-Stampede Racket Flourishes at Expense of Taxpayers," *Spokesman* (Calgary), 13 July 1932.

51. Correspondence dated 21 March 1947, Board of Commissioners Papers, series III, box 13, file folder E-1.

52. Civic and Stampede Dinner Meeting, Fort Calgary House, 10 November 1964, Board of Commissioners Papers, series V, box 84, file folder 4100.1.

53. Correspondence by Andrew Marshall, 20 August 1974, Rod Sykes Fonds RG 2 33.20, file folder 406, CCA.

54. Minutes of the Calgary Industrial Exhibition Co. Ltd., 26, 27 November 1911, Calgary Exhibition and Stampede Fonds, box 1, GMA; also *Morning Albertan*, 27 November 1911.

55. Charles Yule to Mayor Andrew Davison, 12 August 1943, City of Calgary Papers, box 8, file folder 45.

56. City Council Minutes, 16 August 1943, Board of Commissioners Papers, series V, box 84, file folder 4100.1, CCA.

57. "Suggest $20,000 Fair Board Lease," *Calgary Herald*, 31 August 1943.

58. City Solicitor T.W. Collings to Mayor and Council, 20 August 1943, City of Calgary Papers, box 8, file folder 45.

59. "Stampede Limited. Report on Examination of Accounts to Mayor and Council of the Corporation of the City of Calgary," Henderson Teares and Waines, 26 August 1943, City Clerk Files, box 339, file folder 2207.

60. "Aldermen Probing Fair Board Rink," *Calgary Herald*, 17 August 1943; "Suggests $20,000 Fair Board Lease," *Calgary Herald*, 31 August 1943.

61. "Fair Directors Ready to Quit," *Calgary Herald*, 8 September 1943.

62. Finance Director's Report, Annual Report, 1943. Calgary Exhibition and Stampede Fonds, box 2.

63. R.B. Bennett to Ernie Richardson, 25 September 1912, Minutes of the Calgary Industrial Exhibition Co. Ltd., Calgary Exhibition and Stampede Fonds, box 1, GMA.

64. Annual Report, 1948, Calgary Exhibition and Stampede Fonds, box 2.

65. Board of Commissioners Papers, series IV, box 21, file folder 1 of 2, Calgary Exhibition Board 1953–59.

66. For negotiations, see Board of Commissioners Papers, series V, box 84, file folder 4100.1. Claims that Agriculture Minister Harry Hays initiated

the whole Lincoln Park sale in Ottawa on behalf of the Stampede are not supported by evidence. In the summer of 1964, Hays was pushing for the municipal airport.

67. Crown Assets Disposal Corporation, the federal government's agency for disposing of unneeded assets, initially wanted one million dollars for the site. Deciding on the actual boundaries of the area and the need for provincial approval delayed the sale until November 1964.

68. Maurice Hartnett to City Commissioners, 23 October 1964. Hartnett urged haste and indicated that the board wanted to have the new site available by centennial year, 1967. Board of Commissioners Papers, series V, box 84, file folder 4100.1.

69. Board of Commissioners Papers, series IV, box 48, file folder E-1, file 1 of 3. In 1951 General Manager Charles Yule told the city that the Stampede had reached its saturation point with respect to numbers.

70. Meeting between Calgary and Stampede Officials, 14 March 1960. Board of Commissioners Papers, series V, box 22, file folder 175. Steel suggested that the expansion should go as far north as Twelfth Avenue.

71. Board of Directors Meeting, 26 February 1963, Minutes of the Calgary Exhibition and Stampede Board, 1961–76 (hereafter cited as Stampede Minute Book), Calgary Exhibition and Stampede Archives, CS.99.106, box 2.

72. Executive Committee Meeting, 16 October 1964, Stampede Minute Book. The Canadian National Railway (CNR) wanted $690,000 for 20.63 acres. By this time the Stampede had expended about $145,000 to purchase ten properties.

73. Board of Commissioners Papers, box 84, file folder 4100.1.

74. City Council Minutes, 26 October 1964.

75. Board of Directors Meeting, 23 December 1964, Stampede Minute Book.

76. "City Holds Back on Stampede Bid," *Calgary Herald*, 27 October 1964.

77. Board of Commissioners Papers, box 84, file folder 4001.1.

78. Due to the influence of one of the directors, the radio and television broadcasts were free. See Executive Committee Meeting, 7 May 1965, Stampede Minute Book. James H. Gray, *A Brand of Its Own: The 100 Year History of the Stampede* (Saskatoon: Western Producer Prairie Books, 1985), 152.

79. Gray, *Brand of Its Own*, 152.

80. Reports of meetings with Mount Royal College officials, Executive Committee Meetings, 23 April and 5 May 1965, Stampede Minute Book.

81. "Report Picks ATCO for Lincoln Park"; "Stampede Bid For Lincoln Park Led Only In Intangible Benefits," *Calgary Herald*, 18 June 1965.

82. Commissioners' Report to Council, 16 June 1965, City Commissioners Papers, box 84, file folder 4001.1.

83. Special Board of Directors Meeting, 20 June 1965, Stampede Minute Book.
84. "Stampede Drops Lincoln Park Bid," *Calgary Herald*, 22 June 1965.
85. In March 1965 the Stampede Board issued a press release to the effect that its consultant, Gaylord Perry of Findlay, Ohio, had visited all the sites and had determined that Lincoln Park was the most suitable. Although details of these other sites were not given, mention had been made of a site in the northeast near Sixteenth Avenue North and Highway 2, a site near the Burns feedlot in south Calgary, and a site in the vicinity of Ogden.
86. Sites Planning Committee Meeting, 10 December 1965, Stampede Minute Book.
87. City Council Minutes, 25 March 1968; Commissioners' Report, 17 April 1968, Board of Commissioners Papers, series V, box 262, file folder 7200.
88. Board of Commissioners Papers, series V, box 23, file folder 175.
89. Board of Commissioners Papers, series VI, box 72, file folder Stampede Board 1976. The 1968 agreement was amended effective 5 October 1975 to give the city direct responsibility for acquiring land in the expansion area.
90. "Cockroaches Found in City's Suites," *Calgary Herald*, 6 March 1972.
91. Their fears were well founded. The construction of the Saddledome on Stampede property combined with further expansion plans effectively sealed the fate of Victoria Park.
92. Secretary's correspondence dated 4 December 1973. Rod Sykes Fonds, RG 2 33.20, file folder 406. One wonders what a more persuasive approach might have achieved.
93. "The Future of Victoria Park," City of Calgary Planning Department, August 1971, Planning and Building Department, series VIII, box 17413, file folder V2.
94. Correspondence from Director of Planning George Steber to Commissioner George Cornish, 21 March 1974, Rod Sykes Fonds, RG 2 33.20, file folder 406.
95. Board of Commissioners Papers, box 22, file folder 175. See proposal by S. Flock and Company, 29 June 1967.
96. C. Kennedy to Mayor Jack Leslie, 30 May 1968, Board of Commissioners Papers, series V, box 227, file folder Calgary Exhibition and Stampede No. 3, 1968; C. Kennedy to Mayor and Commissioners, 1 January 1968, Board of Commissioners Papers, series V, box 262, file folder 7200.
97. Rebecca Aizenman, presentation to workshop on citizens' participation, Federation of Mayors and Municipalities, Quebec City, 24 May 1972, Board of Commissioners Papers, series IV, file folder Stampede 1972, file 2 of 2. Aizenman castigated both the Stampede Board and the city as middle-class business elitists, and the Stampede as "a middle class drunk

or an anything-goes celebration"; Andrew Marshall, executive assistant to Rod Sykes, to R.J. Benoche, chairman, Victoria Park Family Centre Board, 4 December 1973, Rod Sykes Fonds, file folder 406.

98. Confidential Memo, 7 December 1973, Stampede Minute Book.

99. Meeting between City and Stampede officials,14 March 1960, Board of Commissioners Papers, series V, box 22, file folder Calgary Exhibition Board 1960.

100. The Canada Mortgage and Housing Corporation (CMHC) was already cutting back on urban renewal funding while the province wanted a lengthy and costly city-wide study to see if Victoria Park was the best choice for urban renewal.

101. City of Calgary Planning Department, *The Calgary Plan*, March 1970, page 10.7.

102. City of Calgary Planning Department, *The Calgary Plan*, May 1973, page 10.7.

103. City of Calgary Planning Department, *The Calgary Plan*, June 1977.

104. Board of Commissioners Papers, series V, box 262, file folder 7200. See comments by both the Medical Board of Health and the Chief Building Inspector, 21 and 31 May 1965.

105. "Stampede Park. Calgary Exhibition & Stampede Expansion & Development," August 2004.

106. The community of Victoria Park was merged into the Beltline community. Ironically, West Victoria Park, which had lost most of its houses years earlier to commercial activity, is in the process of being rejuvenated with a high-end residential component.

107. This point is argued in Marilyn Burgess, "Canadian 'Range Wars': Struggles Over Indian Cowboys," *Canadian Journal of Communication* 18 (1993): 351–64.

108. Board of Commissioners Papers, series V, box 23, file folder 125.

109. Cheryl Cornacchia, "A Lady Among the Men," *Calgary Sun*, 12 July 1982. Alderman Naomi Whelan brought pressure to bear to change the rules for the President's luncheon. See correspondence between Naomi Whelan and Mayor Ross Alger, 30 and 31 May, 7 June, and 23 July 1979, Ross Alger Fonds, RG 2, no. 1061, CCA. It was a banner breakthrough year for women; 1979 also saw the first female outrider in the Chuckwagon races.

CHAPTER 7

Riding Broncs and Taming Contradictions: Reflections on the Uses of the Cowboy in the Calgary Stampede

Tamara Palmer Seiler

The Range Rider, c. 1913

Introduction

Calgary is a booming city of just over a million people, its rapid growth and increasingly conspicuous wealth based primarily on its role as the head office centre for the Canadian oil and gas industry. For several weeks before, during, and after its annual Stampede, its downtown streets and suburban shopping malls are filled with images of ranch life, particularly representations of cowboys, as well as with a diverse assortment of urban workers, local revellers, and tourists dressed in cowboy garb as they go about their myriad activities. A thoughtful observer of this scene, particularly one with some appreciation not only of the tensions between rural nostalgia and urban reality, but also of the cowboy's significance in American popular culture, as well as some knowledge of key differences between Canada and the United States and of the degree to which Canadians define themselves as being different from Americans, might be forgiven for being bemused not only by the scene itself, but also by the way in which the apparent contradictions it embodies go largely unremarked upon by cultural analysts as well as local participants.

Building on my previous (collaborative) work on the history and cultural significance of the Calgary Exhibition and Stampede, this article explores the tensions inherent in a Canadian city and region using what is arguably an American cultural icon as its defining symbol.[1] Specifically, the article addresses the following interconnected questions: Who is the cowboy at the heart of Calgary's annual Stampede and its civic iconography, and what social uses does this figure serve? Like the work referred to above, the present study draws on the cultural studies tradition, as delineated by theorists such as Roland Barthes, Stuart Hall, Mikhail Bakhtin, Pierre Bourdieu, Michel de Certeau, and John Fiske, who view the institutions and artifacts of popular culture as sites of struggle over meaning in the context of power relations. However, it is more directly situated at the nexus of several other interconnected scholarly discourses: that of nation and nationalism as delineated by such theorists as Benedict Anderson; that of Canadian studies, with special attention to the considerable body of work on regionalism and Canadian identity; that of western American studies, with special attention to the history of ranching and rodeo and the historical, fictional, and mythological cowboy; and that of comparative Canadian/American history, as exemplified by the work of such scholars as Allan Smith, Sarah Carter, Robert Thacker, Carol Higham, and Elliott West. Thus situated, it attempts to explore directly and in some depth the gap between imported and local culture that haunts Calgary's public iconography.

My point of departure is the framework for comparative American/Canadian studies provided by Elliott West in his insightful "Against the Grain: State-Making, Cultures, and Geography in the American West," the opening chapter in Carol Higham's and Robert Thacker's *One West, Two Myths*. As West explains, the north-south geographical patterns of North America, which suggest a natural division of the continent into three "nations" (which he calls Atlantis, Middle Earth, and Greater Montana), and its current division into three east-west nations (Canada, the United States, and Mexico) are clearly at odds, and nowhere more so than in the North American West. It is here that "the contradictions between landforms and nations seem the most glaring," making "the West the obvious place to look for anything to learn from the odd pattern of modern state-making."[2]

In further exploring this contradiction between geography and history/politics, West notes the longevity and persistence of an earlier congruence between these forces, evident in the cultural patterns of the continent's indigenous peoples. He asserts that "[I]f anyone wonders whether we should expect historical and geographical patterns to overlap in the first place, North America's long past gives an undeniable answer. For most of continental history by far, human activity seems mostly to have followed the broad lay of the land."[3] However, West's discussion also highlights the enormous power of the state-making processes that went against the grain of geography, calling it the "clearest lesson of this ancient north-south alignment." As he puts it, "[O]nce we look at the physical map of North America, the more familiar political map appears stunning. Boundaries that we take for granted today suddenly look arbitrary in the extreme … Most arbitrary of all is the U.S.-Canadian boundary, surely one of the longest nonsensical borders on the planet. "[4] Identifying the three major forces that created these nations as a capitalist economy driven by markets, a technological revolution in transportation and communication, and "the governmental apparatus of the states themselves,"[5] West highlights the paradoxical power of these underlying forces to construct different entities, while emphasizing that the same forces created each nation, and that in both the United States and Canada these forces were brought to bear most powerfully on the western region(s), given the wealth of resources these areas contained.

In thus drawing our attention to the fundamental dynamics of similarity and difference that have shaped the continent's peoples and their social and cultural interaction, West reminds us that in failing to attend to and examine "the obvious," we miss important avenues to insight:

> When we recognize each theme and move them to the
> front of our attention, they suggest a structure for the
> study of the North American West. We can picture it
> as the intersection of influences and trends. One set of
> influences and traditions follows the ancient axis of north
> and south. These influences are rooted in geography and
> deep history … Overrun in some ways by the making of
> two nations, they nonetheless persist. The other forces run
> along the more recent (but now centuries old) axis of east
> and west … These are the influences that swept across the
> continent to create the political map we take for granted.[6]

West moves beyond his delineation of fundamental "themes" in continental history to suggest how they might provide a framework for studying various aspects of Western culture and society, arguing that

> we might approach particular pieces of western history
> and life by sitting them on this grid of influences. We
> might ask in each case about the relative roles of the west-
> erly drive of state-making and the insistent inclinations of
> geography and cultural roots, looking also for differences
> inside these two broad patterns."[7]

West thus provides a remarkably fruitful framework for exploring the questions at the heart of my project about the identity, meanings, and uses of the Calgary Stampede cowboy.[8] My analysis places the Stampede cowboy on the "grid of influences" West delineates and asks, only partly facetiously, if it is accurate to talk about this figure – either the historical cowboy, whose origins are in Spain, who appears, migrates, and evolves in nations throughout the Americas,[9] or the imagined cowboy, created and broadcast globally via a wide range of media, from the Wild West Show and dime novels of the nineteenth century to the plethora of movies in the twentieth and twenty-first – as a "national" figure at all, and most particularly as a "Canadian" figure, given the small space, both literally and mythologically, he occupies in Canada.[10]

In attempting to answer this question of who the Calgary Stampede cowboy is in terms of the countervailing forces of geography and politics, the discussion that follows examines the east-west forces that bear on this figure. That is, I focus primarily on an aspect of the "state apparatus" that, while not strictly "governmental," is arguably central to the state's project of nation-building, namely the discourses that construct the "imagined community" of the nation.[11] I argue that these discourses largely construct the cowboy as being outside the imagined community of Canada. Then I turn my attention to the north-south forces of geography and culture that also bear on this figure, and in juxtaposing these criss-crossing perspectives, I highlight the regional discourse that claims the cowboy as its own, noting several of the major contradictions that this discourse must negotiate to do so in the Canadian context. I end by suggesting that these very contradictions, while rendering the cowboy (particularly the imagined figure, but to some degree even the historical/working cowboy as well) controversial if not inappropriate in the Canadian context, while simultaneously (and paradoxically) lending the figure its considerable power as a symbol of regional identity/resistance and as a powerful marketing tool.

The Cowboy and Canadian Identity: Incompatible Imaginaries?

To assert that the cowboy, despite his multiple origins and hemispheric presence, has a strong American connection – as a historical figure, but most particularly as an imagined one – is hardly to be controversial. In addition to being commonly assumed, this connection between the cowboy and American culture is also the subject of considerable scholarship.[12] Although the nature of that connection, just how it came about and what social uses it serves, is much debated, the idea that the figure of the cowboy embodies key aspects of the American ethos is widely accepted by analysts of American culture.[13] For example, historian Michael Allen argues that the figure of the cowboy emerged and the western genre persists in American popular culture because it taps "deep emotions in the American people," since it tells the "epic story of…[their] crossing a continental frontier and taming its wild forces, planting and nurturing the seeds of American civilization."[14] Further, Allen points to the connection many have made between the values embodied in the "cowboy's code" and the traits that Frederick Jackson Turner famously identified as those nurtured on the American frontier: individualism, a democratic and egalitarian spirit, and ingenuity, to say nothing of physical bravery. Allen sees the figure of the cowboy as providing "a key to understanding American civilization."[15]

Analysts of Canada and of Canadian identity, in contrast, have seldom
made a connection between the cowboy (historical or imagined) and the
Canadian ethos or national mythology. The subject of much discussion and
considerable scholarly analysis, the nature of Canadian identity is widely
agreed to have been shaped not only by such fundamental features as the
nation's vast geography, its northern location, its dual colonial inheritance,
and its diverse population, but also and in very large measure by its long,
somewhat troubled, and asymmetrical relationship with the United States.
Many Americans know very little about Canada and would likely be surprised to learn that the vague notion they may have about its inhabitants
being more or less just like themselves is not widely shared by Canadians.
Most Canadians, however, would be well aware of the differences between
themselves and Americans; indeed, many would be inclined to emphasize
and even exaggerate them. This was made very apparent in 2000 by the way
in which many young Canadians in particular adopted the Molson's "I am
Canadian" beer commercial, with its nose-thumbing rejection of American
stereotypes and its simplistic rendering of the differences between the two
countries (to say nothing of its manipulative commercial agenda), as a kind
of national anthem.[16]

To understand this phenomenon, one must look at least in part to Canada's history, and how it differs from that of the United States. As S.M. Lipset
puts it in his well known comparison of the two societies, "although these
two peoples probably resemble each other more than any other two nations
on earth," there are "consistent patterns of difference between them," which
he attributes to the revolutionary origins of the United States on the one
hand, and the counterrevolutionary origins of Canada on the other.[17] While
the United States, with its successful revolution against Britain, is "organized
around the ideology embodied in the Declaration of Independence, which
proclaimed the validity of egalitarian and universalistic social relations,"[18]
Canada was defined by its loyalty to Britain, and "Canadian identity…in a
sense must justify its raison d'être by emphasizing the virtues of being separate from the United States."[19] Thus, while it would be inaccurate to suggest
that all Canadians are profoundly anti-American, and indeed at least some
analysts stress the moderate nature of Canadian anti-Americanism,[20] most
would agree with Lipset that a combination of "Tory Conservatism and anti-
Americanism" affected not only those regions of Canada originally settled
by Loyalists fleeing the American revolution, but also the political culture of
Canada more generally.[21] J.L. Granatstein makes the point most forcefully
when he asserts that Canadians are the oldest anti-Americans in the world,

and that "Canadian anti-Americanism, just as much as the country's French-English duality, has for two centuries been a central buttress of the national identity."[22] He also points to the way in which a series of events, including perhaps most notably the War of 1812, added to this sentiment, and to what he calls "the Loyalist myth" in Canada, and with it a vein of potential anti-Americanism that lies beneath the surface of Canadian life, to be tapped at any point, or as he puts it, to be "exploited by business, political, or cultural groups for their own ends."[23]

Clearly, in the context of this discussion of the uses to which Canadians in southern Alberta put what is arguably a quintessentially American cultural icon, it is important to appreciate the psychological and emotional implications of Canada's counter-revolutionary past, and in particular the Canadian penchant for harbouring negative attitudes toward the United States. It is even more important to appreciate the nature of the differences between the two societies that reflect their origins as well as the evolution of the United States into a superpower on the global stage. Like Lipset (and several other analysts), John Conway makes the point that Canadian political culture is best understood as embodying the ideas of Burke rather than those of Rousseau and other architects of the Enlightenment, which shaped the American republic. As a result, "Americans cherish individualism and individuality above community. Canadians have exactly the reverse set of political priorities."[24] Exploring the sources of difference in more depth, Conway rightly highlights America's Puritan inheritance, with its emphasis on dissent and on an individual's unmediated relationship with God, both of which "fostered an intense individualism, which lost none of its force as Puritanism became secularized during the eighteenth and nineteenth centuries," eventually merging with social Darwinism to form the potent amalgam of "rugged individualism" that arguably defines the American ethos.[25]

Conway points to the American transcendentalist Henry David Thoreau, whose writings in the 1840s articulated a starkly individualistic perspective, to illustrate what he believes to be the key difference between the United States and Canada. Arguing that although Thoreau's famous statement that "'the only obligation which I have a right to assume is to do at any time what I think right'" was an expression of "fundamental belief [that] was to reverberate through American history in the nineteenth and twentieth centuries," for Canadians, with their emphasis on allegiance and community, the individualism he expressed was almost unthinkable: "[T]here is no counterpart to Thoreau in Canadian history."[26] Far from being arcane, this fact is, I believe, central to my discussion of the Canadian cowboy. Thoreau's world – the pastoral and effete landscape of Concord, Massachusetts – contrasts sharply with that of the American cowboy; nevertheless, when viewed as symbols, the two figures can be seen to merge as they turn away from the (feminized) world of community to "live deliberately" alone, or in the company of men, far away from the constraints of civilization.

Interestingly, while certainly not making this connection between Thoreau and the cowboy, Conway does connect Thoreau's ideas with the development of the American West, which he contrasts with that of the Canadian West:

> Thoreau's musings on man and his place in society were
> written in the full flood of enthusiasm for the westward
> movement, before industrialism, the anarchic violence
> of the West, and the hazards of modern warfare could
> pose serious questions about unchallenged individualism.
> The Canadian frontier experience, when it came, was
> less hopeful, the extension of the frontier more difficult,
> less economically rewarding, than the American. Thus,
> Thoreau's assertion of total freedom is simply incomprehensible to the average Canadian, whether his forbears be
> French, British, or of the newly arrived ethnic communities of this diverse country.[27]

Clearly, this description, cast as it is in the retrospective mode, underscores the possibility of change; that is, in light of a particular historical context, a national ethos and the political culture through which it is expressed can and do evolve. For example, Americans (as well as Canadians) have clearly become much more conscious of the environmental impact of unfettered exploitation than they were in the nineteenth century: witness the efforts on both sides of the border to protect endangered species and, more recently, to reduce carbon dioxide emissions in the effort to stem climate change. In light of their nineteenth- and, particularly, twentieth-century experience with urban crime, Americans may not be quite as unanimously enamoured of their right (forged in the American Revolution) to bear arms as many Canadians might imagine;[28] nor is it as clear as many Canadians would like to believe that Americans are less law-abiding than Canadians and American society more violent.[29]

Similarly, Canadian society has changed considerably since Lipset penned "Revolution and Counterrevolution," in ways too numerous and profound to describe here. One sees evidence of some of these changes in Neil Nevitte's

The Decline of Deference: Canadian Value Change in Cross-National Perspective,[30] which reports in considerable detail on studies designed to measure changes in the attitudes of Canadians on a number of variables (for example, attitudes toward authority) related to political culture. Nevertheless, one can certainly find evidence that the differences in national ethos delineated by the analysts discussed here persist, along with a propensity among Canadians to define themselves against Americans, if not to be overtly anti-American.

Given these underlying patterns of difference, then, it would seem clear that the "imagined national communities" that Canadians and Americans inhabit are also different from each other, if not in terms of the processes whereby they construct these communities, which may indeed be remarkably similar, then clearly in terms of the substance of what they share, that is, of their values and attitudes, and by extension, in terms of their heroes and villains, both real and imaginary. If one follows Benedict Anderson in defining a nation as "an imagined political community – and imagined as both inherently limited and sovereign,"[31] one can imagine the limits of the Canadian national community in terms of the border with the United States, a border that is not only a political reality, defined by guards, the need for official documents and the like, but is also a psycho-cultural one that defines most things American as "other," despite – or perhaps because of – the similarities between the two countries owing to their shared inheritance in particular of British institutions,[32] and to the longstanding and arguably escalating economic, social, and cultural influence of the United States on Canada.[33]

In light of this aspect of Canadian identity – that it is in large measure constructed around not being American – the cowboy at the heart of Calgary's Stampede seems particularly out of place, given the prominent role this figure has played and continues to play as a symbol of American sensibility. Or, to put the matter in terms of Elliott West's grid of influences, the east-west forces shaping the meaning of the cowboy have given this figure a well-recognized place of affection and esteem (and indeed of considerable mythic power) in the United States, broadcasting his image and his heroic exploits as an embodiment of individualism, self-reliance, courage, pragmatic justice, and patriotism not only throughout the American nation, but well beyond to such an extent that the "cowboy" is a globally recognized symbol of American culture and sensibility.[34] Or, as William W. Savage Jr. puts it,

> The cowboy is the predominant figure in American
> mythology. More than the explorer, trapper, soldier, or
> homesteader, the cowboy represents America's westering

> experience to the popular mind, and his image is every-
> where. Accounts of his activities, fictional and historical,
> comprise substantial portions of publishers' lists. His
> virtues – and lately his vices – have become standard fare
> in motion picture theaters and on television…and his
> mystique is evoked by advertising, popular music, and
> amateur and professional sports.[35]

Savage even concludes that "[I]t would…be difficult to imagine the contours of American culture, popular or otherwise, without the figure of the cowboy" and it would "be equally difficult to imagine a replacement for him."[36]

In Canada, the forces of nation-building have made the cowboy clearly "other" because of his strong association with the American ethos, creating instead the figure of the Mountie: the very embodiment of the contrasting Canadian valuing of the collective, the distant source of social order, restraint over action. As literary scholar Dick Harrison puts it when comparing climactic scenes in two quintessential fictions of the American West and the Canadian West, Owen Wister's *The Virginian* (1901) and Ralph Connor's *Corporal Cameron* (1910), "[T]he Virginian draws the gun with which he will enforce the right, while in Connor's scene, it is the man with the gun who backs down."[37] Harrison argues that these patterns are deeply engrained in these two (national) genres of western fiction – that of the cowboy and that of the Mountie – and that while both genres serve to reaffirm the triumph of civilization over wilderness, representations of the Mountie

> embodied most of what was distinctive about the early
> Canadian West. In particular, he represented that faith in
> an encompassing order which was vaguely conceived to be
> at once man-made, natural, and divinely sponsored…he
> represented the West as the Canadian people conceived it
> to be. However wild or rebellious the West might become,
> they preferred to see it as a haven of peace, order and good
> government, watched over by a colonial policeman in a
> red coat: solid, anti-revolutionary, visible proof that order
> would continue to be something which descended deduc-
> tively from higher levels of government and society.[38]

The American cowboy hero, in contrast, resolves the conflict between civilization and wilderness/savagery by responding to the immediate situation, "tilting the balance of power in favour of civilized law" through a violent act that is "almost surgical," thereby reaffirming masculinity (and) individualism."[39] Interestingly, if one sees fictional representation as a "site of struggle," a space wherein versions of the drama of western settlement compete for the allegiance of their readers/viewers, then in this particular space of countervailing narratives, the American version has clearly been the winner, measured in terms of popularity, in Canada as well as elsewhere.[40]

Nevertheless, despite the proliferation and popularity of the imagined cowboy, the figure of the Mountie exerted and continues to exert considerable power in Canadian discourses of nation, as exemplified by the ceremonial uses to which the RCMP are put (including at the Calgary Stampede) and by the pride that many Canadians take in their police forces, and in the persistent predominance of iconic representations of the Mountie (both within and without Canada) as a symbol of the Canadian nation and sensibility. Indeed, the Mountie is the figure at the centre of the westward trek of the North-West Mounted Police in 1874. This is the group credited, both in historical narratives and in national mythology, with bringing British order to the West before the arrival of settlers and thereby literally creating the east-west axis of Canada and distinguishing its West from its supposedly chaotic counterpart in the United States.[41] Thus the Mountie looms sufficiently large in the discourses of Canadian nationhood to leave little or no room for the cowboy, trailing, as he does, so much American baggage.

Moreover, detailed histories of ranching in southern Alberta quite clearly stress the ways in which it was influenced by a distinctively British/Canadian institutional framework that set it apart from the American ranching frontier. The work of David H. Breen, which draws on that of his mentor, L.G. Thomas, develops this thesis most strongly, with Breen arguing in the mid-1970s (and thereby creating a "school" of historical interpretation) against Turnerian continentalist approaches to this history that see the dominant influences as environmental, thereby stressing the similarities between the American and Canadian experiences.[42] Emphasizing the importance in Canada of the police presence, the British social composition and institutional ties, the considerable state control, and the conservative nature of the ranching community of southern Alberta, Breen asserts that

> the ranching frontier in the Canadian and American
> west can hardly be described as culturally homogeneous.
> Further, it is apparent that while there is a certain unity
> of time and physical environment as well as a common

economic enterprise, social and political patterns developed with marked differences on either side of the boundary. This dissimilar development, and the seemingly minor impact of the frontier environment on the Canadian side would seem…to be the consequence of two factors – the character of the in-coming population and the degree of the central government's administrative control. And in the pervasive influence of the central authority, one sees a continuity in western Canadian development that flows through the earlier fur trade period to the closing years of western settlement.[43]

While more recent studies by American and Canadian scholars offer what is arguably a more balanced approach to the history of ranching in Canada, highlighting similarities as well as differences and acknowledging the importance of American as well as British influence, ranching historiography clearly points to the power of east-west (national) forces that have shaped this enterprise.[44] As Simon Evans points out in his detailed history of the Bar U Ranch, "[T]he Canadian government played an important role in the establishment and development of ranching in western Canada," and an important early ranching venture, the North West Cattle Company, "was above all a Canadian enterprise."[45] Similarly, Max Foran rightly reminds us that ranching practices in western Canada have been profoundly shaped by the region's severe northern climate; consequently, ranching in this area "could never approximate its purer essence in the desolate, drier, and more southerly areas of the United States."[46] Thus, even if one sees Breen's interpretation (despite its obvious importance and value) as above all exemplifying the Canadian mentality described by Granatstein that insists upon not being American, there can be no doubt that ranching in southern Alberta was and is distinctive in ways that reflect the impact of powerful east-west forces.

Riding "The Empty Quarter": The Continental Cowboy

Whether labelled as "The Empty Quarter," "Greater Montana," or simply the North American West, the non-coastal western area of North America arguably constitutes a generalized region based on shared geographical features, which in turn provide the basis for shared economic and cultural patterns.[47] Thus viewed, this region clearly runs counter to the east-west national boundaries that run across it, delineating three "counter-intuitive" nations.

As Elliott West points out, one can find longstanding cultural evidence of the existence of such a region in the language families of indigenous peoples across the continent; he notes that "[T]he fifth and sixth language families were in the mountains and arid highlands stretching southward from Canada into Mexico."[48] While the area in question is vast and clearly contains a variety of distinctive sub-regions (Starr, as quoted in Evans, delineates five such regions "from Texas and New Mexico to Wyoming, Nebraska and Nevada with distinct ranching systems"[49]), it is nevertheless characterized by a degree of similarity in terms of its aridity and the nature of its land formations (to say nothing of the sparseness of its population). This similarity not only justifies seeing "the empty quarter" as a significant continental feature, but also provides the basis for particular economic and cultural practices, which, taken together, might be called the "western experience," or "western lifestyle," which in turn engenders a shared mindset, perhaps even "an imagined community" of "westerners."

As to what might define such an imagined community, Molly Rozum's discussion of a series of conferences sponsored by the Rockefeller Foundation in 1942 is suggestive. The project brought together American and Canadian leaders (from North Dakota, South Dakota, Nebraska, Minnesota, Montana, Wyoming, and Colorado and Alberta, Saskatchewan, and Manitoba) to define "a plains sensibility" in North American terms. While nothing very concrete ever came from these deliberations, participants agreed that they felt a sense of unity based on a close connection to the environment, and in particular on a shared sense of space, and on occupying "a beleaguered status" within their respective nations.[50] Interestingly (and not surprisingly, given the similar histories of populist politics north and south of the 49th parallel), Richard W. Slatta argues that one of the defining features of all the cowboy cultures that emerged in various places throughout the western hemisphere was that they developed in remote areas; that is,

> wild livestock hunters were frontiersmen who lived and worked in regions of sparse population, in contact (and often in conflict) with indigenous societies, far from urban, civic authority, and possessing ample natural resources for near self-sufficiency."[51]

Thus, one might argue that the western sensibility (whether or not it is specifically connected with the ranching enterprise) is one shaped by vast spaces and remoteness from centres of power, political and cultural; that as

such, it valorizes independence and self-sufficiency, and the kind of pragmatism that enables survival in an unforgiving environment. Further, it is
one that stresses local loyalties and is suspicious of central authority. My own
experience of living and travelling in various parts of the North American
West for many years tells me that one finds this sensibility throughout the
region, albeit within specific sub-regional contexts. For example, the image
of the "maverick," which Aritha van Herk has used recently to represent the
mentality of Albertans, whom she characterizes in *Mavericks: An Incorrigible
History of Alberta* as uncommonly independent and as incorrigible risk takers, is one that is very familiar to people from my home state of Nevada.
Nevadans tend to regard themselves as the original mavericks, having gone
against the national grain for nearly 150 years, not only in hell-roaring mining camps as Virginia City, Silver City, Tonopah, and many others, but also in
such matters as being residents of the first state to legalize boxing, gambling,
quick divorce, and quick marriage – all in the interests of economic survival
– and the one that refused to institute a speed limit on state highways for as
long as this stance was possible within the framework of federal legislation.
Nor is this image of "maverick" attitudes and behaviour limited to people of
the wide-open "Silver State," however well deserved it is there; it is a label
that would also readily be claimed by many people throughout the American
West, who like to see themselves as tougher and infinitely more self-reliant
than people from the East.[52]

Clearly, as Slatta has suggested, this mindset can be traced in part to the
experiences of those involved in cattle raising and, later, the cattle industry
that has been an economic mainstay of the western hinterland of North
America from the nineteenth century to the present.[53] Those experiences
of the historical/working cowboy generated a specific set of range skills, an
accompanying set of attitudes and values, and even a characteristic mode of
dress. In examining the similarities among cowboys in various parts of the
North American West, Slatta draws on Edward Larocque Tinker, who saw
sufficient similarities to refer to them as "brothers under the skin," asserting
that "[T]hey were all molded, North and South, by the same conditions the
frontier and the cattle business imposed…and naturally developed the same
characteristics of pride, daring, and fierce independence."[54] While Slatta
argues for an understanding of the historical cowboy that takes regional
differences into account, he nevertheless stresses that cowboys constituted a
group with "distinctive cultural values."[55]

The nature of these values is distilled in what Michael Allen refers to as
"the cowboy code," which he describes as "a set of unwritten rules of behavior

that evolved among late-nineteenth-century Great Plains cowboys" that "was subscribed to almost universally by cowboy occupational folk groups,"[56] and which, interestingly enough, echoed the values F.J. Turner had delineated as characteristic of the American frontiersman. As Allen explains it,

> Cowboys were democratic, practical, innovative, and courageous. They disliked intellectuals. Cowboys were individualistic, yet closely bound by the Code mores of their peers. These included an aversion to city life and "civilization," fancy talk, and boasting. Many cowboys spoke only when necessary. They said what they wanted to say in slow, deliberate vernacular, with perhaps a dash of dry humour....A cowboy admired a good horse and took good care of it; he stood by fellow hands and his outfit at all costs. He showed hospitality to cowboys from other outfits and shared important trail information. He was deferential to women, showing an exaggerated courtesy toward "good women" although by and large he shunned the company of "good women" in favor of the prostitutes and bar girls he knew would not "tie him down" and end his wandering lifestyle.[57]

Importantly (and this is the central argument of his book), Allen argues that the rodeo cowboy has inherited the mantle of the historical/working cowboy, often through having an actual connection to ranching, but also through his genuine wrangling skills and through his espousal of the cowboy code.

Calling him a "contemporary ancestor," a paradoxical phrase whereby he attempts to capture the cultural significance of the rodeo cowboy, Allen sees this figure as "painstakingly preserving and honoring cowboy traditions," which offers North Americans a chance to continue their communion with the mythical cowboy.[58] Allen's argument is similar to that of Jack Weston, who asserts that the power of the cowboy myth lies in North Americans' deep longing for a lost Eden. Straddling as he does the gap between nature and civilization, the imagined cowboy can satisfy their longing for the lost pre-industrial world, while at the same time allowing them to embrace the present: the imagined cowboy enables a kind of romantic escapism that "avoid(s) romantic primitivism while recognizing the injuries of progress."[59] For Allen, the rodeo cowboy "acts out the taming of the West ... When his job is done – when he has symbolically tamed the wild frontier to make way

for civilization – the rodeo cowboy hero has to 'move on down the road'…
not astride his horse, but in a pickup truck or aboard a jet airplane."[60]

Thus one begins to see considerable continuity between the cowboy – both
historical/working and imagined – at the centre of the Calgary Stampede and
his counterparts south of the Canadian border. Wallace Stegner insists on this
point in *Wolf Willow*, his reminiscence of growing up in the cowboy country
of southern Saskatchewan, asserting that the cowboy's "costume, the practices, the terminology, the state of mind, came into Canada ready-made, and
nothing they encountered on the northern Plains enforced any real modifications."[61] As Hugh Dempsey notes in his history of the Canadian cowboy, this
figure "inherited much of the Spanish heritage from the American cowboy";
he had the same skills, being "deft with a rope, handy with a branding iron"
and having "an intimate knowledge of cattle, horses and his surroundings."
His clothing was the same as that of his fellows across the border, and he even
"spoke the same lingo, often with the same Texas drawl."[62] Indeed, Dempsey
points out that in the early days of Canadian ranching, most of the cowboys
were Americans,[63] and they generally adhered to the cowboy code mentioned
above, being "tough, hardy, and fiercely loyal."[64] Nomadic by necessity if not
by nature, many did not stay in Canada, some leaving because they found
the general lack of saloons unpalatable.[65]

While Dempsey clearly points to the emergence of a somewhat distinctive
cowboy culture in southern Alberta, and the willingness of most of these men
"to live under Canadian laws and accept them," he acknowledges the presence
of horse thieves and cattle rustlers on the Canadian range.[66] Warren Elofson
develops this theme in considerably more detail in *Cowboys, Gentlemen
and Cattle Thieves*, thereby downplaying the sharp distinction Breen draws
between the supposedly orderly Canadian West and the lawless American
one, and points to the importance of north-south influences.[67] Noting the
diverse origins of Canadian cowboys, who in addition to Americans included
"Ontario farm-boys, English immigrants, and boys born on the western
frontier" along with "Anglos, blacks, Mexicans, Indians, halfbreeds, and men
from every social class," Dempsey emphasizes that "their teachers and…role
models were the cowboys who had learned their trade in Texas, Wyoming
and other centers of America's ranching West."[68] Evans makes a similar point
about the influence of the imagined cowboy, noting that "the Bar U had
extraordinarily close ties to the 'mythic west' created by journalists, novelists,
impresarios, and artists." While Evans points to the "irony" in this particular
ranch (which many regard as the "epitome" of a Canadian ranch) having so
many noteworthy American connections, he nevertheless points out the very

real ties between the people at the Bar U and such American perpetuators of the cowboy myth as the artist Charlie Russell, the writer Owen Wister, and the outlaw Sundance Kid.[69]

Although considerably less scholarly than Dempsey's or Evans's studies, but perhaps in its own way no less authoritative, given his personal experience (and that of his father and grandfather before him) as a working cowboy in southern Alberta, Andy Russell's *The Canadian Cowboy* also stresses the north-south nature of cowboy culture as he knew it and as it was passed down to him. He describes the cowboy as "courageous and physically tough...and inordinately loyal to the brand he worked for" and "generally soft spoken," particularly in the presence of "decent women."[70] He points out that cowboys generally carried a gun "because of the nature of their work," but that "contrary to the popular belief generated first by writers city-born and -raised and then by Hollywood, very few cowboys ever carried more than one pistol for the simple reason that a gun and its...accoutrements were heavy."[71] Interestingly, in describing such historical figures as James Butler (Wild Bill) Hickok, Bat Masterson, and Wyatt Earp, Russell makes no mention of their American connections; rather he presents them as genuine figures of cowboy lore, albeit people whose real stories have been distorted by romanticized representations.[72] Such a presentation of (Canadian) cowboy culture by a popular writer like Russell arguably points to the existence of a cross-border western community, one that claims the cowboy code (and those who have in various ways exemplified it) as its own, regardless of national boundaries.

Conclusion: The Social Uses of the Stampede Cowboy

To this point, I have offered some largely indirect answers to my initial question: Who is the cowboy at the heart of Calgary's annual Stampede and its civic (and regional) iconography? However, placing this figure on Elliott West's grid of influences provides some useful insights. Perhaps the most obvious of these is that the notion of a "Canadian cowboy" (historical and imagined, but perhaps particularly the latter) is one that is fraught with tension, if not contradiction. Viewed from the perspective offered by this countervailing framework, the cowboy has clearly grown out of north-south forces of geography, economics, and culture. Carried north on the waves created by the cattle industry that developed in the United States in the mid-nineteenth century from the trail drives initiated by entrepreneurs such as John Hackett,[73] Joseph G. McCoy, and Charles Goodnight[74] to move thousands of cattle north from Texas to the Great Plains railheads,[75] the cowboy eventually appeared in those few areas in Canada – south-central and western British Columbia, southern Alberta (especially in the foothills of the Rockies), and southwestern Saskatchewan – that could support some form of ranching.

The first herd of cattle to be brought in this way to Canada likely arrived in British Columbia from Washington in 1860.[76] The first roundup in Alberta occurred in 1878 near Fort Macleod, and while it was an initiative of a group of Mounted Police who had decided to stay in the West and who saw an opportunity in the growing need for beef among the Indians (by then almost completely deprived of their mainstay by the slaughter of the great herds of buffalo that had roamed the western plains), this project was ultimately dependent on the presence and skill of American cowboys.[77] In short, the ranching industry, which provided the basis for the establishment of the Calgary Stampede first as a one-off celebration of the working cowboy in 1912 – a figure whose glory days were clearly numbered throughout "the empty quarter" in the wake of agrarian and urban settlement – and then as a yearly celebration of the continued economic power of the country's largest ranching industry,[78] is clearly more the product of continental forces than of national ones, despite the undeniable influence of the latter. Moreover, if one looks at the countervailing forces at work on the historical cowboy, that is, at the discourses of Canadian nation-building, one might say that those discourses attempt to push him aside, if not to erase him completely as they reject all things "American." Or, as a guide at the Bar U Ranch historical site told me confidently when I was visiting there a few years ago, "We didn't have any cowboys here."

Such denials aside, cowboy iconography is a pervasive presence in Calgary and in southern Alberta, not only during Stampede week in July, but also throughout the year. This is amply evidenced by the stylized cowboy hat adopted as a logo by the City of Calgary, by Calgary's White Hat ceremony in its various manifestations,[79] and by the ubiquitous promotional use of the cowboy image by the two major tourism agencies in the area, Travel Alberta and Tourism Calgary, to say nothing of the architecture of Calgary's major stadium, the Pengrowth Saddledome.[80] In short, references to the cowboy clearly dominate the public representation of Calgary and the surrounding region, and indeed, define its – extremely valuable – global brand.[81]

A definitive answer to the question of whether these representations are inflected primarily toward the historical/working cowboy or toward the imagined figure awaits further research; in any case, answering such a question would be challenging if not impossible, since, as many analysts have pointed out, separating these two figures has become increasingly difficult over the past century. What does seem certain is that at both levels – historical and imagined – the cowboy at the centre of all of this activity is primarily the product of continental forces, and in particular of American cultural dynamics. Whether one sees him simply as a legitimate manifestation of the considerable and longstanding presence of Americans and their descendants in (southern) Alberta, that "most American of provinces"; as an unwelcome and simplistic symbol foisted upon unwilling locals by the machinations of (American) capitalism; as a powerful and complex symbol that has been appropriated by Canadians who are quite adept at the art of riding on the coat-tails of Yankee cultural energy and ingenuity while all the while feigning various kinds of moral superiority; or as a combination of all of the above, there is no denying that this figure is dominant and powerful. Why should this be so? What social uses does this figure serve?

Of course at one level, answering this question is easy: the Stampede, embodying as it does the romance and excitement of the Old West, has been a cash cow for most of its existence, and it continues to draw thousands of tourists and millions of dollars to the city and the region. Moreover, the Stampede cowboy with all of his baggage has provided Calgary and environs with an easily reproduced and enormously powerful marketing tool, one that has global resonance. Less obvious is what becomes apparent when one places the figure of the cowboy on West's "grid of influences": that the very negotiations necessitated by the countervailing forces illuminated by such an analysis actually enhance the social/cultural utility of the cowboy in southern Alberta.

That is, the cowboy image is useful as a symbol of the region precisely because it is so profoundly American. The aura of illegitimacy this connection lends the cowboy is one of the figure's most attractive aspects in the Canadian context, enabling Calgarians (and Albertans more generally) to draw on it to evoke their regional identity as the "mavericks" of confederation (as well as to justify a ten-day *carnivale*, replete with a variety of excesses, public and private). At the same time, they are able to draw on the east-west discourses of Canadian identity to attenuate the figure's tantalizingly forbidden connection with the individualism, the wildness, the violence associated in the popular mind (and nowhere more so than in the Canadian popular mind) with America's western frontier. Thus, this negotiation across countervailing forces enables Calgarians to at once have and eat their cake in the figure of the "Canadian cowboy." The social construction of this figure seems to have begun quite early on, with Calgary's booster press remarking in 1884

that unlike his unruly American counterparts, "the genuine Alberta cowboy
is a gentleman." Or, as historian L.G. Thomas insisted many years later, while
this figure might look like an American, he has an English spirit.[82]

I would suggest that the spirit of the Calgary Stampede cowboy is likely
more complex than Thomas allows, and further, that this figure works in the
service of the equally complex and paradoxical dynamics of regionalism. As
Frank Davey has pointed out, regionalism is a multifaceted and contradictory phenomenon. Able to foster both diversity and homogenization, it is "a
strategy" that "operates within a large interplay of power relations," one of
several available "discourses of dissent,"[83] a discourse that can resist "meanings generated by others in a nation state."[84] At the same time, a regional
sensibility is potentially advantageous to the nation state, as, for example,
when a particular regional myth provides a rationale for the national government to avoid taking responsibility for economic problems in the region, or
to downplay the region's growing economic clout. Davey also points to the
crucial role that regionalism can play in nurturing the symbolic resources
and techniques of commodification so essential to "cultural competition and
survival" within the context of global capitalism.[85]

At this point it seems clear that the cowboy serves as just such a symbolic
resource, a tool of resistance for Calgarians, Albertans, and perhaps even for
western Canadians more generally, that works to hide, if not to tame, the
contradictions between being a hinterland and a homeland, between asserting a distinctive regional identity and claiming wholehearted membership
within the national community. American enough to be exciting, the iconic
Stampede cowboy beckons to visitors from across the country and around
the world who have been steeped in the romance of the mythic ("American")
West. While he connotes a maverick identity (one that can be as easily adopted by a newly arrived denizen of Calgary's oil patch as by a fifth-generation
Albertan from ranching country), his promoters can assure those who need
to hear it that Alberta's West is thoroughly Canadian.

Notes

1. Robert M. Seiler and Tamara P. Seiler, "The Social Construction of the Canadian Cowboy: Calgary Exhibition and Stampede Posters, 1952–72," *Journal of Canadian Studies* 33, no. 3 (Autumn 1998): 51–82; Seiler and Seiler, "Ceremonial Rhetoric and Civic Identity: The Case of the White Hat, *Journal of Canadian Studies* 36, no. 1 (Spring 2001): 29–49; Seiler and Seiler, "Managing Contradictory Visions of the West: The Great Richardson-Weadick Experiment," in *Challenging Frontiers: The Canadian West*, ed. Lorry Felske and Beverly Rasporich (Calgary: University of Calgary Press, 2004), 155–80. See also Robert M. Seiler, "M.B. (Doc) Marcell: Official Photographer of the First Calgary Stampede," *American Review of Canadian Studies* 33, no. 2 (Summer 2003): 219–39. As in these other works, my theoretical perspective draws on such works as Raymond Williams, *Culture and Society* (Harmondsworth: Penguin, 1963); Herbert Blumer, "Society as Symbolic Interaction," *Symbolic Interactionism: Perspective and Method* (Englewood Cliffs, NJ: Prentice-Hall, 1969), 78–79; Michel de Certeau, *The Practice of Everyday Life* (Berkeley: University of California Press, 1984); Pierre Bourdieu, "Social Space and Symbolic Power," *Sociological Theory* 7 (Spring 1989): 14–25; John Fiske, *Understanding Popular Culture* (Boston: Unwin-Heyman, 1989); Mikhail Bakhtin, *The Dialogic Imagination* (Austin: University of Texas Press, 1994), 14–25; and Raymond Breton, "Intergroup Competition in the Symbolic Construction of Canadian Society," in *Race and Ethnic Relations*, 2nd ed., ed. Peter S. Li (Don Mills, ON: Oxford University Press, 1999), 291–310.

2. Elliott West, "Against the Grain: State-Making, Cultures, and Geography in the American West," in *One West, Two Myths: A Comparative Reader*, ed. Carol Higham and Robert Thacker (Calgary: University of Calgary Press, 2004), 2.

3. Ibid., 3.

4. Ibid., 6.

5. Ibid., 7.

6. Ibid.

7. Ibid., 9.

8. My inspiration for this approach, one that takes into account the north-south influences on cultural institutions and practices in Canada, also comes from other sources, most notably Joel Garreau's fascinating *The Nine Nations of North America* (New York: Avon Books, 1981). Garreau sees North America in zterms of nine (north-south) regions, and quite compellingly labels the non-coastal western region of the continent "The Empty Quarter." More recent analyses have also documented the degree to which social and cultural

differences between Canada and the United States are considerably less pronounced than the discourses of Canadian nationalism would suggest. See Jeffrey G. Reitz and Raymond Breton, *The Illusion of Difference: Realities of Ethnicity in Canada and the United States* (Toronto: CD Howe Institute, 1994). I have made a similar argument regarding approaches to diversity in both countries in Tamara Palmer Seiler, "Melting Pot and Mosaic: Images and Realities," in *Canada and the United States: Differences that Count*, 2nd ed., ed. David M. Thomas (Peterborough ON: Broadview Press, 2000), 97–120. See also Jeffrey Simpson, *Star Spangled Canadians: Canadians Living the American Dream* (Toronto: Harper-Collins, 2000). Michael Adams, *Fire and Ice: The United States, Canada and the Myth of Converging Values* (Toronto: Penguin Canada, 2004) offers an interesting counterpoint to Simpson's line of argument.

9. See Richard W. Slatta, *Cowboys of the Americas* (New Haven, CT: Yale University Press, 1990), especially Chapter 1, " Introduction," and Chapter 2, "From Wild-Cattle Hunters to Cowboys," 1–27.

10. The following sources (among many others) discuss the role of various media in constructing and purveying the cowboy image and the particular resonance of this figure in the national mythology of the United States: Michael Allen, *Rodeo Cowboys in the North American Imagination* (Reno: University of Nevada Press, 1998); John Cawelti, "Reflections on the Western Since 1970," in *Gender, Language and Myth: Essays on Popular Narrative*, ed. Glenwood Irons (Toronto: University of Toronto Press, 1992), 83–102; Kathryn C. Esselman, "From Camelot to Monument Valley: Dramatic Origins of the Western Film," in *Focus on the Western*, ed. Jack Nackbar (Englewood Cliffs, NJ: Prentice Hall, 1974), 9–18; William H. Forbis, *The Cowboys* (Alexandria, VA: Time-Life Books, 1973); Marcus Klein, "The Westerner: Origins of the Myth," in *Gender, Language and Myth: Essays on Popular Narrative*, ed. Glenwood Irons (Toronto: University of Toronto Press, 1992), 65–82; John Shelton Lawrence and Robert Jewett, *The Myth of the American Superhero* (Grand Rapids, MI: William B. Eerdmans, 2002); Jack Weston, *The Real American Cowboy* (New York: New Amsterdam, 1995).

11. In his well-known book, *Imagined Communities: Reflections on the Origins and Spread of Nationalism* (London: Verso, 1991), Benedict Anderson famously defines the nation as "an imagined political community" that is both limited and sovereign. As he explains, the nation "is imagined because the members of even the smallest nation will never know most of their fellow-members, meet them, or even hear of them, yet in the minds of each lives the image of their communion....Communities are to be distinguished, not by their falsity/genuineness, but by the style in which they are imagined....The nation is imagined as limited because even the largest of them...has finite, if elastic

boundaries, beyond which lie other nations....It is imagined as sovereign because the concept was born in an age in which Enlightenment and Revolution were destroying the legitimacy of the divinely-ordained, hierarchical dynastic realm....Finally, it is imagined as a community, because, regardless of the actual inequality and exploitation that may prevail in each, the nation is always conceived as a deep, horizontal comradeship" (pp. 5–7).

12. See, for example, Jack Weston, *The Real American Cowboy*. See also William W. Savage Jr.'s introduction to *Cowboy Life: Reconstructing an American Myth* (Niwot: University of Colorado Press, 1993), 3–16. Also relevant are: Richard Slotkin, *Gunfighter Nation: The Myth of the Frontier in Twentieth-Century America* (Norman: University of Oklahoma Press, 1992); Philip R. Loy, *Westerns and American Culture, 1930–1955* (Jefferson, NC: McFarland and Company, 2001); Lawrence and Jewett, *The Myth of the American Superhero*, especially Chapter 3, "Buffalo Bill: Staging World Redemption," 49–64, and Chapter 5, "John Wayne and Friends Redeem the Village," 89–105.

13. Various fault lines in this debate are clearly apparent in John Cawelti's "Reflections on the Western Since 1970" (1992), in which he refers to the "Turnerian and post-Turnerian schools," the "myth symbol" school, and the new structuralists. Michael Allen offers a more recent discussion of this debate in *Rodeo Cowboys in the North American Imagination* (1998) and, like Cawelti, calls for a productive synthesis of these various approaches. Jane Tompkins, in "West of Everything," in *Gender, Language and Myth,* 103–23, offers a fascinating feminist interpretation of the cultural significance of the cowboy and the Western. Rather than seeing the popularity of this figure and genre as primarily reflecting a deep nostalgia for a lost pre-industrial world, Tompkins sees it as a reaction to the dominance in the nineteenth century of a feminine perspective in literature and the emerging feminist challenge to male hegemony during the period. She argues quite convincingly that the Western posits a masculine, secular world, with its concentration on death and its disavowal of the Christian worldview and the domestic world. In so doing, it offers a masculine retreat from the feminized world of domesticity and Christianity and valorizes a materialist world and physical force as the ultimate realities.

14. Allen, *Rodeo Cowboys,* 203.

15. Ibid.

16. Robert M. Seiler, "Selling Patriotism/Selling Beer: The Case of the I AM CANADIAN Commercial," *American Review of Canadian Studies* 32 (Spring 2002): 45–66.

17. S.M. Lipset, "Revolution and Counterrevolution: The United States and Canada," in *A Passion for Identity: An Introduction to Canadian Studies*, ed. Eli Mandel and David Taras (Toronto: Methuen, 1987), 81.

18. Ibid., 75.

19. Ibid., 81.

20. J.L. Granatstein, *Yankee Go Home? Canadians and Anti-Americanism* (Toronto: Harper Collins, 1996), 8.

21. Lipset, "Revolution and Counterrevolution," 74.

22. Granatstein, *Yankee Go Home?* Granatstein defines Canadian anti-Americanism as "a distaste for and fear of American military, political, cultural and economic activities that, while widespread in the population, is usually benign unless and until it is exploited by business, political, or cultural groups for their own ends. Added to this is a snippet – and sometimes more – of envy at the greatness, wealth, and power of the Republic and its citizens, and a dash of discomfort at the excesses that mar American life" (p. 4).

23. One sees evidence of this exploitation of latent anti-Americanism on a daily basis in Canada, particularly since 9/11, and most particularly since the American invasion of Iraq. An article by well-known pollster Michael Adams in the context of the disintegration of Paul Martin's Liberal government and Martin's apparent attempt to garner support by "capitalizing on Anti-American sentiment" illustrates the point. Entitled "Bash Thy Neighbor," it appeared (under the heading of "Canada-U.S. Relations") in the *Globe and Mail* on October 19, 2005. Adams asserts that "The last time Canadians so disliked a U.S. President, the Americans were shooting at us" (p. A19). Interestingly, in reporting on Canadian attitudes toward Canada-U.S. relations, thereby highlighting that while Yankee-bashing is a crowd pleaser in Canada, "70 percent (of Canadians) want the government to try to get along," the article illustrates the ambivalence Granatstein refers to in his analysis of anti-Americanism, as implied by his interrogative title.

24. John Conway, "An Adapted Organic Tradition," *Daedalus: Special Issue: In Search of Canada* 117, no. 4 (Fall 1988): 382. Of course Conway is not the first to make this conservative argument. Famously, George Grant evokes Canada's conservative lineage in his *Lament for a Nation: the Defeat of Canadian Nationalism* (Toronto: McClelland and Stewart, 1965).

25. Conway, "Adapted Organic Tradition," 382.

26. Ibid.

27. Ibid., 383.

28. Leslie A. Pal, "Between the Sights: Gun Control in Canada and the United States," in *Canada and the United States: Differences that Count*, 2nd ed., ed. David M. Thomas (Peterborough, ON: Broadview Press, 2000), 68–96.

29. Edward Grabb and James Curtis, *Regions Apart: The Four Societies of Canada and the United States* (Don Mills: Oxford University Press, 2005), 129–30.

30. Neil Nevitte, *The Decline of Deference: Canadian Value Change in Cross-National Perspective* (Peterborough, ON: Broadview Press, 1996).

31. Anderson, *Imagined Communities*, 6.

32. Grabb and Curtis, *Regions Apart*, 157.

33. David Taras, "Surviving the Wave: Canadian Identity in the Era of Digital Globalization," in *A Passion for Identity: Canadian Studies in the 21st Century*, 4th ed., eds. David Taras and Beverly Rasporich (Scarborough, ON: Nelson, 2001), 185–200.

34. Michael Allen, *Rodeo Cowboys*, 62; Loy, *Westerns and American Culture*, 83; Slotkin, *Gunfighter Nation*, 38; Lawrence and Jewett, *Myth of the American Superhero*, 49–64, 89–105.

35. Savage, *Cowboy Life*, 3.

36. Ibid., 5.

37. Dick Harrison, *Unnamed Country: The Struggle for a Canadian Prairie Fiction* (Edmonton: University of Alberta Press, 1977), 78. See also Harrison's edited collection, *Best Mounted Police Stories* (Edmonton: University of Alberta Press, 1996).

38. Harrison, *Unnamed Country*, 158.

39. Ibid., 162.

40. Ibid., 163.

41. R.C. Macleod, *The North-West Mounted Police and Law Enforcement, 1873–1905* (Toronto: University of Toronto Press, 1976).

42. See David H. Breen, "The Turner Thesis and the Canadian West: A Closer Look at the Ranching Frontier," in *Essays in Western History*, ed. Lewis H. Thomas (Edmonton: University of Alberta Press, 1976), 147–56. Breen later produced a book on this topic, *The Canadian Prairie West and the Ranching Frontier, 1874–1924* (Toronto: University of Toronto Press, 1983).

43. Ibid., 155.

44. In addition to Jordan, *North American Cattle-Ranching Frontiers*; and Slatta, *Cowboys of the Americas*, see also Warren Elofson, *Cowboys, Gentlemen and Cattle Thieves* (Montreal: McGill-Queen's University Press, 2000); Simon Evans, *The Bar U: Canadian Ranching History* (Calgary: University of Calgary Press, 2004); and Maxwell Foran, *Trails and Trials: Markets and Land Use in the Alberta Beef Industry, 1881–1948* (Calgary: University of Calgary Press, 2003).

45. Evans, *Bar U*, 300.

46. Foran, "Constancy and Change: Ranching in Western Canada," in *Challenging Frontiers: The Canadian West*, ed. Lorry Felske and Beverly Rasporich (Calgary, University of Calgary Press, 2004), 312.

47. See Garreau, *Nine Nations*; West, "Against the Grain"; Allen, *Rodeo Cowboys*.

48. West, "Against the Grain," 3.

49. Paul F. Starr, *Let the Cowboy Ride: Cattle Ranching in the American West* (Baltimore, MD: Johns Hopkins University Press, 1998), as quoted in Evans, *Bar U*, xvii.

50. Molly P. Rozum, "'The Spark that Jumped the Gap': North America's Northern Plains and the Experience of Place," in *One West, Two Myths*, eds. Carol Higham and Robert Thacker, 137–38.

51. Slatta, *Cowboys of the Americas*, 16.

52. Of course the degree to which this "maverick" mythology accords with the facts of western development is debatable; indeed, one might well argue that on both sides of the border, the myth works in part to hide reality. For example, as Donald Worster points out in "Two Faces West: The Development Myth in Canada and the United States," in *One West, Two Myths*, given the aridity of much of the American West, it was necessary for the federal government to contribute mightily to the irrigation and other infrastructure projects required for development; indeed, "the West of fact rather than romance, became the domain of the Bureau of Reclamation and the Bureau of Land Management (BLM) more than of Wyatt Earp or Billy the Kid" (pp. 33–34). This was and is nowhere more true than in my own "maverick" state of Nevada, where the BLM is the major landholder, and federal control has enabled such projects as the testing of atomic bombs. Similarly, as Todd Babiak points out in "Mavericks? If Only," in a recent issue of *Alberta Views*, there is perhaps more than a bit of sleight of hand in labelling the residents of the essentially one-party province of Alberta as "mavericks."

53. Weston, *Real American Cowboy*, 3–8; Foran, "Constancy and Change," 311–12.

54. In *Cowboys of the Americas*, 5, Slatta cites Edward Larocque Tinker, "The Centaurs of the Americas," in *Centaurs of Many Lands* (London: J.A. Allen, 1964), 50–51.

55. Slatta, *Cowboys of the Americas*, 6.

56. Allen, *Rodeo Cowboys*, 29.

57. Ibid., 29–30.

58. Ibid., 211.

59. Weston, *Real American Cowboy*, 210.

60. Allen, *Rodeo Cowboys*, 211.

61. Wallace Stegner, *Wolf Willow: A History, a Story, and a Memoir of the Last Plains Frontier* (Toronto: Macmillan, 1962), 135–36.

62. Hugh A. Dempsey, *The Golden Age of the Canadian Cowboy: An Illustrated History* (Saskatoon: Fifth House, 1995), 1.

63. Ibid., 11.

64. Ibid., 1.

65. Ibid., 19.

66. Ibid., 2.

67. Warren Elofson, *Cowboys, Gentlemen and Cattle Thieves* (Montreal: McGill-Queens University Press, 2000).

68. Dempsey, *Golden Age,* 20.
69. Evans, *Bar U,* 301.
70. Andy Russell, *The Canadian Cowboy: Stories of Cows, Cowboys and Cayuses* (Toronto: McClelland and Stewart, 1993), 40.
71. Ibid., 40, 41.
72. Ibid., 41, 42.
73. Ibid., 21–25.
74. Weston, *Real American Cowboy,* 35–69.
75. Slatta, *Cowboys of the Americas,* 78–82.
76. Russell, *Canadian Cowboy,* 87.
77. Dempsey, *Golden Age,* 12–23.
78. Foran, "Constancy and Change," 312.
79. Robert M. Seiler and Tamara P. Seiler, "Ceremonial Rhetoric and Civic Identity: The Case of the White Hat," *Journal of Canadian Studies* 36, no. 1 (Spring 2001): 29–49.
80. Donald Den, "The Cowboy and the Business: Travel and Tourism in Southern Alberta" (honours thesis, Faculty of Communication and Culture, University of Calgary, 2007).
81. Although the degree to which the cowboy and the Western genre are on the wane as powerful cultural symbols (and products) is debatable, a number of analysts, artists, and others have pointed to a decline in their popularity. For example, in "Reflections on the Western Since 1970," John Cawelti points to a marked decline, which he attributes in large measure to changes in the West itself, and in the public perception of the region. As he puts it, "[T]he west is becoming just like everywhere else….The geographic frontier is closed and is rapidly receding into the past," to be replaced by "two new landscapes" with similar mythic power – the city and outer space" (p. 92). Cawelti also points to a changing mindset (what one might call the postmodern sensibility) that has emerged since the 1970s, one that reflects "new and conflicting attitudes toward violence, sexism and racism," which has made it difficult for filmmakers, for example, to take the Western genre seriously. One sees this sensibility in such recent Western films as Ang Lee's *Brokeback Mountain* (2005), with its focus on a homosexual relationship between two contemporary cowboys, and in Wim Wenders' *Don't Come Knocking* (2005), which Wenders describes as "'a deconstruction…of the myth of the West…[whose] stories…have been obsolete [and] the iconic American cowboy figure has vanished." (Wenders is quoted in James Adams, "How the West was Spun," *Globe and Mail,* 27 April 2006, R3.). Nevertheless, in *Rodeo Cowboy,* Michael Allen points to the longevity and continued resonance of the Western mythology and the cowboy figure, particularly as embodied in the rodeo cowboy, "a contemporary ancestor," whose popularity stems from his character traits. As he puts it,

this "hero is ubiquitous because he is consummately American, embodying Turnerian traits and complete loyalty to [the] Cowboy Code and to his fellow cowboys" (pp. 211–12). What all this means for the future of the Calgary Stampede is moot, of course, but I would suggest that cowboy/Western iconography is sufficiently powerful (and malleable) to remain useful to the region for many years to come.

82. L.G. Thomas, in Slatta, *Cowboys of the Americas*, 51. With regard to the importance of boosterism as a feature of western Canadian development, see Alan Artibise, "Boosterism and the Development of Prairie Cities, 1871–1913," in *The Prairie West*, 2nd ed., eds. R. Douglas Francis and Howard Palmer (Edmonton: University of Alberta Press, 1999), 515–43.

83. Frank Davey, "Towards the Ends of Regionalism," in *A Sense of Place: Re-evaluating Regionalism in Canadian and American Writing*, ed. Christian Riegel, Herb Wyile, et al. (Edmonton: University of Alberta Press, 1998), 7.

84. Ibid., 4.

85. Ibid., 14.

CHAPTER 8

A Spurring Soul: A Tenderfoot's Guide to the Calgary Stampede Rodeo

Glen Mikkelsen

Rodeo. Sure as bobcats are ornery, it's no tea party. Ask any cowboy who explodes out of a chute biting off a sunfishin' chunk of fury…and then chews it. That, though, is his life…skinned raw from the living flank of adventure. He takes it, tames it and loves it…from raking a saddle bronc to taking on a whole, snorting, pure-out mean ton of enraged bull. Every afternoon of Stampede '78, latigo-tough and arena-wise world champion cowboys compete for a bulging total purse of more than $110,000.

Watch 'em cannonball out aboard twisting, walleyed streaks of sheer hellhorse. See 'em dig in to wrestle down steers whose independence matches their muscle. Hang in as they milk wild cows, race the clock in calf roping, gallop for the finish line astride untamed mustangs in the wild horse race. And grip your seat as daredevil Indians tackle the brute power of plains buffalo. Rodeo. Stampede style! The non-stop action show that leaves hoofprints across hell. Go for it!

1978 Calgary Stampede promotional brochure

The rodeo is to the Calgary Stampede what shadows are to Groundhog Day. Without the rodeo there is no Stampede. It was the rodeo that renewed the Calgary Exhibition's vitality in 1923, and the rodeo has become the foundation of the Stampede's attitude and its community. It holds the imagination for the entire week. The rodeo sustains and nurtures the values of the Calgary Stampede, and it is where the Stampede's traditions are held holy.

The Stampede rodeo is revered as a fabulously grand sensory pageant. Participants and spectators are surrounded by glorious western notions, including beautiful Stampede Princesses bedecked in shimmering sequins atop flowing quarter horses; the taste of jalapeño-laden nachos and cold beer; the smell of dust-laden air rife with manure, hay, and sweat; and the heaving grunts and bellows of kinetic men and beasts. The Stampede rodeo is sensational and unpredictable, and it transcends conceptions with stirring and riveting western moments.

Rodeo competitors face daily peril, and, in fact, the Calgary Stampede rodeo calls upon divine safekeeping prior to each performance. Before the first chute is opened, competitors and fans are united in a communal expression of faith as they stand with hats removed and heads bowed while the Rodeo Cowboy's Prayer is recited.

A Rodeo Cowboy's Prayer

Our gracious and heavenly Father, we pause in the midst of this festive occasion, mindful and thoughtful of the guidance that you have given us. As cowboys, Lord, we don't ask for any special favors, we ask only that you let us compete in this arena, as in life's arena. We don't ask to never break a barrier, or to draw a round of steer that's hard to throw, or a chute fighting horse, or a bull that is impossible to ride. We only ask that you help us to compete as honest as the horses we ride and in a manner as clean and pure as the wind that blows across this great land of ours.

So when we do make that last ride that is inevitable for us all to make, to that place up there, where the grass is green and lush and stirrup high, and the water runs cool, clear, and deep – you'll tell us as we ride in that our entry fees have been paid.

These things we ask. Amen.[1]

With the conclusion of the prayer, the spectacle begins in Canada's largest rodeo, one of the world's most famous. Arguably, it is the most spectacular outdoor rodeo on the planet.

But it is not only the size and show of the Calgary Stampede rodeo that makes it special. The Calgary Stampede is an iconic event within the rodeo circuit, symbolizing western images and themes. The Stampede rodeo is not just sport; it is a tribute to the romanticized sentiments of western North America.

The images evoked daily upon the infield's dirt capture people's fantasies of the West. Through its competitors and its stock, the Stampede rodeo is both propaganda and factual elicitations of the West's savageness. Man vs. beast, life vs. death, luck vs. destiny; each Stampede afternoon the yin and yang of the West's splendor is re-enacted and renewed. As the "Greatest Outdoor Show on Earth," the Calgary Stampede rodeo has played, and continues to play, a pivotal role in preserving and propagating what the West is perceived to be.

The Calgary Stampede also represents the dreams of rodeo cowboys and cowgirls. The best of the best compete at Calgary. What the Masters is to golf, the Calgary Stampede is to rodeo. Its fame, even more than its sizable prize money, pulls rodeo's superlative competitors to Alberta from across continents and around the globe.

Fred Kennedy writes, "Over the gates, which lead into the rodeo arena of the Calgary Stampede, there is room for a sign which could well read: 'through these portals have passed the truly great names in rodeo.'"[2] These include such cowboys as Pete Knight, Herman Linder, Casey Tibbs, Jim Shoulders, Larry Mahan, Fred Whitfield, Dan Mortensen, and Ty Murray, and barrel racer Charmayne James.

Rodeo champions came to Calgary to compete in the rodeo's six major events: Bareback Riding, Saddle Bronc Riding, Bull Riding (collectively known as the rough stock events), Steer Wrestling, Tie-Down Roping (formerly known as Calf Roping), and Ladies Barrel Racing. Also included in the contemporary Stampede rodeo are Novice Saddle Bronc Riding, Novice Bareback Bronc Riding, and Junior Steer Riding. The afternoon rodeo is orchestrated symphonically, beginning with the Grand Entry's pageantry of sponsor flags and contestants and leading to the crescendo of Bull Riding – rodeo's final event.

The Stampede Rodeo Bucks Out

The Stampede rodeo originated with Guy Weadick in 1912. From the beginning, he promised a western show of extraordinary proportions, "entertainment on such a grand scale of magnificence as would be a fitting finale to the glorious history of the justly celebrated range."[3] The 1912 Stampede rodeo celebrated the cowboys' past, without realizing it set the stage for their future.

However, the 1912 show was significantly different from the show seen today. In 1912 Weadick had no regular rodeo circuit from which to draw competitors. Even though the first recorded rodeo took place forty-eight years earlier in Prescott, Arizona (on July 4, 1864), rodeo had not evolved into a regulated sport. There were no rodeo associations, no memberships, and no standardized rules. To entice the West's top ropers and riders,

Weadick used his charisma and prize money. He stated, "The money is here, come and get it."[4]

Weadick also needed to attract an audience to this fledgling, unknown sport. Ticket-buying Calgarians were not familiar with rodeos, but they did understand rodeo's predecessor – the Wild West show. And thus the union between the rodeo "sport" and Wild West "entertainment" was fabricated for the newly urban audience.

Buffalo Bill Cody had brought enormously popular Wild West productions to audiences throughout North America and Europe between 1883 and 1916. His show, and similar troupes such as Colonel Zack Miller's, demonstrated skills such as riding, roping, and shooting, incorporated into dramatic narratives. The Wild West shows blurred the lines between fiction and fact, entertainment and education. Billing themselves as preservers of memory, they regaled audiences with their own romanticized versions of western history.

Wild West promoters and performers created fabricated historical connections, inventing a common western history and culture built entirely upon entertainment. Audiences watched performers who could claim personal experience in the West, but their interpretations of frontier life were based on dime novels and sensational journalism. In a manner familiar to watchers of today's reality television shows, fictional entertainment was taken for "the real thing," and showmanship became inextricably entwined with the ability to sell tickets and put bums in seats.

The legacy of these Wild West performers morphed into the Stampede's rodeo arena. The Stampede rodeo became a reaffirmation of the Old West: the people who knew death on intimate terms, and the men and women who struggled to cheat it. From 1912 onward, the rodeo built upon the values promoted in Wild West show tents: fortitude, independent nobility, and toughness.

Several events demonstrate this; for example, take steer wrestling or bulldogging. On southern Alberta ranches, no cowboys bulldogged as part of their jobs; this rodeo event was invented by black Wild West performer Bill Pickett. Calling himself "The Dusky Demon," Pickett brought steers to their knees by biting on their lips (just like a ranch bulldog). In time, this accomplishment evolved into steer wrestling, became accepted as "sport," and is now one of the six major rodeo events (known as "the big man's event").

The two thrilling and unpredictable events of Wild Cow Milking and the Wild Horse Race are no longer part of the Stampede rodeo. From the 1920s to 2005 they delivered the Wild West show's formula of bravado, conflict, and conquest of the wild.

Wild Cow Milking (or the North American Cow Milking Championship) featured twenty teams of two cowboys competing at the same time. When the horn sounded, the teams chased a herd of wild cows in the arena. One cowboy on horseback roped a long-horned cow, while the other cowboy, the "mugger," took hold of the cow by the horns or neck. The roper then dismounted and attempted to milk the cow into a small-necked bottle. The first milker to run to the judge's stand with the required milk was the daily winner.

The Wild Horse Race (or Stampede Horse Race) featured twelve teams of three cowboys each scrambling to saddle and ride an untamed bucking horse. Simultaneously, all twelve chutes opened. Each man had a specific job: there were the ear-man, the shank-man, and the rider. The horses all wore halters with long shanks. When the horses were released from the chutes, all three-man teams held on to the halter shanks. The ear-man moved up the shank, grabbed the horse by the head, and bit its ear (in later years, the cowboys could only twist the ear). This generally sufficiently distracted and calmed the horse. The rider then moved in to saddle the animal. When the saddle was secured, the ear-man and shank-man released the horse and the rider attempted to ride it across the finish line in front of the grandstand.

> It all sounds straightforward but watch it – with an
> arena full of wild horses, each being saddled by a team
> of cowboys and each team trying to be faster than the
> next, it becomes a dangerous and rugged event, involving
> contestants who must be equally as rugged.[5]

Although the Wild Horse Race is no longer featured, the Wild Pony Race is now included on the event list. But this Stampede event is more amusing than "wild," as teams of three youngsters aged eight to twelve try to tame a wild pony long enough to get a rider aboard for a two-jump ride. The team with the fastest time wins.

The rodeo event that most blurred the lines between reality and entertainment was the Buffalo Riding Championship. For years the Stampede rodeo began with this event. Simultaneously, eight chutes opened to release buffalo ridden by Indian cowboys in traditional regalia. It was truly an unusual western scene as the buffalo – the monarchs of the plains – bucked to rid themselves of their riders. This event would not have taken place historically and was distinctly taken out of the Wild West shows genre. (Robert Altman's 1976 film *Buffalo Bill and the Indians, or Sitting Bull's History Lesson*, filmed outside of Calgary, includes a scene of a cowboy bulldogging a buffalo to the ground, another twisted historical perspective.)

Not all of the Stampede rodeo events merge fiction and fun. Saddle Bronc Riding and Tie-Down Roping are both based on ranching activities, and Bareback Riding originated when cowboys branded young range horses. The horses were held down for branding, but before they were let up, daring cowboys straddled the horses and grasped a handful of mane in each hand. When the horses were released, bronc busters kept their balance by pushing with the front hand and pulling with the back hand.

The "manehold" evolved into riding with a loose rope. A manila rope with a honda (a metal, rope, or rawhide ring) in one end was cinched around the horse's girth and laid across the cowboy's hands (one hand on each side of the horse's withers). The rope was tightened by the chute man and laid back across the rider's hands again. Eventually the rigging matured into a leather strap connected to a handhold resembling a suitcase handle that was fastened to a cinch around the horse. The 1912 Stampede rodeo was notable for hosting one of the world's first bareback riding competitions, and Bareback Riding was recognized as a major rodeo event in 1932.

The First Stampede Stars

The first two celebrities created in the Stampede rodeo arena were Tom Three Persons and Cyclone. Three Persons, apart from Weadick, is the character most feted within the first Stampede's mythology, and Cyclone was his partner. Three Persons, a Blood Indian, drew the famed Cyclone in the 1912 saddle bronc finals. Known as the "Black Terror," Cyclone had thrown 129 of the world's best riders with his frantic pounding style. Cyclone was dangerous and unnerving. The horse would rear as if tumbling backwards (known as sunfishing), then would duck down and leap forward, jerking riders ahead and off into the dirt.INSERT FIG.5

At the 1912 rodeo there were no bucking chutes, and rides lasted until horses stopped bucking (approximately forty seconds). In the infield, horses were blindfolded or held and released. For Three Persons' final ride, Stampede officials held Cyclone steady. As Three Persons settled into the saddle, Cyclone was released and reared backwards. Three Persons recalled, "He starts to raise with me after the fifth jump, and scared the hell right out of me. I thought he was coming over backwards. Without realizing what I was really doin', I started to beller at him. He was so surprised that he flattened out. I knew I had 'im then so I just kept on spurring until I heard the whistle."[6] It was Three Persons' supreme rodeo moment and immortalized him and his outlaw horse into Stampede mythology.

The success and popularity of the 1912 Stampede sparked rodeo's development in southern Alberta. For example, the first known side-delivery rodeo chute was designed and constructed at Welling, Alberta, in 1916. A similar chute was built at New Dayton, Alberta, in 1917, and another in Lethbridge in 1919. The side-delivery chute reversed the chute gate so that it hinged at the horse's head, forcing the horse to turn as the gate opened. This design required only one man to work the chute gate and eliminated the hazard of riders' knees getting hung up. It quickly became standard in rodeos.

In 1927 the Stampede also set a rodeo precedent by reducing a qualifying ride to only ten seconds. This important change allowed the show to run more quickly and cut down the number of horses required. It also prolonged horses' careers. Outstanding bucking horses seldom had their spirits broken in ten seconds. In 1972 the ten-second saddle bronc ride was reduced to eight seconds.

Women in the Infield

Reflecting the Wild West show casts, both women and men participated equally in the 1912 Stampede. Western Canada was still civilizing itself, and women carried the freedoms offered by a new land. According to rodeo accounts, "Prairie Rose" Henderson first opened rough stock riding to women. At Cheyenne, Wyoming, in 1901 Henderson defied the protestations of male judges and completed a bronc-riding performance.

Eleven years later, in the 1912 Stampede, women competed in bucking horse and roping competitions.[7] Fanny Sperry was the first Lady Bucking Horse Champion of the World, and Guy Weadick's wife, Florence LaDue, took the title of Lady Champion Fancy Roper. Although only five feet tall, LaDue could rope a galloping horse with rider from a standing position.[8]

During the 1930s and 1940s women continued to ride in the rough stock events. Cowgirl Tad Lucas earned more than $10,000 riding bucking broncs on the rodeo circuit during the Depression,[9] but after World War II, the rough stock were reserved for men. The rodeo atmosphere was turning masculine, with women considered a performance sideshow. For example, Dixie Reger Mosley, a stunt rider, made a living jumping cars on her palomino.[10]

Modern rodeo remains predominantly a testosterone fraternity. In both the Canadian Professional Rodeo Association and the Pro Rodeo Cowboys Association, women continue to work outside the main events. Often they participate as contracted "Wild West Show" entertainers. For example, as trick riders, women on swift horses wear flashy costumes and enthrall crowds between events.

However, within pro rodeo, women do have one sanctioned event, and have developed a popular following as professional barrel racers. With competitions timed to 1/100th of a second, Barrel Racing is one of the Stampede audience's favourite events. It is easy for rodeo neophytes to understand, and the harmonious partnership between rider and horse is energetic entertainment. Nevertheless, Stampede barrel racers have struggled against the male-dominated world of rodeo. Barrel Racing was not a Stampede prize event until 1979, and although Barrel Racing was part of the daily line-up in 1982, when the $50,000 prize money was awarded in each event, only the events involving cowboys were eligible.

It was not until 1996, when barrel racer Monica Wilson raised $50,000 herself as finals prize money, that the Stampede began paying barrel racers equally and including them in the Sunday Finals. Finally, women and men were equally paid competitors at the Calgary Stampede.[11] For her efforts, Wilson was awarded the coveted Guy Weadick Award, annually given to the rodeo or chuckwagon contestant who combines outstanding accomplishments with personality, sportsmanship, and appearance.[12] The Weadick Award was first presented in 1982, and Wilson was the first woman to receive the trophy.

Bucking Broncs

Within the Stampede culture, the bucking bronc remains the central symbol of rodeo. The bronc represents an outlaw, a force of power over conventional society. Cowboys believe its rebelliousness is genetic and cannot be taught; its power is not controllable. Something within particular horses causes this behaviour and makes them incorrigible. Even when broncs appear docile or calm, they are by nature unpredictable, untameable, and raw. Bulls may be tough, mean, and brutish, but broncs are the wild, renegade spirit beloved in rodeo.

As Louis says in the Alberta motion picture *Road to Saddle River*, "A bucking horse is the meanest, toughest, craziest fifteen hundred pounds of grain-fed

Tilly Baldwin at the 1919 Stampede. Ladies Bucking Horse Riding was one of the premier rodeo events in which women competed in the early 1900s.

animal flesh on the planet. Many a good cowboy has died underneath the hooves of a rank bronc."[13]

To enhance broncs' scoring abilities, the Stampede embarked on producing the world's best bucking horses. In 1961 the Stampede organized the "Born to Buck" program and purchased a ranch near Hanna, Alberta, where it attempted to reverse the centuries-old process of genetic selection for more docile mounts. The Stampede intended to take advantage of economic opportunities and maintain a high level of competition by breeding "hell-horses" for the rodeo circuit.

The Stampede ranch covers about 20,500 acres of leased land and 1,500 acres of deeded property. Fifty mares were the foundation of the breeding program. Presently, more than four hundred horses live at the ranch, including sixty-two brood mares. The Stampede horses are easily identified by the brand (C lazy S) on the left shoulder. The Calgary Stampede is one of the very few rodeos with a registered brand of its own.

One hundred sixty-five of the horses perform in rodeos, and the busiest of those, approximately thirty of them, may be on the rodeo road. The most any horse will buck is about fifteen times. Colts are not moved to rodeos until age five, though they may be ridden twice a year at age three or four. The "top-end" horses, such as the famed Grated Coconut, Papa Smurf, and Guilty Cat, are bucked a maximum of three times during the Stampede.

In appreciation of stock contractors' efforts to produce unrelenting mounts, at every Stampede rodeo performance the horses and bull carrying the day's winning rides and the animals judges deem as the rankest on their scorecards are each awarded $500. On the final Sunday, one bareback bronc, one saddle bronc, and one bull are crowned the overall Calgary Stampede Champion Stock. The contractor receives a bronze trophy, and the animals are let loose in the infield to receive the crowd's praise. These Champion Stock trophies have been awarded since 1979.

In addition to Stampede week, the Calgary Stampede rodeo office produces several rodeos each year in Canada and supplies stock to about twenty other rodeos in western Canada and the United States. It also provides bucking horses for one-day convention rodeos in Calgary and sends its younger stock to rodeo schools and college rodeos. The longest road trip Stampede horses make is to the National Finals Rodeo in Las Vegas each December.

As any cowboy could tell you, riding a bronc is no tea party. The force of a bronc's first jump out of the chute compares to that of the whiplash incurred in an average car accident. Bronc riding hurts. There are reasons why a bucking bronc's saddle is called a "hurricane deck," yet bronc riding has a powerful mystique and pull, as former Calgary Stampede Rodeo Director Winston Bruce, a world champion saddle bronc rider, explains:

> You arrive at the rodeo about a hour to an hour and
> a half before the ride. You start gathering your equip-
> ment together, and your mind changes. It goes to heavy
> concentration to what you're going to do. As the animal is
> brought into the chute, you start preparing, putting your
> saddle and your tack on, becoming more concentrated.
> The outside world starts to shut off more all the time.
>
> By the time you get on the animal, it's almost like being in
> a trance. You're totally alert, really alert, but only alert to
> the things that matter at that moment; things like where
> the pick up men are, where the chute gate openers are,
> where the judges are, where the photographer may be. You
> get that fixed in your mind. And then you feel the animal
> underneath you. He's usually quiet at that time because
> experienced horses are probably thinking the same things
> as you, only in reverse.

By the time the chute gate is opened, the outside world is totally cut away. Your senses are really limited to only what matters at that moment in the arena. As you're riding the animal, you're aware of any movement around you, like the pickup horses or something flickering in the stands, because that could change the direction of the animal. You can usually sense a change of direction in the animal as it's happening.

When you get off the animal, your adrenaline is really running high and you feel good. And because of that, your alertness is on high. So there's a "high" to that in the sense of satisfaction. It's always a personal contest against yourself really. Everybody, I'm sure, has the same goal, and that goal is to make the perfect ride. That's what your goal is. You may never achieve it, but if you ever do, you're probably finished, because what would you want to do the next time?[14]

Rodeo's Seduction

For horses, bulls, and men, an underlying Stampede rodeo theme is the threat of injury or death. As sixteen-time world champion cowboy Jim Shoulders said, "People don't want to see a rodeo cowboy die, but they want to be there

when he does."[15] The Stampede rodeo emphasizes human frailty and the power of nature on a perilous stage; people are drawn into the grandstand like passers-by to an accident.

The first Stampede rodeo of 1912 set the tragic legacy. While preparing stock a few days before the show, cowboy Joe LaMar was trying out bucking horses in the evening arena. Red Wing, a big sorrel from Medicine Hat, fell while bucking. LaMar's chap belt caught on the saddle horn, and Red Wing kicked him.[16] LaMar died en route to the hospital, inciting the first, but not the last, public outcry about the sport's brutality but also piquing the audience's curiosity about cowboys' bravado and dangerous ambitions.

Rodeo fans can determine what events cowboys compete in simply by looking at their injuries. Bareback riders deal with painful elbows from absorbing the pounding shock of riding and sore knees from awkwardly spurring. Bronc riders have knee problems from constant spurring and kinked necks from flying dismounts. Bull riders limp with strained riding arms and pulled groin muscles (the wide backs of bulls are not designed for riding). Steer wrestlers hurt their knees when they jump to the ground from horses going twenty-five to thirty-five miles an hour. Bulldoggers are also prone to shoulder injuries from rotating their arms while grasping the horns of a steer weighing three times their weight. Unlucky ropers can leave a thumb or finger lying in the infield after a shoddy dally (improperly wrapping the rope around the saddle horn).[17]

The spectre of injury is a hook constantly marketed by the rodeo, with the threat not limited to performers. I witnessed this personally in 1978. At that time, there was a children's playground in the middle of the racetrack, behind the infield grandstand. As the rodeo concluded, a bull named USA was released for the clowns and bullfighters to use to demonstrate their skills. USA was chosen for his broad horns, threatening appearance, and speed.

To the crowd's astonishment, this agile 1,300-pound Brahma bull leapt over the infield fence. Running up the racetrack, the bull met a group of exiting fans crossing towards the grandstand. Spooked by the crowd, he jumped the railing towards the playground, where a lone seven-year-old girl played on the swings. The bull, with its eyes alert and horns swinging, pranced towards her. I recall a collective gasp as the panicking grandstand audience helplessly watched the bull trot towards the oblivious child. Jim Knowler said, "The woman beside me was screaming, shrieking, and crying."[18] Finally the girl saw the bull; she took a couple of steps, but could not get out of the way. The bull hit her.

THROWING A STEER IN "BULL-DOGGING CONTEST. STAMPEDE AT CALGARY CAN." OFFICIAL PHOTO #64 MARCELL OF CALGARY.

One upset woman said, "I'll see that as long as I live."[19] Miraculously, the girl suffered only bruising and a cut lip. After toppling the girl, the bull trotted off towards the barns, where a posse of cowboys eventually roped it.

(The image of a rogue bull is not limited to the Stampede. For example, in Billings, Montana, a Brahma bull broke out of the rodeo arena, crashed through the parking lot, and hid out in a city park. For five weeks the city was on a full bull alert. When the bull was finally captured, he was renamed "Longtimenosee."[20])

These scenes of unpredictable danger – western style – fortify the rodeo's image as a theatre of cutting drama. The elements of suspense, injury, and pain are embedded in the sport. Tension is guaranteed every time a chute is opened. It is the perpetual conflict between man and beast. Built upon its dirt, the rodeo infield transforms danger into daring-do, pain into prowess, and death into dignity. The infield manipulates and forges Stampede male, female, bovine, and equine legends.

The risks transform the rodeo cowboy figure into the Stampede emissary. The image of a lone cowboy making his livelihood by luck and skill in one of the last vestiges of an aggressive, untamed, and bestial competition is a key message of the Stampede. From posters to websites, the independent cowboy is the Stampede's ambassador.

Gene Lamb sanctions rodeo as "the last frontier for the individual."[21] Rodeo performers project toughness, endurance, and stoicism. The cowboy's characteristic individualism was reinforced by the structure under which early rodeo contests were conducted. The rodeo cowboy was responsible for all expenses relating to his travels from one rodeo to the next. In this aspect, rodeo differed from many other sports, and it is this element that makes the rodeo cowboy's situation so difficult for the uninitiated to understand. In most rodeos today, the cowboy is still on his own; he pays his way to the rodeo, pays the entry fees and other expenses, and makes money only if he wins or places in the events in which he competes. This only reinforces his sense of independence.[22]

Furthermore, the Stampede rodeo cowboy's success is based on luck – a cowboy crap shoot. Cowboys draw the stock they ride, rope, or wrestle, so the luck of the draw is essential. There is nothing a cowboy can do to dress up a horse or prevent a bull from performing badly or keep a steer from dropping his horns. Each time a rough stock rider blasts out of the chute, he gambles getting hurt and going broke all at once.[23] Even the most skilled cowboy cannot hope to win without a good draw.

Luck also includes surviving the rodeo lifestyle to qualify for the Stampede. Six time all-around world champion Larry Mahan explains rodeo "survival skills." "You have to learn to travel without a car, borrow clothes, and put up with ten men in a motel room. Competitors must also subsist on a diet heavy in 'rodeo steak' [hot dogs]. Contestants pay a fee to compete and earn no salary. On a bad day, riders end up several hundred dollars poorer."[24]

With luck, personal injury, and personal fortitude influencing competitors' success so randomly, cowboys rightly deserve the flattery and attention lavished on them at the Stampede. After all the miles travelled, when cowboys qualify for Calgary, for ten days they are the city's heroes. As the Stampede's pre-eminent personalities, their images and performances dominate local television and print.

In an ironic reflection of urban Calgary's longstanding relationship with rodeo, however, despite their honoured role and their significance in Stampede mythology, the rodeo and chuckwagon cowboys are anonymous superstars. Former professional chuckwagon driver Jim Nevada relates the cowboys' plight: "Chuckwagon drivers are a hero for ten days in Calgary, but the rest of the time we're just some Joe Shmuck cowboy. You see some guys walking around like a peacock, but no one notices you. Some wagon drivers don't realize [they're] not a household name."[25]

Most Calgarians do not know, and do not care, who wins the Stampede events. The cowboys' and cowgirls' names are meaningless, and forgotten. Even Albertan Kelly Sutherland, who is arguably the Stampede's best-known cowboy – a chuckwagon driver for over thirty-five years and record-tying ten-time Rangeland Derby champion – told me he is undetected as a celebrity without a cowboy hat. His black hat and eagle feather give him his recognizable identity. It is the cowboy iconography of hats, buckles, and Wrangler jeans that urbanites seek and crave for one week a year.

Furthermore, by donning their uniform of hats and Wranglers, the lone cowboys identify themselves as a group. As an example, notice the predominance of either black or white cowboy hats behind Stampede rodeo chutes. There is a strong conformist code within rodeo ranks. It is ironic in a sport celebrating individual talents that its men (and women) are perceived collectively.

The cowboys' anonymity stems in part from the Stampede's origins in the Wild West shows, where the athletes were seen as cast members rather than solo performers. The sport is a novelty. The rodeo is still often called a "performance" rather than a "competition," and the cowboys are the cast.

Secondly, cowboys have traditionally received little recognition because they are seen so briefly. Even with the help of a Jumbotron television, an eight-second ride is not long enough for an audience to identify individual cowboys. Typically, cowboys are on their broncs, out of the chute, on the ground, out of the arena, and off down the road, sometimes literally within minutes. With their hats sitting low on their heads, cowboys appear as anonymous, interchangeable figures.

Rodeo organizers recognize that spectators need to empathize with the competitors. It is difficult for new fans to relate to the sport. Urbanites cannot differentiate individual cowboys' rides; apartment dwellers have no shared experiences with a bronc rider.

One tactic rodeo announcers use to build empathy is to introduce cowboys by their hometowns – "Billy Richards, Cochrane, Alberta"; or "Zack Oates, Tonasket, Washington." A connection to the audience is attempted through shared geography. Since experiences are invalid, geography is used to elicit compassion and emotion. Perhaps audience members familiar with the cowboy's hometown, province, or state will support him with a cheer due to the common reference.

Geography is also a constant element in the Stampede rodeo's marketing. The rivalry between Canadian and American cowboys has been emphasized to enliven the show since 1912, when Tom Three Persons was the only

Canadian to win a major event. This competition was also celebrated in the Stampede team rodeo during the 1988 Calgary Winter Olympics. In 2005 a *Calgary Herald* headline proclaimed, "Canadians Rock Stampede's $75,000 Sunday Showdown," and the story added, "When all was said and done at this year's instalment of the world's only regular-season million-dollar rodeo, five out of the six $75,000 bonus round winners were Canadians."[26]

Relieving Tedium

Ironically, even though the rodeo offers numerous opportunities for thrills, much of the performance can be tedious. By its nature, there are ample gaps in a rodeo program. The rough stock events consist of dramatic eight-second rides punctuated by long pauses as cowboys prepare to mount. Even within the timed events, there are gaps between competitors' entrances.

Tedium is not distinctive to the Stampede, as Wayne Wooden and Gavin Ehringer point out. "Boredom is, to be sure, an occupational hazard of the contemporary sport of rodeo and one with which the contestant has to deal, along with a host of other risks inherent in the profession. But boredom has not always been part and parcel of the contest. In fact, rodeo itself was more or less invented to counteract that very condition – the monotony and loneliness of the life of the working cowboy in the days of the cattle drives and the open range."[27]

The tradition of "action gaps" began at the 1912 Stampede, which had no bucking chutes and no time limit on rides. Donna Livingstone writes, "The events themselves were long on promotion and short on delivery ... Most events went on far too long, with unexplained delays ... The steers brought in for the steer roping proved too fast for the Canadian rope horses and had to be chased as much as a quarter of a mile. Competitors often found themselves at the far end of the vast centre field, far from the view of the audience."[28]

The Stampede was not alone in facing timing issues. In rodeo's early years, producers frequently staged poorly organized shows. Often performances were an endless series of slow-moving contests of several hours' duration that stimulated neither the spectators' interest nor the cowboys' cooperation.

Today aficionados understand the nature of the sport and head to the concession or beer garden during the pauses. They appreciate rodeo's rhythm, the short, but climactic, eight seconds competitors have to test their skills. Experienced fans know what events they like and patiently await their arrival.

To preserve the attention of Calgary's greenhorn rodeo fans, "Wild West" acts are hired. Entertainers have included trick riders, whip performers, ostrich races, and First Nations dancers. Bud Munroe, the 1986 World Saddle Bronc Riding Champion, elaborates, "Good acts add to a rodeo. All of us in rodeo are entertainers. Acts break up the monotony of the rodeo, and at the same time give the contractor extra time to do things like run stock in. It's important to have something flamboyant enough to keep the crowd's attention while all this takes place."[29]

Clowning Around

For keeping the crowd entertained, the most significant Stampede rodeo act is the clown. The clown fills in gaps between rides and events and distracts the crowd if a cowboy or animal requires attention in the infield. A regular feature of rodeos since the 1920s, clowns initially did double duty as comedians and cowboy protectors. In addition to entertaining the crowd during lulls, they participated in bull riding, distracting bulls from thrown cowboys. (During this era, "bulls" might be real bulls, range cows, or good-sized steers; in fact, during the 1920s they might be anything that could remotely be considered a "bull.")

In the late 1920s Brahma bulls were introduced. Clowning duties were then split between bullfighters – those fearless men dashing to the cowboy's rescue – and clowns who told jokes, performed skits, and bantered with the announcer. The comedic clowns also often worked within a safety barrel, the "clown lounge," during bull riding.

Whether facing bulls or telling jokes, Stampede clowns are known for their chutzpah. For example, for many years the Stampede held thoroughbred races between rodeo events. During one race, clown Buddy Heaton had a substantial bet on a particular horse. As his horse faded badly around the final turn, Heaton watched from the infield. Infuriated, Heaton sprang on his pet buffalo, an animal used in his acts, rode onto the racetrack, and charged the oncoming horses. Jockeys and horses scattered in every direction, avoiding Heaton and his speeding buffalo.[30]

Apart from spontaneous wild antics, it is up to the clown to entertain the crowd. The rodeo clown is the comic to the announcer's straight man. Jokes rehearsed between the announcer and clown are delivered between events and when a cowboy has trouble saddling a mount. Like Heaton with his buffalo, clowns use chickens, dogs, monkeys, sheep, and other animals in their skits. And few rodeos do not include explosions – exploding outhouses, guns, vehicles, and suitcases are mainstays in rodeo clown skits.

Clown Gene Clark describes rodeo clown humour. "We use common humor that the audience can relate to, especially children. For example, mothers continually fuss at their children about hygiene and manners. One of the simplest jokes kids always love is, 'I stuck my finger up the bull's nose and a booger bit me.'"[31] Coarse humour is a rodeo constant, humour based on homophobia, wife-humiliation, gender bashing, and basic bodily functions. Clowns belittle their wives and draw laughs by embarrassing and tormenting animals and cowboys.

For example, clowning dialogue from a 2006 professional rodeo featured the following lines:

- **Clown asks the announcer:** "What's the difference between my wife and a car battery?"
  Announcer: "I don't know."
  Clown: "A battery has a positive side."

- **Clown:** "You don't want to make my wife mad ... She's big enough to sell shade."

- **Clown:** "Do you know the difference between broccoli and boogers?"
  Announcer: "No."
  Clown: "Kids don't eat broccoli."

- **Clown:** "Constipated people don't give a crap."

- **Clown asks the announcer:** "Do you know the difference between a cow's tail and a water pump?"
  Announcer: "No."
  Clown: "Don't ask me to send you for water."[32]

In another demonstration of clown humour, Jasbo and George Mills lassoed and held a cowboy down in the dirt, While Mills sat upon his chest and held his hands, Jasbo reached into his voluminous patched trousers and pulled out a pair of very pink, very large, very feminine panties. He sat upon the cowboy's kicking legs and tussled the garment over his boots and Levis to its proper position. The clowns stood up to survey their handiwork, staggering about in fits of laughter. The cowboy scrambled out of the rope, and with the overly large legs of the pink underpants flapping, he chased the galloping little clowns out of the arena and around the grandstand.[33]

Throughout the history of rodeo clowning, the humour has reflected rodeo's basic nature as a simple competition between and against men, women, and beasts, a sport without refinements. Its raw personality and culture evoke a certain wildness that makes the clowns' humour tolerable to many spectators. Nevertheless, the clowns' buffoonery reflects sentiments not appreciated by broader urban audiences. Typically, rodeo clown acts have no subtlety, no nuances, and no graciousness; they fail to address society's changing expectations. Without recognizing a modern audience's refinements or tastes, the entertainment potentially alienates rather than amuses spectators.

Dogged by Abuse Accusations

More significant than rodeo clown humour, the main issue dogging the Stampede rodeo is animal abuse. Rodeo everywhere faces accusations constantly; however, in July the world media focus on the action in the Stampede infield (and during the evening, around the chuckwagon track). With each buck and twist, reporters, particularly from those from eastern Canada, pursue any controversial story involving animals.

Questions about animal abuse were raised as early as the 1912 Stampede. Genevieve Lipsett-Skinner, self-appointed spokesperson for "every woman," described in a *Calgary Daily Herald* article "the appalling cruelty to the steers chosen to illustrate the prowess of the cowboys in the manly art of 'bulldogging.'" Her article claimed that a wrestler tore off a steer's horn.[34] How the horn was broken is not recorded. Under normal circumstances, the pain induced by breaking a steer's horn partway compares to that of a human breaking a fingernail. It is nearly impossible for a cowboy to break a steer's horns painfully – by tearing them off the animal's skull. Following their rodeo careers, most steers are dehorned when they are fattened for the beef market.

Lipsett-Skinner's concerns did not stop steer wrestling and steer roping at the 1919 Stampede, but these events were not on the bill in 1923, for two reasons. The first was economic: cattlemen did not like the sports because when their cowboys practised by running steers on the ranch, the wearied cattle lost weight. (In the mid-1960s steer wrestling was re-introduced at Canadian pro rodeos, including the Stampede. The CPRA [Canadian Professional Rodeo Association] wanted integration with the PRCA [Professional Rodeo Cowboy's Association] in the United States, where steer wrestling was still an event, so points won in the event could count in both countries.)

Steer wrestling and steer roping also were not included in the 1923 Stampede as a result of the Calgary Humane Society's incorporation as a charitable organization in 1922. Although claims that steers suffered may have been misguided, the Humane Society offered Calgarians concerned about animal welfare an agency through which to protest perceived cruelties. The incorporation of the society was the beginning of a closer scrutiny of the Stampede's actions.

In rough stock events, animal rights supporters argue that the flank strap inflicts pain to the genitals of a bucking bronc or bull. (A flank strap or scratcher cinch extends around the animal's body at the flanks.) Rodeo proponents argue the flank strap only irritates the animal, inciting it to buck more enthusiastically. Nevertheless, there is an assistant whose job is to pull solidly on the strap when the door opens and the animal leaves the chute. Especially in the finals, when emotion and money are on the line, no effort is spared to make that animal buck.

Stampede rodeo critics take strongest exception to calf roping. With calves literally pushed out of the chute into a run, injuries occur when the rope catches them by the neck, tightens, and pulls them sharply back. In 2003 pro rodeo's public relations advisors recommended that the event be called Tie-Down Roping instead of Calf Roping. The event is unchanged, but the name was changed to make it more marketable.

As a reflection of how this event unnerves spectators, Stampede television broadcasts the "sport" strategically. The initial camera position is set up facing the cowboy and the calf. As the calf leaves the chute, the camera focuses on the cowboy and his horse. Only after the calf is roped does the camera pan down, letting the viewer see the cowboy run to tie the calf. Viewers are intentionally prevented from seeing the rope stop the calf.

Stampede rodeo proponents do their sport no favours by dramatizing its perils. Take Darrell Knight, writing about his famous great-uncle, bronc rider Pete Knight:

> Everyone knew Pete's first ambition was in the bucking
> horse event. That, after all, was the true "lone knight"
> occupation of the stampede – the premier event of every
> rodeo in North America – and Pete's first love. It involved
> the greatest individual danger but reaped the biggest
> rewards for the sole contestant, where one expert rider
> placed all of his skill against one superbly notorious buck-
> ing horse, fully saddled and quickly released.
>
> Charging from an infield chute from 'stand-still' – in a
> fight for supremacy that carried the bronc rider through a
> nightmarish ten seconds – both horse or contestant could
> be battered, bloodied…or killed. Bronc riders losing their
> place in the saddle – an upset to their delicate balance
> and timing with boots spurring in stirrups and buck-rein
> 'see-sawing' in a clenched fist – were often thrown through
> solid wooden railings or wire fences. Horses bucked in a
> maddened frenzy over high walls and through chute gates
> and onto the bleacher seating of stampede grandstands,
> rupturing themselves and often crushing their riders
> in the process. It was a blood-sport born of the plains,
> but an honest depiction of the daily life faced by the
> last western hero – the cowboy – on a frontier that was
> rapidly vanishing."[35]

Such depictions mobilize protesters to march at the Stampede's gates. In 2005 the Stampede faced a hail of criticism after horses drowned near the end of a 206-kilometre trail ride. As part of Alberta's centennial celebrations, some of the Stampede's bucking horses were herded from the Hanna ranch into the congested city. Near the entrance to the Stampede grounds, a train whistled, spooking the herd crossing a Bow River bridge. Horses fell into the unusually high water; three died on impact, five drowned, and one was put down later because of its injuries. No charges were laid in their deaths.

Even some clown acts have historically dealt questionably with animals. For example, Wes Curtis and Sammy Reynosa's routine included tying a Roman candle four inches above a calf's tail. When the calf was released and ran to the ketch pen, one–two–three flares shot up into the air. Announcers prepared the audience by stating, "These Roman candles are specially made and they will not harm the calf in any way,"[36] but undoubtedly they tormented the animal. How would spectators appreciate rockets tied to their buttocks?

The Humane Society of Canada's executive director, Michael O'Sullivan, writes, "Rodeo spectacles are nothing but entertainment for bored 'city slickers.' Horses, calves, steers and bulls suffer during countless hours of practice sessions where riders and ropers train to race against the clock for prize money. People need to find new ways to entertain themselves that don't involve this kind of trauma for animals."[37]

To the Stampede's credit, there is no question the rodeo managers take care of their animals. Stock contractors nurture and coddle their horses and bulls to ensure they are in prime physical and mental condition. Keith Marrington, senior manager of Rodeo and Chuckwagon Racing, states, "They are our friends. We get very emotional, get passionate, we're attached to them. They're like our kids."[38] The animals are equine and bovine athletes. The success and livelihoods of contractors, contestants, the sport, and the Stampede itself lies in the well-being of the animals.

Not all people questioning animal care are animal activists. As one observer noted, "Rodeos are obviously not pleasant for the animals, even though they may not actually be hurt. The flank strap irritates them enough to make them thrash and buck wildly. For a calf, being yanked backwards from a full run by a rope around its neck has got to be a nasty experience. How can we really justify this? And lumping everyone who might be worried about this under the umbrella of animal rights activist seems too easy and an oversimplification."[39]

The Calgary Stampede is not alone in feeling the intensified scrutiny of people concerned about animal welfare. The rodeo in Cloverdale, British Columbia, ranks among the top five Canadian rodeos, but in 2007 a calf was euthanized after a tie-down roping performance. For the 2008 show, in response to tremendous pressure from the Vancouver Humane Society and local politicians, Cloverdale became the first rodeo to ban tie-down roping, team roping, steer wrestling, and wild cow milking.

Roy Call, stock contractor and owner/manager of C-Plus Ranch in 150 Mile House, British Columbia, says, "That got way too much coverage for what it was, but I will say one thing, the cowboys have been very slow to respond to the changing makeup of our spectators."

Call explains the dynamics of tie-down roping:

> How you handle your rope after you catch your calf determines where the calf lands. If you pitch it up his back in a straight line, the calf goes straight over backwards. If you hold the rope off to the side the calf is going to snap around and probably stay on his feet.
>
> You want them to stay on their feet. And where the calves are well-conditioned and fast, you have to do that because if you jerk him off his feet you'll be too slow and you won't place. Where the calves are bigger, or if it's not for a lot of money, you might take a chance and risk that, and that practice needs to be stopped. There's no doubt, injuries to the calves do occur, just like you see with the contestants, and there's no good way to handle those incidents.

Call concludes:

> Very few people in Cloverdale come from rural backgrounds and they're not used to seeing things like that. [Rodeo] has been very slow to make rule changes and bring in extra protection for the animals. This should result in some major changes that will come forward to make it safer for the cattle and make it more palatable for the public."[40]

Unquestionably, the Cloverdale Rodeo faces more intense scrutiny than many other rodeos because it is situated in B.C.'s lower mainland, yet Call's comments reflect animal issues in all rodeos, including the Stampede. Simply, there is greater community compassion for animals. Even in the grocery store, urban cowboys and cowgirls have a broader understanding of animals and are more interested in their lives. They want free-range eggs and organic beef; they want to know the animals have a fair shake. The changes originating from West Coast rodeo may ultimately be recognized within the Calgary Stampede infield as well.

Stampede Rodeo's Challenges

The Stampede rodeo faces other less celebrated but perhaps more pressing issues. Even though the rodeo is so vital to the Stampede, a curious dichotomy is seen in the grandstands. Despite its eminence within the Stampede's raison d'être, the rodeo grandstand is rarely sold out. Even on the final day, seats are available. Although the Stampede revolves around rodeo's men, women, and beasts, Calgarians are not clamoring to buy tickets to the Stampede's showcase event.

The rodeo's odd position within Calgary culture is related to the audience's perception. At its best, the Stampede rodeo is an unequalled western spectacle of cowboys, cowgirls, horses, bulls, calves, and steers. In a fashion not seen in any other sport they compete co-operatively and competitively. At its worst, the rodeo is an insular and closed-minded community competing in a world separate from modern-day Calgary. Regarded as a novelty by visitors and as a historical souvenir by many Calgarians, the rodeo is a ranchland curiosity. To its proponents, the rodeo is misinterpreted; to its detractors, it is brutal, elitist, and anachronistic.

One concern is how to keep the live show compelling when the stock out-competes the cowboys. For example, the hyped bull-riding competition frequently does not meet its billing. Due to the successful breeding of mighty bulls, the bovines often rule the riders. Cowboys are tossed, the rides are short, and although tension is built, commonly the bull riding is tedious. For example, in 2005 only three cowboys out of ten finalists made it to the bonus round. After each of the three cowboys failed to ride two more bulls, the judges used the final round's high scores to determine a winner. Stock contractors have done their task all too well!

Communicating the judging of bulls and horses is another issue faced by the Stampede. Thousands of international tourists attend the rodeo, and most do not understand its judging system. If a sport is complex to understand, it is difficult to nurture a broader fan base.

Rodeo judging is supposed to work like this: In the rough stock events (bareback riding, saddle-bronc riding, and bull riding), the cowboys and the stock are judged equally – 50 points to the cowboy and 50 points to the animal. At many rodeos, two judges are used, but at the Stampede, four judges are used, each calculating 50 points, with the total divided by two.

Judges consider how hard the animal tries to throw the rider, for example, how hard the bull lunges and kicks. Bulls that change directions are scored higher, since spinning animals are harder to ride than ones bucking in straight lines. Likewise, bulls that "belly roll" or "sunfish," exposing their bellies, add another dimension to the bucking actions and are awarded more points.

In scoring animals in the rough stock competitions, judges seek high kicking action with the animals' hind legs fully extended (especially with horses). The higher the kick, the better the score, since high-kicking animals are more difficult to ride. The strength and force of the animal's bucking efforts are also awarded points.

To those attending, the attributes sought by judges are unclear. It is not unusual for an exciting ride to be marked lower than a less thrilling ride. Pro official Jade Robinson explains, "If a wild horse looks hard to ride, it may not be as powerful or difficult. A green or wild horse doesn't have the degree of difficulty, in the sense of power, that you see in a horse that has an even drop and kick style."[41] Even with guidance in the program, it remains difficult for part-time or novice fans (most of the Stampede crowd) to understand the scoring system.

In addition to performance issues, the Stampede rodeo is pressured by Calgary's growth. As Calgary has become an increasingly diversified urban metropolis, its links to rodeo culture have deteriorated, as shown by the following three examples. First, the loss of the stockyards in south Calgary removed a visible, odorous, tangible link to its rodeo roots. Calgarians no longer drive past stockyards full of hundreds of bellowing, milling cattle where they could see, and in particular smell, why Calgary was called "cowtown." The sensory experience was immediate and lasting.

Second, with over a million residents, and thousands more arriving annually, Calgary at the end of the twentieth century became a multicultural city. Families from around the world moved to share the prosperity of southern Alberta, creating a community of different skin colours and languages. As of 2005, 200,000 immigrants were living in Calgary, one-fifth of its population. Calgary prides itself on being an innovative and forward-looking city, but those ideals are reined in at the rodeo chutes.

When one enters the Stampede grandstand and walks up the nine steps to the tarmac level, the first colour seen is white. Sure, the cowboy hats are white, but the majority of people under them are white too. Professional rodeo is a Caucasian man and woman's world; it is not a representation of the Calgary community outside the gates.

The sport's colour was obvious as I sat in the infield's outdoor bar with a long-time friend, a Calgarian born in Bangladesh. As cowboys wrestled steers, my colleague's dark brown skin was an obvious anomaly amid the crowds of limping wild-horse racers and milling fans. The Stampede organization is taking steps to attract new cultural groups, but the rodeo, specifically, is challenged to become meaningful to the non-Caucasian spectator.

Third, when I was growing up in Calgary during the 1970s and 1980s, the whole city seemed to participate in the rodeo festival. Now that I live outside of Calgary and return to visit the Stampede, it is noticeable that the city as a whole no longer embraces the event. Upon driving into the city, except for banners at intersections, it is not immediately apparent that the Stampede is on. People are not commonly "dressing western" throughout neighbourhood communities.

Certainly at social engagements, downtown, and on the Stampede grounds, people are participating. But the city's complete enthrallment with the rodeo festival no longer exists. The sprawling city is metamorphosing, losing its agricultural nucleus of rodeo energy. The sheer size and diversity of the city foretell a greater misunderstanding of and ambivalence towards the Stampede.

The environmental image of the "unending western skyline" is deteriorating around the Stampede grounds. The psychological affect of "space" is prevalent within western mythology, but the new apartment towers around the west of Macleod Trail are changing the "big country" setting. Much like the barbed-wire fences across virgin plains over a century ago, the towers are "fencing in" the Stampede. They are literally casting their developed shadows over the expansive vistas towards the Rocky Mountains. While not affecting the rodeo directly, they reflect the changing atmosphere and environment in which the rodeo exists. As Cole Porter pleads in "Don't Fence Me In,"

> Oh, give me land, lots of land under starry skies above,
> don't fence me in
> Let me ride through the wide open country that I love,
> don't fence me in
> Let me be by myself in the evenin' breeze
> Listen to the murmur of the cottonwood trees
> Send me off forever but I ask you please, don't fence me in
>
> Just turn me loose, let me straddle my old saddle
> Underneath the western skies
> On my cayuse, let me wander over yonder
> Till I see the mountains rise

I want to ride to the ridge where the west commences
And gaze at the moon till I lose my senses
And I can't look at hovels and I can't stand fences
Don't fence me in[42]

With suburban sprawl paving over grazing lands, no tangible cowtown links in the city, and fewer people with agrarian roots, the understanding of a rodeo festival is bound to deteriorate. The rodeo holds the myths so valued by the Stampede's marketing offices, but they are increasingly irrelevant. As the city briskly and recklessly evolves, the rodeo risks reverting to a former cowtown's competition among cowhands – a Wild West anachronism, rather than Calgary's proudest showcase of rodeo's elite athletes.

The Stampede Rodeo Responds

In response to these issues, including the changing demographics, animal activists, entertainment tastes, and the need to re-invigorate rodeo, the Stampede rodeo managers made aggressive changes in 2005. They responded to demands for a faster-paced show, creating relationships with the competitors and fashioning a rodeo more relevant to a modern audience.

In 2005 the American Professional Rodeo Cowboys Association (PRCA) decided not to count Canadian prize money towards the world finals. The Stampede, with its international clout, fought back. In October 2005 the Stampede announced a new rodeo format and an overall increase in prize money to $1.6 million, which includes a $1 million Final Showdown Sunday. No longer sanctioned by the Canadian Professional Rodeo Association or the PRCA, the Stampede made a bold move, with the potential to reshape the sport worldwide.

As of 2006, twenty of the world's highest-rated competitors in each of the six events are invited to participate. Entries are reduced to twenty per event (from fifty in rough stock and sixty in calf roping and steer wrestling). Spectators see these top contestants a minimum of five and a maximum of six times. Contestant entrance fees were eliminated (participants had been paying $400 per event), and each contestant is given a $1,000 travel and living allowance. The two fringe events of Wild Cow Milking and Wild Horse Racing were dropped to create a fast-tempo two-and-a-half-hour show.

The Stampede rodeo is now a tournament, with rodeo's richest prizes. The winner of each event during the final Sunday Showdown walks away with pro rodeo's largest cheques – $100,000. Keith Marrington states, "Everybody in the industry has known – and agrees – rodeo needs to go in a new and innovative direction. We believe we need to create more stars out of our cowboys and cowgirls, get them out in the community to talk about their lifestyle and their background."[43]

Stampede staff and the Rodeo Committee, to their credit, are trying to increase the rodeo's relevancy. They acknowledge they need to make their competitors and their sport valued by a uninitiated audience. By implementing these changes, they are tackling the issues threatening their show, attempting to create a ticket-buying urgency and fill the grandstand. Their task is not an easy one, particularly in a city expanding so rapidly that it is effectively paving over its roots.

Riding Off Into the Sunset

As the Stampede rodeo rides on amid an increasingly challenging metropolitan environment, the vitality of its enduring mythology should ensure its legacy persists. Its legends are iconic fixtures in the history and personality of Calgary. Romantic images of women, horses, men, and bulls, dancing in an infield of jeopardy and bravado remain at the hub of the Calgary Stampede's marketing and story-telling. The Stampede will undoubtedly evolve, but the essential simplicity of its conflicts, in such brilliant spectacle, will continue to reiterate desired western perceptions.

Even if most Calgarians do not go to see the Calgary Stampede rodeo, they want it there. During ten days each summer, Calgary pays attention to rodeo, its symbolism and its ceremony. For most Calgarians, the rodeo's existence justifies community and individual actions taken during the Stampede. The rodeo faces amplified misunderstanding in a swelling urban setting, but it promises to adapt and to endure because its myths and icons are so extraordinary, and their representations so collectively imagined.

Notes

1. Clem McSpadden, "A Rodeo Cowboy Prayer," in memory of Howard Manuel, Jim Moore, and Zachary Vanwhy, http://www.catholic-forum.com/saints/pray0094.htm.

2. Fred Kennedy, *Calgary Stampede: The Authentic Story of the Calgary Stampede and Exhibition, "The Greatest Outdoor Show on Earth," 1912–1964* (Vancouver: West Vancouver Enterprises, 1965), 49.

3. Donna Livingstone, *The Cowboy Spirit: Guy Weadick and the Calgary Stampede* (Vancouver: Greystone Books, 1996), 41.

4. *Calgary Herald*, 29 October 2005, E7.

5. Graham Pike, ed., *The West in Action: Rodeo* (Calgary: Calgary Brewing and Malting Company, 1971).

6. Livingstone, *Cowboy Spirit*, 54.

7. Pike, *West in Action*, 27.

8. Livingstone, *Cowboy Spirit*, 44.

9. Michele Morris, *The Cowboy Life: A Saddlebag Guide for Dudes, Tenderfeet, and Cowpunchers Everywhere* (New York: Simon & Schuster, 1993), 207.

10. Ibid.

11. David Poulsen, *Wild Ride: Three Journeys Down the Rodeo Road* (Toronto: Balmur Book Publishing, 2000).

12. Calgary Stampede Afternoon Program, 2006, 86.

13. *Road to Saddle River*, produced by the Damberger Film and Cattle Company, 1997.

14. Patrick Tivy, *Calgary Stampede and the Canadian West* (Calgary: Altitude Publishing Company, 1995), 60.

15. Wayne S. Wooden and Gavin Ehringer, *Rodeo in America: Wranglers, Roughstock, and Paydirt* (Lawrence: University of Kansas Press, 1996), 3.

16. Livingstone, *Cowboy Spirit*, 47–48.

17. Morris, *Cowboy Life*, 222.

18. *Calgary Herald*, 12 July 1978, 1.

19. Ibid.

20. Morris, *Cowboy Life*, 184.

21. Richard W. Slatta, *The Cowboy Encyclopedia* (Santa Barbara, CA: ABC-CLIO, 1994), 320.

22. Wooden and Ehringer, *Rodeo in America*, 29.

23. Morris, *Cowboy Life*, 188.

24. Slatta, *Cowboy Encyclopedia*, 319.

25. Glen Mikkelsen, *Never Holler Whoa!: The Cowboys of Chuckwagon Racing* (Toronto: Balmur Book Publishing, 2000), 146.

26. *Calgary Herald*, 18 July 2005, 1.

27. Wooden and Ehringer, *Rodeo in America*, 3.
28. Livingstone, *Cowboy Spirit*, 48.
29. Gail Hughbanks Woerner, *Fearless Funnymen: The History of the Rodeo Clown* (Austin: Eakin Press, 1993), 126.
30. Ibid., 62.
31. Ibid., 22.
32. Jokes recorded from the West of the Rockies professional rodeo, October 2006.
33. Ibid., 17.
34. Kristina Fredriksson, *American Rodeo: From Buffalo Bill to Big Business.* (College Station: Texas A&M University Press, 1985), 130.
35. Darrell Knight, *Pete Knight: The Cowboy King* (Calgary: Detselig Enterprises, 2004), 49.
36. Woerner, *Fearless Funnymen*, 49.
37. Humane Society of Canada, 22 August 2005, www.humanesociety.com/newsrel/newsrel.asp?thisrel+12072005&page=1.
38. CBC News, 5 July 2005, www.cbc.ca/canada/story/2005/07/04/stampede050704.html.
39. Wooden, *Rodeo in America*, 130.
40. *Prince George Citizen*, 10 October 2007, 8.
41. Wooden, *Rodeo in America*, 31.
42. Cole Porter and Robert Fletcher, "Don't Fence Me In," 1934.
43. *Calgary Herald*, 29 October 2005, E7.

CHAPTER 9

The Half a Mile of Heaven's Gate

Aritha van Herk

On June 1, 2006, at Grande Prairie, Alberta, two chuckwagon drivers had occasion to reflect on the sport that defines their summers if not their lives. Mark Sutherland and Jason Johnstone, both second-generation members of two venerable chuckwagon racing families, were competing in the same heat when their wagons collided. The result was a spine-chilling, hair-raising ride that beggars the excitement of any Roman chariot race, ancient or modern.

Competing in that heat were Buddy Bensmiller, his son Kurt Bensmiller, Mark Sutherland (son of Kelly Sutherland), and Jason Johnstone (son of Reg Johnstone). These are the royalty of chuckwagon families, names that ring on every track across the West. The horses were restive at the barrels, refusing to stand, nerves and excitement making them eager to go. And take off they did, even though before the horn went Sutherland, fighting to control his horses, yelled for the other wagons to pull up, pull around for another start. But the klaxon sounded, and coming out of the infield, Sutherland discovered that the harness on his right wheeler had broken. In a vain effort, he tried to pull up his horses, but they were already in race mode. Jason Johnstone, with only a split second to make a decision, thought he could get past Sutherland on the rail, but couldn't. His wagon slammed into Sutherland's as they were going around the first turn. A collision between two wagons, pulled by that horse-power at those speeds, is extravagantly forceful. It knocked Johnstone off the seat into the back of his wagon box; unable to fight his way back to the seat, he desperately tried to control his raging horses for the rest of the race from the box. But Sutherland was knocked off of his seat onto the ground. Which might seem anti-climatic – a wicked bump and the end of a race. Except that between wagon, horses, and a melange of dirt and hooves, Sutherland was in mortal danger. "I landed on my head pretty good and bounced. When I was going under and saw the wagon box coming down on me...saw the wheel, I thought, 'this is it.' But I kept my wits about me ... I pushed away from the wagon and luckily, I pushed the right way."[1] As if that wasn't enough of a challenge, Sutherland's right leg had the reins wrapped round it; the left front wheel of the moving wagon struck that same right leg. Knowing he had only one chance to survive, Sutherland grabbed the reach (the pulling pole under the wagon) and hung on, all the while trying to kick the reins off his foot. They caught on his boot, and holding the reach with his arms, he kicked with his left leg, trying to free his foot. When he managed to pry off his boot, he swung both legs around the reach, and then tried to figure out how to climb out from under the still racing wagon. He couldn't get out at the front because the horses' hooves were too close, and at the back he was stopped by the stove box, so he had no choice but to hang on to the reach of that careening wagon, still pulled by thundering, unstoppable horses, to hang on for dear life – and not metaphorically. His outriders raced beside, trying to keep the horses running straight and shouting encouragement to Sutherland to hold on, hold on. When they finally pulled the horses to a stop, far past the finish line, Sutherland emerged, bruised but alive. He gave a thumbs-up to the crowd, and rode back to the barns on a quad. Anxious about his horses' welfare, and determined to check on them first, he declined a trip to the hospital.

Sutherland and Johnstone weren't engaged in some faked and exaggerated feats of showmanship that were set up more than real. They demonstrated, in the heat of a race gone wrong, the powerful strength and quick thinking that separates gladiators from gumshoes. Accidents take only a split second to happen; they take dedicated intelligence to manage. That both men emerged with only bruises and that no horses were hurt speaks volumes about chuckwagon racing as a sport that requires strategy and style as well as speed.

The "chucks" are fast, dangerous, and distinctive. Combining the skittish strength of thoroughbred horses with a driver's rein-control finesse of a weaver, they demonstrate an intricate skill and beauty that isn't always evident in the mud and the dust and the shouts and the thundering hooves of horses and wagons after the klaxon has sounded. To a novice, each heat looks chaotic, a jumble of harness and canvas and hats and horses in the infield before the wagons careen around the barrels and then hit the track. To the discerning fan, outrider, or wagon racer, it is the most incredible spectacle we can witness, and it is our own, born and bred in the West. Mark Sutherland himself has described it best, in a famous summary, almost understated for its precision. "Picture yourself in a ready-made coffin tied by tooth-floss to the tails of four charging dinosaurs. That's wagon racing."[2] Sutherland, clinging to the reach under his wagon in the dust of the horses' hooves, and with his own mortality singing in his ears, probably thought those lines would be inscribed on his tombstone. Or didn't bother to dwell on death. Instead, he used strength and skill to survive.

Chuckwagon racing, or "wagon racing," as the aficionados call it, is the sport of kings adapted to the wiles of the Canadian prairie. Complex and challenging, it is history, technology, the open range, and contemporary horse breeding all rolled up together with sheer speed, nerve, and psychological taunting. While thoroughbred horse races are simply composed of a race between different horses, each horse ridden by one man, wagon races are as tangled and dramatic and earth-bound as their reins. This race is not just a simple test of speed. The chucks require stamina, skill, spirit, and teamwork.

The goal of a chuckwagon race is to win (to be the fastest around the track) without penalty. But this end is remarkably difficult, a chuckwagon race far more complicated than a regular horse race. At the Calgary Stampede, the über-competition of these races, four outfits compete in each of nine heats. The men, horses, and wagon of each chuckwagon comprise an "outfit." An outfit includes a team of four horses, two of them wheelers (the rear pair in the four-horse team), two of them leaders (the front pair of the four-horse team). Those four horses are hooked up to a 1,300-pound wagon, which is precisely weighed and measured and certified to a rigid standard. No more plywood boxes: these are state of the art vehicles. The drivers, who sit on a hard bench with only a tight spring for bounce, manoeuvre four heavy leather reins to control the horses. Complicated enough? There's more. At the Calgary Stampede, each outfit is assisted by four outriders. One holds the two leaders steady until the horn sounds. Three outriders are positioned at the back of the wagon. Two toss in a pair of tent poles and a canvas, and a fourth outrider pitches a (now plastic) stove into the stove rack at the back of the wagon. The outriders, having completed these necessary tasks, then leap onto the backs of their individual horses and follow the wagon, which must turn a tight figure eight around two barrels in the infield before coming onto the track proper and settling into a lane to race.

Gazing down into the infield, a spectator will see a confusion of colourful wagons with drivers, each pulled by four horses, and on the ground four times four outriders, each with his own horse. That makes four wagons, twenty men, and thirty-two horses, milling between eight carefully staggered white barrels. Sixteen of the horses are harnessed to the wagons. Four of the men control the wagons; sixteen men are busy with the work of split-second assistance. Teamwork is essential and timing is crucial. Men must be able to multi-task while remaining aware of their own positions as well as those of every other animal and wagon in the infield. Outriders might hold their horses' reins between their teeth at the same time as they pitch a tarp, then literally spring onto their own horses' backs before chasing the dust of a thundering wagon setting a blistering pace. There is nothing simple about this sport. It defies any reduction to a mere horse race.

Historically, chuckwagon racing was less sport than recreation. Chuckwagons were the movable kitchens that centred every camp. During joint roundups or cattle drives, every ranch was expected to contribute to the enterprise a wagon with a cook, food, and bedding. When the largest general roundup was held in Alberta in the late spring of 1885, it included a hundred riders, fifteen chuckwagons, and five hundred horses.[3] They gathered some 60,000 cattle over several weeks from a huge territory. The men would start as early as 3 a.m., fuelled by a quick breakfast at the chuckwagon. Then the hands would catch their horses and begin to move the herd in the agreed-upon direction. Wagons, horses, and riders would shift, before noon, to the place designated as the next campsite. Once there, the chuckwagons would set up and the cowboys would ride off to gather the scattered cattle, sweeping a huge circle about ten to fifteen miles from the camp inward. When the riders returned late in the day, all the cattle were merged in a large open area, and the chuckwagon served as the workers' home away from home. The combined effort was so complex that large roundups were quickly abandoned in favour of smaller ones, although the same structure of gathering animals applied. And three times a day the camp cook (or camp boss) served up coffee, beans, bread, and bacon or beef from the wagon; cowboys had to be fuelled as much as the horses that they rode.

Charles Goodnight, a Texas cattleman, is credited with inventing the portable kitchen by adapting a Civil War army kitchen wagon or "Conestoga" to supply cooks and workers at roundup time in the 1860s. The

Conestoga wagons, or prairie schooners, which Art Belanger claims were the early forerunners of chuckwagons, "sailed through the waist-high buffalo grass from the mid-eighteenth century to the end of the nineteenth."[4] These heavy, durable wagons had to carry all that migrating settlers required, and so became the moving vans of an earlier era. But as part of cattle drives, the chuckwagon followed the herd and provided a nomadic rest station, water, food, coffee, and a bit of shade. A rough box on the back served as a pantry to carry food, mostly sourdough, coffee, and beans. Add a toolbox and a water-barrel, stretch a long canvas tarp over top, and the travelling kitchen was complete. The wagon also carried harness and slickers and bedrolls (to keep them dry), while a cowhide stretched underneath carried wood and buffalo chips for fuel. The cook drove the wagon horses, made three meals a day, and might even provide haircuts and shaves. At night, the cook's last job was to "point the pole of the wagon toward the North Star, providing a compass heading for the trail boss in the morning."[5] Chuckwagons were used from the 1860s to the 1900s. And of course, despite serving elemental necessities, the wagons and their drivers contributed to the roustering stories of the increasingly mythopoeic West.

The idea of races between these wagons blossomed slowly. All moving vehicles archetypally suggest the notion of a race or a competition, with the first arrival across a finish line earning the cachet of winning. Roman writer and statesman Pliny the Younger wrote in his *Letters*, in the first century CE, of the chariot races.

> I am the more astonished that so many thousands of
> grown men should be possessed again and again with
> a childish passion to look at galloping horses, and men
> standing upright in their chariots. If, indeed, they were
> attracted by the swiftness of the horses or the skill of the
> men, one could account for this enthusiasm. But in fact
> it is a bit of cloth they favour, a bit of cloth that captivates
> them. And if during the running the racers were to
> exchange colours, their partisans would change sides, and
> instantly forsake the very drivers and horses whom they
> were just before recognizing from afar, and clamorously
> saluting by name.[6]

In contemporary terms, the crowd in the bleachers at the Calgary Stampede might not forsake one favourite for another merely for their colours

– or in current terminology their canvasses – but there is enough enthusiasm for the gaily-coloured wagons to make it seem as if two thousand years have not passed. The informal wagering (legal betting on the chuckwagon races is not permitted at the Stampede) in the stands is largely based on visuals or vernacular knowledge, with predictable loyalties. And the wagons do incite spectator loyalty, too: visitors can vote for their favourite driver, and the top rookie driver wins the Orville Standquist Award, while the Guy Weadick Memorial Award is presented annually to the chuckwagon or rodeo competitor who best typifies the Stampede's spirit of showmanship and sportsmanship. More germane, statistics on those watching the Rangeland Derby are huge. During the ten days of the Calgary Stampede approximately 180,000 people watch the chuckwagon races at the track and hundreds of thousands more watch them on television every night.

So how did those ancient horse races arrive, in the outpost of the West, Calgary, Alberta, and the Greatest Outdoor Show on Earth? Promoter Guy Weadick was determined to provide the Calgary Stampede crowd with thrilling events. He was also determined to include racing. Wild horse races were fine, but Weadick could imagine even more compelling competitions. Belanger suggests that "Weadick was looking for a replacement for the Stagecoach Race," a previous entertainment, or that he was inspired by a race he had seen at the Gleichen Stampede, when several farmers "ran their farm wagons with four horse hitches in an exciting match race."[7] They knew too the lore of the American land rush, when the United States opened up thousands of acres in land lotteries. Once a prospective homesteader had won the right to make a claim, he lined up and waited for a starting gun to fire before racing across country to stake a piece of land. And the tradition, at the end of a long roundup, of cooks racing one another to the nearest saloon for a drink was common as well. That informal cross-country race was rough and ready, and accompanied by jangling pots, dust from bags of flour, and rattling tin cups, a source of much merriment. One story contends that in 1892 in Fallon, Montana, when the cooks from the Hog-Eye and the L-Cross ranches were in town to stock up on supplies, someone made a bet on the relative speed of his cook's team of horses. By this time, everybody was well lubricated, and the wagons were loaded with supplies, but they agreed to the six-mile race, and a blaze of gunfire signalled the start. The wagons ran across country, frying pans rattling, everybody shouting, and the Hog-Eye outfit won by one hundred yards. They got the case of whiskey, but one of the cowboys recalled, "'The aftermath of the race was felt and tasted by us for at least the next ten days. We had beans, sugar, coffee, and mica axle grease in our grub.'"[8] Other races were spurred by chuckwagons eager to reach ranch house or saloon, the last one to arrive required to buy everyone else drinks.

In search of an exciting event to cap his hyperbolic rodeo, Guy Weadick figured that some kind of wagon race would be crazy and chaotic enough to guarantee audience interest. The chuckwagons could answer popular desire for a competition. Weadick put out a challenge to the surrounding ranches, and despite understandable reluctance on the parts of ranch owners, he managed to taunt, challenge, and cajole the ranchers of the area into participating. The entrants in that initial race were a variety, mostly "pool" wagons where several owners from a district got together: the Mosquito Creek Pool Wagon (representing ranches owned by Jim Cross, Dan Riley, Jack Drumheller, and Rod MacLeary); the "Double Dishpan" (Sid Bannerman and the Hodgkins Brothers); the VU outfit (from Permez Creek), which was driven by well-known competitor Clem Gardner; the Sheep Wagon (put up by Jack Butler and Ora Demille from Sheep Creek); the V Quarter Circle Ranch outfit (from the Langdon district); and "Sundown" Morton's Gleichen outfit.[9] Six wagons (there were supposed to be two others, but they either threw in with the others or withdrew) comprised the original competitors in the first set of races. These races ran daily, and each outfit had to carry every item necessary to the chuckwagon's traditional job: a water barrel, a stove, a canvas cover, a fly, and a branding iron. Every wagon was pulled by four horses and each driver was to be assisted by four outriders. Those early wagons weighed about a ton, two thousand pounds, meaning that the horses had to be large and strong. Since then, the contents of the wagon have been modified, although now many more rules attend the races themselves.

Running rules for that first race were decided on the ground just before the start. To make the task more difficult, each wagon would cut a figure eight around two barrels set to lead away from the track in front of the grandstand. The wagons would then cut across the infield and enter the racetrack in the middle of the backstretch, which meant that they ran a quarter mile, not the current virtual half a mile (actually a kilometre). At the end, the wagons would turn back into the infield, stop beside their first barrel with the wagon-back to the grandstand, and set up camp, requiring that the crew unhook the team from the wagon, stretch the eight-foot fly, unload the stove, and build a fire. "First smoke decides winner" stated those initial rules. In races to come, lighting the stove incited interesting pyrotechnics, some drivers stuffing the stove with kerosene-soaked straw and tossing a match from a safe distance.

Six wagons meant that the first race was divided into two heats, which ran five nights of the week-long Stampede. The prize money was $300 total,

"$15.00, $10.00 and $5.00 for the first, second and third running times for each evening of racing."[10] The winner overall was long-time Yukon stage-coach driver Bill Somners, in charge of the Mosquito Creek rig owned by Riley, Cross, Drumheller, and MacLeary. Somners' outriders, Dan Fraser, Gus Sonnie, Laurel Millar, and Bill Livingstone, were familiar names in the ranching circuit.[11] For winning the greatest number of races out of five, the Mosquito Creek outfit took home a $25.00 John B. Stetson hat. But that was an understated outcome to the course set that Friday, July 14, 1923. The first ever professional chuckwagon races signalled the launch of the sport. Weadick knew he had a crowd pleaser.

From those rather rude beginnings, the races have gotten faster, more exciting, less forgiving. Changes were implemented quickly. In the interests of time, the team being unhooked, the tent fly stretched, and the campfire starting were dropped in 1925, but gestural elements of those actions remain, although the wagons are streamlined and the equipment is safety engineered. For example, the stove, originally a heavy ranch stove, was replaced by a metal replica, then a wooden one, and now is a rubber imitation (and like the barrels, collapsible). But outriders still toss a tarp and tent poles into the back, still throw a cook stove into the stove rack before jumping onto the backs of what are now thoroughbreds, raring to go. As the years rolled along, rules proliferated. The wagons tried to improve speed by lightening their load, and smaller, lighter wagons and faster horses appeared immediately. The fastest track time in 1923 was 2 minutes and 50 seconds, but although the race was doubled in length in 1924 (to the whole track or half a mile), the fastest time that year was 1 minute and 52 seconds. And to balance the inequity of distance, the barrels were re-positioned in 1925, the starting positions fanned out in front of the grandstand.[12] The chuck box and water barrels came off the wagons in 1946. Whips were outlawed in 1947. In 1948 a growing awareness of safety introduced the rule that each wagon must run in its own lane and could "cut for the rail" only at certain places.[13] The game was becoming a sport.

That transformation was effected by a combination of fast, wily horses and strong, skilful men – and yes, they are all men. This is a male sport, requiring powerful upper-body strength, although wives and mothers, daughters and sisters do a huge amount of behind-the-scenes work. These drivers appear to love risk and to embrace speed and danger. How does a chuckwagon driver start or train? It helps if he belongs to chuckwagon royalty, those families who have driven outfits for generation after generation. Sutherland, Bensmiller, Glass, Vigen, Dorchester, Cosgrave, Walgenbach, Nevada, Willard, Knight, and Lauder – these names ring with their own chuckwagon glamour. But a driver has to be a horse person, has to know horses, their habits and their harness, to be able to hold the reins and imagine a perfect combination of driving and running. An intergenerational sport, drivers are mentored by fathers, grandfathers, and other drivers – Kelly Sutherland often cites Ralph Vigen – or they begin as outriders, a real test of toughness.[14]

The work of the outriders is often unclear to spectators, but they are indispensable to racing and its outcome. An outrider can make the difference between winning and losing. The peg men are responsible for throwing the two tent pegs into the back of the wagon; the peg man closest to the barrel has to ensure that his horse doesn't back into that barrel. The outrider holding the lead horses has to be agile enough to let go and scramble out of the way when the horn sounds, simultaneously leaping onto his own horse, negotiating the figure eight around the barrels, and following the wagon to cross the finish line within a prescribed 150 feet of the wagon crossing. From afar, these movements look effortless, but the athleticism required is astonishing. To identify themselves with the appropriate wagon, the outriders wear matching colours, based on the barrel position. Now the colours are standardized and unmatched shirts result in a penalty (Barrel 1 is white, Barrel 2 is red, Barrel 3 is black, and Barrel 4 yellow), although in the past, outriders and drivers selected their own colours. As is more than evident from the Sutherland accident, outriders are essential to the safety and cohesion of the race, and they can make or break its outcome. If an outrider lifts the stove before the horn goes off, the team earns a 2 second penalty; a 1 second penalty applies if a pole is off the ground or if the fly is not stretched. An outrider must continue straight ahead at the sound of the horn, may not assist the driver after the race starts, must follow the proper figure eight pattern, must not miss a barrel or knock over a barrel, cannot force an injured horse or finish ahead of the wagon team. Every one of these rules targets infractions that will be penalized. And outriders have to work in tandem, recognize one another's body language.

The wagons and drivers too face a particular set of measurements. Stringent controls test drug and alcohol abuse. And the equipment must meet certain criteria of weight and size. On the track, potential penalties abound. Wagons that start ahead of the horn or line up ahead of the barrel are penalized. Creating a false start, missing a barrel or knocking over a barrel (the most common penalty), interfering with another wagon or with other outriders, failing to cooperate with the starter or moving out of an assigned lane, are all subject to penalty. With wagons moving at speeds of more than sixty kilometres per hour, the need for rules is understandable. Largely due to its history of accidents and even fatalities for both man and horse, this has become a much-regulated race. In truth, spectator sports both abhor and scream for blood, and the chucks do not disappoint. Chuckwagons have overturned, drivers and outriders have been dragged or ejected, horses toppled or injured. In July 1986 one chuckwagon cut off another, leading to a spectacular pile-up and claiming the lives of six horses. Even onlookers have been injured and killed. Since 1960 four men have died, and many more have suffered injuries.

The animal rights movement is vocal and vociferous, arguing every year about cruelty to the horses. It is true that the races are dangerous. Six horses were killed in 1986, one in 1999, six in 2002, one in 2004, two in 2006, and three in 2007. There is some compromise: the Humane Society and the SPCA together inspect the horses, observe the races, and keep a watchful eye on the sport. The Stampede officially contends that it has always worked to protect animals, and that part of the ethos of this celebration is the relationship between humans and animals. Yet, the races are called cruel and insensitive, and the controversy surrounding their enactment is fierce and ongoing (see any Internet site for endless discussion about the subject). In response, the drivers argue that thoroughbreds that have been culled from the racetrack face certain euthanasia, and becoming chuckwagon horses gives them a second lease on life. Mikkelson reports Jim Nevada's riposte to accusations of reckless endangerment: "'We don't pay four or five thousand dollars for a horse and try to kill it. You don't win money if you don't take care of your horses. We're drug tested, both us and the horses. Those horses would be in a dog-food can or on a plate in France, if it wasn't for wagon racing.'"[15] That too is a truism. Good wagon racing horses are treasured, even pampered.

Horses are the body of the sport, and it is horses that give the races their excitement. They need, for this particular challenge, to have a certain character and drive. These animals are hooked together in a four-horse hitch in tandem. The leaders, lighter and faster, are in front. The right-hand leader is key to the team: that horse has to be able to carry a line, has to be quick turning, with a will to run and a ready intelligence. On the outside of the first turn, that lead horse must be able to run faster to make the U around the top barrel, must be prepared to turn sharply on the bottom barrel. Only one in twenty horses make good right-hand leaders. The pole team or wheel team closest to the wagon are the muscle, pulling the load behind them. Wheelers are chosen for their size and stamina, while leaders are chosen for speed and leadership. This combination is difficult to configure and even more difficult

CALGARY STAMPEDE
157

J. ROSETTI'S
PHOTO

to measure. It requires careful attention to each horse's skill, training, and ability, a genuine equine knowledge. And it takes practice and patience, the drivers hooking their horses in different combinations in the spring when they begin to train, observing carefully their animals' talents and responses.

Most of the horses now are thoroughbreds, pure blood, although some cold bloods are still used. Some are culled racehorses, saved from the glue factory to enjoy a distinctive and longer life. And they are coddled and cared for, through winter and summer, a chuckwagon family's most valued assets. Some horses stay with individual families for ten to twelve years. Their job is to train in the spring, to run something like a minute every few days in the summer (most horses do about twenty-five to thirty races each year), and to relax in the fall and winter. And it is obvious that the horses love to run: the race is as exciting for them as it is for humans. Outriders' mounts must be fast as well, good saddle horses with speed and dexterity. Every outfit will carry forty to sixty horses, training them, evaluating them, and choosing to run different animals depending on track, temperature, and temper. Drivers will juggle and gnaw over these combinations, trying to achieve the perfect mix. Equipment too is key, and must be cared for and maintained. A chuckwagon outfit moves as a major entourage, requiring a wagon, feed, tack, and at least eight horses, if not more. The gypsy energy of travelling from event to event, hauling horses in semi-trailers and living in motor homes beside barns and corrals, requires a certain flexible temperament on the parts of humans and animals alike. Most important, the whole undertaking of running a chuckwagon is a team effort. One rogue horse, one careless outrider, one slip of the driver's reins, and all is subject to failure.

Despite its difficulty and mysterious chaos, its ineffable cachet, chuck-wagon racing is not a well-sponsored sport, and definitely not a sport that is internationally known. Relatively free of commercial inflection, except for the sponsorship of those companies that buy a wagon tarp, the culture has developed without the monetary pressure and rewards that accrue to other professional athletes. This distinctive activity has more of a flavour of domes-ticity, related partly to the powerful family connections that seem essential, and partly perhaps to the race's origins of being a kitchen on the move. Research on rodeos and on the iconic image of the cowboy (lone, stoic, and individual) tends to sidestep the carnival of wagon racing, as if it does not fit into the historic triangle of man, horse, and cow. Instead, this is a team effort, a community investment, a family undertaking. As Glen Mikkelson argues, "the chuckwagon cowboy personifies the co-operative spirit of Western Canada…[they] remain independent spirits in a communal enterprise. And their sport, which embodies team sportsmanship, community, and collabo-ration, is an apt mirror of the Canadian West and a symbol of the character of western Canadians."[16] The young child standing between his dad's knees and holding the lines of a chuckwagon team in the Calgary Stampede parade might be a more iconic reference for this sport than the buckles and trophies of the rodeo cowboy. More than anything else, chuckwagon racing requires a steady and observant horseperson, and the patience of practice, practice, and practice.

Commercial interest, while it is nowhere near the money tossed at hockey or football, has begun to accelerate. A chuckwagon first carried advertising in 1941, when the Buckhorn Guest Ranch paid Marvin Flett to promote it on his wagon. In 1956 Lloyd Nelson was the last driver to win driving a wagon under his own name.[17] But the expense of racing crept upwards, and in 1979 the first annual canvas auction was held. Organized and formalized by the Stampede, it has accelerated into a gala event. In 2007 all records were shattered, with a total amount of more than four million dollars bid on the thirty-six drivers and their canvasses. The highest bid went to "the King," Kelly Sutherland, whose canvas sold for $205,000. Advertisers who purchase chuckwagons share a unique experience, which goes far beyond the canvas as marketing tool. The social and philanthropic aspect of advertising, the wagon drivers' public appearances and general participation in Stampede celebrations together weave a strange tapestry of competition and coopera-tion. In 2002 Professional Wagon Racing Inc. introduced chuckwagon races at the Las Vegas Stampede, hoping to establish an annual event. The venue and the arena seemed right, but the event has not been repeated. Even Vegas, it seems, cannot accommodate the strange extravaganza of wagon racing.

The characters surrounding the Rangeland Derby both embody and amplify a compelling eccentricity, the layers of a powerful mythology that, for all its hyperbole, is a virtual mystery beyond the western Canadian world. In the early years, the most colourful or foolhardy driver was easily "Sundown" or "Wildhorse" Jack Morton. He was famous for throwing his reins on the ground and grabbing his horses' tails to make them run faster. To light the cook stove, he carried gas on his wagon, but it exploded, and made his horses even crazier. Morton broke his leg, rammed the barrels, and lost a wheel, but he retired only when he was close to sixty, in 1938.[18] Various stories credit him with starting the downtown pancake breakfasts served from the back of the wagons. The voice of the Rangeland Derby, Joe Carbury, has announced the races for more than forty years, and his trademark cry, "They're Offffff," is a benchmark for the event. Dick Cosgrove, who won first in 1926, would win the Derby nine times before retiring twenty years later. His record has been beaten only by "the King," Kelly Sutherland, who has won ten times. These champions are not young men, but wily veterans who have learned from experience. They carry the talismans and markers of gladiators: Kelly's long black feather, the checkered wagon of the Glass family, Dallas Dorchester wearing his father's old felt hat. They are the heroes of inside stories, and yet eternal in terms of their own playful dodges with mortality.

For chuckwagon racing is about staring at mortality, the possibility of death always hovering, the thunder of hooves an apocalypse. Jim Nevada recounts, "I was fifteen years old, it was my second show outriding, and I was nervous. Veteran driver Orville Strandquist said to me, 'Jim, when your card's laid, it's played. It could be on the racetrack or in a car on your way to Calgary, but as long as you're doing something you like, that's what you do. You don't know when you're going to die, and don't push it, but when you card's played, you're dead.' After that I was never nervous."[19] Such fatalism might belong to the world of unpredictability, but it also speaks to an acceptance of danger as a companion to the adrenaline of risk. That calm acceptance might have been what enabled young Sutherland to hold on to the reach of his runaway wagon all the way around the track.

What then to conclude about this unique sport, played out as part of the Calgary Stampede, an event that is powerfully rooted to a place (Calgary, Alberta, and the greater West) and an iconic ethos (ranching and riding). Almost archaic in its origins, almost shyly naive in its development, accidental and local rather than part of the international jockeying that accompanies soccer or basketball, chuckwagon racing is unique in every aspect of its risk and its achievement. It is a living anachronism, and yet beautifully performative. Most of all, every race articulates a hope that out of the complicated danger of these competitions will come a gently persuasive story. This legend might indeed hark back to the ancient chariot races, but it also echoes a yearning to witness the long-lived haunting of a western tradition.

Notes

1. *Calgary Herald*, 3 June 2006, E1.
2. Glen Mikkelson, *Never Holler Whoa!: The Cowboys of Chuckwagon Racing* (Toronto: Balmur Book Publishing, 2000), 2.
3. Warren Elofson, *Cowboys, Gentlemen, and Cattle Thieves: Ranching on the Western Frontier* (Montreal: McGill-Queen's University Press, 2000), 51.
4. Art Belanger, *A Half Mile of Hell* (Aldergrove, BC: Frontier Publishing, 1970), 3.
5. Mikkelsen, *Never Holler Whoa*, 3.
6. H.A. Harris, *Sport in Greece and Rome* (Ithaca: Cornell University Press, 1972), 220–21.
7. Belanger, *Half Mile of Hell*, 6.
8. Mikkelsen, *Never Holler Whoa*, 4.
9. Belanger, *Half Mile of Hell*, 8.
10. Ibid., 11.
11. Ibid.
12. Ibid., 14.
13. Ibid., 43.
14. Mikkelsen, *Never Holler Whoa*, 26.
15. Ibid., 82.
16. Ibid., 19.
17. Glen Mikkelsen, "Greasing the Wheels," in *Grand Souvenir Program* (Calgary: Calgary Stampede, 2004), 19.
18. Joan Dixon and Tracey Read, *Celebrating the Calgary Exhibition and Stampede: The Story of the Greatest Outdoor Show on Earth* (Canmore: Altitude Publishing, 2005), 101.
19. Mikkelsen, *Never Holler Whoa*, 147.

CHAPTER 10

"Cowtown It Ain't":
The Stampede and Calgary's Public Monuments

Frits Pannekoek

Life-size bronze sculpture (1980) by Rick Roenisch is displayed at one of the west entrances
of the Stampede Park

[S]paces of public display and ritual...teach us about our national heritage and our public responsibilities ... [T]he urban landscape itself is the emblematic embodiment of power and memory ... [P]ublic monuments [are not]... innocent aesthetic embellishments of the public sphere.[1]

Nuala C. Johnson, quoted above, is one of many authorities engaged in the study of public monuments and how they both reflect and shape public space and cultural identities.[2] She emphatically agrees with Paul Connerton, the author of *How Societies Remember*, that community elites invent spaces and rituals that claim continuity with their past in order to legitimize their present hegemony.[3] Is Calgary's useable past evidenced in the urban landscape and particularly in its public monuments? Does the Calgary Stampede, considered by many to be a major contributor to the city's identity, fit into its public discourse? If it doesn't, what does that signify?

James Howard Kunstler, in *The Geography of Nowhere: The Rise and Decline of America's Man-Made Landscape*, would agree with Johnson and Connerton, but argues that the North American man-made landscape is unremarkable, homogeneous, and lacking in the particularism of community.[4] He claims that the acres of shopping centres, warehouses, and small businesses, distinguishable only by their signage and neon, are the new public art. If that is the case, is it true of Calgary? What of the past is used to legitimize or "decorate" the present? When searching for a public expression of "hegemonic" art in Calgary, a city that may be the ultimate in post-modern urbanism, we need to look at urban hegemonic expressions in a number of forms, including public monuments, urban commercial signage, and urban toponymy. The urban names imposed by city leaders reflect aspirational values that dominate public signs and life.

Robert J. Belton, author of *Sights of Resistance: Approaches to Canadian Visual Culture*, offers a methodology that might be used to determine whether the claims of Kunstler, Johnson, and Connerton apply to Calgary.[5] What do Calgary's public art, commercial signage, and place names reveal about the city and its values and, perhaps as important, about the elite and their values? Belton suggests that context, form, and history are key to deconstructing and understanding any image. By context, he means the surroundings of an object. How does context reinforce or change meaning? A monument in front of the University of Calgary library might carry different meaning than the same monument in front of a downtown bar. Does the placement of the majority of public art relating to a single theme in one location say anything about the values of a community? The form of any monument matters even more. What, if anything, does the consistent choice of realism versus modernism say about a community? The history of any public art is important because it indicates conceptions and beliefs at the time of its placement. However, context can negate historical purpose and time and time again create new meaning. Has this happened in Calgary?

Taking this methodology and applying it to Calgary is by no means easy. However, by taking one theme, the Calgary Stampede and its public presence in monuments, signage, and toponymy, it might be possible to come closer to the real mental or psychological space the Stampede occupies in the Calgary mind. Why are public monuments that have a connection to the Stampede for the most part confined to the Stampede grounds, the rural hinterland, and the airport? What does this say about the cultural values of Calgary and its elites? What does the fact that Calgary's official subdivision names and street names have little reference to the Stampede or its heritage say about Calgary? What does the fact that commercial signage is the key public manifestation of the Stampede signify? Has the Stampede been rejected because it lacks the dignity for formal public places? Has the Stampede been rejected in subdivision names until recently because it lacked the ability to drive real estate values? Why, then, has it become so common a choice in commercial establishments?

First, what are the physical images in Calgary's public spaces? Who is responsible for these images, who actually made the images, and how are they perceived by the public? Within the city several key areas contain sculptures: City Hall and its environs, Eighth Avenue Mall, Memorial Park Library, the University of Calgary, Fort Calgary, and the Stampede grounds. All are key symbolic areas that reflect and shape the city's identity. Except for the images on the Stampede grounds, few nod in the direction of the ranching or cowboy culture that is celebrated so enthusiastically every July.

What themes were considered "Stampede" in the writing of this essay? Anything involving cowboys and their horses or directly relating to cowboy culture was included, as well as anything commissioned by the Calgary Stampede, since the latter might reveal the values critical to its understanding of Calgary's heritage. Cowboy images definitely include "8 Seconds to Glory" (fig. 1) by Shane R. Sutherland, at Third Street SW, although its modern form may obscure its muse, and "Break Away" (fig. 2) by Robert Keith Spaith at the Calgary International Airport international exit. Both definitely were intended to exude the Stampede theme and the Stampede's perception of the spirit of the West – a wild freedom that must be tamed, but only to a point at which it might become useful.

It is interesting that both "8 Seconds to Glory" and "Break Away" are products of the new millennium. Dixie Jewett's controversial "Metal Horse" (fig. 3) at the Saltlik Restaurant (101 Eighth Avenue SW) is arguably Stampede-related. It is ironic, however, that this presentation of a Clydesdale, a good farm horse, is built from old tractor parts in a genre appropriately known as "steampunk." The juxtaposition of the horse with the bones of its technological replacement – both more farm than ranch – is a puzzle that post-modernists will take great delight in analyzing.[6] This is about it for public sculpture related to the Stampede in public venues outside the Stampede grounds.

There are other horse sculptures; for example, "Family of Horses" (fig. 4) by Harry O'Hanlon (1989) was presented by Spruce Meadows to the city and is located in front of the new City Hall. But these are dressage horses, the gift of the Southern family, hardly symbolic of the rough and ready Stampede. These are as far from the wild broncs at the airport as can be. The other western animal championed in public places is the buffalo, which is found in at least three locations: on the Centre Street Bridge (fig. 5 and 5a), in front of the Shaw building ("Bison," fig. 6), and at Fort Calgary ("The Mighty and Once Many Symbol of the Great Plains," by Don Toney, fig. 6a). But these are historic and symbolize the lost West. They are monuments to sadness and the end of a free animal that represented an unrestrained, yet tamed, Alberta.

The bulk of public sculptures, like those in other Alberta cities, relate to history: the first European Calgarians and the First Nations peoples who, like the buffalo, are depicted as "noble" symbols of "yesterday." Probably the most important public monument of this type is the statue of Sitting Eagle (John Hunt), a respected Stoney who was a key participant in the Calgary Stampede (fig. 7). The 3.6 metre (11 foot, 11 inch), 1,075 kilogram (2,370 pound) statue is located at Cascade Towers on Sixth Street and Seventh Avenue. It was unveiled by Mayor Ralph Klein, Chief John Snow, Elder Lazaras Wesley, its sculptor Don Begg, and Grant MacEwan. But does the representation have anything to do with the Stampede?

The origin of "Sitting Eagle" is ironic at best. The cynic might observe that a people dispossessed of their lands were now celebrated so the developer could add even more square metres to his building. A City of Calgary policy allows higher densities if developers include public art in their projects. "Sitting Eagle," for which the developer paid $250,000, was in effect traded for a one-and-a-half-floor addition to Cascade Towers. Cascade's president at the time was a fan of Nicolas de Grandmaison, one of the great painters of Indians, and so a First Nations theme was chosen. Like the buffalo, Sitting Eagle is part of a Wild West now tamed, a Wild West for show. It could be argued that this monument relates to the Stampede in that the Stampede contains the Indian Village, initially as a symbol of the old captured West. Urban development was dear to the hearts of many of the Stampede's founders.

At the International Airport, Alan Henderson's "Big Head," a bust of Sam Livingston, described under the plaque as Calgary's first citizen, might also be construed to relate to the "wildness" and ranching culture that many historians consider to be part of early Calgary (fig. 8). Henderson himself feels that "Big Head" supports Calgary's western heritage, its openness, its friendliness, and its gregariousness. To him, "Big Head" represents the city's American and European connections. However, that would be a stretch. Sam Livingston was a prospector, farmer, and fur trader; he welcomed the North-West Mounted Police to the city, and now welcomes its visitors. Looking more like a Klondike Gold Rush miner, which he was, than a cowboy, which he was not, he helped found the Alberta Settlers' Rights Association, a group not beloved by the ranching elite – indeed, the antithesis of much of what the Stampede spirit symbolizes.[7]

At Fort Calgary, a statue of North-West Mounted Police Commissioner James Macleod, designed and cast by Don and Shirley Begg in 2005, could also be assigned to the Stampede or at least the western hero genre (fig. 9). The bronze is of Colonel Macleod astride his horse, but the pose is more symbolic of the vision and "majesty" of the police in the western Canadian epic than anything to do with the Wild West image generally projected by the Stampede. Commissioned by the Calgary division of the Royal Canadian Mounted Police Veterans Association, it is intended to symbolize "law and order" and stability rather than the myth of the individual against the environment often associated with the cowboy. However, some Calgarians choose to see the statue as symbolizing not law and order, but the relationship between community of all kinds and the police.[8]

The public monuments of Livingston, the buffalo, Sitting Eagle, and Colonel Macleod all symbolize the end of wilderness, the imposition of law and order, and the triumph of Euro-Canadians. It can be argued that these continue the theme of earlier works of public art, many of which relate to Calgary's imperial connections. The most obvious of these are the famous replica lions on the Centre Street Bridge. Sculpted by James L. Thomson in 1916, the originals are now located at the Calgary municipal building to ensure their preservation. The dominance of the lions over the smaller heads of the buffalo in itself implies conquest (fig. 10). "The South African War" by P. Hebert (1912) at Memorial Park Library is of a mounted soldier, a real Calgarian and his real horse, but it would be a stretch to link it primarily to ranching rather than to the substantial military history of the city (fig. 11).

The most recent public monuments, while historical, have absolutely nothing to do with the spirit of the Stampede. "Gratitude," by Barbara Paterson, an Edmontonian, commemorates the triumph of Alberta's "Famous Five," who successfully fought to have women declared persons in Canada (fig. 12). It is a moving three-dimensional parlour in which Emily Murphy, one of the five women, invites you to enter, sit, and join in their success. Unveiled in 1999, "Gratitude" has pride of place near City Hall in the most symbolic and public of locations. While the statues themselves are far removed from any Stampede theme, their dedication did echo the many ironies of Stampede City. The first person to sit next to Emily Murphy during the unveiling ceremony was a twelve-year-old Peigan girl dressed in traditional clothing. Whether the symbolism of the gesture was understood by Calgarians is not clear.[9] First Nations were not successful in securing the vote, in gaining full citizenship unfettered by enfranchisement laws, until the 1960s. If First Nations people voted before then, they were removed from their reserves and their communities on the grounds that if they could vote, they did not need the social supports offered by treaties. It should be noted that the fight for the First Nations vote was led by two Calgarians, John Laurie and Ruth Gorman, who herself was very much in the mould of the Famous Five. Perhaps the culture of the "strong-minded woman" is more Calgary than that of the cowboy.[10]

More recently oppressed people have found public space in which to celebrate their freedom. "In Search of Gold Mountain" (fig. 13), carved by Chu Honsun from 15 tonnes of granite from China, describes the pursuit of freedom and equality by Chinese Canadians. A companion piece, "Wall of Names" by Ferdinand Spina, also located in Sein Lok Park, was installed two years later to commemorate Chinese males who paid the head tax to enter Canada.

A significant series of public monuments use history to extol a public virtue. They can be described as international in context and generic to any urban environment. Their purpose is to define Calgary as a world city. "Family of Man" (fig. 14) was undertaken by Mario Armengol for the British Pavilion at Expo 67. Donated by Maxwell Cummings, a Calgary and Montreal developer, and dedicated in 1968, this particular piece of public art is symbolic of the kind of contest that sometimes surrounds public art in Calgary. The circle of ten gaunt, expressionless, larger-than-life aluminum (not bronze) men and women attracted the anticipated hysteria from the artistically conservative, but seems to have found a home in the front yard of the Calgary School Board building. It has become so beloved that when the school board moves offices in 2008, it wants to take the naked family with it.[11] No urban environment can do without its nudes.

The trees are probably the most controversial of recent public sculptures. Located on the Eighth Avenue Mall in front of Bankers Hall, they were sponsored by another developer doing penance for increased density (fig. 15). The eight-story trees were to contain street lighting and programmable special light effects. To date this is the only public monument designed by the developer's architect rather than an artist. The trees were intended as highlights of a new downtown meeting place, like the Calgary Tower and Olympic Plaza. Some will argue that the trees are not art, but symbols of excess and disappointment, since they never leafed into the feature that the developers promised. The only link to the Stampede might be that both are the result of a promoter's exuberance.

The University of Calgary, as might be expected, is home to probably the largest collection of modern public sculptures, none of which relate even remotely to the Stampede. The most famous, known on campus as "The Prairie Chicken" (fig. 16), was placed in front of the administration building on Swann Mall. The university commissioned George Norris, a Vancouver-based artist, to undertake the piece to commemorate the city's centennial. To George Norris it is neither an open book nor a chicken; it concerns "revelation, a central concern of any educational institution."[12] Norris also secured the landscaping contract, although the field of marigolds that was to accompany the constructivist piece never materialized. The other sculptures on campus are for the most part of the 1970s and 1980s modernist constructivist movement and are managed by the Nickle Arts Museum as part of the university's outdoor art collections. It is interesting, however, that students tend to find references to the environment – in the case of Norris's contribution, a prairie chicken.

Few, if any, real pieces of public sculpture directly evoking the Stampede have escaped the confines of its grounds. The observation by a press wag that Calgary is beset by bovine and equine statuary simply is not true. Only the art on the Stampede grounds evidences an affinity for the "Remington" or "Russell" schools of western cowboy realism that appear to be so appreciated by ranching and cowboy communities throughout North America and so despised by the scribblers of the third estate.

The most famous sculptures that have come to symbolize the Stampede are Rich Roenisch's "Bronc Twister" (fig. 17) and Linda Stewart's "Roundup" (fig. 18). The Calgary Exhibition and Stampede has always been conflicted about its commemorative role and also celebrates farmers, for example, in "Our Land – Our Future: The Alberta Farm Family" by Vilem Zach (fig. 19). There are also important murals, but the critical point is that they are all confined to the Stampede grounds.

It took until 1980 for the Stampede to bronze its iconic image. Rich Roenisch, who spent a lifetime as a cowboy and came from a founding Alberta ranching family, undertook the "Bronc Twister" that greets visitors to the Stampede. It is based on the famous 1919 Stampede poster by Edward Borein depicting the horse known as "I See U." Roenisch also did the bucking horse relief on the Stampede grandstand and the famous "Question of Survival" bronze, based on Charlie Russell's famous painting, at the Bar U National Historic Site (fig. 20). Symbolically, "Bronc Twister" was unveiled in 1980 by the Honourable Peter Lougheed, premier of Alberta and scion of an old Alberta family, on the seventy-fifth anniversary of the year Alberta became a province. The point is that Calgary got its first Stampede sculpture relatively late in the city's history. Also curious is that while "Bronc Twister" has become the Stampede's symbol, it is seen only in banners, signs, and manhole covers outside the grounds. The appearance of "the Twister" coincided with a considerable increase in the use of Stampede themes in business activities. While there is no evidence of any planned linkage, it helped the Stampede become a greater presence in the public mind.

It is in commercial signage that the Stampede really flourishes as symbol: car dealerships, book companies, grocery establishments, messenger and express companies, pawnbrokers, and dry cleaners all seem to embrace the name with passion. Whether the names have led to greater economic success would require further study. However, these businesses tend to be linked for the most part to service industries – the needs of the everyday. It would be interesting to determine whether businesspeople, particularly owners of small shops, believed this image would benefit their business, or whether they adopted it in order to be city boosters.

A search through Henderson's City Directories for businesses using the Stampede in their signage reveals that there were seven businesses in 1954, thirteen in 1956, eighteen in 1970, twenty in 1985, and twenty-three in 1991 (figs. 22, 23, 24). A few businesses (always in the single digits) used "rodeo" or "Western" in the same years. Today seventy-three businesses in over sixty different categories use Stampede themes in their signage and advertising. The Calgary Yellow Pages also lists three businesses using "cow-boy," three using "bronco," three using "round-up," six using "corral," and thirteen using "maverick."

But for the most part, as previously indicated, Stampede public art is confined to the Stampede grounds. Perhaps this is because the Stampede is not so much an instrument of cultural memory as it is an invented tradition. Guy Weadick himself was key in the creation of an invented tradition based initially on the very successful American Wild West shows. His Stampede included Indians, closed-off streets, and merchant-driven events. His mastery of promotion and creation can be traced to 1923.

Two other manifestations of the Stampede in public imagery are Calgary's two senior sports franchises and the fantastically successful "Udderly Art" charity event of 2000.[13] Individual corporations purchased life-sized fibre-glass Jersey cows for $5,000 and then retained local artists to paint them. Over 200 decorated cows with names such as "Hollywood and Bovine" and "Cowabunga" were auctioned off at Stampede Park, with the proceeds going directly to the charity of the owner's choice. A remnant of the painted herd lives on in the Centennial Parkade, and another fifteen are in the walkway on Ninth Avenue between Fifth and Sixth Streets.

The concept is hardly unique to Calgary. It was invented in Chicago in 1999 and has been adopted around the world, with similar events held in London, New York, and Sydney, Australia. Some cities adapted the cows to their own "culture." While Calgary's cows were unranchmanlike Jerseys, Scotland had highland cattle and Texas had longhorns. "Udderly Art" was an urban undertaking by the socially sexy to raise money. In Calgary the choice of a Jersey cow with little brand identification with the history of ranching or the Stampede did not seem to matter. And in the end, of course, it did not. It was an amusing utilization of an international community-based transitory public art movement that resonated with Calgarians no more than with residents of other major cities. Like commercial signage, it was to be "fun." It was not "serious" public art – that was for those who cast in bronze.

The sports franchises also use "art" or "icons" to associate themselves with the Stampede, but the activities are transitory, much like commercial signage. The Calgary Flames play at the Saddledome – a building cleverly named because it could be construed as reminiscent of a saddle, although it took its shape from engineering formulas. Like many car manufacturers and dealers, the Calgary Stampeders have adopted a bronco as their brand image. Again, this is clever marketing. Stampede themes dominate in the commercial and charity fund-raising realms, but the Stampede is not "serious" enough for "serious" public art. The Stampede lacks gravitas – it lacks "class."

Perhaps this is why city officials are so reluctant to allow the use of public art to commemorate the Stampede. Often those shaping the public spaces in the city were not merely passive about the Stampede, but actually unsympathetic to having it become a dominant element of Calgary's image. Just when business was embracing the Stampede through commercial signage, the city was contemplating "rebranding." The Stampede referred to an invented past, and inventions can be changed.

In 1984 the City of Calgary commissioned a study to determine the importance of the Stampede image in marketing the city. Undertaken just before the Olympics, the study found that seventy percent of visitors stayed with residents and only one in ten visitors saw any attraction at all. The Stampede was hardly the tourist draw that the city thought it was. The conclusion in 1984 was that Calgary did not have an image with any real commercial relevance. The report suggested that a new theme – "Heart of the West" or "Heartbeat of the West" – would integrate western hospitality and western heritage. In other words, the city should keep the white hat, but not the jeans. Calgarians were sophisticated folk whose modernity and urban reality demanded more upscale, more stylish, western wear. Hotel staff in particular were to be encouraged to adopt more "modern" western dress during the Stampede.

The boosters who wanted to rid Calgary of its rough western edges did not succeed. Calgarians like to be thought of as tough rural rustics. Perhaps that is why Ralph Klein was re-elected so often – he understood the importance of image all too well. However, as shall be seen, the sentiments that tried to moderate rampant cowboyism are still alive.

So if the Stampede itself is corralled, and public art only marginally relates to the myths the Stampede has generated, how does the Stampede manifest itself? Robert Venturi, in *Complexity and Contradiction in Architecture* and *Learning from Las Vegas*, offers some insight into how the Calgary Stampede commercial images might be interpreted.[14] Venturi is interested in the creeping "crud" architecture found sprawling all over the urban fringes and rural hinterlands of America. He tries to explain it rather than criticize it. Perhaps that is what we should do with the Stampede. Could it be that Calgary is the first large Canadian city in which buildings no longer matter? Whatever the purpose of a building – motel, casino, carpet warehouse, waterbed store, pizza shop – all are "cinder-block sheds," natural products of freeways and cars. Venturi claims the decorated facades of these buildings and their signage that can be read from a speeding car are the post-modern expression of "architecture," architectural graffiti affixed to modern buildings. Is this any different from putting shutters or siding on a bungalow box to suggest tradition? It can be argued that for the most part history has been stamped out in Calgary; where it still exists it is tolerated as a pastiche of the past.

Perhaps urban manifestations of the Stampede in the form of signage or public art can best be seen as "entertainment architecture" presenting a digestible, readable, and comprehensible context in which to understand the cleansed interpretation of the frontier. New buildings on the Stampede grounds are designed to be user-friendly and promote old-fashioned virtues such as comfort, intimacy, and festiveness. Significant locations become "key urban attractions" and "the show begins on the sidewalk," whether in signage or "re-creations" of trees. The Stampede has been confined to an entertainment park, but its image has escaped to the freeways and landed on the front of Calgary's concrete-block businesses.

The elite, or at least those who control public art, might deny the general public its appetite for Stampede monuments, but the public has created its own symbols. The extent of the use of "Stampede" in commercial imagery suggests that the Stampede and its values are strongly held by "Joe Average" citizens, whose taste for the equine and bovine in their choice of public imagery has been decried by Calgary's third estate.

The "Bronc Twister" symbol is the one most frequently used, seen on manhole covers, Stampede street banners, commercial signs, and signs on the "plus fifteens," the above-street walkways connecting buildings in the city core. It is in Calgary's "architecture" of the modern West that the image of the Stampede flourishes; car dealerships, sports teams, book companies, grocery establishments, messenger and express companies, pawnbrokers, and dry cleaners seem to embrace the name with the greatest passion.

So where does this leave the future of the Calgary Stampede in the physical urban environment? There is really no evidence that the Stampede will have any lasting impact on the physicality of the community. Those responsible for public art in Calgary seem to have no intention of embracing the Stampede in the future. In 2004, for example, Calgary unveiled five projects funded by developers in exchange for density exceptions. Two of the projects had recreational themes and the rest focused on the environment. The city's art committee has decided that an environmental theme will dominate public art.

> Public art plans are essential in ensuring that our visual
> environment and identity be as intentional, deliberate
> and carefully considered as our civic infrastructure
> systems ... Calgary is unique among North American
> cities in its relationship to the Bow River and its watershed.

The river traverses Calgary from the northwest to the
southeast and serves as an organizing principle to the
urban form of the city. The health of the watershed
ecosystem is unprecedented for a river system running
though a city of a million people. The UEP (Utilities and
Environmental Protection Department) Public Art Plan
will move citizens and visitors along the river's path and
watershed, highlighting the excellent successes of UEP, as
well as the unique environmental relationship between the
healthy ecology of the Bow River and our urban needs.
For Calgary, the Bow River is part of our city and our city
is part of the river. The Public Art Plan will celebrate this
complex relationship and call attention to the high quality
of life that our citizens enjoy.[15]

Some might argue that the city boosters are at it again; however, Gail
Anderson, current chair of the Calgary Public Art Committee, conceded
that the federal government had influenced this policy. While there may
not be public support for this decision, there is also really no opposition,
since the policy is not well known. Calgarians have not been meaningfully
involved in any debate on the nature of their public spaces. The most recent
public manifestation of the policy are the 144 concrete trout on the Glenbow
Elbow interchange (fig. 26). Violet Costello, a graduate of Vancouver's Emily
Carr Institute of Art and Design, won the commission in a competition. The
fish are accepted as "nice" decoration, but Calgary newspaper articles focused
on the engineering prowess that produced the concrete cast and colours.[16]
While swimming and jumping fish are environmentally appropriate, equally
vigorous horses and cattle would seem not to be. The Stampede is just not
fashionable, and the rejection of the Stampede myth ensures that any public
expressions of cowboys, horses, and steers will continue to be confined to the
Stampede grounds for the foreseeable future. The values they might evidence
are simply not those the elite want to inculcate in Calgarians. The Stampede
is for amusement; it is not to be associated with reality.

Another key indicator of the role of the Stampede in the urban landscape
might be its impact on Calgary's toponymy. While public art and architecture may be prime indicators of public values, in their absence in the
post-modern city values may be expressed through the place names given
to neighbourhoods and principal geographic features. Generally throughout
North America, eighty percent of everything that has been built, has been

built in the last 50 years: commuter tract housing, shopping plazas, hotel complexes, fast-food joints, office parks, and freeways. Do Calgary's urban place names reflect the ranching and cowboy West, or are echoes of the Stampede manifested only in commercial signage?

The demographic and cultural influences that shape Calgary's urban landscape were recognizable as early as 1913. In that year over four thousand workers were directly employed in manufacturing, in rail yards, in brewing, in abattoirs, and in ceramics. The great boom of this period was predicated on industrial agriculture, not the lone bronc-busting cowboy. In 1914 what would become the heritage infrastructure of the city so beloved by Calgarians today had already been created. That this was to be a modern city, cognizant of its geographic surroundings and the Bow River, is further evidenced by the city's near embrace of the Mawson Plan, which would have made Calgary an ornate garden city of the north, an idealized Arcadia.[17]

In *Calgary Builds: The Emergence of an Urban Landscape, 1905–1914*, Bryan P. Melnyk notes that between 1905 and 1914, when Calgary's population exploded to eighty thousand, over ten thousand buildings were built in dozens of neighbourhoods.[18] These buildings created the urban landscape from which future buildings gained their inspiration, and neighbourhoods their names. A local booster enthusiastically observed:

> Where a few years ago were bare hills and bald-headed
> prairie…are now such beautiful suburbs as Bowness,
> Mount Royal, Elbow Park, Elboya, Glencoe and Rosedale
> … Calgary in recent years has shown the most phenom-
> enal growth of any city on the American continent in the
> same space of time. Million dollar hotels have replaced
> the frontier saloons, million dollar department stores have
> replaced the fur trading posts … [19]

Not a single name reflects a ranching or cowboy culture. It would not be until the 1960s that developers, planners, and city fathers began to embrace a ranching or Stampede heritage in urban toponymics: Chaparral, Ranch-lands, Hanson's Ranch, and Rocky Ridge Ranch.

It is often difficult to determine from urban images where the souls of a community's inspirational elite rested. Were Calgary's elite disconnected from their "wilderness?" Often aspirational values can be determined from an examination of private as well as public spaces. It can be argued, based on heritage house inventories and images in the Glenbow Museum, that the homes of the elite reflected not ranching traditions, but the traditions of wealth. Some of the aspirational homes in Mount Royal would have been acceptable even in Montreal – the other Mount Royal. The Lougheed House in Calgary certainly reflects Montreal tastes. The home of Mr. Robertson, a Calgary entrepreneur with ranching interests, was furnished with the contents of Government House acquired at the Aberhart auction and was decidedly Euro-Canadian, with its red brick exterior and mock Tudor elements.[20] Western Canada entered the decor only in the occasional painting.[21]

However, it should not be assumed that the elite had no connections with the hinterlands. For example, Dr. Margaret Hess, Dr. Ruth Gorman, and Dr. Margaret Cross Dover, like other members of wealthy families, had ranching interests and country as well as city homes. These ties mattered a great deal. The Cross family all had roots in the foothills,[22] and their position in Calgary society was reinforced by their status as landed gentry. The "bronc" and the "cowboy" were not really part of that ranching culture. Dr. Lewis G. Thomas, a leading Alberta historian and a ranching scion himself, argued that the ranching community in Alberta was more genteel, more aristocratic, than elsewhere in the West, and that this tradition informed Calgary's culture. Early ranch homes may have had animal skins as decorations, but these and the rough log walls were abandoned as soon as possible.[23] Perhaps the ranching aristocracy's rejection of the Stampede was a rejection of the wilderness and the lawless cowboy culture that it symbolized. Their reality was not rooted in that past. They may have seen the Stampede as a cynical and inaccurate exploitation of a brief period of history for the purpose of generating revenue.

So, what does the minimal role of the Stampede image in public art and public spaces say about Calgarians' perceptions of their city, their culture, their region, province, and country? Calgary, like many Canadian cities, has created an official past – a useable and commercial past – in part through boosterism, festivals, and public art. Public bronzes, iron sculptures in parks or on streets, and commercial signage are all expressions of what the community determines to be its publicly acceptable past. Public bronzes, in particular, indicate what the community as a whole feels should be validated and acknowledged.

Calgary's public art would seem to convey three key messages. The first and most important is a careful identification of key foundation myths, the second is modernity, and the third – the environment – is still emerging. The foundation values apparent in the public art focusing on the city's heritage are sacrifice, progress, and the taming of a wilderness – the wilderness being symbolized by First Nations peoples (John Hunt) and their environment (the buffalo). Few pieces are related to the Stampede, and the most famous of these are located on the Stampede grounds. For the most part, Stampede images are in commercial signage and sports teams. The Stampede is commercial, not cultural; of the pocketbook, not the soul – although Calgary's soul might well be its pocketbook. Heritage is, however, a key subject in Calgary's public art. It reinforces what most of us believe about Canadian history – that peace, order, and good government were introduced by the North-West Mounted Police, and that they exercised compassion and provided the link that held the West together. The taming of the West involved struggle; "In Search of Gold Mountain" and "Wall of Names" in Sein Lok Park and "Gratitude" celebrate victories over prejudice and marginalization and a new age of equality. However, most public art has one object in mind – to make Calgary appear as a modern city to its citizens and to the visiting public. The dancing circle in front of the school board, the trees on Eighth Avenue Mall, even the fish on the freeway are efforts to make the public see Calgary as a contemporary city with international concerns. The "Udderly Art" phenomenon, born in Chicago and adopted by the fund-raising elite, was almost a mock celebration of Calgary's heritage, focusing as it did on domesticated cows rather than ranchland steers.

The new theme of public sculpture for the city will be the environment, linked always to the Bow River. I suspect that most Calgarians would find this choice surprising; however, I also think few would disagree. Water, air, and energy have become primary concerns for Calgarians. The Stampede, while part of the commercial soul of the city, has no place in modern Calgary, at least not in its public art. It has ever been so.

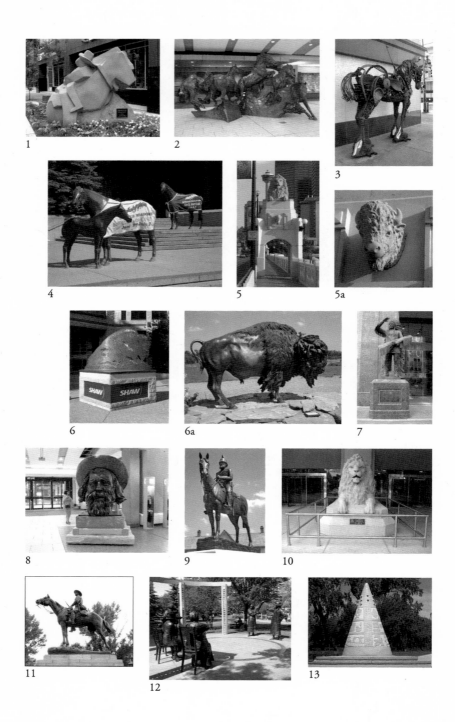

1

2

3

4

5

5a

6

6a

7

8

9

10

11

12

13

14

15

16

17

18

19

20

22

23

24

26

Notes

I would like to thank Fiona Foran for interviewing a number of the artists who have contributed to Calgary's public art landscape. I would also like to thank Stéphane Guevremont for taking the photos.

1. Nuala C. Johnson, "Mapping Monuments: The Shaping of Public Space and Cultural Identities," *Visual Communication* 1, no. 3 (October 2002): 293.

2. The best of the most recent North American studies are on monuments in New York and those relating to the American Civil War. See, for example, Thomas J. Brown, *The Public Art of Civil War Commemoration* (Boston: Bedford/St. Martin's, 2004). See also Nuala Johnson, *Ireland, the Great War, and the Geography of Remembrance* (Cambridge: Cambridge University Press, 2003).

3. Paul Connerton, *How Societies Remember* (Cambridge: Cambridge University Press, 1994).

4. James Howard Kunstler, *The Geography of Nowhere: The Rise and Decline of America's Man-Made Landscape* (New York: Simon and Schuster, 1993).

5. Robert J. Belton, *Sights of Resistance: Approaches to Canadian Visual Culture* (Calgary: University of Calgary Press, 2001).

6. "The Steampunk Gazeteer – Alberta, Canada," in *Steampunk*, n.d., n.p.

7. Sorcha McGinnis, "Livingston's Bust Greets Visitors," *Calgary Herald*, 28 January 2003. See also Interview with Al Henderson, Fiona Foran notes, 6 September 2006.

8. See, for example, *http://members.shaw.ca/rcmpvets.calgary/macleod_statue.htm*.

9. *Calgary Herald*, 19 October 1999.

10. See F. Pannekoek, ed., *Behind the Man: John Laurie, Ruth Gorman, and the Indian Vote in Canada* (Calgary: University of Calgary Press, 2007).

11. *City Centre News*, July 2006. See also *Calgary Herald*, 30 September 1984.

12. *Calgary Herald*, 26 May 1985.

13. Tom Kaplar and Clayton B. Keyser, *Udderly Art: Colourful Cows for Calgary* (Toronto: Fitzhenry & Whiteside, 2000).

14. Robert Venturi, *Complexity and Contradiction in Architecture* (New York: Museum of Modern Art Press, 1966); *Learning from Las Vegas* (Cambridge, MA: MIT Press, 1972).

15. "Draft City of Calgary Utilities and Environmental Protection Department Plan," October 2006.

16. Canadian Precast/Prestressed Concrete Institute, "Jumping Trout Glenmore Interchange (GE5), Calgary, Alberta," Project of the Month, 20 November 2006, http://www.cpci.ca?sc=potm&pn=monthly112006.

17. See a copy of the plan and background at *http://caa.ucalgary.ca/mawson.html*.

18. Bryan P. Melnyk, *Calgary Builds: The Emergence of an Urban Landscape, 1905–1914* (Regina: Canadian Plains Research Center, 1985), 1.

19. B.S. White, *The Story of Calgary, Alberta, Canada: Progress, Resources, Opportunities* (Western Standard Publishing Company, 1914).

20. See F. Pannekoek, M. McMordie, et al., *Heritage Covenants and Preservation: The Calgary Civic Trust* (Calgary: University of Calgary Press, 2004). The Robertson house is referred to in this volume as a key heritage site meriting preservation. I had the good fortune to see the house and its contents prior to Mr. Robertson's passing. It was truly an outstanding example of Calgary's private spaces.

21. An excellent study of interior decoration of ranching houses is Lewis G. Thomas, "Ranch Houses of the Alberta Foothills," in *Canadian Historic Sites Occasional Papers in Archaeology and History*, No. 20 (Ottawa: Parks Canada, 1979), 125–43.

22. For the importance of the ranch in shaping the early culture of Alberta, see Sherrill MacLaren, *Braehead: Three Founding Families in Nineteenth Century Canada* (Toronto: McClelland and Stewart, 1986).

23. Thomas, "Ranch Houses."

CHAPTER 11

"A Wonderful Picture":
Western Art and the Calgary Stampede

Brian Rusted

The Gordon Love Trophy for the North American All Round Cowboy,
design by Charlie Beil for the 1966 Calgary Stampede.

"Not Art but at Least Culture"

In the spring of 2003, John Spittle of Calgary's CBC Radio One woke the city by reporting that the Calgary Stampede was "the biggest detriment to promoting the arts in the province."[1] Spittle was covering a press conference by Robert Palmer, a Scottish arts consultant who had been contracted by the City of Calgary's Civic Arts Policy Review Steering Committee to assist in updating its civic arts policy. There were multiple goals in developing such a policy, derived from the efforts of other cities seeking economic renewal by encouraging creative classes and industries. For Calgary's Review Steering Committee, these goals included providing a greater voice for the arts in the city; having the arts contribute to the city's vitality, sense of identity, and heritage; and having the real economic contribution of the arts be acknowledged in city planning. Oddly, arts associated with the Calgary Stampede – not part of the consultation process – had been caught in the crossfire of such objectives.

Palmer's observation was made in reference to the document that summarized the final Consultant's Report of the Civic Arts Policy Review. His provocative remark reflected opinions heard during focus group sessions, though the Calgary Stampede had little involvement in the process. As an external consultant, he had limited experience with the Stampede itself and limited information on the festival's historic or contemporary connections with and contributions to the city's arts. He was a member of a newly minted class of arts consultants following in the footsteps of Richard Florida[2] and others, whose operational definition of what should be included in the "arts" was universally shared[3] despite an avowed aim of creating "a distinct urban culture" and an "enhanced community identity."[4] Even if such research into the Stampede had been undertaken in developing the city's arts policy, it is unlikely that the view of the Stampede's relation to Calgary's arts would have changed. Despite its commitment to the performing arts (the Young Canadians, its School of Performing Arts, and the Stampede Show Band) and the visual arts (arts and crafts exhibits, the Western Art Show, high school art scholarships, and so forth), the odds would not have been in the Stampede's favour that these activities would have been considered "art" or even arts education. The Stampede received a total of five mentions in the final arts policy document: twice as an international tourist icon, once as a metonymic adjective for the city, once as an event that the (real) arts community might exploit to its own promotional advantage, and finally, once in a delightful expression of taste culture that associates the Stampede with specific arts activities solely to dismiss its relevance. A stakeholder asks of Calgary, "Renowned for what? Best symphony, opera, ballet, visual art gallery, synergy with tourism, Stampede (not art but at least culture)."[5]

Why would arts stakeholders and those invested in city's creative makeover consider the Stampede "not art but at least culture"? This chapter is an effort to answer such a question. The Stampede may serve as a symbolic resource for contemporary art or as a foil for social critique, but there is little need for stakeholders in contemporary art worlds to acknowledge creative practices that fall outside the boundaries of their definitions of art. Answering a question about the boundaries that separate western and contemporary art[6] entails a preliminary consideration of how the contemporary art world defines western art. An indirect consequence of such boundary maintenance has been that the Stampede's contribution to Calgary's visual and performing arts communities has received limited documentation. A second aspect of this chapter, then, will be to sketch distinguishing features of western art and to document some of the roles played by the Stampede in its local expression.

"A Wonderful Picture"

The rain had not yet started on the September afternoon when photographer W.V. Ring set his camera before a group of dignitaries assembled at the start of "The Stampede" in Calgary. Ring made several exposures of this gathering, and his photos have been frequently reproduced.[7] The image of this group at the first Stampede in 1912 was one of the few showing the original "Big Four" founders posed together. The presence of other dignitaries such as the inspector of the RCMP or White Headed Chief might receive mention, but it is the Stampede's original financial backers, George Lane, Archie McLean, Pat Burns, and A.E. Cross, who are most often noted. Two artists, Charles M. Russell and Edward Borein, along with Russell's wife Nancy, the sole woman in the image, are occasionally mentioned. On that September afternoon Charlie Russell looked confidently at the camera, thumb hooked in his trademark sash, as the younger though equally confident Borein clutched at the edge of his vest as if in the midst of the physical labour needed to hoist him into this gathering. What is the significance of the presence of artists among this assembly of Stampede founders?

The Stampede began as a festive celebration of the cowboy, "a wonderful picture of Western sports and the old times"[8] bankrolled by the wealth of these ranchers, developers, and politicians pausing and posing before Ring's camera. The irony that such a group funded the celebration of a

The first Stampede group photo with White Headed Chief (left); George Lane and Mrs. C.M. Russell (3rd and 4th from left); unknown, Pat Burns, Charles M. Russell; A.E. Cross, and Edward Borein (far right).

working-class occupation has never been far below the surface. The event's inception, however, was also due in no small measure to the representational labour of artists such as Russell and Borein. It was not an accident that L.V. Kelly chose the metaphor "picture" to describe this first Stampede in the narrative about Alberta ranching that he published in the following year. Even at that time, the work of myriad writers, musicians, photographers, illustrators, and painters had helped create the image of the West these dignitaries were assembled to celebrate. Although Russell in particular was at the peak of his career and popularity in 1912, it would be a mistake to see his presence in this photograph as either honorific acknowledgment or mere accident due to his commercial capacity as an exhibitor. Ring's photograph demonstrates the degree to which the representation of the North American West had taken hold of the imagination of urban folk. If Guy Weadick's goal with these early Stampedes was to recreate the "atmosphere" of the "frontier days of the west" through a gathering of "western pioneers,"[9] then Russell's presence in this photograph was evidence of his status as a pioneer, but more particularly of his pioneering role in documenting the atmosphere Weadick sought to recreate.

It was not simply access to real capital that earned one a place in this lineup of dignitaries; symbolic capital – the artistic ability to recreate the sights of the West – placed Russell and Borein on an equal footing with the Stampede's backers. To pass over Russell and Borein's participation in this early image of the Stampede is to pass over the significance of western art to the Stampede's inception and to miss its significance in subsequent decades. The task of recovering aspects of the Stampede's relation to western art and accounting for features that mark it as a distinctive art world contributes to answering the question about western art's marginalization by contemporary art institutions.

If It's Western, Is It Art?

In her history of contemporary Alberta art, Mary-Beth Laviolette devotes a portion of one chapter to discussing art by "carving cowboys" that made western themes available to contemporary artists. She naturalizes her view of western art by including it in a chapter discussing documentary photography and folk art. The implication of such a grouping is that these three forms of visual culture share a common ancestor in naive realism. Each form can be characterized in terms of how, as sign, it is bound to place: photography mediates this relation indexically through the camera apparatus, while folk art's mediation is as iconic expression of memory in the absence of technical or formal sophistication. Western art occupies a questionable third space "resolutely narrative, realistic,"[10] its vision of place a more symbolic order of sign somehow distorted by conventions of myth, romance, and nostalgia. Laviolette's account does not cover periods prior to 1970; she does name over a dozen artists making western art before then, but feels that the genre's "boom" in a Canadian context follows "American western art"[11] of the 1970s. Despite a brief mention of Alberta's contribution to the tradition of bronze sculpture, it is the western theme, a kind of natural resource for contemporary art practitioners, that interests Laviolette, and she forges ahead to consider media and installation artists "ready to question, demythologize, play with and respond to the romance and the reality of the West."[12]

Laviolette notes both the absence of scholarly discussions of western art and its general dismissal by the Canadian art establishment.[13] Although an explanation of this state is not a concern in her chapter, her approach to western art suggests why such an absence might be the case. The narrative contour of her discussion connects western art to other, naively realistic, forms of visual culture only to have them shouldered aside by a heroic contemporary art whose muscular, critical engagement redeems viewers and artists alike from the perils and taint of romantic illusions, nostalgia, and Americanism. Such a plot is in turn a romantic narrative about contemporary art's transformative potential, a narrative of visual style and critical discourse that also shares American antecedents. Western subject matter, the self-taught or commercial training of western art's exponents, and the conventionalized treatment of an "idealized way of life"[14] function like Homeric epithets in the discursive practices of art worlds, and conspire alongside such a narrative to marginalize and exclude western art from serious attention.

The discursive force of art history narratives that divide artistic practices along such fault lines points to another order of explanation. The continued presence and vitality of a genre such as western art if not contained and isolated by critical discourses risks destabilizing the authority of the redemptive narrative of contemporary art. Dismissing western art deftly as mere realism inhibits critical consideration and silences disruptive questions about the complexity of social practices of taste associated with art making and viewing. A parallel strategy, noted by Nancy Anderson, is to read western art solely as historical data, its subject oriented towards a past.[15] In considering the Calgary Stampede's relation to western art, it should be possible to glimpse this complexity and to engage the possibility that western art requires a different way of looking, one that falls outside the hegemony maintained by formal art training and elite critical discourses.

Rather than trying to "read" meaning assumed to inhere within images said to represent the West, it is of greater value to explore a social world constituted by the production and consumption of western art, in particular some of the phases in the Stampede's support and exhibition of western art. This chapter considers grounded aesthetic practices that suggest the distinctive ways of looking that western art demands; and it considers how western art is understood in a broader, civic context as an aspect of public culture. Two processes that underlie the dismissal of western art emerge: the slow withdrawal of dominant art institutions from the support, exhibition, and analysis of western art; and the institutional practices in which specific Stampede policies aid in transforming its real engagement in the ongoing re-creation of the West into a form of ocular spectatorship.

How to Savvy Western Art

When asked by a reporter for the *Chicago Evening Post* what he thought about the modern art exhibited in New York's Armory Show in 1913, Charlie Russell said, "Yes, I saw the cubist and futurist exhibit in New York, but can't savvy that stuff. It may be art...but I can't savvy it. Now I may paint a bum horse, but people who know what a horse looks like will know that I tried to paint a horse, at least."[16]

One might conclude from his remark that if art is good for anything, it is good for expressing social boundaries of taste. In his interview, Charlie Russell expressed his view about the boundaries that mark western art: viewers need to be able to "savvy" what he is painting, and they are going to judge the quality of his work by the degree to which it matches their experience with the subject, the referent of his representation. In noting these boundaries, Russell also indicates how such boundaries distinguish western art from the "modern" art of his day and, by extension, of ours. Works of art do not make up a uniform or homogeneous body of creative practice. Art can be "savvied" only with reference to the specific social activities and competencies that mark ways of handling certain subjects, the standards associated with judgment, the institutional contexts and endorsements that go along with exhibition and display, and so forth. Rather than judge western art pejoratively because no special discursive skills appear to be required to "savvy" its stylistic manipulation of the space of the canvas, it is more productive to understand western art as a distinct art world, one that requires a distinctive way of looking.

Thirty years ago, *New York Times* art critic Grace Lichtenstein noted that, "Despite determined inattention by Eastern art critics ... Cowboy art has its own heroes, its own galleries and even its own publishing house."[17] Her comment points to some of the social practices that mark this art world as distinct: its own tradition of exemplars; its own institutions, specifically, its own museums and professional associations dedicated to western art; its own annual shows, sales, and auctions; and as Lichtenstein noted, its own distinctive book and periodical publishing industry.

There are close to two dozen museums in the United States whose curatorial mandate is entirely or predominantly focused on western art. These museums extend from upstate New York, to Oklahoma, and on to California. Some museums, such as the C.M. Russell Museum in Great Falls, Montana, or the Clymer Museum of Art in Ellensburg, Washington, have as their primary focus the work of particular artists. Others, such as the Gene Autry Museum in Los Angeles and the Amon Carter Museum in Fort Worth, Texas, originated from the bequests of private collectors. Some are large museums in urban areas that identify themselves with the West, such as the Phoenix Art Museum; others have more direct connections to regional history, such as the Buffalo Bill Historical Center in Cody, Wyoming. These museums demonstrate a continued fascination with the visual record of the West and create destinations for those seeking the display of western culture.

Although their mandates might be open to political and market pressures,[18] their number continues to grow; in October 2006, for example, the Denver Museum opened the Dietler Gallery of Western Art. In Canada, museums such as the Whyte Museum of the Canadian Rockies and Calgary's Glenbow Museum have substantial collections in the areas of First Nations, settler, and western culture, though their mandates are not exclusively western in focus.

Often connected with such museums and institutions are the various professional associations that support and encourage western artists. The oldest of these, dating from the mid-1960s, is the Cowboy Artists of America. At least two museums represent the work of this group: the Phoenix Art Museum hosts its annual exhibition, while the Western Art Museum in Kerrville, Texas, houses a permanent collection of its work. Artists frequently belong to a variety of professional associations, such as those focused on art practice (plein-air painters or portrait artists, for example) or on various media (watercolours, oils, pastels), but an expanding number of associations serve those whose work is somehow themed on the West.

Many of the museums and associations host annual exhibitions and fundraising galas. Some, such as the C.M. Russell and Buffalo Bill Historical Center auctions, are fundraising events for the parent museums; others, such as the Prix de West and the National Cowboy Museum, celebrate the genre of western art. Events such as the annual exhibition of the Cowboy Artists of America are opportunities to view the exclusive work of premier exponents of this genre. Events such as the Coeur d'Alene art auction, now held in Reno, are entirely commercial ventures and are based primarily on the sale of historical work. The Coeur d'Alene auction sells in excess of $20 million worth of art annually, suggesting something of the economic vitality of work in this genre. There is also a longstanding affiliation of western art sales and auctions with rodeos and livestock shows, the Cheyenne Frontier Days and the Coors Western Art Exhibit being prominent examples. Collectively, these western art shows, sales, and auctions help articulate the boundaries and maintain the standards that define western art. The practices associated with juried selection and the identification of various award winners all help to enact the standards of both tradition and innovation within the genre.

There is a long record of book publications related to the West and western art. The earliest of these publications used art to illustrate aspects of western life. Later, the artists themselves, Remington and Russell being the notable examples, published books dealing with their own artwork. A later generation, artists such as Will James and Dan Muller, combined artistic and prose skills and found ready audiences for their popular rendition of West.

Some, such as Jo Mora, combined art with the skills of folklore collectors to create substantial texts of cowboy lore. Since that time, many studies have attempted to characterize aspects of the world of western art. One of the earliest of these was Robert Taft's 1953 history of western artists.[19] Other authors have worked to document the collections of individuals,[20] the formation of particular institutions,[21] or historical[22] and contemporary trends in western art.[23] It is only in recent decades that a scholarly study of aspects of western life and representation has developed.[24]

More recently, the periodical market has made substantial commitments to western art. Prominent magazines such as *Art of the West* and *Southwest Art* provide information about shows, galleries, artists, and so forth. Publications such as *Cowboys and Indians*, *American Cowboy*, *Western Interiors*, and *Canadian Cowboy Country* offer broader editorial content on western lifestyles, but western art and photography figure prominently. Magazines aimed at horse owners, such as *Western Horseman*, have had longstanding commitments to editorial content on western art. Going back to the first decades of its publication, *Western Horseman* featured decorations by artists such as Joe de Yong, a protege of Charlie Russell. Canadian counterparts such as *Western Horse Review* have recently added editorial content on western art in response to market research on reader interests. Specialized publications aimed at artists themselves include *Equine Vision Magazine*, which combines profiles and instructional content with the promotion of materials and supplies.

All of these books and publications contribute to the terrain of western art. They help in understanding the development of western art and the characteristics that mark it as a distinctive art world. They also map the extent of its contemporary popularity and suggest the appeal that western art has for collectors. This level of social and institutional activity is relatively recent, most of it developing half a century after Russell and Borein posed together at the 1912 Stampede.

The Real Thing and a Lot of It

The participation of Russell and Borein during "The Stampede" of 1912 in Calgary established the parameters of the Stampede's arts-related activities. Russell had been invited by Guy Weadick to exhibit his artwork during the Stampede, while Edward Borein had been recommended by Russell to Weadick for advertising and related promotional illustrations.[25] Such a range of activity demonstrates the foundational presence of western art in the Stampede's heritage. It also suggests that hard and fast distinctions between art and commercial illustration, while evident even at that time, were not of primary importance to these artists, the Stampede, or collectors of western art. Art exhibition and commercial illustration were simply different facets of the visual culture associated with and produced as part of the Stampede's engagement with representations of western heritage. The Stampede's role in providing exhibition space or in commissioning commercial work has been balanced by its roles as a patron and, increasingly, as a collector of western art. It will be useful to outline these as phases in the Stampede's relation to the western art world.

Exhibitor of Western Art

Although a reproduction of Russell's 1909 painting "A Serious Predicament" had been featured on a poster for "The Stampede" in 1912, Russell's work had been shipped north from Great Falls primarily for exhibition. The fact that Russell was able to sell paintings – more than half of those he'd brought, with subsequent commissions generated by the exhibition – for as much as $3,500 in 1912 indicates something about his stature as an artist at the time and his wife's shrewdness in negotiating with buyers.[26] When compared to sales at his New York show a year earlier, it also suggests the effect of exhibiting his paintings for royalty and a ranching elite amid the festive setting of the Stampede. Brian Dippie describes Russell's participation in 1912 as consti- tuting "his first international one man exhibition,"[27] although it is not clear exactly where Russell's work was exhibited during that first Stampede. Some refer to the exhibit as being on the grounds of the Stampede,[28] but others suggest it took place in an exhibition hall in downtown Calgary.[29] Whatever the exact location of this event, it could be considered as the start of western art exhibitions at the Stampede. The Calgary Exhibition's prize books in the years preceding the 1912 Stampede also indicate the presence of art entered for competition along with ladies' crafts and needlework,[30] but there is no evidence of the prominence of western content in its imagery.

If the first phase of the Stampede's exhibition of western art begins in 1912 and carries on into the 1920s, a second phase can be said to begin early in the 1930s. The formation of the Alberta Society of Artists (ASA) in 1931 was the result of nearly a decade's worth of organizational activity in the visual arts in both Edmonton and Calgary. The establishment of local art clubs, the Edmonton Art Association, and the Calgary Sketch Club in the early 1920s were the preliminary steps, but the development of what would even- tually become the Alberta College of Art and Design had greater impact. The founding instructors of art in Calgary, most notably A.C. Leighton, pushed for these various clubs and associations to amalgamate despite differences in their aesthetic standards.

After it had been formally chartered as a society, the ASA held regular art shows. The winter exhibits were hosted by the Hudson's Bay Company, while the summer exhibits were held under the auspices of the Calgary Stampede. This pattern continued until the society banded together with other arts organizations in Alberta and approached the Royal Commission on National Development in the Arts, Letters and Sciences in the late 1940s with the intent of becoming an "allied" arts organization with its own exhibition space, Coste House. Over this period, artists such as Roland Gissing who were involved with the Society also had solo exhibitions at the Stampede. The Stampede's first manager, E.L. Richardson, organized Gissing's debut exhibition at the Calgary Public Library in 1929,[31] and exhibitions of his work occurred during the Stampedes in 1934, 1947, and 1956.

With the formation of the Alberta Society of Artists marking a second phase in the Stampede's exhibition of western art, a third phase might be suggested by the development of the Glenbow Archives in the mid-1950s. Established by collector and philanthropist Eric Harvie, the Glenbow Archives had as its original mandate the collection of works related to the pioneers and aboriginal peoples of southern Alberta. Until construction was completed on its present building in 1976, the Glenbow had no formal exhibition space, nor an exhibition mandate.[32] During the 1950s the Glenbow partnered with Calgary Power, sponsor of Gissing's Stampede exhibit in 1947,[33] to present a display of western art from its collection during the Calgary Stampede. These exhibitions continued until the early 1960s and featured works by artists such as Russell and Rungius and local artists who included John Innes, Roland Gissing, Edward Hagell, Walter Phillips, and Theodore Schintz.

Commissioner of Commercial Art

The year before Borein was approached by Weadick with the opportunity to do commercial design for the Stampede in Calgary, he had already started converting his drawings into etchings and trying to interest New York art galleries in them.[34] He had been living there since 1907 and would continue to maintain a studio there for the next dozen years. Russell visited him in New York in 1908, and by 1912 Borein had built a solid reputation by painting and illustrating magazine covers and advertisements and doing sketches to accompany magazine articles. His focus on western themes characterized by an emphasis on historic action and detail made him an obvious choice for Russell to recommend for the Stampede. Weadick used Borein again to do illustration and commercial work for the second Stampede, held in Winnipeg in 1913; the 1916 Stampede in New York; and the 1919 Calgary Stampede. As Davidson notes, "...the Weadick rodeos became a good source of income for Ed. If nothing else, he would do the cover for the programs."[35] Davidson states that an ink sketch Borein made during the 1919 Stampede was later reproduced as an etching titled "Scratchin' High" and as a lithograph. The lithograph version carries as additional text "I-See-U," variously referred to as its title, the name of the bronc, or a declaration by the rider. Sheilagh Jameson suggests that the image was inspired by W.J. Oliver's photograph of Clem Gardner's ride on High Tower during the 1919 Stampede.[36] However, the "I-See-U" lithograph was used for Stampede posters in 1919 and from 1923 to 1929, so Borein could not have drawn the original during the 1919 Stampede or used Oliver's photograph. There is no evidence that Borein exhibited any of his work during the 1912 Stampede or at subsequent Stampedes, though clearly he would have had etchings available at this time and was actively promoting them in other quarters.

Cover of the souvenir program from the 1919 Stampede

The use of Borein's "I-See-U" lithograph as the basis of the posters promoting the Stampede during the 1920s places the work of western artists at the inception of what has become a long and distinctive tradition of poster design. These early designs have become icons of the Stampede, reproduced and remediated in a variety of ways around the Stampede's grounds as souvenirs and marketing premiums. In the contemporary period, the iconic elements of the posters are unhitched from their primary design and applied to letterhead decorations, components of belt buckles, and so forth. Since 2006 the design of the posters has crossed back into the realm of western art, with paintings by local artists being commissioned as central features.

Patron of Western Art

If Borein established the visual iconography of the Stampede, a young protege of C.M. Russell helped carry it forward into the next three decades. Charlie Beil had made his peripatetic way to Great Falls, Montana, where he earned Charlie Russell's admiration and Nancy Russell's trust. In one of his last recorded interviews, Russell recommends Beil's work to the editor of the *Great Falls Leader*, Ed Cooney, saying, "He is the best I've ever seen at modeling horses and cowpunchers."[37] Beil walked with Russell's horse behind the hearse at Russell's funeral in 1926 and stayed on in Great Falls for several years to help Nancy settle the estate by completing paintings and bronzes.[38]

There is no evidence to suggest that Beil's connection with Russell is what spurred the Calgary Stampede to approach him to design a trophy, but the itinerant cowboy and artist had moved north and was living and working in the Banff area. In the early 1930s he was certainly open to commissions and had already completed work for the Calgary Zoo and Calgary's Model Dairy. In Weadick's final year with the Stampede, Beil was approached to design a trophy for the North American All-Around Champion, the first recipient of which was Herman Linder.[39] By the late 1930s this initial commission had inaugurated a tradition in the world of rodeo: awarding an artist-cast bronze sculpture to winning cowboys in the traditional rodeo contests.[40] Under the sponsorship of Calgary Power, Beil designed a trophy for the winner of the saddle bronc competition and eventually added trophies for the other events, including the chuckwagon races. Beil continued this role into the 1960s, when he designed relief plaques rather than sculptures for the rodeo winners. It is perhaps fitting that Linder returned to the Stampede in 1964 and presented Beil's bronzes to the winning cowboys.[41]

Although the differences may not be boldly marked, the Stampede's role as a client of commercial art and illustration shades into a different role as patron involved in supporting artists through commissions such as the rodeo bronzes. Were these early Beil trophies commercial art, or were they examples of Stampede patronage aimed at establishing a link to western art's heritage? Were Gissing's shows an example of the Stampede's role in exhibiting western art, or was the Stampede acting as a patron who bartered exhibit space in return for the association with an artist who was inspired by Russell and had a personal connection to prominent western artist and writer Will James?[42] If such a distinction between commercial art client and western art patron is to be more than a difference in shading, it should also suggest real differences in organizational and social practices.

Commercial work and the activities of a patron create distinct attitudes towards artwork. On the commercial side, intention is ascribed to the client: the completed artwork is the realization of the client's objectives. In the role of patron, the expressive relationship is reversed. While the patron might still gain promotional benefit from the work, the artist's expressive intentions dominate. In the present, such distinctions can be seen in the organizational practices associated with these various tasks. Despite numerous ambiguous areas where responsibilities overlap, the Stampede's professional marketing staff and employees handle the majority of commissioned work – posters, graphic design, and so forth. Volunteer committees seem to have a greater involvement in activities related to what are identified as the activities of a patron. Although volunteer committees have been significant in the structure of the Stampede since its origins,[43] an important shift from the Stampede's role as a supplier of exhibition space occurs when the Stampede coordinates art exhibitions of its own.

Although the exhibition of western artwork can be traced back to the original Calgary Exhibition, a formal volunteer committee with a mandate to stage an annual art show does not take shape until the late 1970s. Volunteer efforts in two separate spheres contribute to this: one involves the encouragement of high school students to exhibit art during the Stampede, while the other involves the formation of a committee made up of alumni of the Queen's competition. The Queen's Alumni began with an exhibition area known as Women's World. Over time their display came to include cooking and floral arrangements joined by the longstanding arts and crafts exhibition; by 1976 this aggregation was called "Arts Alive." Soon after, these different areas were gathered under a single volunteer committee named Creative Living, with an annual art show and sale. In the early 1980s the show included an annual auction of works by participating artists who attend the show for the duration of the Stampede. More than 100 volunteers work year-round attracting and selecting artists and promoting the event to prospective buyers and collectors who might not otherwise have reason to attend the Stampede.

The development of the Stampede's own Western Art Show is significant here for two reasons: first, it marks a final separation between the Stampede as an organization that provides arts exhibition space and the dominant local art institutions that use the space; second, this event links the artists associated with the Stampede and the western art world. The affinities of the artists who participate and the events that comprise the Western Art Show are no longer with the contemporary, alternative, or avant-garde art worlds. The artists and the event have stronger and more direct affinities with the network of western art shows, auctions, sales, and museums of western art.

Collector of Western Art

By the time Charlie Beil relinquished the task of producing the Stampede's trophy bronzes and plaques, the Stampede had developed a new role as an art collector. Simply keeping each of Beil's bronze sculptures produced what is now perhaps the only complete collection of his trophy works. Almost by accident, the organization amassed works that charted Beil's development as

Calgary Stampede Rodeo Princesses Justine Milner and Coleen Crowe carry present Amy Dryer's painting, *Rider*, at the 2005 Western Art Auction.

a sculptor, although this body of his work was not exhibited as a collection until the late 1970s, when the Queen's Alumni and Women's World were developing their involvement with western art. The volunteers of Women's World gathered up and dusted off the various works that Beil had produced and put them on display during the Stampede. What had started as an expression of the Stampede's commercial needs and over time had become an expression of its role as a patron of western art now became a statement of the Stampede as a collector.

The display of Beil's trophy bronzes coincided with a global interest in heritage.[44] The Stampede as an organization may only just be realizing it has a western art collection acquired through these longstanding practices and innocent archival acts, but for two decades it has been transforming the Stampede from a participant activity into a spectator-driven event. Collections are the coin of the realm in the global market of heritage destinations. Our increasing dislocation from a shared past is patched together by heritage artifacts that help to elicit a sense of history and place. The task of collecting produces identity collateral while at the same time fostering an economy of display and consumption. Collecting builds on routine acquisition and extends it into the self-conscious interpretation of the Stampede's history that can be seen in other features of the Calgary Stampede park such as the Historical Committee's mural project.

The Stampede Historical Committee's murals on the east wall of the Corral building. Completed in 1997, Doug Driediger's work on the upper level portrays Guy Weadick's vision, while Penny Corradine's work on the early parades appears at street level.

Initiated in the mid-1990s, these murals decorate walls, even whole buildings, around the Stampede grounds. Eight murals have been completed to
date, and in their own way they offer both temporal and spatial landmarks
of the Stampede's past. They describe the first winning bronc ride, the
first chuckwagon race, the first parade, the first bull sale, and even the first
entrance to the Stampede grounds. The phenomenon of murals has an
established role in preparing a place for tourist consumption.[45] In the decade
since such commissions began at the Stampede, they have come to form a
distinctive collection, one that serves a double duty: it charts key moments
of display and spectatorship associated with the Stampede, yet at the same
time it makes that history the object of visual consumption for tourists and
visitors alike.

The narrative of the Stampede's involvement in western art moves through
at least four phases. They begin with the exhibition of art but blend into
activities associated with commissioning art and being a patron of the arts.
In its evolution, the mandate of the Calgary Stampede has also shifted from
producing western entertainment to preserving western heritage. Increasingly, this mandate includes components of western art and visual culture
because the preservation of heritage is often synonymous with the display of
the *look* of the West. The design of posters, program illustrations, pageantry,
logos, tourist advertisements, souvenirs, and memorabilia have all played a
part in creating the Stampede's visual discourse on the West. If the Stampede began as a picture of the West, the organization now understands the
West as being embodied through pictures. The Calgary Stampede's recent
effort at "re-branding" in order to create a unified identity that merges with
the mandate "to preserve and promote western heritage and values" was
an exercise in fabricating a visual past: an odd effort given the richness of
the organization's actual visual heritage. If Russell was celebrated in 1912
for offering a documentary link to western heritage, and subsequent artists
associated with the Stampede were in turn celebrated for their links back to
Russell, the Stampede has entered a new phase in which sepia-toned images
and invented myths simulate a relation to the look of a visual past.

"To Provide, Engage and Employ"

At their 2007 meeting Calgary Stampede shareholders passed a special resolution that amended the objectives of the organization. The original wording,
dating from 1978, read very much like a civic arts policy and indicated that
the objects of the Calgary Exhibition and Stampede included a commitment

"to provide, engage and employ...performers, artists" and "generally to promote any activity beneficial to...culture, the arts, education and the City of
Calgary ... "[46] In the revision of these objectives, all references to artists and
art disappeared. Although it is difficult to predict the consequences of such a
change in wording, there has been no apparent reduction in the Stampede's
arts-related activities. As the Stampede inevitably moves away from the
motivations for such a revision, the ambiguity of the Stampede's relation to
art, artists, culture, and the city might increase. Although the word "western"
appears in the revised objectives of the organization, it is defined with reference to words such as integrity, friendliness, and entrepreneurship. Despite
its mandate to preserve western heritage, the organization could potentially
slip free of the halter that has tied it to the heritage of those artists pictured
on the Stampede grounds in 1912. It may be ironic that despite the marginal
treatment of western art, the Stampede's continued support accomplishes
one of the goals of Calgary's Civic Arts Policy, facilitating "ties between the
arts and tourism."[47] The labour begun here of retrieving and reflecting on the
practices that associate the Stampede with western art may help renew a link
with the visual character of western heritage. It is at least one way to savvy
the Stampede's wonderful picture.

Notes

1.	John Spittle, "Calgary Stampede Hurting the Arts: Consultant," *The Arts Report*, CBC Radio (Calgary), 15 April 2003.

2.	Richard Florida, *The Rise of the Creative Class and How It's Transforming Work, Leisure, Community and Everyday Life* (New York: Basic Books, 2000).

3.	For critical assessments of creative industries makeovers, see Max Nathan, *The Wrong Stuff: Creative Class Theory, Diversity and City Performance,* Research Discussion Paper No. 1 (Institute for Public Policy Research, Centre for Cities, 2005), 1–8; Kate Oakley, "Not So Cool Britannia: The Role of Creative Industries in Economic Development," *International Journal of Cultural Studies* 7, no. 1 (2004): 67–77; and Andrew Ross, "Nice Work if You Can Get It: The Mercurial Career of Creative Industries Policy," *Work, Organization, Labour and Globalization* 1, no. 1 (January 2007): 13–30.

4.	Cameron Strategies, Knowledge Navigators, Segue Consulting, *Civic Arts Policy Review: Consultant's Report* (Calgary: City of Calgary, 2003), 16.

5.	Ibid., 48.

6.	Throughout this chapter I distinguish between contemporary art and western art. Both adjectives contain ambiguities. By contemporary art, I am referring to visual art that receives the majority of attention at private and public art galleries, is often supported through public sector arts grants, and is the predominant focus of critical discussion in arts journalism. Western art may not represent solely western subject matter, but is included in western-related art shows and sales and is promoted through western lifestyle publications. Cowboy art is a common synonym for western art but for my purposes implies too narrow a subject range and frequently essentializes the occupation of its exponents.

7.	See, for instance, Harold G. Davidson, *Edward Borein: Cowboy Artist* (Garden City, NY: Doubleday, 1974); James H. Gray, *A Brand of Its Own: The 100 Year History of the Calgary Exhibition and Stampede* (Saskatoon: Western Producer Prairie Books, 1985); Simon Evans, Sarah Carter, and Bill Yeo, eds., *Cowboys, Ranchers and the Cattle Business: Cross-Border Perspectives on Ranching History* (Calgary: University of Calgary Press, 2000).

8.	Leroy V. Kelly, *The Range Men: The Story of the Ranchers and Indians of Alberta* (Toronto: Wm. Briggs, 1913), 433.

9.	Guy Weadick, "Origin of the Calgary Stampede," *Alberta Historical Review* 14, no. 4 (1966): 21.

10.	Mary-Beth Laviolette, *An Alberta Art Chronicle* (Canmore: Altitude Publishing, 2006), 93.

11.	Ibid., 92.

12.	Ibid., 95.

13.	Ibid., 92.

14. Ibid., 93.

15. Nancy K. Anderson, "'Curious Historical Data': Art History and Western American Art," in *Discovered Lands, Invented Pasts: Transforming Visions of the American West*, ed. Jules Prown (New Haven, CT: Yale University Press, 1992), 1–35.

16. John Taliaferro, *Charles M. Russell: The Life and Legend of an American Cowboy Artist* (New York: Little Brown and Company, 1996), 192.

17. Howard Becker, *Art Worlds* (Los Angeles: University of California Press, 1982), 159.

18. Brian Dippie, "'Chop! Chop!': Progress in the Presentation of Western Visual History," *Historian* 66, no. 3 2004): 491–500.

19. Robert Taft, *Artists and Illustrators of the Old West, 1850–1900* (New York: Scribners, 1953).

20. Dorothy Harmsen, *Harmsen's Western Americana*, rev. ed. (Denver: Harmsen Publishing, 1978).

21. Dean Krakel, *Adventures in Western Art* (Kansas City: Lowell Press, 1977).

22. Ed Ainsworth, *The Cowboy in Art*. (New York: World Publishing Company, 1968).

23. Peggy Samuels and Harold Samuels, *Contemporary Western Artists* (New York: Bonanza Books, 1982); Peggy Samuels and Harold Samuels, *The Illustrated Biographical Encyclopedia of Artists of the American West* (Garden City, NY: Doubleday, 1976).

24. Martha Sandweiss, "The Public Life of Western Art," in *Discovered Lands, Invented Pasts: Transforming Visions of the American West*, ed. Jules Prown (New Haven, CT: Yale University Press, 1992), 117–33; Dippie, "Chop! Chop!" See also the symposium "Redrawing Boundaries: Perspectives on Western American Art" held at the Denver Art Museum in March 2007.

25. Throughout this chapter, I characterize this form of activity as commercial art: an artist such as Borein is hired by a client to produce images within contractual specifications for use as advertising, posters, and such.

26. Taliaferro, *Charles M. Russell*, 189.

27. Brian Dippie, "Charles M. Russell, Cowboy Culture and the Canadian Connection," in *Cowboys, Ranchers and the Cattle Business: Cross-Border Perspectives on Ranching History*, ed. Simon Evans, Sarah Carter, and Bill Yeo (Calgary: University of Calgary Press, 2000), 23.

28. Donna Livingstone, *Cowboy Spirit: Guy Weadick and the Calgary Stampede* (Vancouver: Greystone Books, 1996), 42.

29. James H. Gray, *A Brand of Its Own: The 100 Year History of the Calgary Exhibition and Stampede* (Saskatoon: Western Producer Prairie Books, 1985), 37; Taliaferro, *Charles M. Russell*, 189.

30. Gray, *Brand of Its Own*, 42.

31. Max Foran and Nonie Houlton, *Roland Gissing: The People's Painter* (Calgary: University of Calgary Press, 1988), 17.

32. See Hugh Dempsey, *Treasures of the Glenbow* (Calgary: Glenbow Museum, 1991); Fred Diehl, *A Gentleman from a Fading Age: Eric Lafferty Harvie* (Calgary: Devonian Foundation, 1989).

33. Foran and Houlton, *Roland Gissing*, 39.

34. Harold Davidson, *Edward Borein: Cowboy Artist* (Garden City: Doubleday, 1974), 74.

35. Davidson, *Edward Borein*, 78.

36. Sheilagh Jameson, *W.J. Oliver: Life Through a Master's Lens* (Calgary: Glenbow Museum, 1984), 35.

37. Quoted in Banff's *Crag and Canyon*, 4 August 1976, no. 31, 7, but see also, Taliaferro, *Charles M. Russell*, 259–60.

38. Personal communication with Great Falls sculptor and artist Jay Contway, January 2006.

39. Linder's biographer Harold Gunderson reports the year of the award as 1934, although the award was first offered in 1932. See *The Linder Legend: The Story of Pro Rodeo and Its Champion* (Calgary: Sagebrush Publishing, 1996), 123. An article in Banff's *Crag and Canyon* that appears in 1976 following Beil's death reports 1932 as the year when he began sculpting for the Calgary Stampede. Ken Liddell's article in the *Calgary Herald* in 1951 dates the start of Beil's work with the Stampede more informally as "the last 15 years" ("Raffled Jackasses Gave Artist Start," *Calgary Herald*, 9 June 1951, 9.

40. The winner of the saddle bronc competition during the 1925 Cheyenne Frontier Days Rodeo received a bronze sculpture from Hollywood actor William S. Hart. The sculpture, a likeness made some years earlier of Hart in western costume, was awarded to Billie Wilkinson. His name is the only one to appear on the trophy, so Hart's generosity was not repeated in subsequent years and did not initiate a tradition. During the 1920s Calgary Stampede board member and local jeweler David E. Black donated silver trophies for some rodeo contestants. During the 1920s his business had merged with Birks, and he managed its Calgary store.

41. Gunderson, *Linder Legend*, 121.

42. Foran and Houlton, *Roland Gissing*, 6.

43. Gray, *Brand of Its Own*, 69.

44. David Lowenthal, *The Heritage Crusade and the Spoils of History* (Cambridge: Cambridge University Press, 1998).

45. Marilyn McKay, *The National Soul: Canadian Mural Painting, 1930s to 1960s* (Montreal: McGill-Queen's University Press, 2003).

46. Calgary Stampede, "Special Resolution of the Shareholders of the Calgary Exhibition and Stampede Limited," March 2007.

47. Cameron Strategy, *Civic Arts*, 86.

CHAPTER 12

The Social Construction of the Canadian Cowboy: Calgary Exhibitions and Stampede Posters, 1952–1972[*]

Robert M. Seiler and Tamara P. Seiler

[*] *This paper appeared in the* Journal of Canadian Studies *33, no. 3 (1998) and is reprinted here with permission.*

The cowboy as we know him exists on three interrelated levels: the historical, the fictional, and the mythological. In many instances these levels are so inter-related that determining where the historical figure ends and the fictional character begins is difficult, if not impossible. Canadian analysts face another complication: at all three levels, the cowboy is primarily an American invention, in terms of the historical American frontier experience as well as the special role of the "frontier" in the American imagination.[1] At both levels, the Canadian experience has been markedly different;[2] yet, every July Calgary stages the world's most extravagant celebration of the cowboy. That the cowboy, together with his world, should occupy the dominant place he does in the public iconography of Alberta in general and Calgary in particular might seem surprising.

In this paper, we examine selected visual representations of the cowboy, with a view to understanding the Canadian version of this popular stereotype.[3] We take as our corpus the publicity messages (posters) produced for and circulated by the Calgary Exhibition and Stampede board during the period 1952 to 1972. Historians[4] remind us that these were the golden years of the Stampede – the years of its greatest expansion. We focus on the artful organization of the iconographic and the linguistic practices employed in these texts, which we regard as popular cultural artifacts. Popular cultural texts like the texts we examine are relatively open[5] of course, capable of being read in different ways by different people. We try to identify the elements that make up the sign systems asking us to visit the Calgary Stampede, together with the principles according to which these elements are linked, and to suggest the social uses they serve. To begin with, we outline the conceptual apparatus we use to study ephemeral cultural artifacts, and then we sketch the historical dialectic that shaped the discourses at work in the posters.

Theoretical Framework

The approach we have taken builds on the work of a variety of socio-semiotics theorists, including Roland Barthes, Stuart Hall, Michel Bakhtin, Pierre Bourdieu, and Michel de Certeau. It sees popular culture as a site of struggle, focusing on the popular tactics used to evade or subvert the forces of dominance.[6] Analysts who take this approach argue that ordinary people use the resources the elites (who control the cultural industries) provide to produce popular culture. In contrast to the mass cultural model, which conceptualizes artifacts in terms of unified meaning, the popular cultural model conceptualizes cultural artifacts as polysemic, open to a variety of quite different, even contradictory, readings. Some readings support the ideological meanings of cultural elites; others clearly oppose those meanings.[7]

Taking our cue from John Fiske, we treat Calgary Stampede posters as popular cultural artifacts. More precisely, we identify and explain the discursive practices according to which certain individuals are collectively defined via these publicity messages as "cowboys." One could examine such related discursive sites as the Stampede Parade; the street events, including street dances and chuckwagon breakfasts; the layout of the Fairground; the infield (rodeo) events; the Indian Village; and other kinds of official publicity materials, including advertisements and souvenir programs, with this view in mind. To make our project manageable, we examine one kind of official publicity message – the poster – only, in large part because signification in this case is intentional. We take as our corpus twenty-two reproductions (slides) of the posters we obtained from the Glenbow Archives.

Our investigation moved through three stages. First, we examined the socio-cultural discourses by which "the cowboy" was constructed, with particular emphasis on the Wild West Show, which had given way to the rodeo by the end of the First World War. We outline our reflections on this cultural transformation in the following sections.

Second, we examined the posters circulated from 1908 to 1923, the period during which the idea of the Calgary Stampede took shape. The Calgary Exhibition got under way in 1886, justified in part as a means of creating social solidarity in a community divided along a number of lines, including ethnic and occupational.[8] We focus on the years 1908, 1911, 1912, 1919, 1921, and 1923.

Why did we choose these dates? When he visited Calgary in 1908, Guy Weadick approached city officials with the proposition that, if they joined forces, they could stage a week-long tribute to the cowboy, thereby celebrate the role the cowboy played in opening up the West. With the help of four wealthy ranchers, who provided financial backing, Weadick staged the first Calgary Stampede in 1912. In 1919, he staged the Victory Stampede, to mark the official end of the First World War. Finally, in 1923, the Calgary Exhibition and the Calgary Stampede joined forces, thereby becoming an annual event, with Weadick as director. It might be argued that, in fact, the 1923 Exhibition and Stampede set the pattern for all the Stampedes that followed.[9]

Third, we "read" the posters that were circulated by the Calgary Exhibition during the period 1952 to 1972, the golden years of the Calgary Stampede.[10] The years 1952, 1962, and 1972 are important because they mark jubilee celebrations. We have posters for every year except 1956, 1962, 1963, 1964, and 1969.

In terms of format, our corpus can be divided into three groups:

(a) The posters for the years 1908–23 measure 20.50 x 27.00 inches. In many respects, the posters produced today resemble the posters the Calgary Exhibition board produced for those years.
(b) The posters produced during the period 1952–65 measure 13.00 x 47.00 inches. What strikes us about these posters – they were stapled for example to telephone poles – is the very high word-to-image-ratio.
(c) The posters produced during the period 1966–72 measure 22.50 x 34.25 inches. Our discussion is based on a close reading of each text.

Our data base consists of detailed descriptions of the elements that make up these messages, in terms of (i) the linguistic message, denotational and connotational, (ii) the literal image and (iii) the symbolic image. Barthes's seminal essay, "The Rhetoric of the Image" (1964), serves as our point of departure.

Background

The cowboy evolved from an unknown herder into a folk hero in a relatively short period of time. His status grew as he passed through the hands of frontier journalists, dime novelists, wild west promoters, novelists, and artists. In this regard, it is important to remember that virtually all of these early depictions were American, that then as now Canadians were consumers of American popular culture, and that the Canadian experience[11] of the frontier differed markedly from the American[12] suggesting a disjuncture between popular imagery and local experience.

American Context

The historical cowboy played an important role in the development of the American West. He enjoyed a relatively short heyday, ironically, from the late 1860s to the late 1880s.[13] The cattle industry dates from the late 1860s, when entrepreneurs like Joseph G. McCoy realized that the longhorns which roamed southern Texas could be sold to Easterners for a profit.[14] These resourceful people discovered that trailing herds of longhorns north was a cheap way of transporting the animals to market. During the 1870s and the 1880s, millions of animals were driven north, to territories such as Montana, Wyoming, and the Dakotas. American hunters slaughtered millions of bison during this period, opening up these ranges to grazing and thereby forcing the Plains Indians to abandon their traditional way of life.

Cattlemen made huge profits during the period of westward expansion.[15] Along the way, they established the cattle industry going, thereby creating jobs for 40,000 cowboys and keeping a million workers in the East and Midwest busy processing meat products. As William Savage, Jr., and Jack Weston have described him, the historical cowboy was a hired man, a rugged individual without capital in the employ of an enterprising individual with capital. A few, such as Charles Goodnight and Shanghai Pierce, succeeded in becoming cattlemen themselves.[16]

For the most part, the average American cowboy lived a lonely life. An itinerant labourer who worked long hours, he took on whatever task happened to be important at the moment. He might pitch hay, hunt stray animals, clear brush, and break wild horses, but he devoted most of his time and effort to looking after cattle as they grazed on the range. He earned his reputation for strength, endurance, and ingenuity on those long, gruelling cattle drives we have seen portrayed in so many Westerns.

In the early years, cowboys rounded up cattle twice a year and herded them into a central place, to brand calves and to select older cattle and sometimes young bulls not needed for breeding to go to market. The roundup marked that period when a rancher determined how many cattle he actually owned. It was also an important social event, as cowboys visited old friends, challenging one another to tests of skill in such activities as bronco riding, steer wrestling, and calf roping. To be sure, a certain amount of rivalry would surround these contests. On northern ranges, such as in Montana and Wyoming, roundups attracted as many as 300 cowboys.

The economic boom that had fostered the development of ranching ended quite suddenly in the late 1880s, when bad weather (especially the blizzard of 1886–87), poor range management, and plummeting cattle prices put an end to the free-wheeling practices of earlier days.[17] Most importantly, wave after wave of immigrants settled the plains, and thanks to the invention of barbed wire in 1873 a great many set themselves up as small farmers, eventually bringing an end to the open range.

Canadian Context

The heyday of free-range ranching in Canada was brief, extending from the early 1880s to the late 1890s, and ending somewhat dramatically with the disastrous winter of 1906–07.[18] Whereas in the United states ranching dominated a vast territory, in Canada it occupied a fairly small region, including the Columbia basin and the southern interior plateau of British Columbia; southwestern Alberta, around Fort Macleod and the Bow River Valley, near Calgary; and southwestern Saskatchewan, around Swift Current.[19] On the one hand, the American and Canadian ranching frontiers were interconnected in a variety of ways; on the other, the Canadian ranching community stood apart,[20] as did the political cultures of the two countries.

A few very large ranches, owned by an eastern-Canadian and British elite, with strong ties to the Conservative government of the day, dominated Alberta's ranching industry. These ranches, and others established by British immigrants along the foothills in Alberta, became centres of a transplanted British Victorian lifestyle.[21]

The Canadian ranching frontier was not, however, exclusively British and eastern Canadian. American cowboys – and American foremen – had been present from the 1870s. As historian Terry Jordan points out in *North American Cattle-Ranching Frontiers, Origins, Diffusion, and Differentiation* (1990), most of the technology of ranching came from the American West, as well as from Mexico. Nevertheless, the development and overall tone of the Canadian ranching enterprise was in marked contrast to that of the American. Whereas the latter, marked by bitter and violent range wars, the Canadian ranching community was the product of government initiative and developed within a well established legal framework. The ethos of this community was deeply conservative.[22]

The growth of Calgary was closely linked to the ranching industry and to the arrival of the railway in Alberta in 1883. As the main shipping point for livestock, Calgary became the capital of this conservative "Cattle Kingdom." The Liberal government elected in 1896 developed immigration and land policies that paved the way for a massive influx of settlers to "the last best west," North America's last agricultural frontier. While the ranching influence on southern Alberta in general and on Calgary in particular remained strong, and while several large ranches survived, by 1910 ranching was no longer "king."[23]

The Wild West Show and the Image of the American Cowboy

The development of the West marked the end of the era of free-range ranching, and nostalgia soon set in.[24] Many enterprising people took advantage of this mood, including William F. "Buffalo Bill" Cody (1846–1917), who launched and dominated that genre of travelling entertainment called the

Wild West show. Via this medium, Cody "fixed" the romantic image of the cowboy.[25]

Cody lived through nearly every major stage of westward expansion. He was born in a log cabin in Iowa, and with his family he moved in 1853 to Kansas, after which he travelled throughout the West, working at a variety of frontier jobs, including freight company messenger, pony express rider, scout for the Union Army, and buffalo hunter. Legend has it that he killed 4,280 buffalo in eight months, a feat which earned him the nickname "Buffalo Bill." He also served as a scout (1868–72) for the 5th U.S. Cavalry. Russell (1970) claims that he took part in sixteen expeditions against the Native peoples. In 1872, Cody resigned his position to play the lead role in Ned Buntline's melodrama, *Scouts of the Prairie*.

Ned Buntline, the pen name for Edward Z.C. Judson (1823–1886), was an adventurer who turned to writing in the 1860s. He made a fortune fictionalizing the exploits of Cody, beginning with *Buffalo Bill: The King of the Border Men* (1869). Buntline wrote more than 400 of these short, thrilling western stories, thereby creating the genre called the "dime novel," which propagated the image of the cowboy as the rugged tamer of nature. These boisterous tales, which valorized democracy and individualism, were immensely popular during the period from 1860 to 1895. Another prolific writer, Colonel Prentiss Ingraham (1843–1904), also popularized the cowboy as a romantic figure. Ingraham wrote more than 600 dime novels, about 120 of them based on the exploits of Buffalo Bill, as well as several popular plays. He also wrote two plays for Cody, *The Knights of the Plains* and *Buffalo Bill at Bay*.[26]

Ned Buntline persuaded Cody to play himself in *Scouts of the Prairie: And Red Deviltry As It Is* (1872), the first of two western melodramas he wrote expressly for him. This commercially successful venture laid the groundwork for the Wild West Show; however, Cody eventually broke with Buntline[27] and in 1875 formed the "Buffalo Bill Combination," a travelling theatrical troupe, which included Wild Bill Hickock and Texas Jack Omohundro. In 1876, Cody produced and starred in *The Red Hand: or Buffalo Bill's First Scalp for Custer*. This dramatized an incident at Warbonnet Creek, Nebraska, in which Cody is said to have avenged Custer's defeat by shooting and scalping Yellow Hand, the Cheyenne leader. In this way, Cody the man blended with Cody the legend.

When the opportunity presented itself, Cody turned his attention to outdoor performances. In 1882, he was invited to stage a Fourth of July celebration for North Platte, Nebraska, an event which served as the model for his travelling show. The celebration included a series of contests (we would call it a rodeo) that drew no fewer than 1,000 entrants. Clearly, he did not invent rodeo, since these contests had been held at roundups for a generation or so. His innovation was to package them as a road show.[28]

Cody launched the Buffalo Bill Wild West in Omaha, Nebraska, in May of 1883, taking it on the road early in 1884. He set out to revive the events (and the images) of frontier life, insisting on authenticity in almost every detail. To this end he tried to recruit individuals who had taken part in the events he re-created. Any given version of the show included a portrayal of the Pony Express; the Buffalo Hunt; an attack on an emigrant train crossing the Plains; the capture of the Deadwood Mail Coach by "Indians"; an attack on a settler's cabin; and the Battle of Little Big Horn, which was billed as an historically accurate depiction of Custer's Last Fight, together with much trick riding and trick roping and sharp shooting. Annie Oakley appeared second in the program, right after the grand entrance. Cody appeared near the end, which afforded him a moment of dramatic emphasis for showing off his own shooting skills.

Cody's show featured an all-star cast of western notables, including, in addition to Annie Oakley, such figures as Gabriel Dumont, the Métis leader; Dr. William F. Carver, the frontier dentist who became a marksman; and Major Frank North, the frontier scout. Sitting Bull, who in 1876 led the Sioux in the battle of Little Big Horn, toured with the Show during the 1885–1886 season, Toronto being one of the Canadian stops.[29]

For no less than a decade (1887–1896), Cody's Wild West show enjoyed immense popularity. For example, during the 1886 season, it stayed more than six weeks at a summer resort on Staten Island, New York. As well, Cody took his show to London, England, in 1887, to take part in the American Exhibition planned for Queen Victoria's Jubilee. The show thrilled thousands of spectators, among them William E. Gladstone, who marvelled at its graphic depictions of frontier life. Cody staged a number of command performances, including one for Queen Victoria and another for Jubilee guests, such as the kings of Belgium, Denmark, and Saxony. This great success paved the way for two more tours of Europe (1889–92 and 1902–06) that included stops at London, Paris, Rome, and Berlin.

The show enjoyed its greatest season in 1893, the year of the Chicago World's Fair, which honoured the 400th anniversary of the discovery of America, and boasted an attendance of 27.5 million. Cody added the Congress of Rough Riders of the World to his program, which featured expert marksmen and riders from America, England, France, Germany, and

Russia, who dazzled audiences with their military manoeuvres. Although the show was not officially part of the World's Fair, it was conspicuously located just outside the fair gates, and few visitors felt that they had "seen the sights" until they had also visited it Show.[30]

Over the years, Cody varied his program very little. What, then, aroused all this enthusiasm? Millions of people in a dozen countries saw the show, which purported to portray actual events in a truthful, realistic way. Many events showcased riding and racing skills, but much of the show can be described as western pageant and spectacle. People flocked to see Buffalo Bill, the dime novel hero, come to life. His three-hour show neatly fits into the popular myth of the West, which evoked two images: the West as a hostile, barbaric land, and as a place of opportunity.[31] Thanks in no small way to Cody, Europeans[32] developed a great interest in the American west as a far-away land of romance and adventure.[33] Cody eventually suffered a series of setbacks, and in lost his show to creditors.

Throughout this period, many rival shows toured the United States and Europe, including Pawnee Bill's Wild West, Doc W.F. Carver's Wild America, and the Miller Brothers 101 Ranch Wild West Show; for a number of reasons, however, this form of outdoor entertainment barely survived its creator, who died in 1917. Most of the shows in operation at the turn of the century quietly faded from notice before or during the First World War. The major exception was the Miller Brothers 101 Ranch Wild West Show, which seemed to get bigger and better.[34] In many respects, the events that made the Wild West show unique as entertainment continued as "rodeo," a form of entertainment that enjoyed great popularity after the war, thanks in large part to Guy Weadick.

Other Mediums

In addition to the Wild West Show (and the dime novel, which, as we have seen, was closely related to it), by the end of the nineteenth century, four new "western" mediums were consolidating a romantic image of the cowboy: the novel, motion pictures, pulp magazines, and western art. Zane Grey topped all writers of "western" novels in popularity. His sixty novels about cowboy life made the term western generic and the image of the rugged, individualistic cowboy central to American popular culture.[35]

Frederic Remington and Owen Wister were also major popularizers of the romantic cowboy. Remington, best known for his action-filled paintings, drawings, and sculptures of cowboys and Indians, published his first picture in *Harper's Weekly* in 1882[36] and later designed posters for Buffalo Bill's show. In 1893, Remington met Owen Wister, the writer. In Wister, he found an enthusiastic, able collaborator, and for a number of years they produced many articles and illustrations for *Harper's Weekly*. They tried to capture the cowboy as a passing institution before he vanished. They assembled some of these regional sketches as books, including *Red and White* (1895) and *Lin McLean* (1897). The latter anticipated Wister's celebrated novel about the West, *The Virginian* (1902). This fiction created the prototype western, a chronicle of the adventures of a handsome heroic figure, chivalrous and daring, who successfully woos the pretty woman.

Again, the Canadian experience differed from the American experience, in terms of history and myth. The historical Canadian experience differed from the American experience in part because the physical conditions of the ranching areas, including southern Alberta, worked against "pure" open-range ranching and in favour of a more "mixed" operation.[37] As well, the considerable official promotion of the Canadian West via government immigration pamphlets and Canadian popular fiction constructed a "civilized," orderly West that differed markedly from the fictional American West.[38]

Although both fictional traditions "reaffirm the values of progress by re-enacting the triumph of civilized order over a savage wilderness,"[39] they did so in different ways. Whereas the American vision was inductive and individualistic, the Canadian was deductive and communal. Tales of the American west re-affirm the codes of behaviour that developed to suit the local situation and the rough and ready cowboy hero embodied these cultural values. He employs violent means to resolve the conflict between civilization and nature. Tales of the Canadian west celebrate the Mountie who, rather than making the law on the spot, serves as an instrument of law, which like the whole system of order he maintains, together with the code of values he lives by, is created elsewhere. His strength lies in his acceptance of an authority emanating from a remote centre of empire. Rather than employing violent means to resolve conflict, he rejects violence. We see this pattern in the work of such writers as Ralph Connor (Charles Gordon), author of such works as *Sky Pilot* (1899), *Patrol of the Sun Dance Trail* (1910), and *The Major* (1917), and William Lacey Amy, author of the Blue Pete stories, which appeared from 1922 to 1954.[40]

Initially, at any rate, the fictional world of a Wild West, which showcased the cowboy, played only a small part in the work of popular English-Canadian writers.[41] By the turn of the century, however, the cowboy had become one of the most romantic figures[42] in American history,[43] and his influence was felt across the 49th parallel. The newest medium, moving pictures, perfected and disseminated the image, as no medium before it could. From the time the first plotted western movie appeared in 1901 to the high point of the Western in the late 1950s, literally hundreds of evocations of the romantic cowboy were projected to devoted movie, and later television, audiences.[44] Thus, we might say that, very likely, by 1952 many Canadians and most Americans who might think about Western life in general and the cowboy in particular would have trouble differentiating American myth from local reality.

The Birth of the Calgary Stampede

As we said above, the Wild West show gave way to the rodeo, which enjoyed great popularity after the First World War, thanks in large measure to Guy Weadick (1885–1953), the tall, ruggedly handsome impresario who should be viewed as the missing link between these forms of entertainment.

Weadick grew up in Rochester, New York, a thriving commercial and cultural centre. Still in his teens, he moved west. Hoping to become a cowboy, he travelled the western territories of the United States and Canada, finding employment as a cowpuncher wherever he could.[45] He worked on his roping and riding skills, with a view to exchanging an arduous life on the range for a more glamorous one on stage. Barely twenty, he won, in 1905, a spot on the Miller Brothers 101 Ranch Wild West Show, which featured a variety of up-and-coming personalities, including Tom Mix, the future star of low-budget westerns; Bill Pickett, the inventor of a sensational rodeo act called bulldog-ging (a forerunner of steer wrestling); and Lucille Mulhall, the world's lady steer roping champion. Weadick travelled with this important Wild West show for about twenty years, primarily as trick roper.

What set Weadick apart was his driving ambition to stage annually the greatest frontier days celebration and championship cowboy contest the world had ever seen.[46] During his travels, he had realized that, indeed, the time was ripe to pay tribute to the people who had opened up the West. It struck him that staging cowboy contests as an international competition – a rodeo – with huge cash prizes, would ensure that the very best talent would take part in this celebration. He was convinced that a spectacle of the kind he had in mind would make Buffalo Bill's Wild West extravaganza look like a side show. He had the plan, but not the place.

Weadick happened to visit Calgary in July of 1905 during the Industrial Exhibition. He performed rope tricks and provided commentary for Bill Pickett, the black cowboy who dazzled crowds with his dangerous steer-wrestling act. During this visit, he realized that Calgary was just the place: it served as the centre of the ranching industry of western Canada; no less than six tribes of Plains Indians lived nearby; and it exuded a hustling, bustling, progressive spirit.[47]

Weadick proposed his plan on his next visit, in July of 1908, when as trick ropers he and his wife, Flores LaDue, performed at the Dominion Exhibition as part of the Miller Brothers 101 Ranch show. He spent some time with H.C. McMullen, livestock agent for the Canadian Pacific Railway, advancing his plan to bring together all the champion bronco busters, steer ropers, calf ropers, trick and fancy ropers, both male and female, from all parts of Canada and the United States, to compete for prize money totalling $50,000 in gold. He planned to call the show a "Stampede" in order to distinguish it from similar celebrations, including Frontier Days, Rodeos, and Round-ups.[48] City officials, however, argued that the day of the cowboy was a thing of the past; they claimed that, in fact, farming was more important to the area than ranching. The determined promoter argued that the taking over of rangelands by farmers was all the more reason to stage a show in honour of the passing era.

His persistence paid off. Weadick returned to Calgary in March of 1912, at the invitation of McMullen, to formalize his plan for a frontier days celebration and cowboy championship contest. Addison Day, a southern Alberta rancher, offered to put up $10,000 in cash and to supply his top horses for the show Weadick could come up with financial support in Calgary. The most influential cattlemen in the area – George Lane, A.E. Cross, Pat Burns, and A.J. McLean (the Big Four) – agreed to put up $100,000 to stage this show, which was to be billed as a celebration of "The Last and Best Great West."[49]

Ever the promoter, Weadick personally invited champion cowboys and cowgirls from every cattle district in Canada, Mexico, and the United States to compete for $20,000 in prizes.[50] According to plan, he organized the program of fifteen events to conform with "rodeo" style, with standard rules and regular prizes.

It can be argued that, when William F. Cody organized the Fourth of July celebration for North Platte in 1882, he created two forms of entertainment: the Wild West show and the rodeo. Indeed, the basic elements of both forms can be traced to the by-play of early roundups – roping, riding, and shooting – which were labelled "Cowboy Fun."[51] Cody treated these displays of skill as "exhibitions," putting them in historical context, such as "Custer's Last Fight." Of course, his otherwise authentic performances conveyed as sub-text messages about taming the frontier.[52] In stressing context and ritualizing the performance, then, Wild West impresarios might push these demonstrations in the direction of theatre.

A generation later, Weadick proposed to treat these demonstrations as contests,[53] whereby contestants paid to enter and profited only by winning. He too wanted to showcase the genuine frontier performance, and his genius was to turn these contests into international championships.[54] In minimizing the historical context, it might be argued, rodeo impresarios of Weadick's frame of mind might push these demonstrations of skill in the direction of sport.

Weadick launched his Stampede on Labour Day, 2 September 1912, with a massive parade. The population of Calgary was 61,450 at the time; about 75,000 people lined up to watch the procession.[55] He divided the parade into sections, so as to portray the history of the Canadian West: Native peoples, Old-Timers, Hudson's Bay Company Traders, veterans of the Riel Rebellion, original members of the North-West Mounted Police, pioneer settlers, labour union members and craftspeople, and competitors took part. Altogether, 3,000 people made up the procession, which extended over two miles. According to at least one report, it took one hour to pass any given point.[56]

In terms of audience appeal, the show was a success. More than 40,000 people jammed into the Victoria Park fairgrounds on opening day. The Governor-General of Canada opened the show; he enjoyed himself so much that he stayed for the duration. We note that women played a key part in the contests.[57]

The male prize-winners included Jim Massey, from Texas, who won the bareback bronc riding title; Otto Kline, from Montana, who won the cowboys' trick and fancy riding title; and Tex Macleod, from Texas, who won the fancy roping title. The female prize-winners included Fanny Sperry, from Montana, who won the cowgirls' saddle bronc riding title; Dolly Mullens, from New Mexico, who won the cowgirls' trick and fancy riding title; and Flores LaDue, who won the trick and fancy roping title.

The most dramatic moment occurred during the saddle bronc riding event. Only one Canadian cowboy made it to the final round, a Blood Indian named Tom Three Persons. He had drawn the dreaded Cyclone for the final ride of the Stampede. Cyclone had never been ridden; this notorious black horse had thrown more than one hundred riders in his career. He bucked, twisted, and turned, jarring his rider from one side of the saddle to another, but eventually he grew tired and surrendered. Tom Three Persons' prize may not have been huge by today's standards (he received $1,000), but he became a legend, the only Canadian to win a world's championship at the first Stampede.[58]

The outbreak of the First World War killed any possibility of immediately
staging another Stampede in Calgary. At the close of the war, however, the Big
Four invited Weadick to organize the Victory Stampede, which was held in
August of 1919. Yakima Canutt, the leading stuntman for many B-Westerns,
won the saddle bronc riding title. This rodeo was a success, earning a profit,
but to the organizer's disappointment the backers expressed little enthusiasm
for staging another.

Nevertheless, in the fall of 1922, E.L. Richardson, Manager of the Calgary
Industrial Exhibition Co. Ltd., approached Weadick with the idea of staging
the next Stampede as part of the annual agricultural show. Attendance at
the Exhibition had been falling off, and, he argued, Weadick's championship cowboy contests would attract people.[59] This was the opportunity he
had long wished for. He ensured that the 1923 Stampede was organized as
a professional rodeo and to add another element of excitement he put the
chuckwagon race on the program.[60] This event quickly became the hallmark
of the Stampede. From 1923, this joint venture has been billed as "The
Greatest Outdoor Show on Earth."

As producer and manager, Weadick spent six months in Calgary organizing the next program and six months travelling, cultivating rodeo and show
business people, including Hollywood image makers. By way of publicity,
for example, he persuaded Hoot Gibson, the leading cowboy movie star
of the day, to make a feature western, *The Calgary Stampede* (1924), which
spread the fame of the Stampede internationally.[61] Weadick stayed on as
manager until 1932, but after a disagreement with the Stampede Board over
the budget he left the rodeo promotion business altogether. He refused to
have anything to do with the Stampede until 1952, when he was invited to
ride at the head of the parade.

This unpleasantness notwithstanding, what Weadick had created in the
Calgary Stampede was a complex event, one that emerged out of and continues to draw on, an evolving synthesis of many imperatives: historical and
mythological, American and Canadian, folk, and commercial. Like other
analysts, we would argue that one way of making sense of the Calgary Stampede is to regard this celebration of the cowboy as a text, a site of struggle for
control of the meanings of western Canadian history.[62]

Messages and Meanings

So far, we have outlined briefly the historical dialectic that has produced
the romantic figure we recognize as the cowboy. Staging a tribute to this
individual, celebrating the role this individual played in opening up the

West, can never be easy. We have seen how "Buffalo Bill" Cody combined illusion with fact in order to give his "pictures" of frontier life the authenticity he thought they should have. We have seen how, twenty years later, Guy Weadick focused attention on the skills this individual utilized in earning his livelihood. Of course, the outcome of projects like these is a function of the local dynamics of time and place. What piques our interest is how this on-going dialectic has been played out in the publicity messages – the posters – the Calgary Exhibition and Stampede Board circulated during the "golden age" of the Stampede. At a literal level, individual messages invite us to a huge frontier days celebration and cowboy championship competition. Most posters tell us that, in visiting Stampede Park, we will have the time of our lives. At a figurative level, however, they invite us to a communal celebration of our heritage, of "the triumph of civilized order over savage order."[63] We will say more about this point in a moment.

The Posters: The Calgary Exhibition, 1908–23

Our close reading of the exhibition posters that were circulated during the period 1908 to 1923 reveals that two binary oppositions – one might call them two discourses of celebration – run through them: a nature/culture opposition and a past/future opposition. The discourse of the Exhibition was one of progress; the discourse of the Stampede was one of nostalgia. These logically should be at odds with one another. The 1908 poster, which features a rancher bringing his horse quite abruptly to a halt at a barbed-wire fence which crosses the road, erected, we infer, by a farmer, sets up this tension long before the discourse of nostalgia is officially introduced in the 1912 poster (see Fig. 1).

Moreover, the tension between the two discourses pervades the 1919 Dominion Exhibition poster (see Fig. 2), another site of conflict. Here, culture and the present dominate nature and the past by reason of the absence of the latter. In this regard, the neo-classical buildings Calgary and the race cars on the track instead of horses displace nature and the western past.

Overall, however, we found that, rather than contradicting one another, these discourses reinforce one another. We detected this reading in the 1911 poster, which features a cowboy lassoing a bi-plane, thereby bridging the gap between the wild west and the future, i.e., technology. We also read this meaning in the 1912 poster, where (it seems) the cowboy aligns himself with the Big Four in dominating both nature and Native peoples, thereby concealing the tension between legitimate and illegitimate occupation of the land, as well as the tension between town and country.

The harmonizing of these seemingly opposite discourses appears in the later posters. Three interrelated rhetorical strategies seem to bring about this effect; namely, the impression of harmony: (a) the presentation of the cowboy as tamer of nature; (b) the legitimation of the European presence, as signified by a variety of figures, especially the cowboy on the North American frontier; and (c) the commodification or packaging of history, especially the cowboy.

We see that, from the 1912 poster onwards, the cowboy has been juxtaposed with technology, as in: taming or civilizing nature. The posters for 1919 and 1921, for example, feature biplanes (and in 1919 race cars) signifying the latest technology. The 1921 poster features parimutuel betting via the jockey on his fine horse.

The most striking evocation of the idea of taming nature is the image of the cowboy astride the bucking bronco. With only one exception, in the 1960 poster, the cowboy wins the man/animal contest. The 1971 poster, which depicts the Wild Horse race, tells the story of masculine dominance over nature in particularly graphic details.

The Calgary Exhibition and Stampede, 1952–72

The cowboy appears as one of several figures who together legitimate the European presence in and dominance over the North American frontier. Images of marching bands, members of the royal family, Mounted Policemen, flags: all suggest the power of the state. The 1953 poster (see Fig. 3), which features a sea of spectators dressed as cowboys watching an aggressive, action-packed chuckwagon race, speaks of dominance and legitimacy. One might detect some ambiguity in the image of the cowboy vis-à-vis these symbols of state and authority. We might well ask: Is the cowboy their emissary, even their hired hand, or does he stand apart from or in fact above these figures of authority, by virtue of his skills? Do these special qualities align him in a curious way with the "natural" and hence with the Indian?

One important site for the Native/cowboy opposition is the 1959 poster (see Fig. 4), which offers us a view of the Indian village. The juxtaposition of the passive and confined Indian village with the activity and the freedom depicted in the rest of the poster strongly suggests that the Native peoples have lost the struggle to control and to define the West. Clearly, the cowboy wins this contest.

By and large, the posters that were circulated during the period from 1952 to 1966 indicate that conflicting discourses are harmonized via the commodification of past and present experience. We read this in the juxtaposition of events that celebrate technology and events that celebrate the frontier. In the 1959 poster, for example, elements from both discourses are packaged via spokes of a wheel, an image that stands for both past and present. The wheel is central to the chuckwagon, not to mention the automobile or the airplane.

The 1971 poster (see Fig. 9) illustrates this statement via the image of the chuckwagon, apparently thundering into town, perhaps bringing important goods from the East (culture) to the West (nature). We also see in this figure the movement of centre-to-margin that might be said to have defined the Canadian frontier experience.

We notice how this image has been packaged to erase the distinction we might make between authentic and artificial experience. Are we watching a film or are we really living a genuine frontier experience? The dichotomy between authentic and artificial, clearly a subset of the nature/culture tension, becomes increasingly important over the period we study.

As noted above, the 1953 poster packages nature, together with the cowboy and the "Indian." The poster for 1960 (see Fig. 5) packages Hollywood cowboys Roy Rogers and Dale Evans along with rodeo (working?) cowboys. Rex Allen, the singing cowboy, whose fancy, fringed shirt symbolizes that his battles with nature are all staged, occupies the centre position on the poster for 1961 (see Fig. 6). Circus stars and rodeo cowboys share the spotlight in the poster for 1965 (see Fig. 7). By 1970 (see Fig. 8), rodeo cowboy and circus performer have merged in the figure of the working cowboy on his bucking bronco flying across a pink sky alight with fireworks. The frontier and Hollywood have become indistinguishable.

This decontextualization brings to mind the question Northrop Frye asked about Canada, "Where is here?" Has this process of harmonization been at work in these discourses in a way that has removed all "authentic" traces of region or nation? Our reading suggests that, at one level, this appears to be true. Such signifiers as the images of the promoters (or in later years the names of the Stampede officials), the details of ladies' and children's events, disappear from the later posters. Images of the Queen, the Mounties, crowns, the Maple Leaf, pictures of Banff: these are gradually replaced by the dominant, single image of the generic cowboy. Even the 1972 poster (see Fig. 10), which appears to evoke authentic regional history, features a picture of the Pendleton, Oregon, marching band. We might be viewing a pseudo event, if not an identity crisis. Interestingly enough, the strategy used to evoke the Stampede experience during this period (1952 to 1972) is to present a view of the chuckwagon races, together with crowded grandstand, both images of community and joint effort. We would argue that, at some level, what is being asserted here is that elusive "Canadian sensibility," its reputed valorization of communal over individualistic values. Again and again in the posters of the 1950s, order and boundaries are evoked, via images and design features which assert the Canadian counter-revolutionary valuing of "peace, order, and good government" over the unfettered "pursuit of happiness." Thus, vis-à-vis the posters for this period, the answer to Frye's question could be: Canada.

Now and then, we find evidence for an oppositional reading of the cowboy as subversive figure. For example, one can read the cowboy as the "little guy" who makes do with what is available."[64] His mastery is hard won, as the 1960 poster tells us, with its image of a cowboy suspended in the air, thrown by a Brahma bull. The recurring images of the cowboy demonstrating his skill and daring, both as an individual rider and as a member of a team, evoke the democratic ideal of meritocracy, and construct the frontier as a space where the "plucky" are essential, a kind of frontier elite who deserve our respect for their down-to-earth accomplishments.

Overview

As we have pointed out, two binary oppositions run through the discourse of celebration employed in the Stampede posters: (a) the nature/culture opposition and (b) the past/future opposition. In many respects, this distinction is artificial, and we hasten to add that any given message can be inflected in both directions.

When we talk about messages that have been inflected in the direction of the nature/culture opposition, we mean those socially produced ways of thinking and talking about that project commonly known as "winning the West" or "subduing the frontier," so prominent in the Wild West show. The values of one way of life are celebrated at the expense of another. In some instances, the signifiers include representations of the vast prairies/the open range we associate with the early days of ranching, landscapes which may or may not feature Native people, i.e., as a part of the "nature" depicted, or say the rugged Rocky Mountains of southern Alberta. We read these landscapes as hostile or friendly or timeless, depending upon the context in which they are placed.

Often, these signifiers suggest that the European settlement of the West was inevitable and desirable and that the cowboy played a key role in this

process, of the forward march of civilization. On the one hand, such signifiers as "fencing" suggest the order of the British Empire. On the other, such
signifiers as the "open range" suggest the early days of ranching in the United
States. We see, in these images, two versions of the ideal state of nature.

This brings us to "culture," the key element in this binary opposition. In
the earlier messages, those circulated between 1908 and 1923, the signifiers include aeroplanes, airships, and automobiles, which provide us with
examples of the wonders of modern civilization. In the later messages, 1952
to 1972, the signifiers include photos of such figures as Roy Rogers and Dale
Evans, the latest Hollywood icons. We also see conflicting versions of progress, in terms of the buildings represented in the background; for example,
Romanesque buildings on the one hand and Hudson's Bay Company Trading Post on the other.

When we refer to discourses that have been inflected in the direction of
the past/future opposition, we mean those socially produced ways of con-
ceptualizing the history of Alberta, with a view to valorizing/celebrating one
particular period or defining moment. It might be argued that the discourse
of celebration ritualizes two periods only: (a) the distant past, the period
when the Native peoples made the region their home, and (b) the recent past
and the present, the period when Europeans settled the region.[65]

More tensions are at work here; but, the history of Alberta is more complex
than this simple formulation. Whilst it is de-emphasized in the discourse we
studied, this complexity becomes apparent now and then, especially in the
earlier posters, which clearly celebrate progress/technology. The first period
was complex in its own right: it extended over many centuries and two quite
distinct Native groups, the Plains and the Woodlands Indians, lived here.
This complexity is never represented. The second period, encompassed by
the term "European settlement," is likewise more complex than might appear
at first glance. Since the seventeenth century, a series of intruders, such as fur
traders, buffalo hunters, North-West Mounted Police, ranchers (predominantly British), and agricultural settlers successively and in different, often
mutually incompatible ways, altered the lives of the Aboriginal people who
lived in the region. These groups inaugurated technological changes that
intensified the displacement of Native peoples and that formed brief, defining moments in the social, economic, and cultural history of Alberta. This
was hardly a smooth or seamless evolution. The interests of fur traders differed from those of settlers, whether ranchers or farmers, whose interests also
differed, just as the interests of both differed from those of international oil
companies. Thus, the shift from one economic hegemony to another was to
some degree tension laden.

As well, these economic shifts were accompanied by tension-producing demographic shifts; during the period from 1896 to 1914, Canada, especially the West, absorbed the biggest wave of immigrants it has ever received, either before or since, and they were the most ethnically diverse group of people the country had ever absorbed. Alberta was a major destination for immigrants from all parts of Europe and the United States, and the region became a site of struggle over the nature of the society and the culture that would emerge in "the last best West."

The ranching enterprise itself could be seen as a site of struggle between British-oriented and American-oriented social values and cultural assumptions, both of which might be expressed via images of communal celebration; for example, the Queen or the Mountie on the one hand, and the American cowboy on the other. Thus, interpreting and representing the past and looking to the future at the level of communal mythology that celebrates social and cultural achievement via appropriate imagery was a matter of on-going negotiation, both in the years in which the Calgary Stampede was founded (1908–23), and during the years we call its golden era (1952–72), both periods of rapid social change.

Surprisingly, the sets of opposition inscribed in the posters we studied do not come across as being irreconcilable, as one might think. We would argue that the commodification of all these elements, especially the packaging of the cowboy, brings about an illusion of compatibility among the messages. More precisely, this effect is produced by the dissociation of message from its context, a rhetorical strategy quite obvious in the later posters.

Of course, what goes unsaid in these posters is just as important as what is said. First, we notice that women play a very small part in the publicity messages we studied. By contrast, women played a key role in the Wild West Show: they are featured in the Buffalo Bill posters of the 1880s as fancy riders and trick ropers, if not expert marksmen. Annie Oakley is a case in point. Similarly, as we have noted above, in the early days of the Calgary Stampede, women took part in a variety of contests, such as bucking horse riding, wild steer roping, relay race, trick and fancy riding.[66] Bertha Blanchett, Flores LaDue, Lucille Mulhall, and Goldie St. Clair made names for themselves as champions in these events. By 1952, however, the venues for female competitors had been reduced to barrel racing only. In this regard, then, one is tempted to ask the following question: Where in this (western Canadian) landscape are the women? We might answer: This Wild West has been re-constructed as masculine, virile, in large part via the image of the cowboy.

Second, we notice that Native peoples have been portrayed in ways legitimating Euro-Canadian dominance. The exception is the 1918 poster, which offers us a satirical view of life on the foothills of southern Alberta. We see, against a view of the mountains, a big Native person and a small, child-like cowboy standing in front of a huge tipi; the former is painting a message by the entrance that reads: AWAY ALL WEK. GON BEEG FAIR. In this case, we get the impression that nature (the Indian and the land) can co-exist with civilization (the cowboy and industrial technology, indicated elsewhere on the poster). The posters invite us to see the Native peoples before they disappear all together, thereby reinforcing the belief, which was widely held from the mid-nineteenth century to virtually the mid-twentieth century, that Native peoples were disappearing.[67] We develop this notion further when we talk about specific posters.

Again and again, words and images evoke subsets of the binary oppositions we mentioned above, such as progress/nostalgia: man/animal, individual/community, Native/white, real/artificial, and centre/margin. We could not help but notice the ambiguity of the relationship between these mutually exclusive discourses. We could see that, ironically, they are inextricably linked.

Some analysts, interestingly enough, explain the enormous and growing popularity of the cowboy hero over the course of the twentieth century in terms of this opposition. Weston, for example, argues that "[The] only force strong enough to explain such a powerful appetite for the Western is a profound sense of deprivation and loss by the American people and a mass longing for a better world,"[68] a loss engendered by the industrialization of America during the late nineteenth century.

The situation in Canada also generated nostalgia, apparent in the songs written by cowboys,[69] as well as, perhaps most obviously, in Weadick's desire to celebrate the cowboy just as his world was being transformed by the forces of agrarian and urban settlement. We try to throw some light on the role nostalgia plays in the construction of the cowboy via the posters we examine.

Conclusion

The discursive practices that have been employed in the posters we studied bear a strong resemblance to the practices employed by socio-political institutions generally. We see in the harmonization of the discourses of progress and nostalgia via the process of commodification new representations of the master discourse of Euro-centric patriarchal capitalism, which valorize two impulses: to look forward and to look back in the interest of progress, thereby legitimating the European dominance of the North American continent. Along the way, these signs of the historical and the mythical American and Canadian Wests in large part have been emptied of specific meanings, thereby allowing Canadian viewers to insert their own mythic meanings.

Moreover, a paradox lies at the heart of nostalgia, in the sense that nostalgia involves a fantasy that never materializes, one that maintains itself as it were by not being fulfilled. No one can say that the fantasy of reviving the Wild West is an idle dream. Every July, it presses toward indirect fulfilment via the art of spectacle. We detect sufficient ambiguity in our data to suggest a more polysemous discourse than we had anticipated, one in which ordinary people (to paraphrase Fiske) may indeed valorize the dominant discourse, but at the same time insert meanings that subvert it as well. The Calgary Stampede posters we examined are indeed sites of a complex struggle over the meaning of western Canadian experience, and the image of the cowboy that evolves via these popular cultural artifacts is as central to this struggle as it is ambiguous.

1

2

3

4

5

6

7

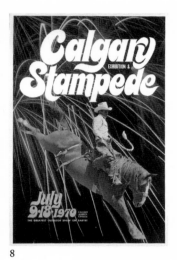

8

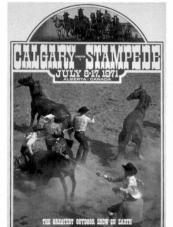

9

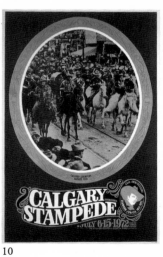

10

Notes

We presented a shorter version of this paper at the Boundaries Conference, held at the University of Edinburgh on 4 May 1996, and the conference on the "Canadian Cowboy: New Perspectives on Ranching History," held at the Glenbow Museum on 28 September 1997. We wish to thank the archivists at the Glenbow Archives and at the Calgary Stampede Board for their help in accessing primary materials, and our colleagues at the university, Donald B. Smith, Max Foran, and Douglas Francis, for their encouragement and helpful criticism.

1. Richard Hofstadter, *Anti-Intellectualism in American Life* (New York: Vintage Books, 1966), 48–49; David H. Breen, *The Canadian Prairie West and the Ranching Frontier, 1874–1924* (Toronto: University of Toronto Press, 1983); Gaile McGregor, *The Wacousta Syndrome: Explorations in the Canadian Landscape* (Toronto: University of Toronto Press, 1985).

2. High H. Dempsey, *The Golden Age of the Canadian Cowboy: An Illustrated History* (Saskatoon: Fifth House, 1995), 1–3.

3. The range of themes and stereotypes presented in western pageants in the United States and Canada was diverse. See Marilyn Burgess, "Canadian 'Range Wars'": Struggles over Indian Cowboys," *Canadian Journal of Communication* 18 (1993): 352. Two central and interrelated images in these pageants were those of the cowboy and the "Indian." If the cowboy came across as "winner," the Indian came across as "loser," although he might be depicted either as the "noble savage" loser or the "ignoble savage" loser. As many analysts have pointed out, Euro-North American writers, artists, and other cultural workers have persistently depicted Native peoples as either the noble or ignoble "Other" and used the images they created either to bolster or to critique their own cultural practises. To paraphrase Francis, Europeans have tended to imagine the Indian rather than to know Native people, to project onto Native people all the fears and hopes they have for the New World, to define themselves in relation to the Other in the form of the Indian. Francis goes on to show how this was effected through a number of cultural forms, including the Wild West Show that was "primarily an allegory depicting the ultimate triumph of civilized values of the anarchy of the wilderness...[which] ended with the cowboys putting the Indians to rout." See Daniel Francis, *The Imaginary Indian: The Image of the Indian in Canadian Culture* (Vancouver: Arsenal Pulp Press, 1992), 8, 94.

4. James H. Gray, *A Brand of its Own: The 100 Year History of the Calgary Exhibition and Stampede* (Saskatoon: Western Producer Prairie Books, 1985), 131–44.

5.   Stuart Hall, "Encoding/Decoding," in *Culture, Media, and Language, ed.* S. Hall, D. Hobson, A. Lowe, and P. Willis (London: Hutchinson, 1980), 128–39; and "Notes on deconstructing 'The Popular,'" in *People's History and Socialist Theory,* ed. E. Samuel (London: Routledge and Kegan Paul, 1981), 227–40; John Fiske, *Understanding Popular Culture,* (Boston: Unwin Heyman, 1989); Wayne Mellinger, "Postcards from the Edge of the Color Line: Images of African Americans in Popular Culture, 1893–1917," *Symbolic Interactionism* 15, no. 4 (1992), 413–33.

6.   Fiske, *Understanding Popular Culture.*

7.   Hall identifies three reading strategies: (a) "dominant readings" are employed by readers who accept the dominant ideology; (b) "negotiated readings" are employed by readers who accept the dominant ideology but who modify it to suit their social position; and (c) "oppositional readings" are employed by readers whose social position is in opposition to the dominant ideology. See Stuart Hall, "Encoding/Decoding."

8.   Gray, *Brand of Its Own,* 9, 10.

9.   Gray, *Brand of Its Own,* 62.

10.   Significantly, following the discovery of oil at Leduc in 1947, Calgary grew dramatically, becoming the oil capital of Canada. This meant, among other things, that a great many Americans immigrated to Calgary during this period, a fact that had an impact on the growth of the Stampede. As Gray puts it, this "immigrant army...came in the main from the south and south-west of the United States and hence were thoroughly familiar with rodeo as an entertainment medium....Not only was there immediate immersion of all concerned in the Stampede week ethos," but also they brought with them the culture and technology of "the outdoor barbecue," which became a central feature of Stampede celebrations. See Gray, *Brand of Its Own,* 136–37.

11.   To paraphrase McGregor, for example, the frontier did not play a positive role in the Canadian experience, the reason being rooted in the essential difference between a "western" frontier and a "northern" frontier. A western frontier, depending on one's perspective, is the limit of knowledge or the limit of control, and as such denotes a temporary and arbitrary boundary that may not only be transcended but actually redefined by human effort. A northern frontier, in contrast, denotes the limits of endurance; while the western frontier is simply a culturally defined interface, the northern frontier is an existential one. In this discussion, McGregor builds, in part, on Northrop Frye's notion of Canadian literature reflecting a "garrison mentality" and on Margaret Atwood's emphasis on survival as its central theme. See Gaile McGregor, *The Wacousta Syndrome: Explorations in the Canadian Landscape* (Toronto: University of Toronto Press, 1985), 282–83.

12. J.M.S. Careless, "Frontierism, Metropolitanism, and Canadian History," *Canadian Historical Review* 35 (March 1954),1–21; Donald Creighton, *The Empire of the St. Lawrence* (Toronto: Macmillan, 1956); McGregor, *The Wacousta Syndrome.*

13. Traditional wisdom has it that, in Alberta, the ranching boom began around 1880 and peaked sometime between 1885 and 1895. Of course, the ranching frontiers – Canadian as well as American – are much more complex than we can possibly indicate in our brief discussion. The recent commentaries of Slatta and Jordan challenge the idea that the historical cowboy enjoyed a very short heyday. These scholars see not so much a collapse of the cattle industry as its contraction, whereby the Texas style of ranching gave way to a much more competitive style of operation. The beef industry survived, buts its relative importance to the total economy declined. Cowboys still tend cattle on horseback and ranching culture remains part of the local scene. See Richard W. Slatta, *Cowboys of the Americas* (New Haven, CT: Yale University Press, 1990); Terry G. Jordan, *North American Cattle-Ranching Frontiers: Origins, Diffusion, and Differentiation* (Albuquerque: University of New Mexico, 1993).

14. Don Russell, *The Wild West: Or a History of the Wild West Shows* (Fort Worth, TX: Amon Carter Museum, 1970), 8.

15. Weston argues convincingly that a bitter class war developed between cowboys attempting to better themselves by becoming homesteaders – generally operators of small ranching or mixed-farming operations – and powerful, large-scale ranchers attempting to maintain their hegemony. The range struggles of the eighties and early nineties were between rich and poor, a war of the classes, cattlemen against blackballed cowboys with greasy-sack shoestring ranches. They involved fence cutting and sheep slaughter but were not fence and sheep wars in themselves. The corporations, having money, fenced first, and often fenced public land; cowboy ranchers cut the fences when they intruded on their ranges. The cattle companies hated sheep as competitors for free grass and sometimes ordered their cowboy employees to drive them off or destroy them; but cowboy settlers often became sheepmen themselves. The popular notion that cowboys hated sheep and sheepmen, like so much of the western myths, reflects the wishes and interests of cattlemen. See Jack Weston, *The Real American Cowboy* (New York: New Amsterdam, 1985), 108.

16. Russell, *Wild West,* 6; Weston, *Real American Cowboy,* 35–69.

17. William H. Forbis, *The Cowboys* (Alexandria, VA: Time-Life Books, 1973), 17.

18. Dempsey, *Golden Age,* 1.

19. Slatta, *Cowboys,* 60–61; Dempsey, *Golden Age,* 1–20.

20. David H. Breen, "The Turner Thesis and the Canadian West: A Closer look at the Ranching Frontier," in *Essays on Western History*, ed. Lewis H. Thomas (Edmonton: University of Alberta Press, 1976), 153; Simon M. Evans, *Prince Charming Goes West: The Story of the E.P. Ranch* (Calgary: University of Calgary Press, 1994), 43, 44; S.M. Lipset, *Continental Divide: The Values and Institutions of the United States and Canada* (London: Routledge, 1990).

21. Sheilagh Jameson, "The Social Elite of the Ranch Community and Calgary," in *Frontier Calgary: Town, City, and Region, 1875–1914*, ed. Anthony W. Rasporich and Henry C. Klassen (Calgary: University of Calgary Press, 1975), 56–70; Breen, "The Turner Thesis"; Howard Palmer and Tamara Palmer, "The Alberta Experience," *Journal of Canadian Studies* 17, no. 3 (Fall 1982): 20–34; Howard Palmer, *Alberta: A New History* (Edmonton: Hurtig Publishers, 1990).

22. Breen, "The Turner Thesis," 153.

23. Palmer and Palmer, "The Alberta Experience."

24. Bruce Patterson and Mary McGuire, *The Wild West* (Banff, AB: Altitude Publishing, 1993).

25. Russell, *Wild West,* 12–13; Slatta, *Cowboys,* 146–47.

26. Henry Nash Smith, *Virgin Land: The American West as Symbol and Myth* (Cambridge: Harvard University Press, 1950).

27. Russell, *Wild West,* 16.

28. Ibid., 9.

29. Daniel Francis, *The Imaginary Indian: The Image of the Indian in Canadian Culture* (Vancouver: Arsenal Pulp Press, 1992).

30. Russell, *Wild West,* 43.

31. Sarah J. Blackstone, *Buckskins, Bullets, and Business: A History of Buffalo Bill's Wild West* (New York: Greenwood Press, 1986).

32. It is instructive to note that, in the latter half of the nineteenth century, both in North America and in Europe, Native peoples were also popular on the entertainment/lecture circuit. Two Canadian-born Native peoples who became lecturers/entertainers illustrate the point. An Ojibway, George Copway (1818–69) travelled widely in North America and Europe after the publication (1847) of his autobiography, the first book written in English by a Native person from Canada. The well-known E. Pauline Johnson (1861–1913), a poet who performed on stage in Native costume, was also part of this tradition of "Indian" as stage performer. A number of Native peoples also participated in Wild West shows, for the most part playing the part of the "aggressive and bloodthirsty attacker of wagons." See Daniel Francis, *Imaginary Indian,* 94.

33. Russell, *Wild West,* 46–47, 70–71.

34. Ibid., 9.

35. Slatta, *Cowboys,* 204–07.

36. Russell, *Wild West,* 12–13.

37. Warren Elofson, "Not Just a Cowboy: The Practice of Ranching in Southern Alberta, 1881–1914," in *Canadian Papers in Rural History* (Ganonoque, ON: Langdale Press, 1996), 205–16.

38. D.J. Hall, "Clifford Sifton: Immigration and Settlement Policy, 1896–1905," in *The Settlement of the West,* ed. Howard Palmer (Calgary: University of Calgary Press, 1977), 60–85.

39. Dick Harrison, *Unnamed Country: The Struggle for a Canadian Prairie Fiction* (Edmonton: The University of Alberta Press, 1977), 157.

40. Ibid., 79.

41. A number of British writers helped construct the image of the Canadian West as "wild and woolly," such as R.M. Ballantyne, H. Jeffs, and Lady Agnes Macdonald, whose work appeared not only in books, but also in periodicals, including *The Boys Own Paper, Murray's Magazine,* and *Wide World Magazine.* See R.G. Moyles and Doug Owram, *Imperial Dreams and Colonial Realities: British Views of Canada, 1880–1914* (Toronto: University of Toronto Press, 1988) 6, 7; and Doug Owram, *Promise of Eden: The Canadian Expansionist Movement and the Idea of the West, 1856–1900* (Toronto: University of Toronto Press, 1992).

42. For a fascinating discussion of the cowboy as romantic hero, see R. McGillis, "Westering of the Spirit: Wordsworth out West," *Journal of Popular Culture* 18 (1984): 85–95. McGillis refers to the idea of cowboy as Arthurian hero, which is developed by Esselman. We should also point out that Kimmel argues that the dynamics of American masculinity are manifest in the cowboy, America's contribution to the world's storehouse of cultural heroes.

43. Buck Rainey, "The 'Reel' Cowboy," in Harris and Rainey, *Unnamed Country,* 18.

44. Weston, *Real American Cowboy,* 210.

45. Donna Livingstone, *The Cowboy Spirit: Guy Weadick and the Calgary Stampede* (Vancouver: Greystone Books, 1996), 3.

46. Ibid., 31.

47. Fred Kennedy, *The Calgary Stampede Story* (Calgary: Commonwealth Press, 1952), 13.

48. Kennedy, *Calgary Stampede,* 11; Guy Weadick, "Origin of the Calgary Stampede," *Alberta Historical Review* 14, no. 4 (1966): 21; Livingstone, *Cowboy Spirit,* 37.

49. The important role played by "boosterism" and its relation to ideology is discussed by a number of historians of the settlement and development of

the West. Friesen notes that the "success" in terms of growth of particular communities over others owed much to these "committed entrepreneurs." He also points out that "It is important to look beneath the boosters' rhetoric to the political and social implications of their message" and that, if we do, we see that booster rhetoric decried the complaints of "knockers," those who "commented publicly" on flaws in the boosters' plans. In a booster atmosphere, class-based debates – that is, serious differences of interest on the spending of public funds and serious differences in perceptions of community needs – were not welcomed. The greatest victory of the boosters was not the creation of their metropolis but the creation of an ethos of community solidarity that transcended class, income, and occupation. See Gerald Friesen, *The Canadian Prairies: A History* (Toronto: University of Toronto Press, 1984), 283–84.

50. Gray, *Brand of Its Own,* 37.

51. Russell, *Wild West,* 2.

52. Blackstone, *Buckskins, Bullets.*

53. In ritualizing these performances, different impresarios might push them in different directions, e.g., theatre or sport. What we notice vis-à-vis the latter (rodeo) is the professionalization of the skills by which individuals can be constructed as cowboys. In the early days of (professional) rodeo, contestants paid their own entry fees and took care of their own transportation and health care. Rules were not standardized, nor were prizes for events. In 1929 a group of cowboys formed the Rodeo Association of America in order to make sense of the chaos. They made no real progress until 1936, when a group of cowboys in Boston formed the Cowboy Turtles Association, which became the Rodeo Cowboy Association in 1945. They created a championship award system that year, which recognized the following "standard" events: saddle-bronc riding, bareback riding, Brahma bull riding, steer wrestling, and calf roping. More than 500 rodeos a year abide by R.C.A. rules. See Russell, *Wild West,* 105–08.

54. Art Belanger, *Chuckwagon Racing: Calgary Stampede's Half Mile of Hell* (Surrey, BC: Heritage House Publishing, 1983).

55. Kennedy, *Calgary Stampede,* 25.

56. Belanger, *Chuckwagon Racing,* 69.

57. Livingstone, *Cowboy Spirit,* 24, 49–50.

58. Burgess provides valuable insight into the problematic of the imaginative space occupied by the Native cowboy. See Burgess, "Canadian 'Range Wars'": Struggles over Indian Cowboys."

59. Belanger, *Chuckwagon Racing.*

60. The chuckwagon races originate in Canada and they represent the only distinctive Canadian contribution to the rodeo.

61. Gray, *Brand of Its Own*, 79.
62. Literary analysts, including Harrison and MacLaren, have argued that our views of the nature/meaning of western experience have been "constructed" by narrative and art. Historians of western Canada, including Francis, Owram, Palmer, Stiles, and Swyripa, have examined how images of the west/western experience have been "constructed" over time. Cultural analysts, drawing on larger frameworks, such as those developed by Edward Said, author of *Orientalism* (1978) and *Culture and Imperialism* (1993), and Homi K. Bhabba, author of *Nation and Narration* (1990), have tried to make sense of western tourist spots and western festivals in terms of the ways they have evolved. For example, Shields "reads" the Banff area as a site that has been named and packaged in a way that provides the "colonial mindset" with "continual repetition of the colonizing act," thereby providing satisfying (and defining) references to European landscape and mythology. Burgess "reads" the entire "discursive and performative apparatus of the Calgary Stampede" as a similar re-enactment of the colonizing moment, a complex "story of origins" that combines several historical stages. In particular, this apparatus combines pre-contact Native history and the history of European settlement in a way that valorizes the European conquest of nature and Native peoples. Burgess, however, argues further that, in its complexity, the Calgary Stampede constitutes a potentially transformative site, one where "narratives of identity and essentialist categories of racial difference" can be "de-stabilized." See R. Douglas Francis, *Images of the West: Changing Perception of the Prairies, 1690–1960* (Saskatoon: Western Producer Prairie Books, 1989).
63. Harrison, *Unnamed Country*.
64. Fiske, *Understanding Popular Culture*, 32–34.
65. Burgess, "Canadian 'Range Wars.'"
66. Kennedy, *Calgary Stampede*, 29–33; Gray, *Brand of Its Own*, 37–40.
67. Penny Petrone, *Native Literature in Canada: From the Oral Tradition to the Present* (Toronto: Oxford University Press, 1990), 43–47, 78–84; Francis, *Imaginary Indian*.
68. Weston, *Real American Cowboy*, 210.
69. Dempsey, *Golden Age*, 150, 151.

CHAPTER 13

Renewing the Calgary Stampede for the 21st Century: A Conversation with Vern Kimball, Stampede Chief Executive Officer

Vern Kimball (centre) with Dr. David Chalack, vice-chairman of the board of directors (left) and George Brookman, president and chairman of the board (right).

The Calgary Stampede's history began in 1884 when the Calgary and District Agricultural Society was formed. The success of the first fair in 1886 set the stage for what would become annual summer fairs. In 1912 the first Calgary Stampede rodeo took the town by storm, and in 1923 the rodeo and the exhibition merged, creating the annual Calgary Exhibition and Stampede. The following decades saw the organization grow beyond the annual celebration to include many programs and venues at Stampede Park. A new brand introduced in 2007 simplified the organization's name to the Calgary Stampede and unified the many aspects of the organization, all focused on preserving and promoting western heritage and values year-round.

The Calgary Stampede is a volunteer-supported not-for-profit organization with a vision to build Stampede Park into a world-class, year-round gathering place. In 2004 the organization unveiled a fifteen-year plan to revitalize Stampede Park. The plan is more than just another construction project – it's about building a better community. Stampede Park will include new trade and entertainment facilities, expanded green space, a youth campus, a new agriculture arena, a hotel, a retail marketplace, and a riverfront heritage park.

Without a doubt, the Calgary Stampede is a best known for its annual ten-day city-wide community celebration. It is the highlight of the summer for Calgarians and their guests. Known as "The Greatest Outdoor Show on Earth," the event has become part of Calgary's culture and attracts over 1.25 million people to Stampede Park each year.

Beyond the July celebration, Stampede Park hosts 1.2 million people each year for trade and consumer shows, weddings, meetings, and a wide range of entertainment options.

As Calgary changes, the Calgary Stampede continues to adapt to its surroundings and contribute to the city's quality of life. For many reasons, it has earned a place deep in the heart of the community.

The following interview was conducted in the spring of 2007 with Vern Kimball, the organization's chief executive officer, who provided a candid perspective from inside the Stampede organization at a time of enormous change and growth.

Q: The Calgary Stampede in many ways has remained remarkably faithful to its roots, with the elements and spirit of the earliest events of the late nineteenth and early twentieth centuries still present today. What is the significance of this historical legacy, and what stories from those early days inspire you the most?

Vern Kimball: Right from the start, the Stampede was more than just a local fair. It was a celebration of the unique character of the people who live here. The entire community participated in making the event come to life. The symbols and traditions clearly represented something meaningful to the community.

When I think of those early years, what really stands out for me is the story of Guy Weadick. He was the inspiration behind most of the vital elements that we associate with the Calgary Stampede today.

Guy was the American impresario who organized a "Calgary Stampede" rodeo in 1912. It was a tribute to the vanishing open range era and cowboy culture – which at the time was thought to be at risk of vanishing. He came back to town to stage a second Stampede in 1919 to celebrate the end of the First World War.

When the agricultural fair and rodeo merged in 1923, Weadick's genius for showmanship came to the forefront. He built up chuckwagon racing as a marquee event, and he attracted the best cowboys in the world for the rodeo. Just as important, he engaged the entire city in Stampede activities. Shopkeepers decorated their storefronts in old western style, people vied for prizes for dressing western, and the street breakfasts and barbeques were a big hit.

This community involvement – continuing to this day – is what makes the Stampede unique.

For sure, Guy was building on a mythology of the untamed West, but his ideas were rooted in the history of the North American West. His Stampede was a real reflection of the excitement and unpredictability of life in the West, and man's relationship to the land and his animals.

Guy Weadick was also remarkable for his foresight in involving the Treaty Seven First Nations. In the early days of settlement of the West, the Canadian government permitted First Nations people to leave their reserves for a maximum of three days at a time. When Weadick conceived of the first Stampede in 1912, he and a few influential Calgary politicians successfully petitioned the federal government to allow the people to come off their reserves for the entire festival. This was enormously important because it meant they were able to practise and showcase their culture at a time when those traditions were at risk. For this reason, this first Stampede is a significant milestone for

the Treaty Seven people. Nearly a century later, our Indian Village continues to be a vital component of the annual festival, and it traces its roots to
Weadick's vision in 1912.

> **Q:** We are now halfway through the first decade of the
> twenty-first century and the Calgary Stampede is in the
> midst of its most exciting period of change since the days
> of Guy Weadick. However, there's an old saying – "If it
> ain't broke, don't fix it." Given the Stampede's considerable
> success historically, why did the organization decide in
> 2000 it was time for change?

> **Kimball:** It's true that by 2000, we had enjoyed tremen-
> dous growth and success. The annual Calgary Stampede
> had grown to become one of Canada's most important
> tourist attractions. And in the rest of the year, Stampede
> Park was busier than ever with hundreds of activities.

However, it was also clear that our community was changing around
us. Thousands of people were – and still are – moving to Calgary each year
from all over Canada and the world. The population in the community was
becoming younger and more diverse, and the city's population was drawing
ever closer to the one-million mark. As an organization we needed to ensure
we were growing and changing in step with the community.

The board of directors commissioned a reputation survey in 2002 to help
us understand how the Calgary Stampede was perceived by the community.
We hired research consultants who surveyed a cross-section of the community, including a large number of Calgarians, community and business leaders, neighbours around Stampede Park, and our employees and volunteers.

The results were both encouraging and revealing.

Respondents really valued the economic and tourism benefits we generate
for the area. They told us they loved the annual celebration in July, but they
didn't know much about what we did the rest of the year. Many didn't know
we were a not-for-profit organization – in fact, a good number thought we
were a for-profit company. We also found that the demographics of our volunteer group did not reflect the "new Calgary" – in other words, we needed
to bring in a younger and more diverse group of volunteers.

Most important, the research – which has been reinforced by subsequent
surveys – found that Calgarians connect to the Stampede at a deeper level.

The Stampede represents a key set of community values...values that are important to them. They told us we did a good job preserving and promoting western heritage and values, and they wanted us to do more.

It was the first time we had ever looked at ourselves formally from the outside in, and the feedback had a tremendous impact on our thinking. It challenged us to remember our roots and reinforced our desire to be more than just a ten-day event in July.

In response to this research, we have set into motion a range of fundamental changes, from how we're structured, to how we operate and communicate.

We established a formal core purpose – "To preserve and promote western heritage and values" – to clarify our mandate for everyone across the organization. We reorganized our board and management structure. The board of directors invited several outside community leaders – people who bring diverse skills and backgrounds – to join the board and other subcommittees. And the board has updated and enhanced our governance policies and processes.

We also took a hard look at our volunteer structure. As a not-for-profit organization, our volunteer system is extremely important to us. Volunteerism is an important legacy from our earliest days. These are people who believe deeply in their community. Volunteers made the first event happen in 1886, and they continue to support the event to this day. Currently we have more than 2,200 active volunteers, and through the years there have been tens of thousands more who have contributed to our growth and success. We have one of the most successful year-round volunteer systems in Calgary, if not the country.

We challenged ourselves to provide volunteer services that would be second to none, and to integrate the volunteers with our paid employees so everyone would function more cohesively as a team.

This assessment resulted in a whole new approach and a new way of thinking. We created a new full-time staff position of volunteer services manager and a professional volunteer management group. Now when we talk about our "human resources," we mean both our paid employees and our volunteers. It's a new, holistic approach.

We also recognized that focused, regular communications would create more transparency with how we make our decisions and how we interact with the community. People wanted to understand us, so there was a need for us to tell our story much more effectively.

So, we created a corporate communications department and hired professionals who are effectively communicating the Stampede's stories. We've taken a new, open approach to two-way communication with our internal and external stakeholders. We're open to new ideas. We're listening and responding. This has had a positive effect throughout the organization and has been well received in the community.

One of the most satisfying things for me is to see how soon after we introduced these changes the organization responded positively. People will tell you that they are functioning on the same page, asking "How can we do things better?" and "How can we work together to build a better organization?'"

We are also approaching our partners in the community, asking them the same questions, and they are helping us find ways and means to improve our participation in community life. As we have reached out, the community has reached back to us.

> **Q:** Did this research lead to the Stampede's plans
> for expansion?

> **Kimball:** Actually, we expressed our desire to expand
> Stampede Park in the 1980s. We finally put forward a
> plan that Calgary City Council approved in 1998 that
> called for the expansion of the Park by an eight-block
> area, extending north to Twelfth Avenue SE, between
> Macleod Trail and Elbow River. In the years that
> followed, we had laid out some general priorities for
> expansion, but the reputation research really caused us
> to stretch our thinking.

We challenged our architects to think not just about the eight-block expansion zone, but to think in terms of the potential for the entire Stampede Park. In turn, our architects challenged us to think big.

Rather than simply expand by 40 acres, we agreed to consider how we could redevelop all 193 acres so Stampede Park could be a gathering place where western heritage and values were celebrated 365 days a year.

All this led to the creation of a sweeping 15-year vision for redeveloping Stampede Park, which we unveiled for the community in 2004. There are about twelve distinct projects within the overall plan, but each piece works as part of the whole. For example, we're working with our Treaty Seven partners to relocate Indian Village to a site physically closer to the original encampments, which were adjacent to Fort Calgary, and restore and enhance access to the Elbow River. This will allow us to create a wonderful inner-city park that will complement other heritage components while also providing a unique destination that will answer people's needs for natural spaces in their lives.

We feel very strongly about our role as stewards of this historic land, including the river that flows through the park. We want Stampede Park to be a green oasis in the middle of a busy metropolitan core. Our comprehensive set of environmental programs protects the natural beauty of the land and the Elbow River and makes us an environmental leader in Calgary. That commitment will continue to guide how we approach projects such as the new trade and entertainment facilities, a youth campus, hotel, new agriculture building, and a retail marketplace.

> **Q:** Every organization has its unique challenges and issues, and the Stampede is no exception. Western Canada is highly urbanized, and our population is more ethnically diverse than it was twenty years ago. What is the Stampede organization doing to address these changing realities and to stay relevant?

> **Kimball:** The changes we are making are about ensuring that the Stampede – as an organization, as a year-round gathering place, including the annual ten-day celebration – remains an integral part of the social and economic fabric of Calgary and southern Alberta.

We are a not-for-profit organization, so our bottom line is not about making money. Our bottom line is about bringing people from all walks of life together and building a better community. This is what the Stampede has done from its earliest days. We continue to represent the community values – western hospitality, integrity, pride of place, and commitment to community – that people define as being fundamental to Calgary's culture and values.

In the spring of 2007 we introduced a new brand identity that integrates the Calgary Stampede name across all parts of the organization, across all events in all times of the year. This will help us communicate who we are, what we do, and what we represent. Most important, this brand communicates that we're more than the annual Stampede – we preserve and promote the community values that lie at the heart of the southern Alberta community.

We are taking many other steps to stay relevant. We are putting a big effort into recruiting more youth and members of Calgary's diverse communities to our volunteer ranks, as well as newcomers to Calgary, whom we are finding to be some of our most enthusiastic supporters.

The board is recruiting more women and representatives of Calgary's corporate and diverse communities, as well as adding more people with governance and financial expertise, which will stand us in good stead as we build out the development plan.

We have also built new bridges with governments at all levels – municipal, provincial, and federal – to the point that our lines of communication with governments are now wide open. As a result, government members now better appreciate the economic and social value of the Stampede – and our still untapped potential.

> **Q:** Agriculture has always been a priority for the Calgary Stampede. What are you doing to ensure that remains the case, particularly given the changing demographics and the increasing urbanization of western Canada?

> **Kimball:** Our commitment to agriculture goes back 120 years and is unwavering. Stampede Park is home to one of the most diverse agriculture showcases that exist anywhere. Each year, we host more than 75 agriculture events and programs for commerce, trade, sports and entertainment, celebration and learning. By connecting people from rural and urban communities, this park continues to be a vital gathering place for southern Alberta.

However, we recognized the agriculture industry is changing, and we are adapting our thinking in response. A major part of our Stampede Park Development Plan is to provide new and innovative ways to link agricultural producers and consumers and rural and urban audiences. For instance, we have partnered with Olds College to create a thriving agriculture college campus right at centre of the city.

Another key development project is a new agricultural facility to replace our nearly 100-year-old barn – this will help us better showcase the industry. This will be a centrepiece of our effort to support Alberta producers as they introduce their products and services to the wider Canadian and international marketplace and to educate and engage diverse audiences about agriculture.

Another unique reputation challenge we face is communicating our care for our animals. Animals were a vital part of the development of the West, and we think it's important that we continue to showcase that heritage. We are very proud of how well we take care of our animals. We work directly with the Calgary Humane Society and the Society for the Prevention of Cruelty to Animals to identify and implement new ways to enhance our animal care measures for the Stampede rodeo and chuckwagon events. As a result, for years we've been the leader in setting stringent rules to ensure the safety of the animals for these events.

Ultimately, however, we will use all 193 acres of the Park to support agriculture-related programming. Olds College, for example, will use the river frontage as part of its environmental stewardship programs. And the expanding Roundup Centre facilities will continue to host national and international industry conferences and meetings that are so important to sharing agriculture knowledge on a global scale.

> **Q:** What do you hope the Calgary Stampede will be in five, ten, twenty, or even one hundred years from now?

> **Kimball:** Today, the organization is in growth mode as we implement our development plan, so I'm expecting that over the next ten years we will, working with our partners, spend $600 million to improve our facilities and programs for the benefit of all Calgarians. That expenditure will encourage subsequent developments. Our $350 million annual economic impact will also increase, and I wouldn't be surprised to see it double in the next few years.

However, even though the physical manifestations of the Stampede will change over time, more important for me than bricks and mortar is keeping the spirit of the Stampede alive throughout the community. We have created a renewed sense of purpose across our organization and a new level of connection with Calgarians. I think these will help the Calgary Stampede to continue to flourish in the decades to come.

We are proud of our success, but we recognize that to maintain our relevance and importance in the future, we have to continue to nurture what has been created. Enduring brands must have a powerful combination of reflecting their past and tying themselves to the future. The Calgary Stampede is very fortunate to have both. However, we are at a pivotal stage in our history, with the opportunity to integrate the power of the Stampede brand across all that we do, 365 days a year.

I said earlier that as we reach out to our community, the community is reaching back. I believe this reflects the enormous change Calgarians are experiencing as their city continues its rapid growth. People want to protect Calgary's unique spirit and identity. Our research finds they consistently talk about a set of values – western hospitality, integrity, pride of place, and commitment to community – that are essential to the character of their community. Calgarians don't want to lose these values. And they are looking to the Stampede, as they have for 120 years, to represent those values. We intend to fulfill that expectation.

Bibliography

Abbott, E.C., and Helena Smith. *We Pointed Them North: Recollections of a Cowpuncher.* Norman: University of Oklahoma Press, 1955.

Adams, Judith. *The American Amusement Park Industry: A History of Technology and Thrills.* Boston: Twayne Publishers, 1991.

Adams, Michael. *Fire and Ice.* Toronto: Penguin, 2004.

Ainsworth, Ed. *The Cowboy in Art.* New York: World Publishing Company, 1968.

Allen, Michael. *Rodeo Cowboys in the North American Imagination.* Reno: University of Nevada Press, 1998.

Anderson, Benedict. *Imagined Communities: Reflections on the Origin and Spread of Nationalism.* rev. ed. London: Verso, 1991.

Anderson, Nancy K. "'Curious historical data': Art History and Western American Art." In *Discovered Lands, Invented Pasts: Transforming Visions of the American West,* edited by Jules Prown, 1–35. New Haven, CT: Yale University Press, 1992.

Angus, Fiona. *Key to the Midway: Masculinity at Work in a Western Canadian Carnival.* Ph.D. Dissertation, Department of Sociology, University of British Columbia, 2000.

Armitage, Shelley. "Rawhide Heroines: The Evolution of the Cowgirl and the Myth of America." In *American Self: Myth, Ideology, and Popular Culture,* edited by Sam B. Girgus, 166–81. Albuquerque: University of New Mexico Press, 1981.

Artibise, Alan F.J. "Boosterism and the Development of Prairie Cities, 1871–1913." In *The Prairie West,* edited by R. Douglas Francis and Howard Palmer, 515–43. Edmonton: University of Alberta Press, 1999.

Barthes, Roland. *Elements of Semiology.* Translated by Annette Lavers and Colin Smith. New York: Hill and Wang, 1967.

"The Rhetoric of the Image" (1964). In *Image–Music–Text.* Translated by S. Heath. London: Wm. Collins Sons, 1977.

Becker, Howard. *Artworlds.* Los Angeles: University of California Press, 1982.

Becker, Howard, and Michel Bakhtin. *The Dialogic Imagination.* Austin: University of Texas Press, 1984.

Belanger, Art. *Chuckwagon Racing: Calgary Stampede's Half Mile of Hell.* Surrey, BC: Heritage House Publishing, 1983.

Bell, Catherine. Ritual: Perspectives and Dimensions. New York: Oxford University Press, 1997.

Belton, Robert J. Signs of Resistance: Approaches to Canadian Visual History. Calgary: University of Calgary Press, 2001.

Blackstone, Sarah J. Buckskins, Bullets, and Business: A History of Buffalo Bill's Wild West. New York: Greenwood Press, 1986.

Boorstin, O.J. The Image: A Guide to Pseudo-Events in America. New York: Harper and Row, 1964.

Bourdieu, Pierre. Distinction: A Social Critique of the Judgment of Taste. Translated by R. Nice. Cambridge, MA: Harvard University Press, 1984.

Breen, David H. The Canadian Prairie West and the Ranching Frontier, 1874–1924. Toronto: University of Toronto Press, 1983.

Breen, David H. "The Turner Thesis and the Canadian West: A Closer Look at the Ranching Frontier." In Essays on Western History, edited by Lewis H. Thomas, 147–56. Edmonton: University of Alberta Press, 1976.

Bruner, Edward. "Abraham Lincoln as Authentic Reproduction: A Critique of Postmodernism." American Anthropologist 96 (1994): 397–415.

Bryan, Dominic. Orange Parades: The Politics of Ritual, Tradition and Control. London: Pluto Press, 2000.

Burgess, Marilyn. "Canadian 'Range Wars': Struggles over Indian Cowboys." Canadian Journal of Communication 18 (1993): 351–64.

Campbell, Colin S. "The Stampede: Cowtown's Sacred Cow." In Stampede City: Power and Politics in the West, edited by Chuck Reasons, 103–20. Toronto: Between the Lines, 1984.

Careless, J.M.S. "Frontierism, Metropolitanism, and Canadian History." Canadian Historical Review 35 (March 1954), 1–21.

Cawelti, John. "Reflections on the Western Since 1970." In Gender Language and Myth: Essays on Popular Narrative, edited by Glenwood Irons, 83–102. Toronto: University of Toronto Press, 1992.

Cohen, A.P. The Symbolic Construction of Community. London and New York: Tavistock, 1985.

Connerton, Paul. How Societies Remember. Cambridge: Cambridge University Press, 1989.

Davey, Frank. "Toward the Ends of Regionalism." In A Sense of Place: Re-Evaluating Regionalism in Canadian and American Writing, edited by Christian Riegel et al., 1–17. Edmonton: University of Alberta Press, 1998.

Davidson, Harold G. *Edward Borein, Cowboy Artist: The Life and Works of John Edward Borein, 1872 [sic]–1945.* Garden City: Doubleday, 1974.

Davis, Susan G. *Parades and Power: Street Theater in Nineteenth-Century Philadelphia.* Philadelphia: Temple University Press, 1986.

de Certeau, Michael. *The Practice of Everyday Life.* Berkeley: University of California Press, 1984.

Dempsey, Hugh A. "Calgary and the Riel Rebellion." *Alberta History* 33, no. 2 (Spring 1985): 7–18.

———. "Deerfoot and Friends." In *The Amazing Death of Calf Shirt and Other Blackfoot Stories: Three Hundred Years of Blackfoot History,* 161–85. Saskatoon: Fifth House, 1994.

———. *The Golden Age of the Canadian Cowboy: An Illustrated History.* Saskatoon: Fifth House, 1995.

———. *Treasures of the Glenbow.* Calgary: Glenbow Museum, 1991.

Derry, Kathryn. "Corsets and Broncs: The Wild West Show Cowgirl, 1890–1920." *Colorado Heritage* (Summer 1992): 2–16.

Dicks, Bella. *Culture on Display: The Production of Contemporary Visitability.* London: Open University Press, 2003.

Diehl, Fred. *A Gentleman from a Fading Age: Eric Lafferty Harvie.* Calgary: Devonian Foundation, 1989.

Dippie, Brian. "Charles M. Russell, Cowboy Culture and the Canadian Connection." In *Cowboys, Ranchers and the Cattle Business,* edited by Simon Evans, Sarah Carter, and Bill Yeo. Calgary: University of Calgary Press, 2000.

———. "'Chop! Chop!': Progress in the Presentation of Western Visual History." *Historian* 66, no. 3 (2004): 491–500.

———. "One West, One Myth: Transborder Continuity in Western Art." *American Review of Canadian Studies* 33, no. 4 (2003): 509–41.

Dunning, Eric. *Sport Matters: Sociological Studies of Sport, Violence and Civilization.* London: Routledge, 1999.

Eamer, Claire, and Thirza Jones. *The Canadian Rodeo Book.* Saskatoon: Western Producer Prairie Books, 1982.

Elofson, W.M. *Cowboys, Gentlemen and Cattle Thieves: Ranching on the Western Frontier.* Montreal: McGill-Queen's University Press, 2000.

———. *Frontier Cattle Ranching and the Life and Times of Charlie Russell.* Montreal: McGill-Queens University Press, 2004.

———. "Not Just a Cowboy: The Practice of Ranching in Southern Alberta, 1881–1914." In *Canadian Papers in Rural History*, edited by Donald H. Akenson, 205–16. Ganonoque, ON: Langdale Press, 1996.

English, Linda Christine. "The Calgary Exhibition and Stampedes: Culture, Context and Controversy, 1884–1920." M.A. Thesis, Department of History, University of Calgary, 1999.

Esselman, Kathryn C. "From Camelot to Monument Valley: Dramatic Origins of the Western Film." In *Focus on the Western*, edited by Jack Nackbar, 9–18. Englewood Cliffs, NJ: Prentice Hall, 1974.

Evans, Simon. *The Bar U: Canadian Ranching History*. Calgary: University of Calgary Press, 2004.

———. *Prince Charming Goes West: The Story of the E.P. Ranch*. Calgary: University of Calgary Press, 1994.

Evans, Simon, Sarah Carter, and Bill Yeo, eds. *Cowboys, Ranchers and the Cattle Business: Cross-Border Perspectives on Ranching History*. Calgary: University of Calgary Press, 2000.

Fiske, John. *Understanding Popular Culture*. Boston: Unwin Heyman, 1989.

Florida, Richard. *The Rise of the Creative Class and How It's Transforming Work, Leisure, Community and Everyday Life*. New York: Basic Books, 2000.

Foran, Maxwell. "Coalitions and Demolitions: The Destruction of Calgary's East Victoria Park, 1960–1998." *Prairie Forum* (May 2005): 17–45.

———. "Constancy and Change: Ranching in Western Canada." In *Challenging Frontiers: The Canadian West*, edited by Lorry Felske and Beverly Rasporich, 311–28. Calgary: University of Calgary Press, 2004.

———. *Trails and Trials: Markets and Land Use in the Alberta Beef Cattle Industry, 1881–1946*. Calgary: University of Calgary Press, 2003.

Foran, Maxwell, and Sheilagh Jameson, eds. *Citymakers: Calgarians After the Frontier*. Altona, MB: Historical Society of Alberta, Chinook Chapter, 1987.

Forbis, William H. *The Cowboys*. Alexandria, VA: Time-Life Books, 1973.

Francis, Daniel. *The Imaginary Indian: The Image of the Indian in Canadian Culture*. Vancouver: Arsenal Pulp Press, 1992.

Francis, R. Douglas. "Rural Ontario West: Ontarians in Alberta." In *Peoples of Alberta: Portraits of Cultural Diversity*, edited by Howard Palmar and Tamara Palmer, 123–42. Saskatoon: Western Producer Prairie Books, 1985.

Frantz, Joe B., and Julian Ernest Choate, Jr. *The American Cowboy: The Myth and the Reality*. Norman: University of Oklahoma Press, 1955.

Fredriksson, Kristine. *American Rodeo – From Buffalo Bill to Big Business*. College Station: Texas A&M University Press, 1985.

Friesen, Gerald. *The Canadian Prairies: A History*. Toronto: University of Toronto Press, 1984.

Garreau, Joel. *The Nine Nations of North America*. Boston: Houghton Mifflin, 1981.

Godard, Barbara. "The Politics of Representation." In *Native Writers and Canadian Writing*, edited by W. H. New. Vancouver: University of British Columbia Press, 1991.

Grabb, Edward, and James Curtis. *Regions Apart: The Four Societies of Canada and the United States*. Don Mills: Oxford University Press, 2005.

Graham, William M. *Treaty Days: Reflections of an Indian Commissioner*. Introduction by James Dempsey. Calgary: Glenbow Museum, 1991.

Granatstein, J.L. *Yankee Go Home? Canadians and Anti-Americanism*. Toronto: Harper Collins, 1996.

Gray, James H. *A Brand of its Own: The 100 Year History of the Calgary Exhibition and Stampede*. Saskatoon: Western Producer Prairie Books, 1985.

———. "Unlikely Partners in a Grand Vision: Guy Weadick and E.L. Richardson." In *Citymakers: Calgarians after the Frontier*, edited by Maxwell Foran and Sheilagh Jameson, 59–69. Altona, MB: Historical Society of Alberta, Chinook Chapter, 1987.

Gunderson, Harold. *The Linder Legend: The Story of Prorodeo and Its Champion*. Calgary: Sagebrush Publishing, 1996.

Hall, D.J. "Clifford Sifton: Immigration and Settlement Policy, 1896–1905." In *The Settlement of the West*, edited by Howard Palmer. Calgary: University of Calgary Press, 1977.

Hall, Stuart. "Encoding/Decoding." In *Culture, Media, and Language*, edited by S. Hall, D. Hobson, A. Lowe, and P. Willis, 128–39. London: Hutchinson, 1980

———. "Notes on Deconstructing the 'The Popular.'" In *People's History and Socialist Theory*, edited by R. Samuel, 227–40. London: Routledge, 1981.

Harmsen, Dorothy. *Harmsen's Western Americana*. rev. ed. Denver: Harmsen, 1978.

Harris, Charles W., and Buck Rainey, eds. *The Cowboy: Six Shooters, Songs, and Sex*. Norman: University of Oklahoma Press, 1976.

Harris, H.A. *Sport in Greece and Rome*. Ithaca: Cornell University Press, 1972.

Harrison, Dick. *Best Mounted Police Stories*. Edmonton: University of Alberta Press, 1996.

———. *Unnamed Country: The Struggle for a Canadian Prairie Fiction*. Edmonton: University of Alberta Press, 1977.

Hobsbawm, Eric. "Mass Producing Traditions: Europe 1870–1914." In *Representing the Nation: A Reader: Histories, Heritage and Museums*, edited by David Boswell and Jessica Evans, 61–86. London and New York: Routledge and the Open University, 1999.

Hobsbawm, Eric, and Terence Ranger, eds. *The Invention of Tradition*. Cambridge: Cambridge University Press, 1983.

Higham, Carol, and Robert Thacker, eds. *One West, Two Myths II: Essays on Comparison*. Calgary: University of Calgary Press, 2006.

Hofstadter, Richard. *Anti-Intellectualism in American Life*. New York: Vintage Books, 1966.

Hopkins, Monica. *Letters from a Lady Rancher*. Calgary: Glenbow Museum, 1982.

Howell, Colin D. *Blood, Sweat and Cheers: Sport and the Making of Modern Canada*. Toronto: University of Toronto Press, 2001.

Hunter, Virginia Lee. *Carny: Americana on the Midway*. Brooklyn, NY: Umbridge Editions, 2007.

Jameson, Sheilagh. "The Social Elite of the Ranch Community and Calgary." In *Frontier Calgary: Town, City, and Region, 1875–1914*, edited by Anthony W. Rasporich and Henry C. Klassen, 56–70. Calgary: University of Calgary Press, 1975.

Johnson, Nuala C. "Mapping Monuments: The Shaping of Public Space and Cultural Identities." *Visual Communication* 1, no. 3 (2002): 293–90.

Jones, David C. *Midways, Judges, and Smooth-Tongued Fakirs: The Illustrated Story of Country Fairs in the Prairie West*. Saskatoon: Western Producer Prairie Books, 1983.

Jordan, Teresa. *Cowgirls: Women of the American West*. Lincoln: University of Nebraska Press, 1992.

Jordan, Terry G. *North American Cattle-Ranching Frontiers: Origins, Diffusion, and Differentiation*. Albuquerque: University of New Mexico, 1993.

Joslin, Mark. *The Alberta Society of Artists: Sixty Years*. Edmonton: Edmonton Art Gallery, 1982.

Kaplar, Tom, and Clayton B. Keyser. *Udderly Art: Colourful Cows for Calgary.* Toronto: Fitzhenry & Whiteside, 2000.

Kearns, Gerry, and Chris Philo, eds. *Selling Places: The City as Cultural Capital, Past and Present.* Oxford: Pergamon Press, 1993.

Kelly, Leroy V. *The Range Men: The Story of the Ranchers and Indians of Alberta.* Toronto: Wm. Briggs, 1913.

Kennedy, Fred. *Calgary Stampede: The Authentic Story of the Calgary Stampede and Exhibition, "The Greatest Outdoor Show on Earth," 1912–1964.* Vancouver: West Vancouver Enterprises, 1965.

———. *The Calgary Stampede Story.* Calgary: Commonwealth Press, 1952.

Kimmel, Michael S. "The Cult of Masculinity: American Social Character and the Legacy of the Cowboy." In *Beyond Patriarchy: Essays by Men on Pleasure, Power, and Change,* edited by M. Kaufman, 277–97. Toronto: Oxford University Press, 1987.

Kinser, Samuel. *Carnival, American Style: Mardi Gras at New Orleans and Mobile.* Chicago: University of Chicago Press, 1990.

Klassen, Henry C. *A Business History of Alberta.* Calgary: University of Calgary Press, 1999.

Klein, Marcus. "The Westerner: Origins of the Myth." In *Gender Language and Myth: Essays on Popular Narrative,* edited by Glenwood Irons, 65–82. Toronto: University of Toronto Press, 1992.

Knight, Darrell. *Pete Knight: The Cowboy King.* Calgary: Detselig Enterprises, 2004.

Konrad, Herman W. "Barren Bulls and Charging Cows: Cowboy Celebration in Copal and Calgary." In *The Celebration of Society: Perspectives on Contemporary Performance,* edited by Frank E. Manning, 145–64. Bowling Green: Bowling Green University Press, 1983.

Kotler, Phillip, Donald H. Haider, and Irving Rein. *Marketing Places: Attracting Investment, Industry and Tourism to Cities, States and Nations.* Don Mills: Maxwell Macmillan Canada, 1993.

Krakel, Dean. *Adventures in Western Art.* Kansas City: Lowell Press, 1977.

Kunstler, James Howard. *The Geography of Nowhere: The Rise and Decline of America's Man-Made Landscape.* New York: Simon & Schuster, 1993.

Lamar, Howard R., ed. *The New Encyclopedia of the American West.* New Haven, CT: Yale University Press, 1998.

LaRoque, Emma. "When the 'Wild West' is Me: Re-viewing Cowboys and Indians." In *Challenging Frontiers: The Canadian West,* ed. Lorry Felske and Beverly Rasporich, 136–55. Calgary: University of Calgary Press, 2004.

Laviolette, Mary-Beth. *An Alberta Art Chronicle: Adventures in Recent & Contemporary Art.* Canmore, AB: Altitude Publishing, 2005.

Lawrence, John Shelton, and Robert Jewett. *The Myth of the American Superhero.* Grand Rapids, MI: William B. Eerdmans, 2002.

LeCompte, Mary Lou. "Home on the Range: Women in Professional Rodeo, 1929–1947." *Journal of Sport History* 17, no. 3 (Winter 1990), 318–46.

Leslie, Jean. "Don H. MacKay, Mayor 1950–59." In *Past and Present: People, Places, and Events in Calgary*, edited by Herb Surplis, 181–82. Calgary: Century Calgary Publications, 1975.

Livingstone, Donna. *The Cowboy Spirit: Guy Weadick and the Calgary Stampede.* Vancouver: Greystone Books, 1996.

Logan, John R., and Harvey Molotch, *Urban Fortunes: The Political Economy of Place.* Berkeley: University of California Press, 1987.

Lounsberry, Lorain. "Wild West Shows and the Canadian West." In *Cowboys, Ranches, and the Cattle Business*, edited by Simon Evans, Sarah Carter, and Bill Yeo, 139–52. Calgary: University of Calgary Press, 2000.

Lowenthal, David. *The Heritage Crusade and the Spoils of History.* Cambridge: Cambridge University Press, 1988.

Loy, R. Philip. *Western and American Culture, 1930–1955.* Jefferson, NC: McFarland & Company, 2001.

MacCannell, D. *The Tourist: A New Theory of the Leisure Class.* New York: Shocken, 1976.

MacLaren, I.S. *The Influence of 18th Century British Landscape Aesthetics on Narrative and Pictorial Responses to the British North American North and West.* Ottawa: National Library of Canada, 1983.

Macleod, R.C. *The NWMP and Law Enforcement: 1873–1905.* Toronto: University of Toronto Press, 1976.

McGillis, Roderick. "Westering of the Spirit: Wordsworth Out West." *Journal of Popular Culture* 18 (1984): 85–95.

McGregor, Gaile. *The Wacousta Syndrome: Explorations in the Canadian Landscape.* Toronto: University of Toronto Press, 1985.

McKay, Ian. *The Quest of the Folk.* Montreal: McGill-Queen's University Press, 1994.

McKay, Marilyn. *The National Soul: Canadian Mural Painting, 1930s to 1960s.* Montreal: McGill-Queen's University Press, 2003.

McKennon, Joe. *A Pictorial History of the American Carnival.* Sarasota, FL: Carnival Publishers of Sarasota, 1972.

Mellinger, Wayne Martin. "Postcards from the Edge of the Color Line: Images of African Americans in Popular Culture, 1893–1917." *Symbolic Interactionism* 15, no. 4 (1992): 413–33.

Melnyk, Bryan P. *Calgary Builds: The Emergence of an Urban Landscape, 1905–1914.* Regina: Canadian Plains Research Center, 1985.

Mikkelsen, Glen. *Checkered Courage: Chuckwagon Racing's Glass Family.* Calgary: Johnson Gorman, 2002.

———. "Indians and Rodeo." *Alberta History* 35, no. 3 (Summer 1987): 13–19.

———. *Never Holler Whoa!: The Cowboys of Chuckwagon Racing.* Toronto: Balmur Book Publishing, 2000.

Morris, Michelle, *The Cowboy Life: A Saddlebag Guide for Dudes, Tenderfeet, and Cowpunchers Everywhere.* New York: Fireside, 1993.

Moyles, R.G., and Doug Owram. *Imperial Dreams and Colonial Realities: British Views of Canada, 1880–1914.* Toronto: University of Toronto Press, 1988.

Nathan, Max. *The Wrong Stuff: Creative Class Theory, Diversity and City Performance.* Research Discussion Paper No. 1, 1–8. London: Institute for Public Policy Research, Centre for Cities, 2005.

Oakley, Kate. "Not So Cool Britannia: The Role of Creative Industries in Economic Development." *International Journal of Cultural Studies* 7, no. 1 (2004): 67–77.

O'Neil, Paul. *The End and the Myth.* Alexandria, VA: Time-Life Books, 1979.

Owram, Doug. *Promise of Eden: The Canadian Expansionist Movement and the Idea of the West, 1856–1900.* Toronto: University of Toronto Press, 1992.

Pal, Leslie A. "Between the Sights: Gun Control in Canada and the United States." In *Canada and the United States: Differences that Count,* edited by David M. Thomas, 68–96. Peterborough, ON: Broadview Press, 2000.

Palmer, Howard. *Alberta: A New History.* Edmonton: Hurtig Publishers, 1990.

Palmer, Howard, and Tamara Palmer. "The Alberta Experience." *Journal of Canadian Studies* 17, no. 3 (Fall 1982): 20–34.

Pannekoek, F., M. McMordie, et al. *Heritage Covenants and Preservation: The Calgary Civic Trust.* Calgary: University of Calgary Press, 2004.

Patterson, Bruce, and Mary McGuire. *The Wild West.* Banff, AB: Altitude Publishing, 1993.

Petrone, Penny. *Native Literature in Canada: From the Oral Tradition to the Present*. Toronto: Oxford University Press, 1990.

Pike, Graham, ed. *The West in Action: Rodeo*. Calgary: Calgary Brewing and Malting Company, 1971.

Poulsen, David. *Wild Ride!: Three Journeys Down the Rodeo Road*. Toronto: Balmur Book Publishing, 2000.

Rainey, Buck. "The 'Reel' Cowboy." In *The Cowboy: Six Shooters, Songs, and Sex,* edited by Charles W. Harris and Buck Rainey, 17–55. Norman: University of Oklahoma Press, 1976.

Read, Tracey, and Joan Dixon. *Celebrating the Calgary Exhibition and Stampede*. Calgary: Altitude Publishing, 2005.

Reasons, Chuck, ed. *Stampede City: Power and Politics in the West*. Toronto: Between the Lines, 1984.

Richardson, E.L. *The Calgary Exhibition: 1884–1920*. Calgary: The Calgary Exhibition, 1921.

Ross, Andrew. "Nice Work if You Can Get It: The Mercurial Career of Creative Industries Policy." *Work, Organization, Labour and Globalization* 1, no. 1 (January 2007): 13–30.

Rozum, Molly P. "'The Spark that Jumped the Gap': North America's Northern Plains and the Experience of Place." In *One West, Two Myths: A Comparative Reader*, edited by Carol Higham and Robert Thacker, 133–48. Calgary: University of Calgary Press, 2004.

Russell, Andy. *The Canadian Cowboy: Stories of Cows, Cowboys, and Cayuses*. Toronto: McClelland & Stewart, 1993.

Russell, Don. "The Cowboy: From Black Hat to White." In *The Cowboy: Six Shooters, Songs, and Sex*, edited by Charles W. Harris and Buck Rainey, 5–15. Norman: University of Oklahoma Press 1976.

———. *The Wild West: Or a History of the Wild West Shows*. Fort Worth, TX: Amon Carter Museum, 1970.

Samuels, Peggy. *The Illustrated Biographical Encyclopedia of Artists of the American West*. Garden City, NY: Doubleday, 1976.

Samuels, Peggy, and Harold Samuels. *Contemporary Western Artists*. New York: Bonanza Books, 1982.

Sandweiss, Martha. "The Public Life of Western Art." In *Discovered Lands, Invented Pasts: Transforming Visions of the American West*, edited by Jules Prown, 117–33. New Haven, CT: Yale University Press, 1992.

———. "Views and Reviews: Western Art and Western History." In *Under an Open Sky: Rethinking America's Western Past*, edited by William Cronen, George Miles, and Jay Gitlin, 185–202. New York: Norton, 1992.

Savage, Candace. *Cowgirls.* Vancouver: Greystone Books, 1996.

Savage, William W., Jr. "The Cowboy Myth." In *The Cowboy: Six Shooters, Songs, and Sex*, edited by Charles W. Harris and Buck Rainey, 154–63. Norman: University of Oklahoma Press, 1976.

Scott, Guy. *Country Fairs in Canada.* Markham: Fitzhenry & Whiteside, 2006.

Seiler, Robert M. "M.B. (Doc) Marcell: Official Photographer of the First Calgary Stampede." *American Review of Canadian Studies* 33, no. 2 (Summer 2003): 219–239.

———. "Selling Patriotism/Selling Beer: The Case of the 'I AM CANADIAN' Commercial." *American Review of Canadian Studies* 32, no. 1 (Spring 2002): 45–66.

Seiler, Robert M., and Tamara P. Seiler. "Ceremonial Rhetoric and Civic Identity: The Case of the White Hat." *Journal of Canadian Studies* 36, no. 1 (Spring 2001): 29–49.

———. "Managing Contradictory Visions of the West: The Great Richardson-Weadick Experiment." In *Challenging Frontiers: The Canadian West*, edited by Lorry Felske and Beverly Rasporich, 155–80. Calgary: University of Calgary Press, 2004.

Silverman, Eliane Leslau. *The Last Best West: Women on the Alberta Frontier, 1880–1930.* Calgary: Fifth House, 1998.

Slatta, Richard W. *Cowboys of the Americas.* New Haven, CT: Yale University Press, 1990.

Slotkin, Richard. *Gunfighter Nation: The Myth of the Frontier in Twentieth-Century America.* Norman: University of Oklahoma Press, 1998.

———. *Regeneration Through Violence: The Mythology of the American Frontier, 1600–1860.* Norman: University of Oklahoma Press, 1973.

Smith, Henry Nash. *Virgin Land: The American West as Symbol and Myth.* Cambridge, MA: Harvard University Press, 1950.

Stegner, Wallace. *Wolf Willow: A History, a Story, and a Memory of the Last Plains Frontier.* Toronto: Macmillan, 1962.

Stiles, Joanne A. "Descended from Heroes: The Frontier Myth in Rural Alberta." *Alberta* 2, no. 2 (1990): 27–46.

Taft, Robert. *Artists and Illustrators of the Old West, 1850–1900*. New York: Scribners, 1953.

Taliaferro, John. *Charles M. Russell: The Life and Legend of an American Cowboy Artist*. New York: Little Brown and Company, 1996.

Thomas, L.G., "Ranch Houses of the Alberta Foothills." In *Canadian Historic Sites, Occasional Papers in Archaeology and History*, No. 20. Ottawa: Parks Canada, 1979.

Tompkins, Jane. "West of Everything." In *Gender Language and Myth: Essays on Popular Narrative*, edited by Glenwood Irons, 103–23. Toronto: University of Toronto Press, 1992.

Truzzi, Marcello. "Introduction: Circuses, Carnivals and Fairs." *Journal of Popular Culture* 6, no. 3 (Spring 1973): 531–34.

Turner, Victor. "Variations on a Theme of Liminality." In *Secular Ritual*, edited by Sally Moore and Barbara Myerhoff, 36–52. Amsterdam: Van Gorcum, 1977.

Van Herk, Aritha. "Leading the Parade." *American Review of Canadian Studies* 33, no. 4 (Winter 2003): 487–96.

———. *Mavericks: An Incorrigible History of Alberta*. Toronto: Penguin Canada, 2001.

———. "Shooting a Saskatoon: (Whatever Happened to the Marlboro Man?)." In *Challenging Frontiers: The Canadian West*, edited by Lorry Felske and Beverly Rasporich, 15–25. Calgary: University of Calgary Press, 2004.

Varga, Vincent. "Gentleman Ranchers: High Class Cowboys." *Journal of the West* 23, no. 4 (1984): 48–56.

Walden, Keith. *Becoming Modern in Toronto: The Industrial Exhibition and the Shaping of a Late Victorian Culture*. Toronto: University of Toronto Press, 1997.

Waters, H.W. *History of Fairs and Expositions: Their Classifications, Functions and Values*. London, ON: Reid Bros., 1939.

Weadick, Guy. "Origin of the Calgary Stampede." *Alberta Historical Review* 14, no. 4 (1966): 20–23.

West, Elliott. "Against the Grain: State-Making, Cultures, and Geography in the American West." In *One West, Two Myths: A Comparative Reader*, edited by Carol Higham and Robert Thacker, 1–21. Calgary: University of Calgary Press, 2004.

Weston, Jack. *The Real American Cowboy*. New York: New Amsterdam, 1995.

Wetherell, Donald G., and Irene Kmet. *Useful Pleasures: The Shaping of Leisure in Alberta, 1896–1945*. Regina: Canadian Plains Research Center, 1990.

Wooden, Wayne S., and Gavin Ehringer. *Rodeo in America: Wranglers, Roughstock, and Paydirt.* Lawrence: University of Kansas Press, 1996.

Worster, D. "Two Faces West: The Development Myth in Canada and the United States." In *One West, Two Myths: A Comparative Reader*, edited by Carol Higham and Robert Thacker, 23–46. Calgary: University of Calgary Press, 2004.

Zimon, Kathy. *Alberta Society of Artists: The First Seventy Years.* Calgary: University of Calgary Press, 2000.

Contributors

Fiona Angus currently teaches sociology at MacEwan College in Edmonton, Alberta, after having taught for several years at the University of British Columbia. She obtained her Ph.D. in sociology at the University of British Columbia in 2000. Her doctoral thesis is based on extensive participant-observation research she conducted on a western Canadian carnival, during which she worked as a carny, living and travelling with the carnival over the four western provinces. She continues to conduct research on Canadian carnivals and frequently gives guest lectures on carnival life and culture.

Hugh A. Dempsey is chief curator emeritus of the Glenbow Museum and the author of a number of books on the Canadian West, including *Tom Three Persons: Legend of an Indian Cowboy* and *The Golden Age of the Canadian Cowboy: An Illustrated History*. He has been editor of the quarterly *Alberta History* since 1958. He received the Order of Canada in 1975, and in October 2005 Canada's National History Society honoured his lifetime achievements with a special centenary award.

Lorry Felske is the coordinator of the Canadian Studies Program in the Faculty of Communication and Culture at the University of Calgary. His research interests focus on the history of local communities, especially their origins, and the social, cultural, economic, and political forces at work in new communities.

Max Foran is a professor in the Faculty of Communication and Culture at the University of Calgary. He has written several books and articles on Calgary's development and in 2004 published a history of the Alberta beef cattle industry up to 1948. He has just completed a manuscript on the relationship between the City of Calgary and land developers in the post-1945 period of suburban sprawl.

Vern Kimball joined the Calgary Stampede in 1986 and has been chief executive officer of the organization since 2006. Vern played a key role in the design and implementation of the Stampede's twenty-year development plan, which is focused on transforming Stampede Park into a year-round gathering place for Calgarians and visitors to the city. Vern has M.B.A. and B.A. degrees from the University of Calgary.

Glen Mikkelsen is the author of *Never Holler Whoa!: The Cowboys of Chuckwagon Racing* and *Checkered Courage: Chuckwagon Racing's Glass Family*. For over ten years he has been a feature writer for the Calgary Stampede Rodeo and Grandstand programs. He has also written articles for *Western Horseman, Canadian Rodeo News,*

Canadian Cowboy Country, Alberta History, and Oklahoma City's National Cowboy Hall of Fame. As an event manager in Prince George, British Columbia, he assists in the planning and production of amateur rodeos and the West of the Rockies Pro Rodeo Finals. For over a decade his family has hosted an annual Calgary Stampede breakfast, bringing horses, roping cowboys, singing cowgirls, and free flapjacks to the suburbs of northern British Columbia!

Frits Pannekoek is president of Athabasca University. He is also an adjunct professor in the Department of History and an adjunct professor in the Faculty of Communication and Culture at the University of Calgary. He has written widely on western Canadian history, heritage studies, digital environments, and information management. He was a founding member of the Calgary Civic Trust and the 2005 winner of the Calgary Stampede Western Legacy Award.

Brian Rusted is an associate professor in the University of Calgary's Faculty of Communication and Culture. He teaches courses in visual culture, folklore, and performance studies. His recent research on visual culture and the performance of place has appeared in journals such as *Cultural Studies, Text and Performance Quarterly,* and *Visual Studies.* As an active volunteer with the Calgary Stampede, Brian has helped coordinate aspects of the annual Western Art Show and has lectured on the history of the Stampede as part of the Smithsonian Folklife Festival in Washington, D.C.

Tamara Palmer Seiler is a professor and division head of Culture Studies in the University of Calgary's Faculty of Communication and Culture. She has a Ph.D. in Canadian literature with a particular interest in narratives about immigrant experience in Canada. She has also published books and articles on Alberta history and culture. Although she has spent her adult life in Canada, she was born and raised in the United States and has an academic and personal interest in the North American West.

Robert M. Seiler is an associate professor emeritus in the University of Calgary's Faculty of Communication and Culture. He has a Ph.D. in English from the University of Liverpool, where he specialized in Victorian studies, and has written three books on the British cultural critic Walter Pater. His research interests include media and cultural studies, with a focus on the social construction of meaning. He is currently completing a book on the history of film exhibition in western Canada.

Donald Wetherell has an M.A. from the University of Saskatchewan and a Ph.D. from Queen's University. He is a professor and director of the Historical Resources

Intern Program at Athabasca University. He is co-author with Irene Kmet of *Useful Pleasures: The Shaping of Leisure in Alberta, 1896–1945*; *Town Life: Main Street and the Evolution of Small Town Alberta, 1880–1947* (named Scholarly Book of the Year by the Book Publishers Association of Alberta in 1995); and *Alberta's North: A History, 1890–1950* (winner of the Clio Award [Prairies], 2001), among other books. Most recently, he was one of the editors of *Alberta Formed – Alberta Transformed*, the centennial history of Alberta, and edited *Architecture, Town Planning and Community: Selected Writings and Public Talks by Cecil Burgess, 1909–1946*. He lives in Calgary.

Aritha van Herk has been an avid spectator of chuckwagon races for thirty years. She is the author of nine books, including five novels and two works of criticism. Her irreverent history of Alberta, *Mavericks: An Incorrigible History of Alberta*, won the Grant MacEwan Author's Award and frames the new permanent exhibition at the Glenbow Museum. She is a University Professor and professor of English at the University of Calgary.

Index